Robin Geiß / Anna Petrig

Piracy and Armed Robbery at Sea

Max Planck Research on International, European, and Comparative Criminal Law

General Editor: Prof. Dr. Dr. h.c. mult. Ulrich Sieber

Volume 1

Robin Geiß / Anna Petrig,
Piracy and Armed Robbery at Sea

This series presents results of research conducted at or in cooperation with the Max Planck Institute for Foreign and International Criminal Law in Freiburg/Germany. The Institute's research program focuses on the challenges to criminal law in the global risk and information society that are leading to new paradigms: The global nature of the 21st century defies the traditional territorial limits of national criminal law and requires new forms of transnationally effective regulation; the modern risk society with its emerging security law poses a challenge to the functional limits of traditional criminal law and threatens the delicate balance of security and liberty. These developments are especially apparent in complex criminal activity such as terrorism, cybercrime, organized, economic, and international crime. Comparative legal research and the analysis of national, international, and private regulative approaches as carried out by the Max Planck Institute in Freiburg are essential to the successful and timely resolution of these fundamental issues.

MAX-PLANCK-GESELLSCHAFT

Robin Geiß • Anna Petrig

Piracy and Armed Robbery at Sea

The Legal Framework for Counter-Piracy Operations in Somalia and the Gulf of Aden

OXFORD
UNIVERSITY PRESS

OXFORD

UNIVERSITY PRESS

Great Clarendon Street, Oxford OX2 6DP

Oxford University Press is a department of the University of Oxford.
It furthers the University's objective of excellence in research, scholarship,
and education by publishing worldwide in

Oxford New York

Auckland Cape Town Dar es Salaam Hong Kong Karachi
Kuala Lumpur Madrid Melbourne Mexico City Nairobi
New Delhi Shanghai Taipei Toronto

With offices in

Argentina Austria Brazil Chile Czech Republic France Greece
Guatemala Hungary Italy Japan Poland Portugal Singapore
South Korea Switzerland Thailand Turkey Ukraine Vietnam

Oxford is a registered trade mark of Oxford University Press
in the UK and in certain other countries

Published in the United States
by Oxford University Press Inc., New York

© R Geiß and A Petrig, 2011

The moral rights of the authors have been asserted

Crown copyright material is reproduced under Class Licence
Number C01P0000148 with the permission of OPSI
and the Queen's Printer for Scotland

Database right Oxford University Press (maker)

First published 2011

British Library Cataloguing-in-Publication Data
Data available

Library of Congress Cataloging in Publication Data
Data available

Typeset by The Max Planck Institute for Foreign and International Criminal Law
Printed in Great Britain
on acid-free paper by
CPI Antony Rowe, Chippenham, Wiltshire

ISBN HB 978–0–19–960952–9

1 3 5 7 9 10 8 6 4 2

Preface

This new series, "International, European, and Comparative Criminal Law," published by Oxford University Press presents the results of research conducted at or in cooperation with the Max Planck Institute for Foreign and International Criminal Law in Freiburg/Germany. The Institute's research program focuses on the challenges to criminal law in the global risk and information society that are leading to new paradigms: The global nature of the 21st century defies the traditional territorial limits of national criminal law and requires new forms of transnationally effective regulation. The modern risk society with its emerging security law poses a challenge to the functional limits of traditional criminal law and threatens the delicate balance of security and liberty, especially in the context of such complex crimes as terrorism, organised crime, and cybercrime. In today's interconnected world, solutions to these challenges must be derived from comparative law and basic research on the models of international crime control and its regulation.

These central challenges are clearly apparent in the area of sea piracy. Since 2008, the international community has witnessed a sharp increase in pirate activities off the coast of Somalia, in the Gulf of Aden, and in the Western Indian Ocean. The roots of this development lie in Somalia's socio-economic problems, which are fostered by extensive international exploitation of its neighbouring fishing grounds, and in the collapse of state institutions, the paralysis of governance, and the breakdown of law and order in Somalia. These problems are no longer merely national and have led to a global threat to security at sea and to the security of international trade routes. They illustrate how highly interconnected the world has become and show that the emergence of global problems requires a reconceptualization of the traditional mechanisms of national law.

Present international attempts to repress piracy in the larger Gulf of Aden and in Somalia also provide an ideal area of study with respect to the development of models for a security law that reaches beyond the territory of the nation State. The reactions of the international community to sea piracy showcase the need for such new security concepts and can be interpreted against the background of the two main models for such a transnational security law: the *development of international law* and the *extension of national laws* to extraterritorial conduct. The international *policing approach* to sea piracy in the Gulf of Aden aiming at the prevention of future crimes, which uses the international model, albeit with explicit caveats not to create "new" law, is based on the United Nations Convention on the Law of the Sea and various UN Security Council Resolutions, and it is currently enforced by an international armada of warships. It is partly successful at sea but has yet to be enforced on the territory of Somalia. Most importantly, this "executive" international policing approach lacks a corresponding concerted international judicial approach. Thus, the judiciary, particularly in the area of *"repressive" criminal law* aiming at the sanctioning of past crimes, must rely on the second model, that of applying national criminal law, mainly by using the national criminal law systems of regional States. Yet this national approach is limited by the capability and willingness of nation States to assume responsibility for prosecution.

In more general terms, the UN Security Council approach to sea piracy is an incomplete solution and shows that the international community lacks a coherent system of transnational security law beyond the limits of the nation State and one that effectively protects human rights by means of judicial remedies. Thus, as in the case of UN Security Council Resolutions against terrorism, international regulation by the UN against piracy illustrates the need for new concepts on the basis of which a global security law can be established that is transnationally effective and at the same time guarantees international human rights standards.

In the context of this ongoing debate, this book fills a major gap. *Robin Geiß* and *Anna Petrig* present the first monograph that specifically deals with the various legal challenges pertaining to the repression of piracy in the larger Gulf of Aden region. The authors have skillfully untangled the intricate meshwork of applicable regulations, and they provide a concise analysis of the entire spectrum of applicable legal regimes. Their study develops a number of innovative ideas that will influence and promote future debate on the prevention and prosecution of piracy. The book shows that, in the global risk and information society, just as at the national level, the effectiveness of law enforcement operations and rule-of-law abidance should not be regarded as mutually exclusive; ultimately, they are the best guarantees to achieving long-term success. Robin Geiß' and Anna Petrig's pioneering work addresses these issues comprehensively and offers new insights into and solutions to the myriad challenges posed by sea piracy.

The authors should be commended for making a serious and significant contribution to the corpus of international law governing the prevention and prosecution of piracy and armed robbery at sea. Their analysis of the complex operational, political, and legal challenges of sea piracy is also exemplary of the issues surrounding the coordinated efforts of the international community to repress international criminal phenomena as a whole. For this reason, this book should be of great interest not only to those dealing specifically with piracy but also to scholars and practitioners working on the regulation of international criminal phenomena in general.

Freiburg/Germany, October 2010   *Prof. Dr. Dr. h.c. mult. Ulrich Sieber*
                                            Director at the Max Planck Institute for
                                            Foreign and International Criminal Law

Acknowledgments

The upsurge of piracy off the coast of Somalia and in the Gulf of Aden since 2008 has generated a significant amount of new legal instruments and State practice in a rather short period of time. The current efforts to counter piracy in the Gulf of Aden, therefore, provide an excellent opportunity to study the international legal framework pertaining to the repression of piracy, as it stands in 2010. In addition, the tools devised and the practices employed to repress piracy in the Gulf of Aden may be used in the future when dealing with other criminal phenomena in the maritime context in the future. Thus, the findings of the research at hand may have validity beyond the piracy context.

This book was written with the aim of providing an overview on the current legal framework pertaining to the repression of piracy and armed robbery at sea, both in general, and with regard to the specific context of Somalia and the Gulf of Aden. An Appendix containing the most relevant legal instruments for the repression of piracy off the coast of Somalia – some of which are hard to come by even in the internet era – should help the reader to find some orientation in the rather complex tangle of norms pertaining to the repression of piracy and armed robbery at sea. The work reflects the law as it stood in August 2010.

We wish to express our deep gratitude to Prof. Dr. Dr. h.c. *Ulrich Sieber*, Director at the Max Planck Institute for Foreign and International Criminal Law in Freiburg (Germany), who made this publication possible. We are also very grateful for the meticulous work done by the publication team of Oxford University Press and the various proof-readers (especially *Ellen Weaver*, *Indira Tie*, and *Justin Bachmann*) as well as the professional support we received from the staff of the Max Planck Institute's publication department (namely *Ines Hofman*, *Irene Kortel* and *Petra Lehser*).

We would also like to thank the practitioners and scholars, who participated in the *Criminal Law & Sea Piracy Scholarship Program* at the Max Planck Institute for Foreign and International Criminal Law in fall 2009. Dr. *Henri Fouché* from South Africa, *Aïd Ahmed Ibrahim* from Djibouti, *Raphael Kamuli* from the United Republic of Tanzania and Dr. *Paul Wambua* from Kenya provided us with excellent insights into the various national legal frameworks, judicial proceedings and generally the domestic practices in dealing with piracy in the Gulf of Aden.

During the *Expert Meeting on Multinational Law Enforcement and Sea Piracy* held at the Max Planck Institute for Foreign and International Criminal Law in November 2009, we gained valuable insights into the operational challenges that counter-piracy missions in the Gulf of Aden region face. We thus owe special thanks to the practitioners (namely Lt. Colonel *Gavin Davies*, Legal Advisor to the NATO, Commander *Marc Lemoine* assigned to the European Union Operation Atalanta and *Jacob Skude Rasmussen* of the Danish Ministry of Foreign Affairs) and academics (namely Prof. Dr. *Claus Kreß* of the University of Köln, Dr. *Max Meija* from the World Maritime University of Sweden and Prof. Dr. *Wolfgang Schomburg*) for attending the Expert Meeting and contributing to the fruitful discussions. A special debt of gratitude goes to *Tilman Rodenhäuser* who greatly assisted the organization of the Expert Meeting.

Moreover, warm thanks are due to the various other experts who provided us with invaluable information. In particular, we would like to mention *Wambui Mwangi*, who is the United Nations Political Affairs Officer for the Somalia Planning Team at the Department of Peacekeeping Operations, and *Thomas Unger*, who is a Legal Officer at the Office of the Legal Adviser for the Austrian Federal Ministry for European and International Affairs.

Finally, the list of acknowledgments would not be complete without mentioning all those persons who contributed in one way or the other to the realization of the book at hand – be it for providing us with up-to-date information, by reading draft versions, by giving us help with formal corrections or the layout or by simply encouraging us to write this book.

Geneva & Freiburg/Germany, October 2010   *Robin Geiß & Anna Petrig*

Contents

List of abbreviations

a.o.	and others
Abl.	Amtsblatt der Europäischen Union
AJIL	American Journal of International Law
AJP	Aktuelle Juristische Praxis
AMISOM	African Union Mission in Somalia
ARD	Arbeitsgemeinschaft der öffentlich-rechtlichen Rundfunkanstalten der Bundesrepublik Deutschland
Art. / Arts.	article / articles
ASEAN	Association of Southeast Asian Nations
ASIL	American Society of International Law
BBC	British Broadcasting Corporation
CAT	Committee against Torture
CFSP	Common Foreign and Security Policy
CGPCS	Contact Group on Piracy off the Coast of Somalia
cit.	cited
CTF	Combined Task Force
Doc.	document
e.g.	for example
ECHR	Convention for the Protection of Human Rights and Fundamental Freedoms (European Convention on Human Rights)
ed.	edition / editor
eds.	editors
EJIL	European Journal of International Law
EMRK	Konvention zum Schutze der Menschenrechte und Grundfreiheiten (Europäische Menschenrechtskonvention)
EPIL	Encyclopedia of Public International Law
et al.	and others
EU	European Union
EUNAVFOR	European Union Naval Force
FDP	Freie Demokratische Partei

G.A. Res.	United Nations General Assembly Resolution
GASP	Gemeinsame Außen- und Sicherheitspolitik
HRC	Human Rights Committee
ICC	International Chamber of Commerce
ICC	International Criminal Court
ICC-IMB	International Chamber of Commerce – International Maritime Bureau
ICCPR	International Covenant on Civil and Political Rights
ICJ	International Court of Justice
ICLQ	International and Comparative Law Quarterly
ICTR	International Criminal Tribunal for Rwanda
ICTY	International Criminal Tribunal for the former Yugoslavia
id.	idem
IMB	International Maritime Bureau
ILM	International Legal Materials
I.L.R.	International Law Reports
IMO	International Maritime Organization
IMO Doc.	International Maritime Organization Document
INTERPOL	International Criminal Police Organization
IRRC	International Review of the Red Cross
IRTC	Internationally Recommended Transit Corridor
ISC	Information Sharing Center
ITLOS	International Tribunal for the Law of the Sea
KFOR	Kosovo Force
L	legislation
lit.	litera
M/V	Motor Vessel
MARLO	Maritime Liaison Office
MSCHOA	Maritime Security Centre – Horn of Africa
NATO	North Atlantic Treaty Organization
No./no.	number
NPR	National Public Radio
O.J.	Official Journal of the European Union
p. / pp.	page / pages
para. / paras.	paragraph / paragraphs
PSC	Political and Security Committee

PSI	Proliferation Security Initiative
publ.	publisher
ReCAAP	Regional Cooperation Agreement on Combating Piracy and Armed Robbery against Ships in Asia
S.C. Res.	United Nations Security Council Resolution
S.S.	Steam Ship
SHADE	Shared Awareness and Deconfliction Group
SOFAs	Status of Forces Agreements
SUA Convention	Convention for the Suppression of Unlawful Acts against the Safety of Maritime Navigation
SWP	Stiftung Wissenschaft und Politik
TEU	Twenty-Foot Equivalent Units
TFG	Transitional Federal Government
U.N. Doc.	United Nations Document
U.N./UN	United Nations
U.N.R.I.A.A.	United Nations Reports of International Arbitral Awards
U.N.T.S.	United Nations Treaty Series
U.S.	United States of America
UK	United Kingdom
UNCLOS	United Nations Convention on the Law of the Sea
UNCTAD	United Nations Conference on Trade and Development
UNMIK	United Nations Interim Administration Mission in Kosovo
UNODC	United Nations Office on Drugs and Crime
USA	United States of America
USS	United States Ship
v. / vs.	versus
Vol.	volume

Introduction

Pirates are long-standing pariahs of the international legal order. Although often perceived as an 18th century-phenomenon, since 2008, increasing pirate activities in the Gulf of Aden and more recently the Western Indian Ocean have once more drawn the international community's attention to piracy and armed robbery at sea.[1] *Prima facie*, two lessons can be learned from the recent upsurge of piracy and armed robbery at sea off Somalia's coast: Firstly, ignoring failed States is not an option. Sooner or later the absence of effective governmental control will lead to intolerable problems, forcing the international community to act. Secondly, piracy is not an archaic relict of long gone times. It is a lucrative business, thriving not only in the Gulf of Aden, but also in Asia. In the context of an exponentially growing worldwide shipping industry,[2] there are ample opportunities to commit acts of piracy and armed robbery at sea. It appears quite likely that piracy will remain a problem in the 21st century. This raises the question of how to best repress piracy and armed robbery at sea in its modern form and whether the existing legal framework on piracy, primarily laid out in the United Nations Convention on the Law of the Sea (UNCLOS),[3] is still up to the task.

The current situation off Somalia's coast and in the Gulf of Aden has spurred the international community into action. Various Chapter VII-based Security Council

---

[1] A precise legal definition of the term "pirate" does not exist. Rather, Art. 101 UNCLOS defines piracy by reference to specific acts. The definition of piracy is analyzed in depth further below, see p. 59 *et seq.* Colloquially, the term "pirate" is often used more broadly, not only to include persons having committed acts defined in Art. 101 UNCLOS, but also persons having committed piracy like attacks in the territorial waters, i.e. "armed robbers at sea." For more on the definition of armed robbery at sea, see p. 73 *et seq.* As far as consistency was possible, the word "pirate" is used in this book to denote someone who has committed any of the acts laid out in Art. 101 UNCLOS. For persons having committed violent acts against ships or persons in the territorial sea, the term "armed robbers at sea" is used in the book at hand.

[2] In 2011, global containerized trade alone is forecast to reach 134 million Twenty-Foot Equivalent Units (TEU), 2.3 times as much as the 58 million TEU recorded in 2001: *Levinson*, Container Shipping and the Economy – Stimulating Trade and Transformations Worldwide, TR News 46 (2006), 11.

[3] United Nations Convention on the Law of the Sea, *adopted* Dec. 10, 1982, 1883 U.N.T.S. 3 [hereinafter: UNCLOS]. The piracy relevant provisions of the UNCLOS are reprinted on p. 233 *et seq.* of this book (Appendix).

Resolutions,[4] the authorization to use "all necessary means,"[5] and the proclaimed objective of the "full eradication of piracy and armed robbery at sea off the coast of Somalia"[6] send a clear message. There can be no doubt, the international community is firmly resolved to repress piracy in Somalia and the Gulf of Aden.

Various law enforcement operations – namely, European Union Naval Force Operation Atalanta, NATO Operation Ocean Shield and Combined Task Force-151 – have been deployed to the Gulf of Aden. In addition, numerous States are independently contributing to the international counter-piracy efforts.[7] The Security Council has authorized their operations in Somalia's territorial waters and has even paved their way onto the Somali mainland. Indeed, the Security Council has been active in expanding the geographical scope of enforcement powers against pirates, thereby remedying some of the oft-lamented shortcomings of the counter-piracy enforcement regime contained in the UNCLOS. Yet it is still not always easy to discern precisely what, in practice, States are currently allowed to do in their quest to repress piracy in the Gulf of Aden, nor where nor against whom. What kind and degree of force is permissible in maritime interception operations? What is armed robbery at sea? Are counter-piracy operations in the region based on a coherent set of enforcement powers or does it make a difference whether pirates or armed robbers at sea are pursued on the high seas, within territorial waters of Somalia and other littoral States or on the Somali mainland? As will be shown, some lacunae and ambiguities still remain as to the precise scope and proper limitations of the enforcement powers granted.

---

[4] United Nations, Security Council, S.C. Res. 1816, U.N. Doc. S/RES/1816 (June 2, 2008) [hereinafter: S.C. Res. 1816; reprinted on p. 251 *et seq.* of this book (Appendix)]; S.C. Res. 1838, U.N. Doc. S/RES/1838 (Oct. 7, 2008) [hereinafter: S.C. Res. 1838]; S.C. Res. 1846, U.N. Doc. S/RES/1846 (Dec. 2, 2008) [hereinafter: S.C. Res. 1846; reprinted on p. 254 *et seq.* of this book (Appendix)]; S.C. Res. 1851, U.N. Doc. S/RES/1851 (Dec. 16, 2008) [hereinafter: S.C. Res. 1851; reprinted on p. 258 *et seq.* of this book (Appendix)]; S.C. Res. 1897, U.N. Doc. S/RES/1897 (Nov. 30, 2009) [hereinafter: S.C. Res. 1897; reprinted on p. 261 *et seq.* of this book (Appendix)]; S.C. Res. 1918, U.N. Doc. S/RES/1918 (April 27, 2010) [hereinafter: S.C. Res. 1918; reprinted on p. 265 *et seq.* of this book (Appendix)]. Notably, S.C. Res. 1844, U.N. Doc. S/RES/1844 (Nov. 20, 2008) [hereinafter: S.C. Res. 1844] could possibly be mentioned as another Security Council Resolution relating to piracy. However, in S.C. Res. 1844, preambular para. 5, the Security Council merely expresses "its grave concern over the recent increase in acts of piracy and armed robbery at sea against vessels off the coast of Somalia" and notes "the role piracy may play in financing embargo violations by armed groups" without taking any action in relation to piracy.

[5] S.C. Res. 1816, para. 7(b), and S.C. Res. 1846, para. 10(b).

[6] S.C. Res. 1846, preambular para. 10, and S.C. Res. 1897, preambular para. 13.

[7] United Nations, Secretary-General Report on S.C. Res. 1846, Nov. 13, 2009, para. 27, lists the following States: Japan, China, the Russian Federation, India, Malaysia, the Republic of Korea, Saudi Arabia, the Islamic Republic of Iran and Yemen; all of them have deployed naval ships and/or aircraft to fight piracy in the Gulf of Aden.

The respective Security Council Resolutions are conspicuously silent as to the legal confines of the enforcement powers so authorized. Discussion of limitations may be considered inappropriate when seeking to show resolve in the struggle against a *hostis humani generis*. Merely Security Council Resolution 1851 tentatively insinuates the application of human rights and international humanitarian law,[8] albeit only in relation to enforcement operations conducted on Somali mainland. In addition, in counter-piracy operations the application of international humanitarian law would not necessarily always act as a constraint. Where the use of force is concerned, the application of international humanitarian law could set aside some more protective human rights prescriptions. The Security Council Resolutions' silence with respect to legal constraints on enforcement powers is worrying because, as far as maritime interception operations are concerned, the applicable legal confines are neither clear nor comprehensively established. In particular the extraterritorial application of human rights law at sea, as well as the attribution of possible human rights violations in the context of United Nations-mandated multinational operations that involve the NATO and the European Union, raise issues of considerable complexity. It is, therefore, hardly surprising that in the current public debate over how to best deal with pirates, at one end of the spectrum of opinions the outright sinking of pirate ships has been contemplated, whereas the opposite extreme view has called for strict adherence to domestic police-custody periods of maximal 48 hours, even in relation to arrests on the high seas.

The Security Council has set itself an ambitious objective: the full[9] and durable eradication[10] of piracy. Evidently, in the pursuance of this aim, enforcement powers allowing the initial arrest of persons suspected of having committed piracy and armed robbery at sea, only amount to a first step. The instigation of criminal proceedings and the effective prosecution of alleged perpetrators are equally important for ensuring the long-term success in the repression of piracy and armed robbery at sea. Thus far, a number of captured pirates and armed robbers at sea have been released; in recent times, mostly for a lack of evidence that could support prosecution. The majority of captured suspects have been transferred for prosecution to States in the region; and a few have been brought before domestic trials of States participating in the law enforcement operations in the Gulf of Aden. In total, prosecutions of acts of piracy committed in the Gulf of Aden region are currently ongoing in 10 States, namely Kenya, Seychelles, Somalia (however, only in the Somaliland and Puntland regions), the Maldives, Yemen, the Netherlands, the United States of America, France, Spain and Germany.[11] Some States have proposed the establishment of an international piracy tribunal. Discussions continue as to which

---

[8] S.C. Res. 1851, para. 6.

[9] S.C. Res. 1846, preambular para. 10.

[10] S.C. Res. 1897, preambular para. 13.

[11] United Nations, Secretary-General Report pursuant to S. C. Res. 1918, July 26, 2010, para. 19.

venue would be the most suitable for the prosecution of piracy and armed robbery at sea. In this context, a recent Report from the Secretary-General has identified no less than seven different options for consideration by the Security Council. A clear understanding of the scope of adjudicative jurisdiction over piracy and armed robbery at sea is crucial, therefore, but is not easily achieved. The UNCLOS is widely perceived to contain a jurisdictional basis for adjudication, but the various Security Council Resolutions have also invoked a range of other equally relevant treaties such as the Convention for the Suppression of Unlawful Acts against the Safety of Maritime Navigation,[12] the United Nations Convention against Transnational Organized Crime[13] and the International Convention against the Taking of Hostages.[14] Moreover, the Security Council has explicitly called for the conclusion of so-called shiprider agreements with regional States, presumably in order to facilitate the criminal prosecution of piracy suspects *in situ*.

It is against this background that the following contribution sets out to analyze the international legal framework applicable to the counter-piracy operations in Somalia, off its coast and in the larger Gulf of Aden region. The analysis is in four main parts.

In Part I, the current situation in the Gulf of Aden is brought into focus. We consider the regional development of piracy and armed robbery at sea since 2008, the situation in Somalia and the various multinational enforcement operations deployed to the area as well as international coordination mechanisms.

In Part II, a brief history of the evolution of legal rules pertaining to piracy and armed robbery at sea is provided. Piracy ranks among one of the old subject matters of public international law and contemporary rules on piracy laid out in the UNCLOS have thus a long history.

In Part III, we scrutinize the scope of enforcement powers granted to States by Articles 110 and 105 United Nations Convention on the Law of the Sea and by virtue of the various Security Council Resolutions (Chapter I). The guiding questions in this section are: What kind of enforcement measures are States currently allowed to employ? Against whom can these enforcement powers be used? What is the geographical scope of the enforcement powers now granted? In particular, is a coherent and uniform regime of enforcement powers in place or does it make a

---

[12] Convention for the Suppression of Unlawful Acts against the Safety of Maritime Navigation, *adopted* March 10, 1988, 1678 U.N.T.S. 221 [hereinafter: SUA Convention]. Piracy relevant provisions of the SUA Convention are reprinted on p. 239 *et seq.* of this book (Appendix).

[13] United Nations Convention against Transnational Organized Crime and the Protocols Thereto, *adopted* Nov. 15, 2000, 2225 U.N.T.S. 209 [hereinafter: Organized Crime Convention].

[14] International Convention against the Taking of Hostages, *adopted* Dec. 18, 1979, 1316 U.N.T.S. 205 [hereinafter: Hostage Convention]. Piracy relevant provisions of the Hostage Convention are reprinted on p. 247 *et seq.* of this book (Appendix).

difference whether pirates and armed robbers at sea are pursued on the high seas, within Somalia's or other States' coastal waters or on the Somali mainland? Secondly, given that the Security Council has explicitly called for the use of shipriders in the present context, this rather novel mechanism is also examined (Chapter II). Thirdly, the analysis aims to identify the applicable legal constraints that confine and regulate the execution of enforcement powers in relation to piracy and armed robbery at sea off the coast of Somalia and in the larger Gulf of Aden region. Are such constraints to be found in the respective Security Council Resolutions, the international law of the sea, human rights law or possibly even international humanitarian law, as Security Council Resolution 1851 seems to insinuate? In the pursuance of these questions, particular attention is devoted to the emergence of certain general standards pertaining to maritime interception operations and to the (extraterritorial) application of human rights law at sea. In addition, the attribution of possible human rights violations in the United Nations-mandated multinational counter-piracy operations is considered (Chapter III).

Finally, Part IV focuses on the criminal prosecution of alleged pirates and armed robbers at sea. Here we discuss on what substantive criminal norms the prosecution of acts of piracy and armed robbery at sea could be based. Further, we attempt to distil the applicable jurisdictional basis from the complex mesh of international treaties potentially applicable to the various offenses typically committed in the context of piracy and armed robbery at sea. Thereby, we analyze whether the various counter-piracy Security Council Resolutions had an impact on the criminal prosecution of pirates and armed robbers at sea (Chapter I). In a next step, the different propositions and arguments as to the most suitable venue for the criminal prosecution of pirates and armed robbers at sea are then examined (Chapter II). For the time being, the majority of persons suspected of having committed acts of piracy or armed robbery at sea are prosecuted in regional States. The transfer of alleged offenders from States carrying out maritime enforcement operations in the Gulf of Aden and apprehending persons suspected for piracy or armed robbery at sea to regional States willing to prosecute them is a prerequisite for the commencement of any criminal proceedings. Thus, the legality of transfers of alleged pirates and armed robbers to regional States, especially in the light of the principle of *non-refoulement*, is a highly topical issue in the present context. It is the focus of the last chapter (Chapter III).

Part 1

Current Efforts to Counter Piracy in Somalia and the Gulf of Aden

I. Piracy in the Gulf of Aden

A. The Gulf of Aden

The Gulf of Aden, named for the seaport of Aden in southern Yemen, is a sea lane of strategic significance. Located in the Arabian Sea between Yemen on the south coast of the Arabian Peninsula and Somalia in the Horn of Africa, the Gulf of Aden is part of the important Suez Canal shipping route between the Mediterranean Sea, the Red Sea, the Arabian Sea and the Indian Ocean. The Gulf is roughly 900 kilometers long; its width varies. Littoral States of the Gulf are Djibouti, Egypt, Jordan, Saudi-Arabia, Somalia, Sudan and Yemen.[15]

It is estimated that the Gulf of Aden is used by approximately 22,000 vessels annually, carrying around 8% of the world's trade, including more than 12% of the total volume of oil transported by sea. Hence, it forms an essential oil transport route between Europe and the Far East.[16]

B. The Upsurge of Pirate Attacks in the Gulf of Aden since 2008

Piracy is not new to the Gulf of Aden.[17] The narrowness of the Gulf, which separates Somalia and Yemen by merely 170 nautical miles at its widest point and by

---

[15] Encyclopædia Britannica Online, Gulf of Aden, *available at* www.search.eb.com/eb/article-9003716 (last visited Aug. 30, 2010).

[16] European Space Agency, Earth from Space: The Gulf of Aden – The Gateway to Persian Oil, April 13, 2006, *available at* www.esa.int/esaEO/SEMWOXNFGLE_index_2.html (last visited Aug. 30, 2010).

[17] ICC-IMB, Piracy Report 2009, p. 25. In recent years, the Gulf of Aden has also received worldwide attention due to terrorist attacks. In October 2000, suicide bombers attacked and nearly sank the United States navy destroyer *Cole* in the Gulf of Aden: Globalsecurity.org, USS Cole Bombing, *available at* www.globalsecurity.org/security/profiles/uss_cole_bombing.htm (last visited Aug. 30, 2010). In 2002, the French tanker *M/V Limburg*, carrying Persian Gulf crude oil, was attacked: Globalsecurity.org, Limburg Oiltanker Attacked, www.globalsecurity.org/security/profiles/limburg_oil_tanker_attacked.htm (last visited Aug. 30, 2010).

merely 100 nautical miles at other points, together with the density of traffic on this important waterway, have long rendered this region prone to pirate attacks. All traffic is forced to pass within striking distance of the Somali coast.[18] In 2008, pirate attacks in the Gulf of Aden reached unprecedented dimensions, as shown by statistics from the International Maritime Organization, a specialized agency of the United Nations[19] and the International Maritime Bureau, a specialized division of the International Chamber of Commerce.[20]

Figures compiled by the International Maritime Organization demonstrate that in the first quarter of 2008, there were 11 pirate attacks in the region, rising to 23 in the second quarter and rocketing to 50 in the third and 51 in the fourth quarter. This amounts to a total of 135 attacks during 2008, resulting in the seizing of 44 ships by pirates and more than 600 seafarers being kidnapped and held for ransom.[21] The International Maritime Bureau's Piracy Reporting Centre arrived at similar, albeit slightly lower figures, estimating that in 2008 a total of 111 vessels were targeted by Somali pirates resulting in 42 hijackings.[22] Variations of figures in the different reports stem from the fact that different geographical areas may have been considered and that they are based on the number of incidents reported to the respective organizations. Traditionally, the estimated number of unreported cases has been quite high.

From 2006 to 2009, attacks by pirates and armed robbers at sea in Somali waters developed from a common domestic nuisance, aimed mainly at illegal fishing vessels, into a sophisticated and well-organized industry.[23] For the year 2006, the International Maritime Organization reported a total of only 31 (attempted or successful) incidents of piracy or armed robbery at sea in the entire East African Region[24] and a total of 53 incidents in the entire Indian Ocean.[25] However, in 2009, according to the Annual Piracy Report issued by the International Maritime

---

[18] United Nations, Monitoring Group on Somalia, Report, Dec. 10, 2008, para. 126.

[19] For more information about the International Maritime Organization (IMO), see www.imo.org (last visited Aug. 30, 2010).

[20] The International Maritime Bureau (IMB) is a non-profit organization, which was established in 1981 to act as a focal point in the fight against all types of maritime crime and malpractice; for more information about the International Maritime Bureau, see www.icc-ccs.org (follow hyperlink "International Maritime Bureau") (last visited Aug. 30, 2010).

[21] Figures *available at* www.imo.org (follow "Safety" hyperlink, then follow "Piracy and Armed Robbery against Ships" hyperlink, then follow "Piracy in Waters off the Coast of Somalia" hyperlink) (last visited Aug. 30, 2010).

[22] ICC-IMB, Piracy Report 2009, p. 25.

[23] United Nations, Monitoring Group on Somalia, Report, Dec. 10, 2008, para. 122.

[24] IMO, Piracy Report 2006: 18 incidents took place in international waters, 10 in territorial waters and 3 in port areas.

[25] *Id.*: Two incidents took place in international waters, 16 in territorial waters and 35 in port areas.

Bureau's Piracy Reporting Centre, 222 incidents occurred in East Africa.[26] It appears that in 2009, 217 incidents could be attributed to Somali pirates alone, with 47 vessels hijacked and 867 people (crew members and passengers) taken hostage. Thus, Somali pirates and armed robbers at sea account for more than half of the world-wide 2009 figure of 406 incidents of piracy and armed robbery against ships.[27]

The Secretary-General's Report pursuant to Security Council Resolution 1846 as well as the International Maritime Bureau's Annual Report for 2009 point out that while the number of incidents (comprising successful as well as unsuccessful and merely attempted attacks) has further increased, the proportion of successful hijackings has decreased.[28] The reports attribute this to the increased presence of international maritime forces in the area. Heightened awareness and preparedness by the shipmasters transiting these waters certainly also played a role in this regard.[29]

A significant shift in the area of attacks can be observed. Throughout 2008, attacks predominantly occurred in the Gulf of Aden. In 2009, pirates increasingly broadened their range of operation. According to the International Maritime Bureau's Piracy Report for the period between January and September 2009, Somali pirates extended their reach to the Red Sea and Bab el Mandab Straits.[30] Most importantly, since October 2009, an increasing number of attacks have been observed in the Western Indian Ocean towards the Seychelles and off the coast of Oman.[31] Between October and December 2009, the International Maritime Bureau counted 33 incidents, including 13 hijackings in the Indian Ocean.[32] Many of these attacks occurred at distances of approximately 1,000 nautical miles off the Somali shore, including in the territorial waters of the Seychelles.[33] This suggests, *prima facie*, that the problem of piracy in the region is as pertinent as ever. It seems likely that if

---

[26] IMO, Piracy Report 2009. For the period from 1 January to 30 September, 2009, 160 incidents in the East African area had been reported according to the United Nations, Secretary-General Report on S.C. Res. 1846, Nov. 13, 2009, which relies on figures compiled by the International Maritime Organization. According to figures of the International Maritime Organization for this period, in the waters off the coast of Somalia 34 ships had been hijacked and more than 450 seafarers had been taken hostage.

[27] ICC-IMB, Piracy Report 2009, p. 25; the last time piracy figures exceeded 400 incidents was in 2003. The year 2009 marks the third successive year in which the number of reported incidents has increased. The number of reported incidents was 239 for 2006, 263 for 2007 and 293 for 2008.

[28] United Nations, Secretary-General Report on S.C. Res. 1846, Nov. 13, 2009, para. 5.

[29] ICC-IMB, Piracy Report 2009, p. 25; United Nations, Secretary-General Report on S.C. Res. 1846, Nov. 13, 2009, para. 5.

[30] ICC-IMB, Piracy Report January-September 2009, p. 27; ICC-IMB, Piracy Report 2009, p. 25.

[31] United Nations, Secretary-General Report on S.C. Res. 1846, Nov. 13, 2009, para. 6.

[32] ICC-IMB, Piracy Report 2009, p. 25.

[33] United Nations, Secretary-General Report on S.C. Res. 1846, Nov. 13, 2009, para. 6; ICC-IMB, Worldwide Piracy Figures Surpass 400, Jan. 14, 2010, *available at* www.icc-ccs.org (follow "News" hyperlink) (last visited Aug. 30, 2010).

the maritime presence in the Gulf of Aden region were to decrease, the number of successful attacks would instantaneously rise again.

C. Somali Pirates: Who Are They?

Somali pirates and armed robbers at sea often appear to be closely connected to the coastal fishing communities of north-eastern and central Somalia, and their organization reflects Somali clan based social structure.[34] The Monitoring Group on Somalia points out that it "has found no evidence to support allegations of structured cooperation between pirate groups and armed opposition groups, including Al-Shabaab."[35] Moreover, the Monitoring Group emphasized that it "considers Somali-based piracy to be a fundamentally criminal activity attributable to specific militia groups and families."[36]

Illicit overfishing by foreign vessels and the dumping of toxic waste into Somalia's territorial waters, combined with general economic hardship, are widely presumed to be among the factors that have led these groups to resort to piracy as a source of revenue. Nevertheless, the Monitoring Group on Somalia has stated that "[e]xploitation of Somali marine resources is a reality, but it is by no means a preoccupation of Somali pirates or their backers."[37] Still, it appears that foreign exploitation has been brought forward as a justification for carrying out acts of piracy.[38] It is for this reason that during the Security Council debates on the Resolutions pertaining to piracy and armed robbery at sea, various States have emphasized the importance of devising a communication strategy to explain international maritime efforts against piracy in Somalia's territorial waters to coastal communities.

Initially, Somali pirate groups were only loosely organized, partially ill-equipped and fluid in membership. However, according to the Monitoring Group on Somalia, the extraordinarily lucrative nature of piracy has transformed rag-tag, ocean-going militias into well-resourced, efficient and heavily armed syndicates, employing hundreds of people in north-eastern and central Somalia. Some of these groups now appear to rival or surpass established Somali authorities in terms of their military capabilities and resources.[39] External financiers typically provide the boats, fuel, arms and ammunition, communication equipment and pirate salaries.

---

[34] United Nations, Monitoring Group on Somalia, Report, Dec. 10, 2008, para. 131.
[35] United Nations, Monitoring Group on Somalia, Report, March 10, 2010, para. 129.
[36] *Id.* at para. 130.
[37] *Id.* at para. 127.
[38] United Nations, Monitoring Group on Somalia, Report, Dec. 10, 2008, para. 125.
[39] *Id.* at para. 122.

D. Pirate Attacks: The *Modus Operandi*

Piracy has emerged as a highly lucrative business. The *modus operandi* of pirates has, accordingly, become more and more sophisticated.[40] Increasingly, scouts appear to be used to provide intelligence on the movement of vessels and to monitor major ports in neighboring countries.[41] It also appears that pirate groups are engaged in the systematic corruption of local officials.[42]

It seems that certain vessels, particularly fishing vessels, have been hijacked with the specific intention of converting them into "mother ships." Captured vessels whose owners are unable to meet ransom demands may likewise be used as "mother ships." According to the NATO Shipping Center's description of piracy operations in the Gulf of Aden, "mother ship" supply ports exist at Al Mukallah, Al Shishr, Sayhut, Nishtun, Al Ghaydah on the Yemeni coast and Bossaso, Aluula and Mogadishu on the Somali coast.[43]

The use of "mother ships" that can launch smaller crafts, allows pirates to extend the range and endurance of their attacks and to operate far off the coast. Attacks as distant as 1,000 nautical miles off shore have been reported, which allow the hijacking of larger vessels, including oil tankers.[44] On April 18, 2010, three Thai fishing vessels from Djibouti were hijacked 1,200 nautical miles east of the coast off Somalia. Reportedly, this has been the furthest east pirate attack thus far.[45] The International Maritime Bureau advises that vessels not making scheduled calls to ports in Somalia should keep as far away as possible from the Somali coast, preferably more than 600 nautical miles from the coast line, and when routing north or south to consider keeping east of the Seychelles.[46]

Attacks are commonly conducted with a number of readily maneuverable smaller crafts (skiffs or fiberglass speedboats) that are equipped with powerful outboard engines. According to the Report of the Monitoring Group on Somalia pursuant to Security Council Resolution 1811,[47] arms seized by the Danish military

---

[40] United Nations, Secretary-General Report on Somalia, Jan. 8, 2010, para. 23.

[41] United Nations, Monitoring Group on Somalia, Report, Dec. 10, 2008, para. 136.

[42] United Nations, UNODC, Piracy-Background, *available at* www.unodc.org/eastern africa/en/piracy/background.html (last visited Aug. 30, 2010).

[43] United Nations, Monitoring Group on Somalia, Report, Dec. 10, 2008, para. 137.

[44] *Id.*

[45] European Union, Council of the European Union, News in Brief, Pirates Head East to Counter EUNAVFOR Success, April 20, 2010, *available at* http://consilium.europa.eu/ showPage.aspx?id=1567&lang=en (last visited Aug. 30, 2010).

[46] ICC-IMB, Piracy Prone Areas and Warnings, *available at* www.icc-ccs.org (follow "IMB Piracy Reporting Center" hyperlink, then follow "Piracy Prone Areas and Warnings" hyperlink) (last visited Aug. 30, 2010).

[47] United Nations, Security Council, S.C. Res. 1811, U.N. Doc. S/RES/1811 (April 29, 2008). Pursuant to S.C. Res. 1519, U.N. Doc. S/RES/1519 (Dec. 16, 2003), para. 2, the

ship *Absalon* on September 19, 2008 provide a typical sample of the weapons employed by pirate teams: Kalashnikov assault rifles, rocket-propelled grenade-7V
launchers, Tokarev TT-33/7.62 mm pistols, a French LRAC F1/89 mm anti-tank
rocket launcher and M76 rifles.[48] The pirates and armed robbers at sea were also in
possession of mobile phones, a global positioning system device and extra fuel
tanks. Pirates frequently carry high-power binoculars, grappling hooks, telescopic
aluminum ladders and small boat radars that help them to detect targets, particularly at night, and to keep track of the vessel traffic around them.[49]

The acquisition of these arms, ammunition and equipment almost certainly involves violations of the arms embargo first imposed on Somalia by the Security
Council on January 23, 1992.[50] The Monitoring Group on Somalia estimates that
most serviceable weapons and almost all ammunition currently available in the
country have been delivered since 1992 in violation of the embargo. Although provision exists for exemptions to the embargo to be granted by the Security Council
under the various Resolutions,[51] notably regarding efforts to combat piracy and
armed robbery at sea off the coast of Somalia, no exemption for the delivery of
arms and ammunition to any Somali armed group has ever been granted. Consequently, the Monitoring Group believes that every armed group in Somalia, its
financiers and active supporters are currently in violation of the arms embargo.[52]
Indeed, Security Council Resolution 1897 explicitly mentions the lack of enforcement of this arms embargo as a factor that is fueling the growth of piracy in the
region.[53] The Monitoring Group on Somalia, in its Report of December 10, 2008,

---

Secretary-General established a Monitoring Group on Somalia composed of four experts
for a period of six months. The mandate of the Monitoring Group has continuously been
extended since. By S.C. Res. 1853, U.N. Doc. S/RES/1853 (Dec. 19, 2008) [hereinafter:
S.C. Res. 1853], the Security Council decided to extend the mandate of the Monitoring
Group, requesting the Secretary-General to re-establish the Monitoring Group for a period
of twelve months and to add a fifth expert to the group of four. According to S.C. Res.
1853, para. 3, the current mandate of the Monitoring Group includes, *inter alia*, continuing
to investigate the implementation of the arms embargo, all activities which generate rev-
enues used to commit arms embargo violations and any means of transport, routes, seaports,
airports and other facilities used in connection with arms embargo violations. The Monitoring
Group is further mandated to assist in identifying areas where the capacities of States in the
region can be strengthened to facilitate the implementation of the arms embargo.

[48] United Nations, Monitoring Group on Somalia, Report, Dec. 10, 2008, para. 138; see
also United Nations, UNODC, Piracy-Background, *available at* www.unodc.org/eastern
africa/en/piracy/background.html (last visited Aug. 30, 2010).

[49] United Nations, Monitoring Group on Somalia, Report, Dec. 10, 2008, para. 138.

[50] *Id.* at para. 122.

[51] United Nations, Security Council, S.C. Res. 1356, U.N. Doc. S/RES/1356 (June 19,
2001); S.C. Res. 1725, U.N. Doc. S/RES/1725 (Dec. 6, 2006); S.C. Res. 1744, U.N. Doc.
S/RES/1744 (Feb. 21, 2007) [hereinafter: S.C. Res. 1744]; S.C. Res. 1772, U.N. Doc.
S/RES/1772 (Aug. 20, 2007); S.C. Res. 1816; S.C. Res. 1846; S.C. Res. 1851.

[52] United Nations, Monitoring Group on Somalia, Report, Dec. 10, 2008, para. 9; S.C.
Res. 1846, para. 12; and S.C. Res. 1851, para. 11.

[53] S.C. Res. 1897, para. 2.

emphasized that leading figures in piracy syndicates are responsible for arms embargo violations and should be considered for individual targeted sanctions under Security Council Resolution 1844 of November 20, 2008.[54]

The Secretary-General's Report of November 13, 2009, pursuant to Security Council Resolution 1846, states that no significant, observable change occurred during the reporting period in the *modus operandi* of pirate attacks.[55] With regard to piracy incidents worldwide, the International Maritime Bureau's Report notes that the level of violence towards crews has increased, along with the number of crew injuries.[56] According to the International Maritime Bureau's Piracy Report for the period between January and September 2009, pirate attacks in which firearms were used increased in 2009 by more than 200 compared to 2008.[57] More and more, there appears to be an intersection between piracy and other criminal activities, such as arms trafficking and human trafficking, both of which involve the movement of small craft across the Gulf of Aden.[58]

E. Ransom Payments: A Factor Fueling the Growth of Piracy

Piracy is an increasingly important source of revenue in the Gulf of Aden region, because of considerable ransom payments.[59] Indeed, Security Council Resolution 1897 speaks of "escalating ransom payments" fueling the growth of piracy off the coast of Somalia.[60]

In this regard it should be noted that the payment of ransom to pirates potentially amounts to financing of terrorism. Article 2(1) of the International Convention for the Suppression of the Financing of Terrorism, which entered into force in 2002,[61] stipulates that:

Art. 2 International Convention for the Suppression of the Financing of Terrorism

1. Any person commits an offense within the meaning of this Convention if that person by any means, directly or indirectly, unlawfully and willfully, provides or collects funds with the intention that they should be used or in the knowledge that they are to be used, in full or in part, in order to carry out:

---

[54] United Nations, Monitoring Group on Somalia, Report, Dec. 10, 2008, para. 123.

[55] United Nations, Secretary-General Report on S.C. Res. 1846, Nov. 13, 2009, para. 6.

[56] ICC-IMB, Piracy Report 2009, p. 25.

[57] ICC-IMB, Piracy Report January-September 2009, p. 27. See also the statistics provided in the IMO, Piracy Report 2009.

[58] United Nations, Monitoring Group on Somalia, Report, Dec. 10, 2008, para. 143.

[59] *Id.* at para. 266.

[60] S.C. Res. 1897, para. 2; see also S.C. Res. 1846, para. 2.

[61] International Convention for the Suppression of the Financing of Terrorism, *adopted* Dec. 9, 1999, 2178 U.N.T.S. 197.

(a) An act which constitutes an offense within the scope of and as defined in one of the treaties listed in the annex; or

(b) Any other act intended to cause death or serious bodily injury to a civilian, or to any other person not taking an active part in the hostilities in a situation of armed conflict, when the purpose of such act, by its nature or context, is to intimidate a population, or to compel a government or an international organization to do or to abstain from doing any act.

[…]

Notably, the SUA and Hostage Conventions figure among the treaties that are listed in the annex of the International Convention for the Suppression of the Financing of Terrorism and mentioned in the provision cited above. Since ransom payments are made to persons who have typically committed some of the offenses described in Article 1 of the Hostage Convention and Article 3 of the SUA Convention, such payments arguably amount to the financing of terrorism, as defined in Article 2 of the International Convention for the Suppression of the Financing of Terrorism. Moreover, such payments would appear to fall within the ambit of Security Council Resolution 1373 of September 28, 2001,[62] which is also aimed at the prevention and suppression of the financing of terrorist acts.

Admittedly, these findings may at first sight seem rather far-fetched. However, on the face of the relevant legal provisions, leaving the possibility of justifying such payments as a means of freeing hostages aside, the conclusion that ransom payments fulfill the legal requirements for the financing of terrorism is tenable. It is evidence that there is still a long way to go to achieve coordinated international responses to global criminal phenomena.

F. The Situation in Somalia

As is well known, since the collapse of Siad Barre's authoritarian socialist rule in 1991, Somalia has faced constant unrest. Although the Somali Transitional Federal Government was created in 2004, two semi-autonomous provinces, Puntland and Somaliland, have separated themselves from the mainland. Independence was declared by Somaliland in 1991, followed by Puntland in 1998. To date, however, these entitites have not been recognized by any State.[63] The situation in Somalia continues to be defined by the Security Council as a threat to the peace in the sense of Article 39 of the United Nations Charter.[64] The socio-economic situation in

---

[62] United Nations, Security Council, S.C. Res. 1373, U.N. Doc. S/RES/1373 (Dec. 28, 2001) [hereinafter: S.C. Res. 1873], para. 2(e).

[63] United States of America, Central Intelligence Agency, The World Fact Book, Somalia, *available at* https://www.cia.gov/library/publications/the-world-factbook/geos/so.html (last visited Aug. 30, 2010).

[64] S.C. Res. 1897.

Somalia is dire, as indicated by its gross domestic product per capita ratio and life expectancy, which are among the lowest in the world.[65] Somalia is the most often cited example of a failed State.[66]

In 2004, the Somali Transitional Federal Government was installed, but its support in Somalia soon waned. In 2006, the Ethiopian military intervened to drive the rival Islamic Courts Union out of Mogadishu and to uphold the Transitional Federal Government's rule. The Transitional Federal Government is internationally recognized as the official government of Somalia and currently represents Somalia in the United Nations, the African Union and the Organization of the Islamic Conference. However, its capacity to act on the international level is arguably greater than its ability to act within Somalia. The respective Security Council Resolutions relating to piracy and armed robbery at sea off Somalia's coast confirm that the Transitional Federal Government is unable to maintain order within Somalia where a non-international armed conflict is ongoing. Opposition to the Transitional Federal Government is distributed across a wide spectrum of armed groups. These groups share some common objectives, but they lack unified command and are openly divided over a number of issues.[67] The total strength of opposition groups is unknown. The Monitoring Group on Somalia estimates that the various groups collectively control or exercise influence over more than 90% of the territory of Somalia south of the town of Gaalka'yo.[68]

The armed conflict in Somalia is of low-intensity, with simmering but omnipresent violence, characterized by small-scale engagements of limited duration and poorly disciplined irregular forces that are armed with conventional infantry weapons. This is sustained by a constant, low-level flow of weapons and ammunition in contravention of the arms embargo.[69] The armed groups are typically self-financing, with the proceeds from piracy and kidnapping used to procure arms, ammunition and equipment.[70]

In February 2007 the Security Council in Resolution 1744, authorized member States of the African Union to establish the African Union Mission in Somalia (AMISOM) for an initial period of six months.[71] The African Union Mission in

---

[65] United States of America, Central Intelligence Agency, The World Fact Book, Somalia, *available at* https://www.cia.gov/library/publications/the-world-factbook/geos/so.html (last visited Aug. 30, 2010).

[66] *Geiß*, Failed States, p. 44.

[67] United Nations, Monitoring Group on Somalia, Report, Dec. 10, 2008, para. 56.

[68] *Id.* at para. 57.

[69] See also *Geiß*, Qualifying Armed Violence in Fragile States – Low Intensity Conflicts, Spill Over Conflicts and Sporadic Law Enforcement Operations by External Actors, IRRC 91 (2009), 127.

[70] United Nations, Monitoring Group on Somalia, Report, Dec. 10, 2008, para. 6.

[71] S.C. Res. 1744.

Somalia was authorized to take all necessary measures as appropriate, *inter alia*, to support reconciliation in Somalia, to provide protection to the Transitional Federal Government to help it carry out its functions of government and to contribute, as may be requested and within its capabilities, to the creation of the necessary security conditions for the provision of humanitarian assistance. The mandate of the African Union Mission in Somalia has been extended several times, most recently by Security Council Resolution 1910, until January 31, 2011.[72]

In 2009, insecurity remained widespread throughout Somalia.[73] Similarly, the humanitarian situation remained dire. It is estimated that more than 3.6 million Somalis (compared to 3.2 million in January 2009), or nearly 50% of the total population, will continue to require humanitarian assistance or livelihood support into 2010.[74] By November 2009, the total number of internally displaced persons in Somalia had reached 1.55 million, 93% of whom were concentrated in the southern and central areas, including 524,000 in the Afgooye corridor. According to a more recent Report, the figure had slightly fallen to 1.4 million internally displaced persons during the period from December 2009 to January 2010.[75]

The link between the situation on the Somali mainland and the upsurge of piracy off Somalia's coast is evident. The Contact Group on Piracy off the Coast of Somalia, a coordination mechanism established on January 14, 2009 pursuant to United Nations Security Council Resolution 1851,[76] pointed out that piracy was a symptom of a wider lack of security and rule of law in Somalia and continues to constitute a threat to regional stability.[77] Security Council Resolution 1872 emphasizes that "the ongoing instability in Somalia contributes to the problem of piracy and armed robbery at sea off the coast of Somalia, stressing the need for a comprehensive response by the international community to tackle piracy and its underlying cause."[78] Furthermore, the Secretary-General has pointed out that "the long-term solution to piracy can come only by re-establishing the rule of law in Somalia."[79]

---

[72] United Nations, Security Council, S.C. Res. 1910, U.N. Doc. S/RES/1910 (Jan. 28, 2010).

[73] United Nations, Monitoring Group on Somalia, Report, Dec. 10, 2008, para. 16. See also United Nations, Security Council, Statement by the President of the Security Council, U.N. Doc. S/PRST/2009/31 (Dec. 3, 2009).

[74] United Nations, Secretary-General Report on Somalia, Jan. 8, 2010, para. 24.

[75] United Nations, Secretary-General Report on Somalia, May 11, 2010, para. 15.

[76] S.C. Res. 1851, para. 4; on the Contact Group on Piracy off the Coast of Somalia, see p. 26 *et seq.*

[77] United States of America, Africa Command, Policy Statement: Contact Group on Piracy off the Coast of Somalia, Jan. 14, 2009, *available at* www.africom.mil/getArticle.asp?art=2466 (last visited Aug. 30, 2010). United Nations, Monitoring Group on Somalia, Report, March 10, 2010, paras. 11–13.

[78] S.C. Res. 1872, para. 72.

[79] United Nations, Security Council, Official Records, 64th Session, 6197th Meeting, U.N. Doc. S/PV.6197 (Oct. 8, 2009).

Against this background, it is astounding that the Secretary-General's latest Report on the situation in Somalia of January 8, 2010, notes that "[d]espite the fact that humanitarian needs have increased in 2009, there has been a significant drop in humanitarian funding. At the end of November, the 2009 Somalia consolidated appeals process was 60 percent funded, with $512 million having been received out of the $851 million required. The slow release of new funding and the overall reduction in total funding have had a direct impact on humanitarian action in Somalia."[80]

In spite of the repeated affirmation that the solution to the piracy problem not only lies at sea but also on land, thus far States have not made use of the authorization of Security Council Resolution 1851 as prolonged by Security Council Resolution 1897 to conduct law enforcement operations on the Somali mainland. Apparently, the Somali Transitional Federal Government has not provided any advance notification to the Secretary-General, as is required by Security Council Resolution 1851, with regard to any State that wishes to operate on the Somali mainland.[81] Notably, the law enforcement operation that was executed by French forces in the context of the so-called *Ponant Affair* in April 2008 took place before Security Council Resolution 1851 was adopted and was based on the specific consent of the Somali Transitional Federal Government. After the French yacht *Ponant* and its passengers had been hijacked and taken hostage by Somali pirates, French forces freed the passengers and subsequently pursued and arrested six alleged pirates, apparently on Somali mainland.[82]

Therefore, it seems safe to conclude that (despite the presence of the African Union Mission in Somalia and the singular example of the *Ponant Affair*) on the whole, States remain as reluctant as ever to become engaged on Somalia's mainland. This attitude may change in the near future, as the need to develop long-term solutions to prevent, repress, and prosecute acts of piracy and armed robbery at sea will become more pressing. Clearly, the costs for the current maritime presence off Somalia's coast and in the Gulf of Aden are not sustainable over a significant number of years. It may be seen as a harbinger of such a development in the near future that France recently submitted a proposal to the European Union suggesting the training of African Union security personnel to conduct counter-piracy operations on the Somali mainland.[83]

---

[80] United Nations, Secretary-General Report on Somalia, Jan. 8, 2010, para. 26.

[81] S.C. Res. 1851, para. 6.

[82] The New York Times, French Troops Seize Somali Pirates after Hostages are Freed, April 11, 2008, *available at* www.nytimes.com/2008/04/11/world/africa/11iht-yacht .4.11921315.html (last visited Aug. 30, 2010).

[83] *Diekhans*, ARD, Die Anti-Piraten-Mission "Atalanta" – Erfolgreich oder überfordert? Dec. 9, 2010, *available at* www.tagesschau.de/ausland/atalanta110.html (last visited Aug. 30, 2010).

II. Efforts to Counter Piracy in the Gulf of Aden

A. Naval Enforcement Missions Operating in the Region

The Secretary-General's Report of November 13, 2009, pursuant to Security
Council Resolution 1846, concludes that the combined efforts of the international
naval forces operating off the coast of Somalia have considerably reduced successful incidents of piracy and armed robbery at sea in the region.[84] At the same time
the Monitoring Group on Somalia points out that "[a]rguably the main effect of
international counter-piracy efforts has been to shift pirate areas of operation away
from the Gulf of Aden into the Indian Ocean and towards hunting grounds increasingly distant from the Somali coast."[85]

Three multinational missions, the European Union Operation Atalanta, NATO
Operation Ocean Shield and the United States-led Combined Task Force 151, are
currently deployed in the area. In addition, several States are operating independently, albeit usually in coordination with the multinational coalitions, in the region.
Japan, China, the Russian Federation, India, Malaysia, the Republic of Korea,
Saudi Arabia, the Islamic Republic of Iran and Yemen have deployed naval ships
and/or aircraft to fight piracy in the Gulf of Aden.[86]

These various forces operate under different command structures, but in accordance with the respective Security Council Resolutions. Thus, they share the common objectives of deterring and preventing piracy and armed robbery at sea off
the coast of Somalia, ensuring the safe delivery of humanitarian assistance to the
region (namely shipments of the World Food Program and logistical support to the
African Union Mission in Somalia) and facilitating safe navigation for all merchant
shipping.

To this end, since February 1, 2009, the so-called Internationally Recommended
Transit Corridor (IRTC) has been established. It is intended to allow merchant vessels to transit the Gulf of Aden safely. The corridor is supported by vessels involved in counter-piracy activities in the region, including European Union Operation Atalanta, the Combined Maritime Forces, NATO, China, Japan, the Republic
of Korea and some regional countries. The Internationally Recommended Transit
Corridor was endorsed by the International Maritime Organization in 2009 and
enables commercial shipping, registered in advance using the Maritime Security
Centre – Horn of Africa,[87] to transit "high risk" seas at agreed times, protected by

---

[84] United Nations, Secretary-General Report on S.C. Res. 1846, Nov. 13, 2009, para. 18.

[85] United Nations, Monitoring Group on Somalia, Report, March 10, 2010, para. 122.

[86] *Id.* at para. 27.

[87] For further information on the Maritime Security Centre – Horn of Africa (MSCHOA),
see p. 28 *et seq.*

naval forces patrolling the relevant area.[88] By grouping merchant shipping by speed, with staggered starting points, the mechanism allows for close monitoring and quicker response by the nearest military ships in case of emergency. In comparison with convoys and escorts, group transit has proved to be a very effective means of protection with limited resources for a maximum number of vessels.[89]

The enforcement powers of these various maritime forces derive from Security Council Resolutions 1846 and 1851 and the UNCLOS.[90] Upon their expiry in December 2009, the time limited authorizations of Security Council Resolutions 1846 and 1851 (notably it is not the Resolutions as a whole that are time limited but the specific operative paragraphs) were prolonged for a period of 12 months until December 2010 by virtue of Security Council Resolution 1897. The relevant operative paragraphs of Security Council Resolutions 1846 and 1851 require that the Somali Transitional Federal Government provide advance notification to the Secretary-General with respect to any State that wishes to operate in Somalia's territorial waters or upon its mainland.[91] As stated above, as far as can be seen, until now no such (officially recorded) notification has been transmitted to the Secretary-General with respect to Security Council Resolution 1851, i.e. with regard to States intending to operate on Somalia's mainland. As of October 31, 2009, Somalia has received 16 notifications from States and regional organizations in accordance with Security Council Resolution 1846, that is, notifications indicating the wish to operate in Somalia's territorial waters. In addition to the European Union and NATO, the following 14 States have submitted notifications: Canada, India, China, Turkey, the Russian Federation, the United States of America, Denmark, France, the Netherlands, Spain, the United Kingdom of Great Britain and Northern Ireland, Australia, the Islamic Republic of Iran and the Republic of Korea.[92]

1. European Union Naval Force Operation Atalanta

The European Union Naval Force (EUNAVFOR) Operation Atalanta was established by a Council Joint Action on November 10, 2008.[93] Operation Atalanta is

---

[88] *Petretto*, in: Mair (ed.), Piraterie und Maritime Sicherheit, 14–15; International Maritime Organization, Piracy and Armed Robbery against Ships in Waters off the Coast of Somalia, Information on Internationally Recommended Transit Corridor (IRTC) for Ships Transiting the Gulf of Aden, IMO Doc. SN.1/Circ.281 (Aug. 3, 2009); International Maritime Organization, Resolution A.1026(26), adopted on December 2, 2009, Piracy and Armed Robbery against Ships in Waters off the Coast of Somalia, IMO Doc. A.26/Res. 1026) (Dec. 3, 2009).

[89] United Nations, Secretary-General Report on S.C. Res. 1846, Nov. 13, 2009, para. 37.

[90] *Id.* at para. 17.

[91] S.C. Res. 1846, para. 10; S.C. Res. 1851, para. 6.

[92] United Nations, Secretary-General Report on S.C. Res. 1846, Nov. 13, 2009, para. 17.

[93] European Union, Council Joint Action 2008/851/CFSP of November 10, 2008 on a European Union Military Operation to Contribute to the Deterrence, Prevention and

the first European Union-led maritime operation and is being conducted within the framework of the European Security and Defense Policy (ESDP).[94] Notably, the Council Joint Action on Operation Atalanta also provides for the participation of third (non-European Union) States in the naval deployment.[95] Thus far, the participation of Norway, Croatia, Montenegro and Ukraine in the European Union Operation Atalanta has been approved by the Political and Security Committee.[96]

Operation Atalanta was launched on December 8, 2008 and became operational on the 13th of the same month, with its operational headquarters at Northwood in the United Kingdom.[97] Initially scheduled for a period of one year, Operation Atalanta has been extended until December 12, 2010.[98] As of October 2009, the operation included 11 vessels and 3 aircraft.[99] For the extended mission until 2010, all together more than 20 vessels and maritime patrol aircraft, with more than 1'800

Repression of Acts of Piracy and Armed Robbery off the Coast of Somalia, 2008 O.J. (L 301) 31–37 (EU) [hereinafter: EU Council Joint Action Operation Atalanta]. The EU Council Joint Action Operation Atalanta is reprinted on p. 267 *et seq.* of this book (Appendix).

[94] According to Art. 6 EU Council Joint Action Operation Atalanta the Political and Security Committee (PSC) exercises the political control and strategic direction of the European Union military operation. According to the Europa Glossary, Political and Security Committee, *available at* http://europa.eu/scadplus/glossary/political_security_committee_ en.htm (last visited Aug. 30, 2010), the Political and Security Committee is the permanent body in the field of common foreign and security policy mentioned in Art. 25 of the Treaty on European Union as amended by the Treaty of Lisbon. It is made up of the political directors of the member States' foreign ministries. Its remit is to monitor the international situation in the areas covered by the common foreign and security policy; to contribute to the definition of policies and to monitor implementation of the Council's decisions. Under the responsibility of the Council, the Committee exercises political control and strategic direction of crisis management operations. It may thus be authorized by the Council to take decisions on the practical management of a crisis.

[95] Art. 10 EU Council Joint Action Operation Atalanta.

[96] Art. 1 of the Political and Security Committee Decision ATALANTA/1/2010 of 5 March 2010 amending Political and Security Committee Decision ATALANTA/2/2009 on the acceptance of third States' contributions to the European Union military operation to contribute to the deterrence, prevention and repression of acts of piracy and armed robbery off the Somali coast (Atalanta) and Political and Security Committee Decision ATALANTA/3/2009 on the setting up of the Committee of Contributors for the European Union military operation to contribute to the deterrence, prevention and repression of acts of piracy and armed robbery off the Somali coast (Atalanta), 2010 O.J. (L 83) 20–21 (EU).

[97] European Union, Council Decision 2008/918/CFSP of December 8, 2008, on the Launch of a European Union Military Operation to Contribute to the Deterrence, Prevention and Repression of Acts of Piracy and Armed Robbery off the Somali Coast (Atalanta), 2009 O.J. (L 330) 19–20 (EU).

[98] European Union, Council Decision 2009/907/CFSP of December 8, 2009 amending Joint Action 2008/851/CFSP on a European Union Military Operation to Contribute to the Deterrence, Prevention and Repression of Acts of Piracy and Armed Robbery off the Somali Coast, 2009 O.J. (L 322) 27 (EU).

[99] European Union, Council of the European Union, Operation EUNAVFOR, Current Total Strength of EU-NAVFOR Atalanta, *available at* http://consilium.europa.eu/uedocs/ cmsUpload/naviresOCTOBRE.pdf (last visited Aug. 30, 2010).

military personnel from the Netherlands, Spain, Germany, France, Greece, Italy, Sweden, Belgium and Luxembourg, are expected to participate. Operation Atalanta's current area of deployment is up to 500 nautical miles off the coast of Somalia. In practice, the European Union Naval Force operates in a zone comprising the south of the Red Sea, the Gulf of Aden and part of the Western Indian Ocean, which represents an area comparable in size to that of the Mediterranean Sea.[100]

Operation Atalanta's mandate is to protect vessels chartered by the World Food Program, including by means of the presence of armed units on board those vessels and the protection, based on a case-by-case evaluation of needs, of merchant vessels cruising in the areas where it is deployed. Moreover, Operation Atalanta is tasked with keeping watch over areas off the Somali coast, including Somalia's territorial waters, in which there are dangers to maritime activities, in particular to maritime traffic. The mandate also encompasses taking the necessary measures, including the use of force, to deter, prevent and intervene, in order to bring to an end acts of piracy and armed robbery at sea, which may be committed in the areas where it is present. Furthermore, Atalanta is mandated to arrest, detain and transfer persons who have committed, or are suspected of having committed, acts of piracy or armed robbery at sea in the areas where it is present. Atalanta may also seize the vessels of pirates or armed robbers at sea, or the vessels caught following an act of piracy or an armed robbery at sea and which are in the hands of the pirates, as well as the goods on board. To this end, Operation Atalanta liaises with organizations and entities, as well as States, working in the region to combat acts of piracy and armed robbery at sea off the Somali coast.[101]

According to the Report of the Secretary-General pursuant to Security Council Resolution 1846, during the reporting period from January 1 to October 31, 2009, Atalanta provided 47 escort missions and allowed for the safe arrival of all World Food Program and United Nations related shipments.[102]

In order to fulfill its counter-piracy mandate effectively, the European Union concluded a number of Status of Forces Agreements (SOFAs). A Status of Forces Agreement is an agreement that establishes the framework under which armed forces operate within a foreign country. Typically, a Status of Forces Agreement provides for rights and privileges of the forces while in the foreign jurisdiction. In particular, the Council has approved Status of Forces Agreements between the European Union and Somalia as well as between the European Union and

---

[100] Art. 1(2) EU Council Joint Action Operation Atalanta; European Union, Council of the European Union, EU Naval Operation against Piracy, Factsheet, Feb. 1, 2010, *available at* http://consilium.europa.eu/showPage.aspx?id=1521&lang=en (last visited Aug. 30, 2010), p. 2.; see also United Nations, Secretary-General Report on S.C. Res. 1846, Nov. 13, 2009, para. 20.

[101] Art. 2 EU Council Joint Action Operation Atalanta.

[102] United Nations, Secretary-General Report on S.C. Res. 1846, Nov. 13, 2009, para. 21.

Djibouti.[103] In October 2009, the Council of the European Union also approved a Status of Forces Agreement between the European Union and the Republic of Seychelles.[104] These agreements regulate the privileges and immunities granted by the host State to personnel of the European Union-Led Naval Force, issues relating to identification, border crossing and movement within the host State's territory, as well as questions relating to criminal jurisdiction over personnel of the European Union-Led Naval Force, the wearing of uniforms and arms during the mission and possible claims for death, injury, damage and loss.[105]

Besides concluding Status of Forces Agreements, the European Union also entered into agreements with regional States, regulating the conditions of transfers of piracy suspects to any such State, in view of their criminal prosecution. The Council of the European Union approved an Exchange of Letters between the European Union and the government of Kenya on the conditions and modalities for the transfer of suspected persons and seized property.[106] Further, on October 23, 2009, the Council approved the signing and provisional application of the Exchange of Letters between the European Union and the Republic of Seychelles regarding the conditions and modalities for the transfer of suspected pirates and armed robbers at sea from the European Union-Led Naval Force to the Republic of Seychelles and for their treatment after such transfer.[107]

---

[103] European Union, Council Decision 2009/29/CFSP of December 22, 2008 Concerning the Conclusion of the Agreement between the European Union and the Somali Republic on the Status of the European Union-Led Naval Force in the Somali Republic in the Framework of the EU Military Operation Atalanta, 2009 O.J. (L 10) 27–28 (EU) [hereinafter: Council Decision, EU-Somalia SOFA]; Council Decision 2009/88/CFSP of December 22, 2008 Concerning the Conclusion of the Agreement between the European Union and the Republic of Djibouti on the Status of the European Union-Led Forces in the Republic of Djibouti in the Framework of the EU Military Operation Atalanta, 2009 O.J. (L 33) 41–42 [hereinafter: Council Decision, EU-Djibouti SOFA].

[104] European Union, Council Decision 2009/916/CFSP of October 23, 2009 Concerning the Signing and Conclusion of the Agreement between the European Union and the Republic of Seychelles on the Status of the European Union-Led Force in the Republic of Seychelles in the Framework of the EU Military Operation Atalanta, 2009 O.J. (L 323) 12–13 [hereinafter: Council Decision, EU-Seychelles SOFA].

[105] See, for example, the Agreement between the European Union and the Republic of Djibouti on the Status of the European Union-Led Forces in the Republic of Djibouti in the Framework of the EU Military Operation Atalanta, 2009 O.J. (L 33) 43–48 (EU).

[106] Exchange of Letters between the European Union and the Government of Kenya on the conditions and modalities for the transfer of persons suspected of having committed acts of piracy and detained by the European Union-Led Naval Force (EUNAVFOR), and seized property in the possession of EUNAVFOR, from EUNAVFOR to Kenya and for their treatment after such transfer, 2009 O.J. (L 79) 49–59 (EU) [hereinafter: EU-Kenya Transfer Agreement]. Excerpts of the EU-Kenya Transfer Agreement are reprinted on p. 276 et seq. of this book (Appendix). The Exchange of Letters was approved by the Council of the European Union, Council Decision 2009/293/CFSP, 2009 O.J. (L 79) 47–48 (EU).

[107] European Union, Exchange of Letters between the European Union and the Republic of Seychelles on the Conditions and Modalities for the Transfer of Suspected Pirates and

2. Consecutive NATO Operations

Three different NATO operations have been deployed in the region, namely NATO Operation Allied Provider, Operation Allied Protector and Operation Ocean Shield. Operation Ocean Shield is ongoing at the time of writing.

a) Operation Allied Provider

Operation Allied Provider took place from October 24 to December 13, 2008 and was conducted in direct response to a request by the United Nations Secretary-General of September 25, 2008, to the Secretary-General of NATO. It was carried out on the basis of Security Council Resolutions 1814, 1816 and 1838.[108] In a letter dated October 21, 2008, the Somali Transitional Federal Government informed the United Nations Secretariat that it had authorized NATO to provide naval escorts to vessels chartered by the World Food Program and to undertake counter-piracy functions in the region, including within Somali territorial waters. In addition, on October 23, 2008, the Somali Transitional Federal Government advised that it had authorized NATO to provide naval escorts to one ship transporting critical supplies through Somali waters to Mogadishu in support of the African Mission in Somalia.[109] Operation Allied Provider started to operate on October 24, 2008, when four ships from the NATO Standing Maritime Group 2 reached the assigned area and began operational activities.[110]

During the short period that Operation Allied Provider was operative in the region, it provided protection on eight occasions, namely in the form of naval escorts, to ships chartered by the World Food Program, which resulted in the safe delivery of 30,000 metric tonnes of humanitarian aid to Somalia. Moreover, Operation Allied Provider conducted deterrence patrols in the area most susceptible to criminal acts against merchant shipping. In the course of those patrols, NATO ships disrupted several pirate attacks against merchant vessels and deterred numerous others.[111] Operation Allied Provider was terminated on December 13, 2008, when

---

Armed Robbers from EUNAVFOR to the Republic of Seychelles and for their Treatment after such Transfer, 2009 O.J. (L 315) 37–43 (EU) [hereinafter: EU-Seychelles Transfer Agreement]. Excerpts of the EU-Seychelles Transfer Agreement are reprinted on p. 280 *et seq.* of this book (Appendix). The Exchange of Letters was approved by the Council of the European Union, Council Decision 2009/877/CFSP, 2009 O.J. (L 315) 35–36 (EU).

[108] United Nations, Security Council, S.C. Res. 1814, U.N. Doc. S/RES/1814 (May 15, 2008); S.C. Res. 1816; S.C. Res. 1838.

[109] United Nations, Secretary-General Report on S.C. Res. 1846, March 16, 2009, para. 26.

[110] NATO, Operation Allied Provider, *available at* www.manw.nato.int/page_operation _allied_provider.aspx (last visited Aug. 30, 2010).

[111] United Nations, Secretary-General Report on S.C. Res. 1846, Nov. 13, 2009, paras. 22 and 23.

the European Union Operation Atalanta (which was launched with similar aims) was declared operational.[112]

b) Operation Allied Protector

From March 24 until June 29, 2009, Operation Allied Protector was conducted by Standing NATO Maritime Group 1 vessels.[113] According to the official NATO website, "Operation Allied Protector helped to deter, defend against and disrupt pirate activities in the Gulf of Aden and off the Horn of Africa." Under Operation Allied Provider five NATO ships assisted the international efforts to repress piracy off the coast of Somalia and in the Gulf of Aden region.[114] Standing NATO Maritime Group 2 took over responsibility from Standing NATO Maritime Group 1 for conducting counter piracy operations off Somalia on June 29, 2009 and continued Operation Allied Protector.[115]

c) Operation Ocean Shield

Operation Ocean Shield was approved by the North Atlantic Council and commenced on August 17, 2009, replacing Operation Allied Protector.[116] Building on the two previous counter-piracy missions, Operation Ocean Shield focuses on at-sea counter-piracy operations in the area.[117] In the course of this operation, NATO has broadened its approach towards combating piracy and armed robbery at sea by introducing a new element to its mission. It is offering assistance to regional States that request it in developing their own capacity to counter piracy activities. The operation continues to comprise five NATO vessels from Standing Maritime Group 2, which patrol the waters off the Horn of Africa and along the Internationally Recommended Transit Corridor, in concert with European Union Operation Atalanta and the Combined Maritime Forces.[118]

---

[112] NATO, Allied Maritime Component Command Naples, *available at* www.afsouth. nato.int/organization/CC_MAR_Naples/operations/allied_provider/index.htm (last visited Aug. 30, 2010).

[113] NATO, Counter-Piracy Operations, *available at* www.nato.int/cps/en/natolive/topics _48815.htm#Protector (last visited Aug 30, 2010).

[114] NATO, NATO Resumes Counter-Piracy Mission, News, March 24, 2009, *available at* www.nato.int/cps/en/natolive/news_52016.htm?selectedLocale=en (last visited Aug. 30, 2010).

[115] NATO, NATO's Standing Maritime Group 2 Takes Over Counter Piracy Mission, News, June 29, 2009, *available at* www.nato.int/cps/en/natolive/news_56035.htm?select edLocale=en (last visited Aug. 30, 2010).

[116] NATO, Operation Ocean Shield – Current News, *available at* www.manw.nato.int/ page_operation_ocean_shield.aspx (last visited Aug. 30, 2010).

[117] NATO, Counter-Piracy Operations, *available at* www.nato.int/cps/en/natolive/topics _48815.htm#Protector (last visited Aug. 30, 2010).

[118] United Nations, Secretary-General Report on S.C. Res. 1846, Nov. 13, 2009, para. 22.

Between January 1 and October 31, 2009, NATO escorted over 50 merchant vessels, including several ships chartered by the World Food Program and delivering humanitarian assistance to the region. NATO forces were also involved in some 46 incidents whereby NATO units boarded suspicious small craft, provided humanitarian assistance to beleaguered merchant vessels and responded to emergency calls, including from vessels under pirate attacks.[119]

3. United States-Led Combined Maritime Forces

The Combined Maritime Forces are a United States-led international naval coalition, whose intended mission is to conduct integrated and coordinated operations in the Gulf of Aden, the Gulf of Oman, the Arabian Sea, the Arabian Gulf, the Red Sea and parts of the Indian Ocean. The Combined Maritime Forces cover over 2.5 million square miles of international waters.[120] The Combined Maritime Forces' general task is to create a lawful maritime order and conduct maritime security operations to help develop security in the maritime environment. The forces comprise three principal Combined Task Forces (CTFs): CTF-150, CTF-151, and CTF-152, the first two of which have specifically undertaken efforts to combat piracy off the coast of Somalia.

CTF-150 was the first multinational naval force to contribute to the fight against piracy off the coast of Somalia, operating from late 2008 to January 2009.[121] Although countering piracy is not part of the explicit mandate of CTF-150, it nevertheless assumed this function under the umbrella of its general mandate to conduct maritime security operations. This Combined Task Force stood under the rotating command of the United States, Denmark and Germany. CTF-150 passed on its counter-piracy tasks to CTF-151 on January 22, 2009.

CTF-151, unlike CTF-150, was specifically established in January 2009 to conduct counter-piracy operations in and around the Gulf of Aden, the Arabian Sea and the Indian Ocean.[122] CTF-151 is "mission specific" and without geographical restrictions; its geographical area of operation is dependent on the activities and operational area of the pirates and armed robbers at sea.[123] CTF-151 is designed to

---

[119] *Id.* at para. 23.

[120] *Id.* at para. 24. For more information on Combined Task Force 150, see www.cusnc.navy.mil/cmf/150/index.html (last visited Aug. 30, 2010); for Combined Task Force 151, see www.cusnc.navy.mil/cmf/151/index.html (last visited Aug. 30, 2010); and for Combined Task Force 152, see www.cusnc.navy.mil/cmf/152/index.html (last visited Aug. 30, 2010).

[121] United Nations, Secretary-General Report on S.C. Res. 1846, Nov. 13, 2009, para. 25.

[122] United Nations, Secretary-General Report on S.C. Res. 1846, March 16, 2009, para. 19.

[123] United Kingdom, Royal Navy, Combined Maritime Forces, Combined Task Force 151, *available at* www.royalnavy.mod.uk/operations-and-support/operations/united-king

be a dedicated international arrangement combining military force, intelligence sharing and coordinated patrols.[124] From January to October 2009, the Combined Maritime Forces continued to ensure tactical "deconfliction" between all ships and States operating in the Gulf of Aden, including a good level of shared awareness and optimal allocation of assets.[125]

Depending on operational requirements, CTF-150 and CTF-151 have both had assigned to them between five and eight ships and aircraft from various naval forces as well as personnel from several nations. Several NATO member States have contributed to the Combined Maritime Forces in the fight against piracy, including Australia, France, Canada, Denmark, Germany, Italy, Pakistan, the Republic of Korea, Singapore, Turkey, the United States and the United Kingdom.[126] The Report of the Secretary-General, pursuant to Security Council Resolution 1846, concludes that the operations of the various Combined Task Forces have successfully deterred several pirate attacks, responded to emergency calls from vessels in distress and seized large quantities of contraband, including weapons.[127]

B. Coordination of National and Multinational Efforts to Counter Piracy

The various national and multinational forces are operating under different command structures. In order to ensure the effectiveness of the collective efforts to counter and repress piracy in the region, coordination and close cooperation are essential. To this end, Security Council Resolution 1846 generally calls upon States and regional organizations to coordinate their efforts to deter acts of piracy and armed robbery at sea off the coast of Somalia.[128] In Security Council Resolution 1851, the Security Council encourages all States and regional organizations fighting piracy and armed robbery at sea off the coast of Somalia to establish an international cooperation mechanism.[129] Specifically, Security Council Resolution 1851 encourages States and regional organizations to consider creating a center in the region to coordinate information relevant to piracy and armed robbery at sea.[130] As a consequence of this, the Contact Group on Piracy off the Coast of Somalia, the

---

dom-component-command-ukmcc/coalition-maritime-forces-cfmcc/ctf-151/combined-task-force-151 (last visited Aug. 30, 2010).

[124] United Nations, Secretary-General Report on S.C. Res. 1846, March 16, 2009, para. 30.

[125] United Nations, Secretary-General Report on S.C. Res. 1846, Nov. 13, 2009, para. 24.

[126] *Id.* at para. 25.

[127] *Id.* at para. 26.

[128] S.C. Res. 1846, para. 7.

[129] S.C. Res. 1851, para. 4.

[130] *Id.* at para. 5.

Shared Awareness and Deconfliction (SHADE) group, and the Maritime Security Centre – Horn of Africa (MSCHOA) have been established.

1. Contact Group on Piracy off the Coast of Somalia

The Contact Group on Piracy off the Coast of Somalia has been established as an international cooperation mechanism to act as a common point of contact between and among States and regional and international organizations on all aspects of combating piracy, in line with paragraph 4 of Security Council Resolution 1851. The Contact Group is not to be confused with the Monitoring Group on Somalia, which has been vested with a specific Security Council mandate.[131] The Contact Group is a forum where a considerable number of States meet to discuss issues related to the effective repression of piracy and armed robbery at sea off Somalia's coast.[132] Several meetings took place in 2009 and 2010.[133] The Contact Group is assisted by the United Nations Secretariat and the International Maritime Organization and it is supported by four Working Groups, which address specific thematic issues.[134]

Working Group 1, chaired by the United Kingdom, focuses primarily on the operational coordination of military naval activities in the region and regional capacity development.[135]

Working Group 2, chaired by Denmark, focuses on legal issues aiming to provide specific guidance to members of the Contact Group on the legal framework pertaining to the fight against piracy, including the prosecution of suspected pirates. To this end, the Working Group has begun to develop a set of practical tools with the aim of providing support to States and organizations. Working Group 2 also serves as a forum for the sharing of information and best practices. The United Nations Office on Drugs and Crime has provided support in various ways to the

---

[131] S.C. Res. 1853.

[132] 45 States and seven international and regional organizations participated, for example, in the meeting of 10 September, 2009: United Nations, Secretary-General Report on S.C. Res. 1846, Nov. 13, 2009, para. 8. The meeting held on November 26, 2009 was reportedly attended by some 50 countries and organizations.

[133] For an overview over the activities and meetings of the Contact Group on Piracy Off the Coast of Somalia, see www.state.gov/t/pm/ppa/piracy/contactgroup/c32666.htm (last visited Aug. 30, 2010).

[134] United States of America, Department of State, Bureau of Political and Military Affairs, First Plenary Meeting of the Contact Group on Piracy Off the Coast of Somalia, New York, Jan. 14, 2009, *available at* www.state.gov/t/pm/rls/fs/130610.htm (last visited Aug. 30, 2010).

[135] United States of America, Department of State, Office of the Spokesman, Sixth Plenary Meeting of the Contact Group on Piracy off the Coast of Somalia, June 11, 2010, *available at* www.state.gov/r/pa/prs/ps/2010/06/143010.htm (last visited Aug. 30, 2010); United Nations, Secretary-General Report on S.C. Res. 1846, March 16, 2009, para. 14.

Working Group, such as an analysis of the legal and practical challenges to prosecuting suspected pirates; it gathers information on relevant national legal systems, including those of coastal States. Working Group 2 also commissioned an independent academic expert to facilitate a common understanding of the relevant legal provisions within the Working Group.[136] The United Nations Office of Legal Affairs has likewise actively supported States in Working Group 2, in particular with regard to the international legal regime applicable to piracy, international tribunals and the applicability of international human rights obligations to the detention of suspected pirates at sea and their transfer to regional States.[137] Notably, at its meeting on September 10, 2009, the Contact Group approved the terms of reference of an international trust fund, which is designed to help defray the expenses associated with the prosecution of piracy suspects as well as other activities undertaken to combat the phenomenon of piracy.[138]

Working Group 3, chaired by the United States, focuses on the strengthening of shipping self-awareness and interrelations with the shipping industry. In August 2009, twelve industry organizations, representing the vast majority of ship-owners and operations of the seafarers working on ships transiting the region, had updated the document entitled "Best Management Practices to Deter Piracy in the Gulf of Aden and off the Coast of Somalia." In September 2009, the International Maritime Organization circulated the document to all member States and the shipping industry, urging them to follow these new guidelines.[139]

Working Group 4, chaired by Egypt, aims to coordinate communication activity addressing piracy off the coast of Somalia and to inform the wider international community of all Contact Group policies, recommendations and activities. At its third meeting on May 29, 2009, the Contact Group endorsed the communication and media strategy proposed by Egypt, which foresees that key messages should be delivered to various target audiences, including Somalis in and outside Somalia, neighboring States and the international community, as well as the shipping industry.

2. Shared Awareness and Deconfliction

The Shared Awareness and Deconfliction (SHADE) group is a voluntary international military group, established in December 2008, as a means of sharing best

---

[136] *Guilfoyle*, Treaty Jurisdiction over Pirates: A Compilation of Legal Texts with Introductory Notes, Prepared for the 3rd Meeting of Working Group 2 on Legal Issues, Copenhagen, August 26–27, 2009.

[137] United Nations, Secretary-General Report on S.C. Res. 1846, Nov. 13, 2009, para. 14.

[138] United States of America, Department of State, Office of the Spokesman, Fourth Plenary Meeting of the Contact Group on Piracy off the Coast of Somalia, Sept. 11, 2009, *available at* www.state.gov/r/pa/prs/ps/2009/sept/129143.htm. (last visited Aug. 30, 2010).

[139] International Maritime Organization, Piracy and Armed Robbery against Ships in Waters off the Coast of Somalia, IMO Doc. MSC.1/Circ.1335 (Sept. 29, 2009), para. 11.

practices, conducting informal discussions and "deconflicting" the activities of the nations and organizations involved in military counter-piracy operations in the region.[140] SHADE's monthly meetings in Bahrain provide a working-level opportunity for navies to come together to share information. Initially, SHADE participation involved only the Combined Maritime Forces, the European Union Naval Force and NATO. However, over time SHADE has expanded to include many regional nations and navies operating under independent mandates, such as those of China, India, Japan and the Russian Federation. In more recent meetings close to 30 countries participated.[141]

According to the Report of the Secretary-General pursuant to Security Council 1846, SHADE has significantly furthered coordinated and focused military naval operations off the coast of Somalia. As a result of SHADE's coordination efforts, command opportunities and assets have been shared across SHADE participants, e.g. Singaporean and Turkish commanders have operated from United States warships. Moreover, coordination through SHADE has contributed to the establishment of the Internationally Recommended Transit Corridor in the Gulf of Aden and it has significantly improved coordination with the shipping industry.[142]

3. Operation Atalanta Maritime Security Centre – Horn of Africa

The Operation Atalanta Maritime Security Centre – Horn of Africa (MSCHOA) has been set up by the European Union as part of the European Security and Defense Policy initiative to combat piracy and armed robbery at sea in the Gulf of Aden region. MSCHOA is a civil-military coordination center with the task of safeguarding merchant shipping operating in the region by preventing and deterring acts of piracy in the Gulf of Aden, off the Horn of Africa and in the Somali Basin.[143] The Center's Internet portal enables the European Union Naval Force to liaise and communicate with the international merchant community, allows vessels to register their movements and receive advice on best practices and updates on piracy activity in the region.[144]

---

[140] United Nations, Secretary-General Report on S.C. Res. 1846, Nov. 13, 2009, para. 29. United Kingdom, Foreign & Commonwealth Office, The International Response to Piracy, CGPCS (Contact Group on Piracy off the Coast of Somalia), *available at* www.fco.gov.uk/en/global-issues/conflict-prevention/piracy/international-response (last visited Aug. 30, 2010).

[141] United States of America, Central Command, Pirate Attacks on Rise off Somalia Coast, Sept. 29, 2009, *available at* www.centcom.mil/press-releases/pirate-attacks-on-rise-off-somalia-coast (last visited Aug. 30, 2010).

[142] United Nations, Secretary-General Report on S.C. Res. 1846, Nov. 13, 2009, para. 30.

[143] For more information on Maritime Security Centre – Horn of Africa (MSCHOA), see www.mschoa.org (last visited Aug. 30, 2010).

[144] United Nations, Secretary-General Report on S.C. Res. 1846, Nov. 13, 2009, para. 31.

4. United Kingdom Maritime Trade Organization Office in Dubai and the Maritime Liaison Office

Other relevant cooperative frameworks and arrangements include the United Kingdom Maritime Trade Organization office in Dubai, which also acts as a point of contact for merchant vessels and liaison with military forces in the region. Information gathered by the Dubai office is passed to the Combined Maritime Forces and European Union Operation Atalanta headquarters, enabling relevant information affecting commercial traffic to be passed directly to ships, improving responsiveness and saving time.[145]

The Maritime Liaison Office (MARLO), yet another cooperation mechanism, facilitates the exchange of information between the United States Navy, Combined Maritime Forces and the commercial maritime community in the United States Central Command's (CENTCOM) area of responsibility. The Maritime Liaison Office was originally established in 1987, during the so-called Iran-Iraq "Tanker Wars," to promote cooperation between the United States Navy and the commercial maritime community.[146] Today, according to the Maritime Liaison Office's own website, it operates as a conduit for information focused on the safety and security of shipping and is committed to assisting all members of the commercial maritime community. It describes itself as an "active advocate for commercial mariners."[147] Currently, the Maritime Liaison Office serves as a secondary emergency point of contact (after the United Kingdom Maritime Trade Organization) for mariners in distress and also disseminates transit guidance.[148]

C. Criminal Repression of Piracy and Armed Robbery at Sea

1. Catch-and-Release-Practices

Instituting criminal proceedings constitutes an indispensable component in the quest for a "durable eradication of piracy and armed robbery at sea off the coast of Somalia."[149] So far, however, States, having captured suspected "pirates and armed robbers at sea," have frequently and for various reasons either been unable or unwilling to commence domestic criminal proceedings against alleged perpetrators. In these cases, alleged pirates and armed robbers at sea were released after being disarmed.

---

[145] *Id.* at para. 32.

[146] Maritime Liaison Office, History of MARLO, *available at* www.cusnc.navy.mil/marlo/History/marlo-history.htm (last visited Aug. 30, 2010).

[147] Maritime Liaison Office, Marlo Mission, *available at* www.cusnc.navy.mil/marlo/Mission/marlo-mission.htm (last visited Aug. 30, 2010).

[148] United Nations, Secretary-General Report on S.C. Res. 1846, Nov. 13, 2009, para. 33.

[149] S.C. Res. 1897, preambular para. 13.

The Secretary-General's Report pursuant to Resolution 1918 states that "[t]he commanders of the European and NATO naval forces off the coast of Somalia estimate that around 700 suspects apprehended by the ships under their command have been released between January and June 2010."[150] Indeed, as recently as in April 2010, in Resolution 1918, the Security Council expressed its concern "over cases when persons suspected of piracy are released without facing justice" and affirmed "that the failure to prosecute persons responsible for acts of piracy and armed robbery at sea off the coast of Somalia undermines anti-piracy efforts of the international community."[151]

2. Criminal Prosecutions in Seizing States and Non-Seizing Victim States

Thus far the States carrying out the seizure of alleged pirates have only rarely instigated criminal proceedings against the arrested suspects. Only a handful of seizing States – namely France, Spain, the United States of America, the Seychelles as well as Somalia (Somaliland and Puntland)[152] and Yemen[153] – have brought alleged offenders they had arrested before their own domestic courts. Generally, in these cases, national interests were involved.[154]

Thus, France currently prosecutes the alleged hijackers of the French yachts *Le Ponant*,[155] *Carré d'As*[156] and *Tanit*[157] in its domestic criminal courts. Spain commenced criminal proceedings in its Audiencia Nacional in Madrid against two men allegedly involved in the hijacking of the fishing ship *Alakrana*, the crew of which

---

[150] United Nations, Secretary-General Report pursuant to S.C. Res. 1918, July 26, 2010, para. 20.

[151] S.C. Res. 1918, preambular para. 17 and para. 1.

[152] United Nations, Secretary-General Report pursuant to S.C. Res. 1918, July 26, 2010, para. 19.

[153] BBC News, Yemen Sentences Somali Pirates to Death, May 18, 2010, *available at* http://news.bbc.co.uk/2/hi/middle_east/8689129.stm (last visited Aug. 30, 2010).

[154] United Nations, Secretary-General Report pursuant to S.C. Res. 1918, July 26, 2010, para. 22.

[155] The New York Times, French Troops Seize Somali Pirates after Hostages are Freed, April 11, 2008, *available at* www.nytimes.com/2008/04/11/world/africa/11iht-yacht.4.119 21315.html (last visited Aug. 30, 2010); L'Express.fr, Les six pirates du *Ponant* sont arrivés en France, April 16, 2008, *available at* www.lexpress.fr/actualite/monde/les-six-pirates-du-i-ponant-i-sont-arrives-en-france_472071.html (last visited Aug. 30, 2010).

[156] LeMonde.fr, «Carré-d'As»: les six pirates somaliens placés en garde à vue en France, Sept. 23, 2008, *available at* www.lemonde.fr/afrique/article/2008/09/23/carre-d-as-les-six-pirates-somaliens-places-en-garde-a-vue-en-france_1098819_3212.html (last visited Aug. 30, 2010).

[157] LeMonde.fr, Les trois pirates somaliens du «Tanit» placés en garde à vue en France, April 14, 2009, *available at* www.lemonde.fr/afrique/article/2009/04/14/les-trois-pirates-somaliens-du-tanit-places-en-garde-a-vue-en-france_1180728_3212.html (last visited Aug. 30, 2010).

included more than a dozen Spanish nationals.[158] In the United States of America, the first piracy prosecution in decades is approaching its end: In May 2010, a Somali pleaded guilty to charges that he hijacked the United States-flagged cargo ship *Maersk Alabama* and kidnapped its captain. The defendant also pleaded guilty to conspiracy and hostage taking. The count for the crime of piracy as defined by the law of nations was dropped in exchange for his plea. Sentencing in this case before the Federal District Court of New York is scheduled for October 2010.[159] Meanwhile, the grand juries in the Federal District Court of Virginia have returned two separate indictments in April 2010, charging 11 Somali men with, *inter alia*, engaging in piracy. They are accused of having exchanged fire with the frigate *USS Nicholas* in the Indian Ocean and for having attacked the amphibious dock landing ship *USS Ashland* in the Gulf of Aden.[160] However, the piracy charges against the six Somali men of having attacked the *USS Ashland* were later dismissed with the argument that the government had not shown that the men's actions violated American piracy law. Judge Jackson further argued that "the definition of piracy in the international community is unclear" and that "the court's reliance on these international sources as authoritative would not meet constitutional muster and must therefore be rejected."[161] In Yemen, a court has sentenced six Somali pirates to death and jailed six other persons in May 2010 for the hijacking of a Yemen-flagged oil tanker, which had been liberated by Yemeni forces.[162] Thus, a look at the current practice reveals that seizing States only exceptionally, usually only when national interests are involved, prosecute piracy suspects in their domestic criminal courts.

---

[158] *Cala*, The New York Times, Spain Arraigns Somalis Suspected of Piracy, Oct. 13, 2009, *available at* www.nytimes.com/2009/10/14/world/europe/14iht-spain.html (last visited Aug. 30, 2010).

[159] United States of America, Department of Justice, United States Attorney's Office, Southern District of New York, Somalian Pirate Brought to U.S. to Face Charges for Hijacking the Maersk Alabama and Holding the Ship's Captain Hostage, Press Release, April 21, 2010, *available at* http://newyork.fbi.gov/dojpressrel/pressrel09/nyfo042109.htm (last visited Aug. 30, 2010); *Rivera*, The New York Times, Somali Man Pleads Guilty in 2009 Hijacking of Ship, May 19, 2010, *available at* http://query.nytimes.com/gst/fullpage html?res=990CE6DB153EF93AA25756C0A9669D8B63&ref=abduwali_abdukhadir_muse (last visited Aug. 30, 2010).

[160] United States of America, Department of Justice, United States Attorney's Office, Eastern District of Virgina, Alleged Somali Pirates Indicted for Attacks on Navy Ships, Press Release, April 23, 2010, *available at* http://norfolk.fbi.gov/dojpressrel/pressrel10/nf042310.htm (last vistited Aug. 30, 2010); *Flintoff*, NPR, Prosecuting Pirates May Not Be Easy, April 23, 2010, *available at* www.npr.org/templates/story/story.php?storyId=126218804 (last visited Aug. 30, 2010).

[161] *Schwartz*, The New York Times, Somalis No Longer Face Federal Piracy Charges, Aug. 17, 2010, *available at* www.nytimes.com/2010/08/18/us/18pirates.html?_r=1&ref=piracy_at_sea (last visited Aug. 30, 2010).

[162] BBC News, Yemen Sentences Somali Pirates to Death, May 18, 2010, *available at* http://news.bbc.co.uk/2/hi/middle_east/8689129.stm (last visited Aug. 30, 2010).

In cases where the seizing State decides not to prosecute the arrested persons, it generally offers to surrender arrested persons to the victim State, i.e. either to the State whose flag the victim vessel flies or to the State whose nationals have been the victims of the attack. However, current practice also shows that victim States often decline the offer to take over suspects for criminal prosecutions. As far as can be seen, only two non-seizing victim States have taken alleged pirates over for prosecution. Firstly, the Netherlands requested the extradition from Denmark of five piracy suspects, who were involved in the attack of the Dutch Antilles-flagged cargo ship *Samanyolu* and have been arrested by the Danish frigate *Absalon*.[163] They were sentenced in a Dutch court in Rotterdam to five years in prison in June 2010.[164] Secondly, Germany requested the extradition from the Netherlands of ten piracy suspects allegedly involved in the attack against the German-flagged *Taipan* in June 2010.[165]

It can thus be concluded that to date only a small proportion of all apprehended piracy suspects have been prosecuted by the seizing State and only two non-seizing victim States were willing to receive alleged offenders for proesecution. Since releasing captured piracy suspects after disarming them (so-called catch-and-release strategy) runs counter to the goal of a full and durable eradication of piracy and armed robbery at sea,[166] the search for alternative judicial *fora* has been a predominant feature of the international debate over the effective repression of piracy in the Gulf of Aden region. While the idea of an international(ized) piracy tribunal has not yet seen the light of day, the majority of arrested pirates is for the time being prosecuted in domestic courts of so-called regional States, i.e. African States of the Gulf of Aden region that are affected by piracy and armed robbery at sea.

3. Criminal Prosecutions in Regional States

Currently, a considerable number of piracy suspects are undergoing criminal trials in regional States. It seems safe to say that the most common *modus operandi* is the transfer of piracy suspects apprehended by patrolling naval States to regional

---

[163] Agence France Press, Dutch Seek Extradition of Somali Pirates, Jan. 15, 2009, *available at* www.google.com/hostednews/afp/article/ALeqM5hMfTxjAVudEutFTdRutw zyRn5nKA (last visited Aug. 30, 2010); BBC News, Somali "Pirates" Face Dutch Court, Feb. 11, 2009, *available at* http://news.bbc.co.uk/2/hi/europe/10342547.stm (last visited Aug. 30, 2010).

[164] BBC News, Five Somali Men Jailed for Piracy by Dutch Court, June 17, 2010, *available at* http://news.bbc.co.uk/2/hi/europe/10342547.stm (last visited Aug. 30, 2010).

[165] Der Spiegel, Somalische Piraten in Deutschland eingetroffen, June 10, 2010, *available at* www.spiegel.de/politik/deutschland/0,1518,700035,00.html (last visited Aug. 30, 2010).

[166] S.C. Res. 1846, preambular para. 10, and S.C. Res. 1897, preambular para. 13.

African States.[167] At the time of writing there are only about 40 prosecutions taking place outside the region.[168]

Various agreements have been concluded with regional States willing to receive piracy suspects for criminal prosecution. The European Union, for example, concluded a transfer agreement with Kenya in which the latter undertakes that it "will accept, upon the request of the EUNAVFOR, the transfer of persons detained by EUNAVFOR in connection with piracy (...) and will submit such persons and property to its competent authorities for the purpose of investigation and prosecution."[169] Kenya entered into similar agreements with various States, namely the United Kingdom,[170] the United States,[171] Denmark, China and Canada.[172] As of May 2010, 123 prosecutions following arrests by patrolling naval States were reported to take place in Kenya. It is currently the only State where *all* prosecutions are a result of arrests by other States.[173]

Moreover, the Seychelles is also becoming a regional prosecution center.[174] The Seychelles currently holds over thirty suspects apprehended by the European Union Naval Force[175] and the island has concluded transfer agreements with the European Union[176] and the United Kingdom.[177] The Seychelles are carrying out prosecutions

---

[167] United Nations, UNODC and Piracy, *available at* www.unodc.org/unodc/en/piracy/index.html (last visited Aug. 30, 2010). On transfers of piracy suspects in view of their prosecution, see p. 186 *et seq*. On the various implications of conducting large-scale prosecutions of alleged pirates in regional States such as Kenya, see p. 174 *et seq*.

[168] United Nations, Secretary-General Report pursuant to S.C. Res. 1918, July 26, 2010, para. 22.

[169] Art. 2(a) EU-Kenya Transfer Agreement.

[170] United Kingdom, Foreign and Commonwealth Office, Prisoner Transfer Agreements, www.fco.gov.uk/en/global-issues/conflict-prevention/piracy/prisoners (last visited Aug. 30, 2010).

[171] Reuters, Kenya Agrees to Prosecute U.S.-Held Pirates: Pentagon, Jan. 29, 2009, *available at* www.reuters.com/article/worldNews/idUSTRE50S4ZZ20090129 (last visited Aug. 30, 2010).

[172] United Nations, Secretary-General Report pursuant to S.C. Res. 1918, July 26, 2010, para. 23.

[173] *Id.* at para. 19.

[174] *Jay*, Jurist, Seychelles Announces Creation of UN-backed Piracy Court, May 6, 2010, *available at* http://jurist.org/paperchase/2010/05/seychelles-announces-creation-of-un-backed-piracy-court.php (last visited Aug. 30, 2010); United Nations, News Centre, UN Opens New Courtroom to Try Pirate Suspects in Kenyan Port, June 25, 2010, *available at* www.un.org/apps/news/story.asp?NewsID=35156&Cr=UNODC&Cr1= (last visited Aug. 30, 2010).

[175] United Nations, Secretary-General Report pursuant to S.C. Res. 1918, July 26, 2010, para. 19.

[176] EU-Seychelles Transfer Agreement.

[177] United Kingdom, Foreign and Commonwealth Office, Prisoner Transfer Agreements, www.fco.gov.uk/en/global-issues/conflict-prevention/piracy/prisoners (last visited Aug. 30, 2010).

both with regard to suspects captured by their own forces and by patrolling naval States.

Puntland, Somaliland and Yemen are also prosecuting alleged pirates and armed robbers at sea. Puntland has received almost 60 piracy suspects from third States for prosecution.[178] It is further reported that prosecutions of pirates and armed robbers at sea take place in Somaliland, which has thus far received 20 alleged offenders in order to criminally prosecute them. In addition, Puntland (148 persons) and Somaliland (80 persons) each prosecute a significant number of alleged offenders seized by their own forces.[179] Finally, it appears that Yemen has also commenced criminal proceedings against piracy suspects and alleged armed robbers at sea seized by other States and later handed over to it.[180]

As far as regional prosecutions are concerned, the first convictions have already been issued and a number of persons are serving their sentences. For example, in Kenya 10 pirates transferred by the United States have each been sentenced to eight years of imprisonment, and eight pirates transferred by the United Kingdom have each been sentenced to 20 years of imprisonment.[181]

The United Nations is helping regional States to address weaknesses in their piracy legislation and to improve their criminal procedures and (judicial) capacities. In particular, the United Nations Office on Drugs and Crime, is providing targeted support and capacity-building to regional countries, such as Kenya and the Seychelles, as called for in Security Council Resolution 1851 and pursuant to its mandates to assist States in their struggle against serious crime.[182]

In sum, criminal prosecution of pirates in third States, i.e. States other than the seizing State, is currently the norm rather than the exception. Prosecution by third States, be it the victim State or any other so-called regional State, requires that the piracy suspect is brought from the jurisdiction of the seizing State into the prosecuting State's jurisdiction. Various means and methods are used or could

---

[178] *Middleton*, Pirates and How to Deal With Them, Chatham House, Africa Programme and International Law Discussion Group, London, April 22, 2009, *available at* www.chathamhouse.org.uk/files/13845_220409pirates_law.pdf (last visited Aug. 30, 2010), p. 6; United Nations, Secretary-General Report pursuant to S.C. Res. 1918, July 26, 2010, para. 19.

[179] *Id.* See also Brunei News.Net, Somali Court Hears of Pirate Activity, Feb. 14, 2010, *available at* www.bruneinews.net/story/601492 (last visited Aug. 30, 2010).

[180] *Gros-Verheyde*, Comment les pirates arrêtés sont jugés ? May 26, 2010, *available at* http://bruxelles2.over-blog.com/article-comment-sont-juges-les-pirates-arretes-le-point--42 673756.html (last visited Aug. 30, 2010).

[181] United Nations, Secretary-General Report pursuant to S.C. Res. 1918, July 26, 2010, para. 21.

[182] United Nations, UNODC, Counter Piracy Programme, November 2009, *available at* www.unodc.org/documents/easternafrica//piracy/UNODC_Counter_Piracy_Programme.pdf (last visited Aug. 30, 2010).

potentially be used in the piracy context to transfer suspects from the jurisdiction of the seizing State into another State's jurisdiction with a view to their criminal prosecution.[183]

III. Conclusion

At the time of writing, the problem of piracy persists in the Gulf of Aden and increasingly spreads into the Indian Ocean. Although the various international maritime operations have been rather successful in discouraging piracy and armed robbery at sea off Somalia's coast and in the Gulf of Aden, the number of piracy incidents in the wider region remains high. Thus, it seems safe to conclude that the maritime deployments in the Gulf of Aden have been effective in the immediate reduction of successful pirate attacks in their specific operative region and that the Internationally Recommended Transit Corridor is an effective mechanism for ensuring unimpeded transit through the Gulf of Aden. At the same time, it is submitted that maritime counter-piracy operations thus far have largely had a "crowding-out effect," rather than repressing piracy and armed robbery at sea in the area on a long term or sustainable basis. As a result of successful efforts in the Gulf of Aden, the locus of pirate attacks is now shifting to the Western Indian Ocean and towards the vast coastal waters of the Seychelles. There appears to be widespread agreement that if naval deployments were to be decreased, piracy off Somalia's coast would resurge, almost instantaneously. Piracy has become an increasingly important source of revenue in the region and it thus seems quite likely that piracy and armed robbery at sea will persist in the wider region for some time to come. Simultaneously, it may well be that over time, the international community's readiness to sustain naval operations on the current scale could decline. The current operations are costly and, if unimpeded passage via guarded corridors can be ensured, the inclination to further invest in the repression of piracy may gradually abate.

Thus, priority for the year 2011 and beyond will be the development of sustainable, long-term solutions. Increasingly, military deployments on board merchant ships may emerge as a less cost-intensive and more sustainable alternative to the large-scale deployment of military vessels aiming to patrol a vast area, which, in its entirety, is unmanageable. The "undesired option" of private military and security companies carrying out the task is also on the table. While this approach could certainly help to lower the costs of current counter-piracy operations, it too would only address the symptoms, but not the causes of piracy and armed robbery at sea. Debates in the Security Council, preceding the adoption of the various piracy-related Resolutions, indicate widespread agreement that a long-term solution to the

---

[183] On transfers of piracy suspects and alleged armed robbers at sea, see p. 186 *et seq.*

problem of piracy and armed robbery at sea off Somalia's coast and in the Gulf of Aden region can only be found if the situation on the Somali mainland is addressed. For the time being, the absence of any significant practice in relation to Security Council Resolution 1851 certainly evidences that the readiness to become engaged in law enforcement operations on Somalia's mainland remains as remote as ever. France has tabled the idea of creating a European Union unit to train security personnel of the African Union in preparation of counter-piracy operations in Somalia, but as far as can be seen this idea has not yet materialized.[184] Meanwhile, a strong emphasis is being put on the strengthening of regional capacities. The Regional Cooperation Agreement on Combating Piracy and Armed Robbery against Ships in Asia (ReCAAP) is widely regarded as an important step towards the repression of piracy in Asia and hopes are high that the Djibouti Code of Conduct, which is largely modeled upon the ReCAAP, could eventually have a similar impact in the wider Gulf of Aden region. This will hinge, first and foremost, on a speedy and comprehensive implementation of the Djibouti Code of Conduct that will require further assistance from the international community. Certainly, in the long run it would also seem conducive if the participants in the Djibouti Code of Conduct entered into a legally binding agreement as envisaged in Article 13 of the Code.

---

[184] *Diekhans*, ARD, Die Anti-Piraten-Mission "Atalanta" – Erfolgreich oder überfordert? Dec. 9, 2009, *available at* www.tagesschau.de/ausland/atalanta110.html (last visited Aug. 30, 2010)

Part 2

Historic Evolution of Legal Rules Relating to Piracy, Armed Robbery at Sea and Other Forms of Maritime Violence

I. Codification of Piracy Rules in the 20th Century

Piracy is an ancient phenomenon and it ranks among the older subject-matters of public international law.[185] However, contemporary international treaty provisions on piracy, namely those enshrined in the UNCLOS, date back to the beginning of the 20th century. Therefore, the following brief description of the evolution of treaty rules pertaining to piracy starts with the codification efforts on piracy initiated by the League of Nations at the beginning of the last century.[186]

A. Codification Efforts under the Auspices of the League of Nations

In 1924, the Assembly of the League of Nations requested the Council of the League to convene a Committee of Experts for the Progressive Codification of International Law. The Committee of Experts was vested with the specific mandate of identifying "subjects of international law, the regulation of which by international agreement would seem the most desirable and realizable at the present moment."[187] Piracy was among the subjects chosen for codification by the Committee of Experts.[188] A Sub-Committee consisting of the Japanese Rapporteur

---

[185] *Rubin*, Law of Piracy, pp. 1–70.

[186] Earlier draft conventions going back to private initiatives of scholars, such as those elaborated by *Field* (1876), *Fiore* (1890) and *Bluntschli* (1876) are not analyzed below. These draft conventions are reprinted as appendix to the ASIL-Commented Harvard Draft Convention on Piracy, p. 876, p. 880 and p. 882.

[187] League of Nations, Records of the Fifth Assembly, Plenary Meetings, p. 125, cited in ASIL, Harvard Research, General Introduction, p. 1. The League of Nations promoted specific international agreements, but also tried to approach the codification of international law in a more systematic way. Therefore, in 1924, the League started to work towards a Codification Conference, which was finally held in The Hague in 1930. Reports prepared by the Committee of Experts on the Progressive Codification of International Law and by a Preparatory Committee formed the basis for the Hague Codification Conference: *Tams*, in: Wolfrum (ed.), EPIL-League of Nations, para. 38.

[188] ASIL, Harvard Research, General Introduction, pp. 1–2.

Matsuda and the Chinese representative Wang Chung-Hui henceforth elaborated a draft treaty on piracy, the so-called Matsuda Draft.[189] However, this draft was not further pursued. Instead, piracy was dropped from the list of topics to be codified with the argument that the conclusion of a universal agreement on piracy would have been difficult at the time. It was further argued that the problems arising from piracy were not important enough to warrant the topic's insertion in the agenda of the 1930 Codification Conference of the League of Nations in The Hague.[190]

B. Harvard Draft Convention on Piracy of 1932

The codification process initiated by the League of Nations prompted the faculty of the Harvard Law School to commence a research project of its own, with a view to contributing towards future codification. The project's objective was to scrutinize the issues that the League of Nations had identified as being ripe for codification independently from the work of the international organization and it aimed to prepare a draft convention for each subject.[191] For that purpose, an Advisory Committee was set up at Harvard, under which the research on the various topics to be tabled at the 1930 Codification Conference of the League of Nations in The Hague was to be carried out.[192] With the approval of the Advisory Committee, a Reporter was named for each subject.[193] For the topic of "piracy," Professor Bingham of Stanford University was appointed.[194] Together with a group of experts, he elaborated what henceforth became known as the Harvard Draft Convention on Piracy.[195]

While the Matsuda Draft had not cited any doctrine, State practice or case law, and, therefore, did not allow for a distinction between well-settled principles of existing international piracy law and *de lege ferenda* elements,[196] the Harvard Draft Convention on Piracy[197] was accompanied not only by a document which exhaust-

---

[189] The Matsuda's Draft Provisions for the Suppression of Piracy are reprinted as appendix to the ASIL-Commented Harvard Draft Convention on Piracy, p. 873.

[190] *Rubin*, Law of Piracy, pp. 333–335.

[191] For an overview on topics other than piracy, which were studied by the Harvard Research Program and on which draft conventions were prepared, see ASIL, Harvard Research, General Introduction, p. 10.

[192] *Id.* at 5.

[193] *Id.* at 10.

[194] *Id.* at 12–13; *Rubin*, Law of Piracy, p. 335.

[195] The full text of the ASIL-Commented Harvard Draft Convention on Piracy can be found on p. 229 *et seq.* of this book (Appendix).

[196] *Rubin*, Law of Piracy, p. 333.

[197] ASIL-Commented Harvard Draft Convention on Piracy, p. 798 and p. 857.

ively set out the relevant piracy laws of the time,[198] but also by a report summariz-
ing the doctrinal debate on piracy as it stood in 1932.[199] This might be the reason
why the Harvard Draft Convention received far more attention from scholars than
the Matsuda Draft. It may also explain why the Harvard Draft Convention had a
major impact on the development of the law on piracy throughout the 20th century.[200] Henceforth, the Harvard Draft Convention served as a basis for the International Law Commission's work on piracy starting in the early 1950's, which later
led to the Convention on the High Seas of 1958, which in turn strongly influenced
the negotiations leading to the adoption of UNCLOS.[201]

C. Convention on the High Seas of 1958

In 1954, the International Law Commission was mandated by the United Nations
General Assembly to elaborate a text that could form the basis for an international
agreement on the law of the sea.[202] The text entitled *Regime of the High Seas*,
which was prepared by the Dutch Rapporteur François and published in 1954, contained only six articles dealing with piracy. All provisions were a French translation of the Harvard Draft Convention on Piracy.[203] The International Law Commission later adopted François' draft text and thus basically endorsed the findings of
the Harvard research project.[204]

In 1957, the General Assembly decided to convene a United Nations Conference
on the Law of the Sea.[205] The Conference took place in Geneva from February 24
to April 27, 1958. During the conference, at which a total of 86 States participated,
together with specialized United Nations agencies and other intergovernmental

---

[198] ASIL, A Collection of Piracy Laws in Various Countries, pp. 887–1013.

[199] ASIL-Commented Harvard Draft Convention on Piracy, pp. 749–872.

[200] *Rubin*, Law of Piracy, p. 341.

[201] United Nations, International Law Commission, Commentary on the Law of the Sea Draft Convention, p. 282.

[202] United Nations, General Assembly, G.A. Res. 899 (IX), U.N. Doc. A/RES/899 (IX) (Dec. 14, 1954), para. 2.

[203] The definition of piracy is François's French translation of Art. 3 ASIL-Commented Harvard Draft Convention on Piracy, the other five articles are French translations of Art. 4(1), 5, 6, 10 and 12 of the said Draft: *Rubin*, Law of Piracy, pp. 348–349.

[204] United Nations, International Law Commission, Commentary on the Law of the Sea Draft Convention, p. 282: "In its work on the articles concerning piracy, the Commission was greatly assisted by the research carried out at the Harvard Law School, which culmin-ated in a draft convention of nineteen articles with commentary, prepared in 1932 under the direction of Professor Joseph Bingham. In general, the Commission was able to en-dorse the findings of that research." *Lagoni*, in: Ipsen/Schmidt-Jortzig (eds.), Piracy, 512; *Rubin*, in: Bernhardt (ed.), EPIL-Piracy, 261.

[205] United Nations, General Assembly, G.A. Res. 1105 (XI), U.N. Doc. A/RES/1105 (XI) (Feb. 21, 1957).

organizations,[206] the legal regime on piracy did not receive a great deal of attention. Piracy was perceived first and foremost as a historical phenomenon rather than an acute or potential threat. In that vein, the Uruguayan delegation (unsuccessfully) proposed[207] to delete the provisions on piracy altogether, contending that piracy "no longer constituted a general problem."[208] A joint amendment of Czechoslovakia and Albania,[209] which was finally rejected, asked for the merger of the piracy draft provisions into one single article reading: "All States are bound to take proceedings against and to punish acts of piracy, as defined by present international law, and to cooperate to the full possible extent in the repression of piracy."[210] This amendment was supported with the argument that "it would be out of all proportion for the present draft to contain eight articles dealing with an eighteenth century concept."[211] Also, the delegation of Romania "considered that the International Law Commission had been mistaken in devoting so many articles to piracy, which was no longer a very real problem" and that "States could be relied upon to take the necessary steps for protecting navigation on the high seas."[212] However, a majority of States participating at the diplomatic conference was not willing to marginalize the legal regime on piracy to such an extent. Thus, the provisions contained in the draft of the International Law Commission, in an amended form, entered into the Convention on the High Seas of April 29, 1958,[213] as Articles 14 to 21. The Convention entered into force on December 30, 1962 and has 63 parties, as of August 2010.

D. United Nations Convention on the Law of the Sea of 1982

The interest devoted to piracy was equally marginal during the Third United Nations Conference on the Law of the Sea, held between 1973 and 1982, which led

---

[206] *Rosenne/Gebhard*, in: Wolfrum (ed.), EPIL-Conferences on the Law of the Sea, para. 13. United Nations, Conference on the Law of the Sea, 1958, *available at* treaty.un .org/cod/diplomaticconferences/lawofthesea-1958/lawofthesea-1958.html (last visited Aug. 30, 2010).

[207] United Nations, Conference on the Law of the Sea, Summary Record of the 29th Meeting, U.N. Doc. A/CONF.13/C.2/L.78 (Feb. 24 to April 27, 1958), para. 4.

[208] United Nations, Conference on the Law of the Sea, Feb. 24 – April 27, 1958, Official Records: Volume IV: Second Committee (High Seas: General Régime), p. 78 (statement by Uruguay) and at 84 (vote), U.N. Doc. A/CONF.13/40 (Feb. 24 to April 27, 1958).

[209] *Id.* at p. 128 (proposal by Czechoslovakia: A/CONF.13/C.2/L.46).

[210] *Id.* at p. 78 (statement by Czechoslovakia) and at 84 (vote).

[211] *Id.* at p. 78.

[212] *Id.* at pp. 78–79.

[213] Convention on the High Seas, *adopted* April 29, 1958, 450 U.N.T.S. 11 [hereinafter: Convention on the High Seas]. The piracy relevant provisions of the Convention on the High Seas are reprinted on p. 233 *et seq.* of this book (Appendix).

to the adoption of the UNCLOS in Montego Bay on December 10, 1982.[214] The piracy provisions as contained in the Convention on the High Seas of 1958, with some (largely unexplained) minor changes,[215] were simply imported into the UNCLOS as Articles 100 to 107.[216]

As of September 2010, 160 States were party to the UNCLOS. The earlier Convention on the High Seas was thus largely superseded by UNCLOS. However, until now, certain States are bound merely by the Convention on the High Seas, such as the United States.[217] However, as far as the repression of piracy is concerned this is only of minor relevance. The piracy regime of the 1958 Convention is almost identical to the one of UNCLOS and, what is more, there is widespread agreement that the piracy rules contained in the UNCLOS reflect customary international law.[218] With respect to the Gulf of Aden, it may be noteworthy that Somalia, the Seychelles, Kenya, the United Republic of Tanzania, Djibouti, and Yemen are all parties to the UNCLOS. The latest ratifications of UNCLOS were deposited in 2009 by Chad, the Dominican Republic and Switzerland.[219]

II. Counter-Terrorism Rules Relevant for Violence against Ships and Persons on Board

The piracy rules of the Convention on the High Seas and the UNCLOS do not cover each and every type of violence against ships and persons on board. Over the years, a range of other rules have evolved, mainly deriving from treaties drafted in

---

[214] *Rubin*, Law of Piracy, p. 393; see also *travaux préparatoires* to the Third United Nations Conference on the Law of the Sea (1973–1982), *available at* http://untreaty.un.org/cod/diplomaticconferences/lawofthesea-1982/lawofthesea-1982.html (last visited Aug. 30, 2010).

[215] The wording of Art. 107 UNCLOS, for example, was amended compared to Art. 21 Convention on the High Seas in order to narrow the scope for possible abuses; *Rubin*, Law of Piracy, p. 372.

[216] *Id.*

[217] United Nations, Treaty Collection, Status of Treaties, Chapter XXI, Law of the Sea, 2. Convention on the High Seas, *available at* http://treaties.un.org/Pages/ParticipationStatus.aspx (last visited Aug 30, 2010).

[218] *Lagoni*, in: Ipsen/Schmidt-Jortzig (eds.), Piracy, 524. Rubin asserts that there is not a *customary* piracy law at all, i.e. a "public international law of piracy divorced from specific treaties:" *Rubin*, in: Bernhardt (ed.), EPIL-Piracy, 261; extensively argued in *Rubin*, Law of Piracy, pp. 373–396. However, that there exists no customary international piracy law seems to be a minority view.

[219] For the consolidated table of ratifications and accessions to UNCLOS, see United Nations, Treaty Collection, Status of Treaties, Chapter XXI, Law of the Sea, 6. United Nations Convention on the Law of the Sea, *available at* http://treaties.un.org/Pages/ParticipationStatus.aspx (last visited Aug. 30, 2010).

response to terrorist acts, which likewise address violence at sea in various forms. In this regard, two treaties appear to be of particular relevance: the Convention for the Suppression of Unlawful Acts against the Safety of Maritime Navigation (SUA Convention) and the International Convention against the Taking of Hostages. Partially, these rules have filled specific loopholes inherent in UNCLOS' definition of piracy.[220] At the same time, there may also be overlap between the forms of maritime violence covered in these treaties and by the definition of piracy contained in the UNCLOS.

A. SUA Convention

The Convention for the Suppression of Unlawful Acts against the Safety of Maritime Navigation, the so-called SUA Convention, is a treaty specifically dealing with violent acts against ships and persons on board. Broadly speaking, it obliges States to suppress unlawful acts against the safety of maritime navigation.[221] It was adopted in Rome in 1988 and entered into force on March 1, 1992.

The impetus for the drafting of the SUA Convention came from a major maritime terrorist incident, which occurred in 1985. The Italian cruiser *Achille Lauro*, sailing in the Mediterranean Sea, was hijacked by members of the Palestine Liberation Front, who had boarded the ship in Italy pretending to be tourists. The offenders held the crew and passengers hostage and killed one person when their demands (the release of 50 Palestinian prisoners by Israel) were not met.[222] This incident revealed some important gaps and limitations in the piracy rules, as contained in the Convention on the High Seas and the UNCLOS. For example, the definition of piracy contained in these instruments requires the involvement of two ships for an act of piracy to occur.[223] This so-called two-ship-requirement was not fulfilled in the *Achille Lauro* incident, which merely involved a single ship. The SUA

---

[220] On the definition of piracy under the UNCLOS, see p. 59 *et seq.*

[221] The specific offenses are defined in Art. 3 SUA Convention; see p. 153 *et seq.*

[222] *Halberstam*, Terrorism on High Seas: The Achille Lauro, Piracy and the IMO Convention on Maritime Safety, AJIL 82 (1988), 269–270 and 291–292: In the aftermath of the *Achille Lauro* incident Italy, Austria and Egypt proposed a convention on maritime terrorism and submitted a draft modeled on existing counter-terrorism conventions to the International Maritime Organization. In 1986, the Council of the International Maritime Organization decided that the matter required its urgent attention. In order not to delay the process, the Council established an Ad Hoc Preparatory Committee open to all States instead of submitting the draft prepared by Italy, Austria and Egypt to the already overburdened Legal Committee. Its mandate was to prepare, on a priority basis, a draft convention. The Committee met for a week in March 1987 in London and for a week in May 1987 in Rome, where they agreed on the SUA draft convention. Not even a year later, the SUA Convention was adopted by the diplomatic conference convened in Rome.

[223] On the two-ship-requirement, see p. 62 *et seq.*

Convention was adopted to close the loopholes inherent in the piracy definition, which were revealed in the course of the *Achille Lauro* affair.

As of September 2010, 156 States, representing 95% of the gross tonnage of the world's merchant fleet, were party to the SUA Convention. Among them are many States of the larger Gulf of Aden and Horn of Africa region, namely Kenya, the Seychelles, the United Republic of Tanzania, Djibouti, Yemen and Oman. However, Somalia did not ratify the SUA Convention.[224]

B. Hostage Convention

Many pirate attacks involve the taking of hostages in order to compel the payment of ransom. In 2009 alone, Somali pirates hijacked 47 vessels and took 867 persons hostage.[225] In light of these numbers, the importance of the Hostage Convention in relation to the present context is clear. Interestingly, none of the Security Council Resolutions relating to piracy and armed robbery at sea explicitly mention the Hostage Convention. The treaty obliges State parties to criminalize hostage taking under their domestic law[226] and to establish jurisdiction over this particular offense.[227]

The Hostage Convention originated from a request by the Federal Republic of Germany in 1976, presumably stimulated by the terrorist attacks during the 1972 Summer Olympics in Munich. Germany had asked that the agenda of the United Nations General Assembly include the drafting of an international instrument against the taking of hostages. Three years later, in 1979, the Hostage Convention was adopted. It entered into force on June 3, 1983. Similar to other treaties elaborated in the wake of the international community's counter-terrorism efforts, the Hostage Convention deals exclusively with a specific phenomenon and well-delineated aspect of terrorism. Earlier efforts to deal more comprehensively with all forms of terrorism in one and the same legal instrument had failed.[228]

---

[224] International Maritime Organization, Status of Multilateral Conventions and Instruments in Respect of which the International Maritime Organization (IMO) or its Secretary-General Performs Depositary or Other Functions as at 31 December 2009, *available at* www.imo.org (follow "legal" hyperlink, then follow "IMO Conventions" hyperlink, then follow "Depositary Information on IMO Conventions" hyperlink) (last visited Aug. 30, 2010), pp. 385–387.

[225] On the number of persons taken hostage by pirates and armed robbers at sea, see p. 6 *et seq.*

[226] Art. 2 Hostage Convention.

[227] Art. 5 Hostage Convention.

[228] *Rosenstock*, International Convention against the Taking of Hostages, Another International Community Step to Counter Terrorism, Denver Journal of International Law and Policy 9 (1980), 172–173.

With 167 State parties as of September 2010, the Hostage Convention is widely ratified. With the exception of Somalia, most regional States, including Djibouti, Kenya, Oman, the Seychelles, Yemen, and the United Republic of Tanzania, are contracting parties.[229]

III. Regional Instruments

The importance of regional cooperation in the quest to effectively repress piracy is widely recognized. The United Nations General Assembly, in Resolution 63/111 of February 12, 2009, explicitly pointed out the crucial role of international cooperation at the global, regional, sub-regional and bilateral levels in combating threats to maritime security, including piracy and armed robbery at sea through bilateral and multilateral instruments and mechanisms.[230] Similarly, the International Maritime Organization's Code of Practice for the Investigation of the Crimes of Piracy and Armed Robbery against Ships invites governments to develop agreements and procedures to facilitate cooperation in applying efficient and effective measures to prevent acts of piracy and armed robbery against ships.[231]

In particular, formalized regional cooperation has been commenced in Asia under the framework of the Regional Cooperation Agreement on Combating Piracy and Armed Robbery against Ships in Asia (ReCAAP), adopted in 2004. The United Nations General Assembly Resolution 60/30 of March 8, 2006, welcomed "the progress in regional cooperation" in Asia and urged States to "give urgent attention to adopting, concluding and implementing cooperation agreements at the regional level in high risk areas."[232] Against this background, the International Maritime Organization, in November 2007, specifically called upon governments in the Gulf of Aden region to conclude and implement as soon as possible a regional agreement to prevent, deter and suppress piracy and armed robbery against ships.[233] It appears that this call has now been heeded. In January 2009, the Djibouti Code

---

[229] United Nations, Treaty Collection, Status of Treaties, Chapter XVIII, Penal Matters, 5. International Convention against the Taking of Hostages, *available at* http://treaties.un.org/Pages/ParticipationStatus.aspx (last visited Aug. 30, 2010).

[230] United Nations, General Assembly, G.A. Res. 63/111, U.N. Doc. A/RES/63/111 (Feb. 12, 2009), para. 61.

[231] International Maritime Organization, Code of Practice for the Investigation of the Crimes of Piracy and Armed Robbery against Ships, IMO Doc. A22/Res.922 (Jan. 22, 2009).

[232] United Nations, General Assembly, G.A. Res. 60/30, U.N. Doc. A/RES/60/30 (March 8, 2006), para. 57.

[233] International Maritime Organization, Resolution A.1002(25), adopted on November 29, 2007, Piracy and Armed Robbery against Ships in Waters off the Coast of Somalia, IMO Doc. A25/Res. 1002 (Nov. 27, 2007).

of Conduct, which is largely modeled upon the ReCAAP, was adopted by States in the Gulf of Aden.

A. Regional Cooperation Agreement on Combating Piracy and Armed Robbery against Ships in Asia (ReCAAP)

The Regional Cooperation Agreement on Combating Piracy and Armed Robbery against Ships in Asia (ReCAAP) is an international treaty that resulted from a series of negotiations and calls for a multilateral approach to combating piracy in Southeast Asia.[234] According to its preamble, the ReCAAP aims to "significantly contribute towards the prevention and suppression of piracy and armed robbery against ships in Asia."[235]

The text of the ReCAAP was drafted by representatives of the ten members of the Association of Southeast Asian Nations (ASEAN) and six other countries from South (Bangladesh, India and Sri Lanka) and East Asia (China, Japan and South Korea). The agreement was adopted on November 11, 2004 and entered into force on September 4, 2006. Initially, it was open for signature only to regional States, but upon entry into force, in accordance with its Article 18(5), ReCAAP became open for accession by any State. Currently, ReCAAP has fifteen contracting parties, namely Bangladesh, Brunei, Cambodia, China, India, Japan, Laos, Myanmar, Norway, Philippines, Singapore, South Korea, Sri Lanka, Thailand and Vietnam. The fact that two important players in the region, Indonesia and Malaysia, are not parties to the agreement is seen as a significant challenge for the ReCAAP.[236] As far as non-Asian States are concerned, Denmark and the Netherlands announced their intention to accede to the ReCAAP in February 2009.[237] Norway recently joined the ReCAAP in August 2009.[238]

---

[234] The Regional Cooperation Agreement on Combating Piracy and Armed Robbery against Ships in Asia [hereinafter: ReCAAP] is *available at* www.recaap.org/about/pdf/ReCAAP%20Agreement.pdf (last visited Aug. 30, 2010). Generally, see *Mejia*, in: Petrig (ed.), Sea Piracy Law – Droit de la piraterie maritime; *Guilfoyle*, Shipping Interdiction, p. 57; *Hayashi*, Introductory Note – Regional Cooperation Agreement on Combating Piracy and Armed Robbery against Ships in Asia, ILM (4) 2005, 826–829.

[235] Preamble of the Regional Cooperation Agreement on Combating Piracy and Armed Robbery against Ships in Asia (ReCAAP).

[236] *Mejia*, in: Petrig (ed.), Sea Piracy Law – Droit de la piraterie maritime, Section I.A.

[237] ReCAAP, The ReCAAP ISC Makes Further Progress and Will Co-Operate with the IMO in the Effort against Piracy in the Western Indian Ocean and the Gulf of Aden, Press Release, Feb. 27, 2009, *available at* www.recaap.org/news/pdf/press/2009/Press%20Release-3GC%20Mtg.pdf (last visited Aug. 30, 2010).

[238] *Id.* at para. 5. In August 2009, Norway has become the fifteenth contracting party to the Regional Cooperation Agreement on Combating Piracy and Armed Robbery against Ships in Asia (ReCAAP): ReCAAP, Report for August 2009, *available at* www.recaap.org/incident/pdf/reports/2009/ReportAug09_O_180909.pdf (last visited Aug. 30, 2010), p. 1.

In Article 1 ReCAAP, the definition of piracy of UNCLOS and the definition of armed robbery against ships as entailed in the International Maritime Organization's Code of Practice for the Investigation of Armed Robbery against Ships are adopted.[239] The general obligations of the contracting parties are laid out in the following provision:

Art. 3(1) ReCAAP – General Obligations

1. Each Contracting Party shall, in accordance with its national laws and regulations and applicable rules of international law, make every effort to take effective measures in respect of the following:

a) to prevent and suppress piracy and armed robbery against ships;

b) to arrest pirates or persons who have committed armed robbery against ships;

c) to seize ships or aircraft used for committing piracy or armed robbery against ships, to seize ships taken by and under the control of pirates or persons who have committed armed robbery against ships, and to seize the property on board such ships; and

d) to rescue victim ships and victims of piracy or armed robbery against ships.

Against the background of these general obligations, ReCAAP envisages the sharing of information, cooperation and capacity building among contracting parties. To this end, Article 4 ReCAAP creates an Information Sharing Center (ISC). The Information Sharing Center is an international organization with a Governing Council, composed of a representative from each contracting party, and a Secretariat. It is located in Singapore and was officially launched on November 29, 2006.[240] Article 7 ReCAAP lays out the functions of the Information Sharing Center. It serves as an information exchange platform and it collects and analyzes information transmitted by the contracting parties, which by Article 9 ReCAAP are required to designate national focal points responsible for the communication with the Information Sharing Center. The Information Sharing Center prepares statistics and reports on the basis of the information gathered and it provides alerts against imminent threats of piracy or armed robbery against ships. In accordance with Article 10 ReCAAP, contracting parties may request other contracting parties, through the Information Sharing Center or directly, to cooperate in detecting persons who have committed acts of piracy or armed robbery against ships.

Article 12 ReCAAP is entitled "Extradition" and provides that contracting parties, subject to their national laws, shall endeavor to extradite pirates or persons who have committed armed robbery against ships, and who are present in their territory, to other contracting parties that have jurisdiction over them, at the request of that contracting party. However, it should be emphasized that Article 12 ReCAAP is couched in rather cautious language. It does not stipulate a strict obligation to prosecute or extradite piracy suspects but merely requires that contracting parties

---

[239] International Maritime Organization, Code of Practice for the Investigation of the Crimes of Piracy and Armed Robbery against Ships, IMO Doc. A22/Res.922 (Jan. 22, 2009).

[240] *Mejia*, in: Petrig (ed.), Sea Piracy Law – Droit de la piraterie maritime, Section I.A.

shall, subject to their national laws and regulations, endeavor to extradite pirates. Notably, Article 13 ReCAAP which deals with mutual legal assistance and the sharing of evidence contains a similar *caveat*, referring to national laws and regulations. Finally, it should be pointed out that Article 12 ReCAAP, contrary to the transfer agreements concluded by the European Union with certain regional States,[241] does not speak of transfers, but explicitly refers to the more formalized procedure of extradition.

ReCAAP does not provide for any enforcement powers going beyond what is provided for in UNCLOS, nor does it envisage coordinated patrols or joint law enforcement operations at sea. In particular, the ReCAAP does not facilitate the pursuit of suspicious vessels that enter the territorial waters of another State. On the contrary, the ReCAAP contains an explicit saving clause:

Art. 2(5) ReCAAP – General Provisions

5. Nothing in this Agreement entitles a Contracting Party to undertake in the territory of another Contracting Party the exercise of jurisdiction and performance of functions which are exclusively reserved for the authorities of that other Contracting Party by its national law.

While the wording of this provision is admittedly somewhat ambiguous,[242] the intention to bar law enforcement operations in littoral States' coastal waters or upon their mainland seems rather clear. ReCAAP, therefore, may best be described as an effort towards enhanced law enforcement cooperation and coordination.

Although couched in cautious terms and without significant innovations in the field of joint maritime law enforcement operations, ReCAAP has potential to evolve. Notably, according to Article 7(g) ReCAAP, the Information Sharing Center may also perform such other functions as may be agreed upon by the Governing Council, which according to Article 4(6) ReCAAP decides by consensus, with a view to preventing and suppressing piracy and armed robbery against ships. However, given that the Governing Council is only authorized to enlarge the functions of the Information Sharing Center, it would not seem possible for the Governing Council to set up novel enforcement powers exceeding the enforcement regime of the UNCLOS or entirely innovative mechanisms in contravention of the safeguard clause contained in Article 2 ReCAAP. For the time being, it seems safe to conclude that ReCAAP still lacks teeth but that it usefully formalizes cooperation and coordination in the field of maritime law enforcement with a view to prevent and repress piracy and armed robbery at sea in Southeast Asia. Continuous cooperation under the umbrella of the ReCAAP may enhance mutual confidence among the contracting parties and may thus pave the way for a gradual enlargement of the

---

[241] On the transfer agreements concluded between the European Union and regional States, see p. 33 *et seq.* and p. 199 *et seq.*

[242] *Guilfoyle*, Shipping Interdiction, p. 59.

functions of the Information Sharing Center and ultimately perhaps to joint patrols and the negotiation of extended enforcement powers.

B. Djibouti Code of Conduct

On January 29, 2009, the Code of Conduct Concerning the Repression of Piracy and Armed Robbery against Ships in the Western Indian Ocean and the Gulf of Aden (Djibouti Code of Conduct) was adopted at a high-level meeting attended by States from the Western Indian Ocean, the Gulf of Aden and the Red Sea areas, convened in Djibouti by the International Maritime Organization.[243] It entered into force on January 29, 2009, with the initial signatures of nine regional States.[244] It is open for signature only by the 21 States referred to as "Participants" in the Preamble of the Code.[245] On March 10, 2010, Saudi Arabia signed the Code, thereby becoming the 13th country to do so.[246]

The Djibouti Code of Conduct aims to promote greater regional cooperation between signatories and, thereby, to enhance their effectiveness in the prevention, interdiction, prosecution, and punishment of persons engaging in piracy and armed robbery against ships.[247] The Codes's main objective is cooperation in sharing and reporting relevant information, with a view to the repression of piracy and armed robbery against ships.[248] The Djibouti Code of Conduct has already been praised as

---

[243] Code of Conduct Concerning the Repression of Piracy and Armed Robbery against Ships in the Western Indian Ocean and the Gulf of Aden, advance copy *available at* www.fco.gov.uk/resources/en/pdf/pdf9/piracy-djibouti-meeting (last visited Aug. 30, 2010) [hereinafter: Djibouti Code of Conduct; the document is reprinted on p. 284 *et seq.* of this book (Appendix)]. The high-level meeting was attended by ministers, ambassadors, senior officials and legal experts from the Comoros, Djibouti, Egypt, Ethiopia, France, Jordan, Kenya, Madagascar, Maldives, Oman, Saudi Arabia, Seychelles, Somalia, South Africa, Sudan, the United Republic of Tanzania and Yemen, as well as observers from other member States of the International Maritime Organization, United Nations specialized agencies and bodies, as well as international and regional inter-governmental and non-governmental organizations; see International Maritime Organization, High-Level Meeting in Djibouti Adopts a Code of Conduct to Repress Acts of Piracy and Armed Robbery against Ships, Jan. 30, 2009, *available at* www.imo.org/newsroom/mainframe.asp?topic_id=1773&doc_id=10933 (last visited Aug. 30, 2010).

[244] United Nations, Secretary-General Report on S.C. Res. 1846, Nov. 13, 2009, para. 16.

[245] Art. 16 Djibouti Code of Conduct. According to the Preamble of the Djibouti Code of Conduct, "Participants" to the Code are the governments of the Comoros, Djibouti, Egypt, Eritrea, Ethiopia, France, Jordan, Kenya, Madagascar, Maldives, Mauritius, Mozambique, Oman, Saudi Arabia, Seychelles, Somalia, South Africa, Sudan, the United Arab Emirates, the United Republic of Tanzania and Yemen.

[246] International Maritime Organization, Saudi Arabia Signs Djibouti Anti-Piracy Code, Press Release, March 10, 2010, *available at* www.imo.org/inforesource/mainframe.asp?topic_id=1859&doc_id=12603 (last visited Aug. 30, 2010).

[247] Preambular para. 11 of the Djibouti Code of Conduct.

[248] International Maritime Organization, High-Level Meeting in Djibouti Adopts a Code of Conduct to Repress Acts of Piracy and Armed Robbery against Ships, Jan. 30, 2009,

a milestone development and a central instrument in the development of regional capacity to combat piracy. In Resolution 1918, in the context of the prosecution of suspected pirates and armed robbers at sea and the imprisonment of convicted pirates apprehended off the coast of Somalia, the Security Council explicitly welcomed "the progress being made to implement the IMO Djibouti Code of Conduct, and calls upon its participants to implement it fully as soon as possible."[249]

As explicitly stated in the preamble, the Djibouti Code of Conduct was inspired by and, partially based upon, the ReCAAP. Various regulations of the Djibouti Code of Conduct resemble provisions of the ReCAAP. Thus, for example, Article 3 Djibouti Code of Conduct regarding protection measures for ships is modeled upon Article 16 ReCAAP.[250] Similarly, Articles 8, 9 and 10 Djibouti Code of Conduct regarding information sharing, incident reporting and general assistance among participants are based on Articles 9 and 10 ReCAAP. Thus, like the ReCAAP, the Djibouti Code of Conduct envisages to facilitate a coordinated flow of information through a system of national focal points and piracy information exchange centers in Kenya, the United Republic of Tanzania and Yemen.[251] The development of uniform reporting criteria, in accordance with Article 9 Djibouti Code of Conduct, is intended to ensure an accurate assessment of the threat of piracy and armed robbery at sea in the Western Indian Ocean and the Gulf of Aden.[252]

However, unlike the ReCAAP, the Djibouti Code of Conduct is not a legally binding instrument. According to its Article 15(a), nothing in the Djibouti Code of Conduct is intended to create a binding agreement. However, Article 13 Djibouti Code of Conduct stipulates, somewhat elliptically, that within two years of the effective date of the Code (i.e. January 29, 2009) and having designated the national focal points referred to in Article 8 Djibouti Code of Conduct, the participants

---

available at www.imo.org/newsroom/mainframe.asp?topic_id=1773&doc_id=10933 (last visited Aug. 30, 2010).

[249] S.C. Res. 1918, para 3.

[250] See also the following recommendations: International Maritime Organization, Piracy and Armed Robbery against Ships, Recommendations to Governments for Preventing and Suppressing Piracy and Armed Robbery against Ships, IMO Doc. MSC/Circ.622/Rev.1 (June 16, 1999); and, International Maritime Organization, Piracy and Armed Robbery against Ships, Guidance to Shipowners and Ship Operators, Shipmasters and Crews on Preventing and Suppressing Acts of Piracy and Armed Robbery against Ships, IMO Doc. MSC/Circ.623/Rev.3 (May 29, 2002).

[251] International Maritime Organization, High-Level Meeting in Djibouti Adopts a Code of Conduct to Repress Acts of Piracy and Armed Robbery against Ships, Jan. 30, 2009, *available at* www.imo.org/newsroom/mainframe.asp?topic_id=1773&doc_id=10933 (last visited Aug. 30, 2010).

[252] International Maritime Organization, Piracy and Armed Robbery against Ships, Recommendations to Governments for Preventing and Suppressing Piracy and Armed Robbery against Ships, IMO Doc. MSC/Circ.622/Rev.1 (June 16, 1999); International Maritime Organization, Piracy and Armed Robbery against Ships, Guidance to Shipowners and Ship Operators, Shipmasters and Crews on Preventing and Suppressing Acts of Piracy and Armed Robbery against Ships, IMO Doc. MSC/Circ.623/Rev.3 (May 29, 2002).

intend to consult, with the aim of arriving at a binding agreement. Moreover, unlike the ReCAAP, the Djibouti Code of Conduct[253] is not open for accession by any State.[254]

Article 4 Djibouti Code of Conduct lays out the range of enforcement measures for the repression of piracy. It is based on the respective UNCLOS provisions and does not extend the scope of enforcement powers. Rather, Article 4(5) Djibouti Code of Conduct reiterates that any pursuit of a ship extending in and over the territorial sea of a Participant is subject to the authority of that Participant, and that no Participant should pursue such a ship in the territorial sea of any coastal State without the permission of that State. Possibly with a view to facilitating law enforcement cooperation between the pursuing State and the State whose territorial waters are concerned in such a scenario, Article 7 Djibouti Code of Conduct provides for the embarkation of authorized law enforcement officials (so-called shipriders)[255] of one State on the patrol ships or aircraft of another participating State.

Article 15 Djibouti Code of Conduct (similar to Article 2 ReCAAP) and Security Council Resolutions 1846 and 1851, as prolonged by Resolution 1897) contains a number of safeguard clauses. According to Article 15(b) Djibouti Code of Conduct, nothing in the Code is intended to affect in any way the rules of international law pertaining to the competence of States to exercise investigative or enforcement jurisdiction on board ships not flying their flag. Moreover, according to its Article 15(d), the Djibouti Code of Conduct does not affect enforcement competencies granted under international law against pirates on the high seas. Further, Article 15(j) Djibouti Code of Conduct stipulates that nothing in the Code entitles a Participant to exercise jurisdiction in the territory of another Participant, which is exclusively reserved for the authorities of that other Participant. Finally, according to Article 15(k) Djibouti Code of Conduct, the Code does not intend to prejudice in any manner the positions and navigational rights and freedoms of any Participant regarding the international law of the sea.

The Djibouti Code of Conduct aims to ensure that persons committing, or attempting to commit, acts of piracy or armed robbery against ships are apprehended and prosecuted.[256] Article 11 Djibouti Code of Conduct requires that "[i]n order to allow for the prosecution, conviction and punishment of those involved in piracy or armed robbery against ships, and to facilitate extradition or handing over when

---

[253] The Djibouti Code of Conduct is, according to its Art. 16(1), open for signature by Participants on January 29, 2009 and at the Headquarters of the International Maritime Organization from February 1, 2009.

[254] Art. 18(5) of the Regional Cooperation Agreement on Combating Piracy and Armed Robbery against Ships in Asia (ReCAAP).

[255] On the definition and use of shipriders, see p. 85 *et seq.*

[256] United Nations, Secretary-General Report on S.C. Res. 1846, Nov. 13, 2009, para. 38.

prosecution is not possible, each Participant intends to review its national legislation." In particular, Article 11 Djibouti Code of Conduct envisages this review so as to ensure that there are adequate national laws in place to criminalize piracy and armed robbery against ships on the domestic level. Moreover, review is foreseen so as to ensure that adequate guidelines for the exercise of jurisdiction, conduct of investigation and prosecution of alleged offenders are in place. Notably, in this regard the Report of the Secretary-General pursuant to Security Council Resolution 1846, notes that the International Maritime Organization secretariat has recently undertaken a review of national legislation from contracting governments. The secretariats of the International Maritime Organization and the United Nations Office on Drugs and Crime have drawn a number of preliminary conclusions, which indicate a lack of appropriate implementation, especially as far as domestic provisions implementing universal jurisdiction are concerned. According to the Report, the United Nations Office of Legal Affairs and the International Maritime Organization will be working closely with the United Nations Office on Drugs and Crime to complete the legislative review and to consider how best to assist States in taking appropriate steps under their national law to facilitate the apprehension and prosecution of those who are alleged to have committed acts of piracy.[257]

The International Maritime Organization provides continuous assistance in the implementation of the Djibouti Code of Conduct in cooperation with the United Nations Office on Drugs and Crime, INTERPOL, the Information Sharing Center of the ReCAAP, a number of its member States and a number of navies.[258] The International Maritime Organization's activities to implement the Djibouti Code of Conduct, currently funded through the organization's technical cooperation program, will be funded through the Djibouti Code of Conduct trust fund, a multi-donor fund established following significant donations from Japan.[259]

IV. Conclusion

Throughout the 20th century, codification efforts relating to piracy were largely determined by the perception that piracy amounts to an historical phenomenon hardly in need of elaborate codification, rather than an imminent problem of the modern world. To some extent, piracy was not even perceived as being worthy of any specific codification at all and, accordingly, the rules that ultimately found their way into UNCLOS' piracy regime, were never the subject of any in-depth discussions. For the most part, the rules relating to piracy were simply imported

---

[257] *Id.* at para. 42.

[258] *Id.* at para. 38.

[259] *Id.* at para. 41.

from previous draft conventions or earlier treaties, with all their intricacies and loopholes. Presumably, this is what led Alfred Rubin to conclude rather bluntly that the treaty provisions on piracy in force today "are incomprehensible and codify nothing."[260]

Yet, despite the perception of piracy's outdatedness prevailing at the diplomatic conferences on the law of the sea in 1958, 1960 and 1982, violence against ships and persons on board, continued to pose a threat throughout the 20th century. This is likely to hold true in the 21st century. There will be plenty of opportunities given that in the course of globalization the international shipping industry has grown exponentially, becoming itself a motor of globalization.[261]

Every major upsurge in maritime violence in the more recent past has brought to the fore the failure to remedy the deficiencies and shortcomings of the legal framework pertaining to piracy during earlier drafting exercises. Yet, there has been little, if any, momentum towards a reform of the piracy regime contained in the UNCLOS. Maritime interception operations (in particular in view of the ever increasing importance of unimpeded navigation of a growing ship industry) are an especially sensitive issue, touching directly upon States' sovereign interests over their coastal waters and over ships flying their flag.

UNCLOS is traditionally perceived to reflect a subtle balance of extensively negotiated compromises that is only acceptable to States parties as a package deal. Thus, a widely held perception is that a modification of singular elements or even entire sections would off-set the negotiated compromise and would necessitate modifications of UNCLOS in its entirety. For the time being, States appear to be strongly committed to uphold this package-deal. In fact, the reaffirmation of UNCLOS as the legal framework applicable to combating piracy at sea in the various Security Council Resolutions relating to the situation in the Gulf of Aden proves this continuous commitment.[262] Similar reaffirmations are contained in the Djibouti Code of Conduct and the ReCAAP.[263] What is more, in light of the present political atmosphere, it appears even less likely that a reform of the UNCLOS may be attempted. Despite the seriousness of the piracy problem and its current acuteness in the Gulf of Aden, the section within the UNCLOS dealing with piracy is

---

[260] *Rubin*, Law of Piracy, p. 393.

[261] *Erie*, Globalizing L.A.; *Krugman/Cooper/Srinivasan*, Growing World Trade: Causes and Consequences, Brookings Papers on Economic Activity (1) 1995, 341; *Broda/Weinstein*, Globalization and the Gains from Variety, Quarterly Journal of Economics (121) 2006.

[262] See only the reaffirmation in the most recent counter-piracy Resolution, S.C. Res. 1918, preambular para. 3, which reaffirms that "international law, as reflected in the United Nations Convention on the Law of the Sea of 10 December 1982 (…), in particular its articles 100, 101 and 105, sets out the legal framework applicable to combating piracy and armed robbery at sea, as well as other ocean activities."

[263] Art. 15(k) Djibouti Code of Conduct; Art. 2(2) of the ReCAAP.

arguably not where the greatest contemporary concern lies. After all, these are times in which competing continental shelf claims to the North Pole are at issue.[264] This contentious debate would seem to act as an additional disincentive for States to reopen the negotiations of UNCLOS with a view to reform.

Thus, in response to increasing pirate activities in certain areas, region-specific solutions have commonly been sought, rather than a universal solution by way of reforming the UNCLOS' counter-piracy provisions. An increase in acts of piracy in Southeast Asia resulted in the ReCAAP. The threat posed by piracy in the Gulf of Aden region has, likewise, led to the adoption of a regional instrument, the Djibouti Code of Conduct. In addition, in view of the latter upsurge, a considerable number of context-specific Security Council Resolutions have been adopted.

The finding that States commonly accord preference to situation-specific solutions over a universal approach appears to hold true not only with regard to piracy. The largely consent-based, context-specific *modus operandi* pursued in relation to piracy can also be observed with regard to other maritime security threats, such as the smuggling of drugs or weapons and the trafficking of persons. Various bilateral agreements between the United States and numerous Caribbean States, for example, concerning the repression of illicit drug trafficking, underline a geographically limited and context-specific approach that is tailored towards a particular maritime problem. Similarly, under the umbrella of the Proliferation Security Initiative (PSI),[265] bilateral agreements have been favored over a more general expansion of universal maritime enforcement competencies by way of further codification.

Of course, over time these various initiatives will lead to an increasing amount of State practice that could in theory ultimately result in the evolution of customary law rules relating to law enforcement powers against acts of violence at sea.[266] However, one may remain doubtful with regard to any such evolution in practice. Thus far, practice in relation to bilateral drug interdiction treaties that predate the Proliferation Security Initiative (PSI) has, as far as can be seen, not led to the development of novel customary law. Although some of these treaties are rather similar and drafted on the basis of the same model, overall their number remains limited, differences in drafting exist and all of these treaties are fundamentally

---

[264] *Matz-Lueck*, Planting the Flag in Arctic Waters: Russia's Claim to the North Pole, Göttingen Journal of International Law (1) 2009, 235–256.

[265] Announced by President of the United States of America, George W. Bush, in Krakow (Poland) on May 31, 2003, the Proliferation Security Initiative (PSI) is a United States-led multinational initiative to counter the trafficking of weapons of mass destruction. Under the umbrella of the PSI, a number of States have agreed to exchange information concerning suspected proliferation of weapons of mass destruction, to review and strengthen their national laws and to undertake a number of specific interdiction measures at sea, so far typically based on the respective flag State's consent. See *Byers*, in: Wolfrum (ed.), EPIL-Proliferation Security Initiative, para. 6.

[266] *Byers*, Policing the High Seas: The Proliferation Security Initiative, AJIL (98) 2004, 534.

premised on the consent of the flag State. Certainly, for the time being, nothing on the universal level confirms the evolution of customary law rules that would go beyond the enforcement competencies laid out in UNCLOS.

In the past, the counter-piracy regime of the UNCLOS has often proven to be too narrow to target various other forms of maritime violence. The *Achille Lauro* incident is, perhaps, the epitome in this regard. Henceforth, codification efforts undertaken in the wake of counter-terrorism initiatives, such as the SUA and Hostage Conventions, helped to remedy some of the UNCLOS' shortcomings. The Security Council, arguably in an attempt to cover the acts of violence in the Gulf of Aden region as comprehensively as possible, has invoked a number of these Conventions in its various Resolutions dealing with piracy. Yet, as will be shown in detail further below, the SUA and Hostage Conventions do not contain a boarding provision or enforcement powers akin to, let alone going beyond, the UNCLOS. Moreover, they are primarily terrorism-tailored in that the offenses described and defined in Article 3 SUA Convention usually relate to specific terrorism acts, such as placing explosive devices on a ship or destroying navigational facilities. Therefore, from the outset it can be concluded that the legal framework pertaining to piracy and armed robbery at sea remains fragmented and complex. At the same time, the emergence of a new and integrated set of rules dealing with the whole phenomenon of maritime violence against ships and persons on board seems unlikely at the present juncture.

The focus of the following analysis will, therefore, be on the context-specific legal regime that currently applies to counter-piracy operations in the Gulf of Aden region. This legal regime is made up of different components, namely the general regime pertaining to counter-piracy operations as it derives from the UNCLOS and customary law, counter-terrorism rules laid out in the SUA and Hostage Conventions and the various Security Council Resolutions pertaining to piracy and armed robbery at sea off the coast of Somalia.

Part 3

Counter-Piracy Enforcement Powers and their Legal Constraints

I. Scope of Counter-Piracy Enforcement Powers

Security Council Resolution 1897, like all previous Security Council Resolutions relating to the fight against piracy and armed robbery at sea off the coast of Somalia, reaffirms "that international law, as reflected in the United Nations Convention on the Law of the Sea of 10 December 1982 (UNCLOS), sets out the legal framework applicable to combating piracy and armed robbery at sea."[267]

A. Enforcement Powers Granted by UNCLOS

1. Article 110(1)(a) UNCLOS: The Right of Visit

Article 110 UNCLOS is entitled "right of visit." According to Article 110(1)(a) UNCLOS, a warship that encounters a foreign ship on the high seas is not justified in boarding it, unless there is reasonable ground for suspecting that the ship is engaged in piracy. The word "unless," together with the negative formulation of Article 110(1) UNCLOS, indicate that the right of visit is an exceptional measure. The right exists as an exception to the generally exclusive jurisdiction of the flag State over ships flying its flag.[268] Against this background, it would seem that Article 110 UNCLOS should be interpreted restrictively rather than broadly.

The wording of Article 110(1)(a) UNCLOS begs two central questions. Firstly, what are reasonable grounds for suspecting that a ship is engaged in piracy; in other words, under which circumstances a ship may be visited (a.)? Secondly, which specific enforcement measures are entailed in and, therefore, conferred by, the right of visit under Article 110 UNCLOS or, in other words, which specific enforcement measures are States authorized to employ under the right of visit (b.)?

---

[267] S.C. Res. 1897, preambular para. 4; S.C. Res. 1918, preambular para. 3. Strictly speaking, of course, UNCLOS has nothing to say about armed robbery at sea, which is not a standing legal term but a notion commonly used to designate activities that take place in a State's territorial sea and, therefore, do not fall within the ambit of the piracy definition in Art. 101 UNCLOS. On the definition of armed robbery at sea, see p. 73 *et seq.*

[268] Art. 92 UNCLOS; see also Art. 6 Convention on the High Seas. *Nandan*, in: Nordquist (ed.), UNCLOS-Commentary, Article 110, 238–239.

a) Ships that May be Visited

Article 110 UNCLOS does not specify what is meant by the phrase "reasonable ground for suspecting" in the context of identifying which ships are engaged in piracy. In the Gulf of Aden, the identification of pirate vessels poses a veritable operational challenge. For example, it is not uncommon that shipping crews of regular fishing or merchant vessels cruising in the region are armed with light weapons. Moreover, a lot of vessels in the Gulf of Aden could be said to be "dual-use vessels." Fishing vessels are temporarily converted into pirate ships and *vice versa*. Similarly, merchant bulk carriers captured by pirates have reportedly been used as "mother ships" for the purpose of carrying out acts of piracy further from the coastline. Thus, a great number of ships transiting the Gulf of Aden could, in some regards, be deemed to be suspicious.

With regard to the question when there are reasonable grounds for suspecting that a ship is engaged in piracy, triggering the right of visit, some guidance may be derived from a comparison between Articles 110 and 105 UNCLOS. The first sentence of Article 105 UNCLOS grants enforcement powers against pirate ships that go beyond the mere right of visit laid out in Article 110 UNCLOS. Article 105 UNCLOS, for example, authorizes the arrest of the crew of a pirate ship. However, unlike Article 110 UNCLOS, Article 105 UNCLOS only grants these enforcement powers vis-à-vis pirate ships as defined in Article 103 UNCLOS (i.e. an identified pirate ship). On the basis of the wording of Article 105 UNCLOS, a mere suspicion that a ship might be engaged in piracy would not seem to suffice to trigger the enforcement powers provided by Article 105 UNCLOS. These different standards in terms of suspicion in Articles 110 and 105 UNCLOS are in line with the graduation of enforcement competencies laid out in these provisions.

Article 110 UNCLOS grants a (mere) right of visit, in order to verify an initial suspicion. The logic of Article 110(2) UNCLOS is that as the initial suspicion is gradually substantiated, the range of enforcement powers against the suspicious ship is proportionally extended.

Art. 110(2) UNCLOS – Right of Visit

2. In the cases provided for in paragraph 1, the warship may proceed to verify the ship's right to fly its flag. To this end, it may send a boat under the command of an officer to the suspected ship. *If suspicion remains* after the documents have been checked, it may proceed to a further examination on board the ship, which must be carried out with all possible consideration.[269]

Ultimately, once the suspicion has been confirmed and the ship can be identified as a pirate ship in accordance with Article 103 UNCLOS, the enforcement measures granted by Article 105 UNCLOS become available.[270] Alternatively, of course, the

---

[269] Emphasis added.

[270] Of course, even the first sentence of Art. 105 UNCLOS does not require absolute certainty or a level of proof beyond reasonable doubt as is required for conviction in criminal proceedings.

initial suspicion which led to the visit of the suspicious vessels may turn out to be unfounded, in which case Article 110(3) UNCLOS provides the following:

Art. 110(3) UNCLOS – Right of Visit

3. If the suspicions prove to be unfounded, and provided that the ship boarded has not committed any act justifying them, it shall be compensated for any loss or damage that may have been sustained.

From Article 110(3) UNCLOS it may be inferred that an initial suspicion justifying a right of visit may arise even if the ship in question has not committed any suspicious act. It follows that, as far as the powers laid out in Article 110 UNCLOS are concerned, indicative criteria, such as the bearing of arms or the use of ships that are typically used to commit acts of piracy in a specific region, may suffice to grant a right of visit. In other words, an armed fishing vessel encountered in the Gulf of Aden may be visited under Article 110 UNCLOS, even if it is not currently engaged in any particularly suspicious activity. Although Article 110(1) UNCLOS, generally, would seem to require a rather restrictive interpretation, this view appears arguable in light of the regionally increased risk of pirate attacks, given that a right of visit in and of itself entails only a rather temporary interference with the freedom of navigation and, furthermore, because Article 110(3) UNCLOS explicitly provides for compensation for any loss or damage caused by the interception, if the suspicion turns out to be unfounded.

b) Types of Enforcement Measures Authorized: Stopping, Boarding and Searching

The right of visit implicitly comprises a right to stop a suspicious vessel in order to enable a visit.[271] On the face of its wording, Article 110(2) UNCLOS merely allows the verification whether a ship is entitled to fly its flag. However, in line with the object and purpose of Article 110 UNCLOS to ensure the unimpeded freedom of navigation on the high seas and in line with Article 110(1)(a) UNCLOS, which explicitly refers to piracy, it seems plausible to argue that Article 110 UNCLOS grants such powers as are necessary to verify whether a ship is in fact a pirate ship, in the sense of Article 103 UNCLOS.

Against this background, the second sentence of Article 110(2) UNCLOS allows a boat under the command of an officer to be sent to the suspected ship and, if suspicion remains, a further examination on board the ship as may be required. Therefore, once a suspicious ship has been boarded and, if suspicion that the ship might be engaged in piracy remains, the right of visit granted by Article 110 UNCLOS also comprises a right to search the vessel and, arguably, also its crew for purposes

---

[271] United Nations, International Law Commission, Commentary on the Law of the Sea Draft Convention, p. 284.

of verifying or dispelling the suspicion.[272] In practice, it appears to be common upon boarding suspected pirate vessels to conduct a preliminary security sweep of the boat to identify possible threats, including hidden persons and weapons. This practice is not explicitly mandated by UNCLOS and tends to somewhat blur the line between visit and search under Article 110(2) UNCLOS. However, it responds to imminent security needs of the operating personnel and it does not significantly prolong the visit. Therefore, it seems feasible to argue that an initial security sweep is comprised already by the right of visit.

Hypothetically, irrespective of Article 110 UNCLOS, as far as the right to stop, board and search vessels is concerned, in the case of Somali ships encountered in the Gulf of Aden, the Somali Transitional Federal Government could consent to a general right of visit of Somali ships encountered in the region. Common practice in relation to high seas law enforcement, however, would seem to require the express consent of a State for enforcement operations against its vessels on the high seas. Similarly, the Transitional Federal Government could consent into a right of visit of Somali ships already on the basis of a minimal suspicion. Although implied consent in this regard could possibly be derived from the Somali Transitional Federal Government's numerous requests to the Security Council and its clearly expressed interest to effectively repress piracy and armed robbery at sea off its coast, for the sake of legal certainty and in line with common practice, the better view would seem to be to require explicit consent.

2. Article 105 UNCLOS: The Right to Arrest and Seize Pirate Ships

Like Article 110 UNCLOS, the first sentence of Article 105 UNCLOS is an exception to the generally exclusive jurisdiction of the flag State over vessels flying its flag.[273] It authorizes all States to take enforcement measures against pirate ships or ships taken by piracy and under the control of pirates.[274]

Art. 105 UNCLOS – Seizure of a Pirate Ship or Aircraft

On the high seas, or in any other place outside the jurisdiction of any State, every State may seize a pirate ship or aircraft, or a ship or aircraft taken by piracy and under the control of pirates, and arrest the persons and seize the property on board.

Article 107 UNCLOS specifies that the enforcement powers laid out in Article 105 UNCLOS may only be carried out by warships, military aircraft or other ships or aircraft clearly marked and identifiable as being on government service

---

[272] *Nandan*, in: Nordquist (ed.), UNCLOS-Commentary, Article 110, 244.

[273] Art. 92 UNCLOS.

[274] According to the first sentence of Art. 105 UNCLOS, these enforcement powers also apply vis-à-vis pirate aircraft or aircraft taken by piracy and under the control of pirates. The focus of this analysis is exclusively on ships. The first sentence of Art. 19 Convention on the High Seas is almost identically worded with the sole exception that it makes not mention of aircraft.

and authorized to that effect.[275] Thus, in order to determine the scope of enforcement powers granted by virtue of Article 105 UNCLOS, three questions need to be addressed: What is the personal scope of enforcement powers under Article 105 UNCLOS (a.)? What is the geographical scope of enforcement powers under Article 105 UNCLOS (b.)? And what types of enforcement measures are authorized under Article 105 UNCLOS (c.)?

a) Personal Scope of Enforcement Powers under Article 105 UNCLOS

The enforcement powers laid out in the first sentence of Article 105 UNCLOS only apply vis-à-vis pirate ships as defined in Article 103 UNCLOS (aa.), ships taken by piracy and under the control of pirates (bb.), and against persons and property that are found on board such ships (cc.).

aa) Article 103 UNCLOS: The Definition of Pirate Ships

According to Article 103 UNCLOS, two categories of ships qualify as pirate ships: Firstly, ships that have not (necessarily) yet been involved in "acts of piracy" but are intended to be used to commit an "act of piracy" (first sentence); and secondly, ships that have already been used to commit an "act of piracy", so long as the ship remains under the control of the persons guilty of that act (second sentence). It follows that the definition of "piracy" (and more specifically "acts of piracy") laid out in Article 101 UNCLOS is central to the identification of a "pirate ship" or a "ship taken by piracy."

(1) Article 101 UNCLOS: The Definition of Piracy

The definition of piracy in Article 101 UNCLOS, while generally accepted, is intrinsically convoluted. Its ambiguity has been the subject of much criticism. This may be partly because piracy was largely regarded as an archaic 18th century phenomenon, which was not worthy of prolonged diplomatic deliberation when the definition was incorporated into UNCLOS.[276] The intricacies inherent in this definition, arguably, also reflect overly ambitious attempts to capture a criminal phenomenon in its entirety in one offense, while simultaneously making allowance for the preservation of States' sovereign interests.

---

[275] Even though Art. 107 UNCLOS only explicitly mentions seizure, it can be deduced that it applies to the entire panoply of enforcement powers contained in the first sentence of Art. 105 UNCLOS, which is entitled "Seizure of a Pirate Ship or Aircraft."

[276] *Rubin*, Law of Piracy, p. 393; *Dickinson*, Is the Crime of Piracy Obsolete? Harvard Law Review 38 (1925), 360. On the perceived outdatedness of the phenomenon of piracy during drafting of the UNCLOS, see p. 40 *et seq.*

The limitations and ambiguities in the definition of piracy in Article 101 UNCLOS have repercussions also on Article 105 UNCLOS, in that they limit and blur the scope of enforcement powers defined in the first sentence of this provision. In addition, the cross-references between Article 105 UNCLOS, Article 103 UNCLOS and, finally, Article 101 UNCLOS further amplify some of these ambiguities. The definition of piracy in Article 101 UNCLOS thus deserves specific attention.

Art. 101 UNCLOS – Definition of Piracy

Piracy consists of any of the following acts:

(a) any illegal acts of violence or detention, or any act of depredation, committed for private ends by the crew or the passengers of a private ship or a private aircraft, and directed:

(i) on the high seas, against another ship or aircraft, or against persons or property on board such ship or aircraft;

(ii) against a ship, aircraft, persons or property in a place outside the jurisdiction of any State;

(b) any act of voluntary participation in the operation of a ship or of an aircraft with knowledge of facts making it a pirate ship or aircraft;

(c) any act of inciting or of intentionally facilitating an act described in subparagraph (a) or (b).

(i) Illegal Acts of Violence

Almost all of these defining criteria of piracy carry specific problems of their own. First of all, Article 101(a) UNCLOS, by referring to "acts", seems to require a plurality of "acts." A systematic comparison with Article 101(b) and (c) UNCLOS, both of which refer to a singular act, however, evidences that a single act would suffice.

The explicit reference to "illegal" acts of violence is similarly imprecise. It is tautologous because grounds for justification of acts of violence committed between private actors, such as individual self-defense under domestic law, cannot be found in public international law.[277] "Illegality", as mentioned in Article 101(a) UNCLOS, thus merely refers to the self-evident, namely, to the illegality of the acts under the law of the State which decides to exercise its adjudicative jurisdiction over acts of piracy and to prosecute alleged offenders under its domestic laws.[278] As far as the scope of enforcement powers is concerned, the criterion of "illegality" is, therefore, irrelevant.

---

[277] During the drafting process Greece had proposed to delete the word "illegal," see *Nandan*, in: Nordquist (ed.), UNCLOS-Commentary, Article 101, 216.

[278] *Lagoni*, in: Ipsen/Schmidt-Jortzig (eds.), Piracy, 513.

(ii) Acts Committed for Private Ends

Article 101(a) UNCLOS further requires that acts amounting to piracy be "committed for private ends." This element has sparked ample debate in the past.[279] The words "for private ends" were originally included in the definition of piracy to acknowledge the historic exception for civil-war insurgencies that attacked solely the vessels of the government they sought to overthrow.[280] This historic interpretation of the wording "for private ends" has been perceived as overly narrow. Subsequently, broader definitions of the "private ends" requirement have been endorsed. Some authors maintain that the requirement simply excludes all acts committed for political reasons from the ambit of piracy.[281] Such a reading of the "private ends" requirement, however, appears to be overly broad and has been sharply criticized.[282] Indeed, it has convincingly been argued that the test lies not in the pirates' subjective motivation, but in whether the acts in question qualify as public acts authorized by (or more broadly attributable to) a State.[283] From this line of argument, it follows that all acts of violence that lack State sanction, are acts undertaken "for private ends."

Still, despite this predominantly academic debate, it remains to be seen how the "private ends" requirement will play out when tested in practice. In the Gulf of Aden context, thus far, there have been no indications that the relevant acts had not been committed for private ends or that this criterion has been of any particular relevance. This could change, however, if arrested piracy suspects in the course of judicial proceedings started to argue that their acts were politically motivated; an avenue which, in theory, could offer them an easy excuse against any allegations of having committed piracy. Somali suspects could argue that they are insurgents in conflict with the Somali Transitional Federal Government, since it is undisputed that there is presently a non-international armed conflict taking place on Somalia's

---

[279] *Halberstam*, Terrorism on High Seas: The Achille Lauro, Piracy and the IMO Convention on Maritime Safety, AJIL 82 (1988), 290; *Lagoni*, in: Ipsen/Schmidt-Jortzig (eds.), Piracy, 518. See also *Menefee*, Foreign Naval Intervention in Cases of Piracy: Problems and Strategies, International Journal Marine and Coastal Law 14 (1999), 358.

[280] ASIL-Commented Harvard Draft Convention on Piracy, p. 798 and p. 857; *Halberstam*, Terrorism on High Seas: The Achille Lauro, Piracy and the IMO Convention on Maritime Safety, AJIL 82 (1988), 290; *Lagoni*, in: Ipsen/Schmidt-Jortzig (eds.), Piracy, 518. The Rapporteur of International Law Commission suggested to also exclude acts of violence from unrecognized insurgents without combatant status in armed conflict from the definition of piracy: United Nations, International Law Commission, Yearbook, 1955, Volume 1, p. 40.

[281] *Crockett*, Toward a Revision of the International Law of Piracy, DePaul Law Review 26 (1976), 80.

[282] *Guilfoyle*, Shipping Interdiction, p. 36.

[283] *Id.*; *Halberstam*, Terrorism on High Seas: The Achille Lauro, Piracy and the IMO Convention on Maritime Safety, AJIL 82 (1988), 290; *Lagoni*, in: Ipsen/Schmidt-Jortzig (eds.), Piracy, 517.

mainland, in which the Transitional Federal Government is involved. Moreover, suspects could argue that in attacking other vessels they acted with an exclusively political motivation, aiming to fight off illegal fishery or the dumping of waste and that, consequently, their acts do not amount to piracy within the meaning of Article 101(a) UNCLOS.[284] Conversely, if it is accepted that without State sanction or without the possibility to attribute private acts to a State, acts are undertaken "for private ends," such defensive lines of argumentation could easily be refuted. Without the authorization of the Somali Transitional Federal Government for committing acts of piracy and armed robbery at sea, activities of Somali nationals could hardly be said to amount to public acts falling outside the ambit of the UNCLOS' piracy definition.

(iii) The "Two-Ship-Requirement"

Article 101(a) UNCLOS requires that a "private ship" be used against "another ship" which does not necessarily need to be a private ship.[285] Whether or not the second (attacked) ship flies the same flag as the first (attacking) ship, is irrelevant. However, crew seizures, mutiny or passenger takeovers of one and the same vessel do not satisfy the so-called "two-ship-requirement." They are thus excluded from the piracy definition's ambit.[286] The jurisdictional loopholes inherent in the "two-ship-requirement" were brought to the fore during the *Achille Lauro* incident, in response to which the SUA Convention was adopted.[287]

Article 101(a) UNCLOS does not contain any specific requirements regarding the size of either the offender or victim ship. Given the object and purpose of Part VII of the UNCLOS, in which Article 101 UNCLOS is found, namely, to protect free navigation on the high seas, it seems arguable that even small vessels and crafts (skiffs) are included within the meaning of the word "ship." As far as the offender ship (pirate ship) is concerned, the decisive criterion would seem to be

---

[284] *Guilfoyle*, Shipping Interdiction, p. 36.

[285] The reference to a "private ship" in Art. 101 UNCLOS in contrast to Art. 102 UNCLOS is to be understood broadly and comprises any ship, which is not a warship or a government ship. According to Art. 102 UNCLOS acts committed by a warship, government ship or government aircraft whose crew has mutinied and taken control of the ship or aircraft are assimilated to acts committed by a private ship or aircraft.

[286] Unlike Art. 101(a)(i) UNCLOS, Art. 101(a)(ii) UNCLOS does not refer to "another" ship. Yet, even though the high seas mentioned in Art. 101(a)(i) UNCLOS amounts to a place outside the jurisdiction of any State as mentioned in Art. 101(a)(ii) UNCLOS, equating Art. 101(a)(i) and (ii) UNCLOS and thereby dropping the "two-ship-requirement" in Art. 101(a)(i), as has been suggested, is probably not maintainable in view of the clear distinction of these two subparagraphs. But see *Menefee*, Foreign Naval Intervention in Cases of Piracy: Problems and Strategies, International Journal Marine and Coastal Law 14 (1999), 358.

[287] *Halberstam*, Terrorism on High Seas: The Achille Lauro, Piracy and the IMO Convention on Maritime Safety, AJIL 82 (1988), 269–310.

whether a vessel (whatever its size and irrespective of whether it was dispatched from a "mother ship") is capable of interfering with free navigation on the high seas. Similarly, as far as the victim ship is concerned, it would seem to suffice that the ship is seaworthy enough to be out on the high seas where UNCLOS' piracy regime applies. Therefore, the definition of piracy in Article 101(a) UNCLOS includes attacks against smaller crafts and yachts (so-called "yacht-jacking"),[288] as well as the use of maneuverable outboard engine driven long-boats, which are apparently particularly effective for carrying out attacks at sea and, therefore, for interfering with free navigation.

(iv) Acts Committed on the High Seas or in a Place Outside the Jurisdiction of Any State

Most importantly in the present Somali context, the definition of piracy contains a geographical limitation. In order to amount to piracy, acts in the sense of Article 101(a) UNCLOS must be committed either on the high seas or in a place outside the jurisdiction of any State. The latter limitation has little significance for the purposes of the present analysis, despite Somalia's often-cited status as a prototype of a failed State, which has no government capable of maintaining control over its territory and coastal waters.[289] Somalia's sovereignty has, nevertheless, remained unquestioned and Somalia's territorial waters thus cannot qualify as "a place outside the jurisdiction of any State."[290] The International Law Commission has pointed out that "a place outside the jurisdiction of any State" refers to an island constituting *terra nullius* or the shores of an unoccupied territory,[291] in other words, places that are not under the sovereignty of any State. Such an understanding of the phrase "a place outside the jurisdiction of any State" is also supported by the wording of Article 101(a) and the first sentence of Article 105 UNCLOS, which speak of "the high seas or (...) any *other* place outside the jurisdiction of any State."[292] Thus, as far as the identification of a "place outside the jurisdiction of any State" is concerned, sovereignty is decisive whereas the existence or absence of actual governmental control is irrelevant.

The restriction of the definition of acts of piracy to acts carried out on the high seas is, however, extremely relevant in the present context. According to Article 3 UNCLOS, every State has the right to establish the breadth of its territorial sea up to a limit not exceeding 12 nautical miles, measured from baselines determined in

---

[288] *Lagoni*, in: Ipsen/Schmidt-Jortzig (eds.), Piracy, 516.

[289] *Geiß*, Failed States, p. 162.

[290] S.C. Res. 1816, preambular para. 6; S.C. Res. 1846, preambular para. 3; S.C. Res. 1851, preambular para. 3.

[291] United Nations, International Law Commission, Commentary on the Law of the Sea Draft Convention, p. 282.

[292] Emphasis added.

accordance with UNCLOS. It follows that by definition acts of piracy cannot occur within the coastal area. Meanwhile, acts of piracy committed in the exclusive economic zone, the zone adjacent to the territorial sea, are treated as though they had been committed on the high seas.[293]

From the high seas-limitation it follows that conduct which fulfils all the substantive requirements of Article 101(a) UNCLOS but is committed within the territorial waters of a State (Somalia), does not qualify as an act of piracy. Thus, a ship that has engaged in criminal acts within Somalia's territorial waters that is subsequently encountered on the high seas, could not be intercepted or seized under the first sentence of Article 105 UNCLOS, because such a ship would not qualify as a "pirate ship" in the technical sense of Article 103 read together with Article 101 UNCLOS. Pirate-like attacks against vessels in territorial waters do not amount to piracy in the legal sense. In the parlance of the International Maritime Organization and of the Security Council, these attacks are commonly referred to as armed robbery against ships or as armed robbery at sea.[294]

(2) Remaining Definitional Ambiguities with Regard to Pirate Ships

Given that Article 103 UNCLOS refers to the piracy definition in Article 101 UNCLOS *in toto*, in theory a ship also qualifies as a pirate ship, if it has been used, or is intended to be used, to commit the acts described in Article 101(b) and (c) UNCLOS. These references lead to some almost inextricable problems: First of all, the reference of Article 103 UNCLOS to the acts described in Article 101(b) UNCLOS is a circular reference. Article 101(b) UNCLOS requires involvement in the operation of a "pirate ship," which Article 103 UNCLOS aims to define by reference to Article 101 UNCLOS. Secondly, contrary to Article 101(a) UNCLOS, the acts described in Article 101(b) and (c) UNCLOS pertaining to participation and incitement respectively, are not geographically limited to the high seas. Notably, the acts referred to in Article 101(c) UNCLOS, unlike the acts mentioned in Article 101(a) and (b) UNCLOS, need not even take place aboard a ship. Arguably the acts laid out in Article 101(c) UNCLOS also encompass activities of accomplices ashore or within a State's territorial waters. After all, according to Article 101(c) UNCLOS any act of inciting or of intentionally facilitating an act described in subparagraph (a) of Article 101 UNCLOS, irrespective of where it is undertaken,

---

[293] Art. 58(2) UNCLOS provides that Arts. 88 to 115 UNCLOS, pertaining to the high seas, also apply to the exclusive economic zone in so far as they are "not incompatible" with Part V of UNCLOS on the exclusive economic zone. Generally, there is no indication that the provisions pertaining to piracy would be incompatible with Part V of UNCLOS. Piracy normally does not interfere with the specific exclusive economic zone rights of the coastal State as laid out in Art. 56 UNCLOS. In exceptional cases, violence between private fishery vessels within the exclusive economic zone may lead to such incompatibility, see *Lagoni*, in: Ipsen/Schmidt-Jortzig (eds.), Piracy, 515.

[294] On the definition of armed robbery at sea, see p. 73 *et seq.*

amounts to an act of piracy. Thirdly, perhaps the epitome of this convoluted reference system is the following: Ships used to incite or facilitate acts of piracy would amount to pirate ships, even if the act of inciting or facilitating took place in territorial waters. This leads to an illogical discrepancy. Article 101(c) UNCLOS, in combination with Articles 103 and 105 UNCLOS, defines a ship that facilitates acts of piracy from within territorial waters as a pirate ship. Therefore, if such a ship is subsequently encountered on the high seas, the first sentence of Article 105 UNCLOS would grant enforcement powers against such a ship. However, such enforcement powers would not be granted against a ship that directly engaged in pirate-like acts, in the sense of Article 101(a) UNCLOS, within territorial waters.

A possible solution to this complicated reference system could be derived by way of a restrictive interpretation of the reference in Article 103 UNCLOS to Article 101 UNCLOS. Given that the acts described in Article 101(b) and (c) UNCLOS relate to activities of individuals that need not be carried out aboard a ship, rather than acts for the commission of which a ship needs to be used, one could argue that, by way of a teleological reduction, the sweeping reference in Article 103 UNCLOS, which aims to define a pirate ship, to all acts described in Article 101 UNCLOS, is in fact restricted to acts described in Article 101(a) UNCLOS, i.e. acts that by definition require the utilization of a ship. This would avoid the various ambiguities contained in a more global reference that comprises the acts laid out in Article 101(b) and (c) UNCLOS. However, at the present juncture, there is remarkably little discussion and no established consensus on the matter.

Thus, in the most "straightforward" case possibly imaginable, a private ship committing violent acts against another ship beyond the 12 mile zone in the Gulf of Aden would be committing piracy, in the sense of Article 101(a)(i) UNCLOS and would thus qualify as a "pirate ship" in the sense of Article 103 UNCLOS. Enforcement powers, authorized by Article 105 UNCLOS may be taken against such a ship, on condition that, at the time when enforcement measures are carried out, the ship remains under the control of the persons guilty of that act, as required by the second sentence of Article 103 UNCLOS or, alternatively, that the ship is intended to be used again to commit such acts, in accordance with the first sentence of Article 103 UNCLOS.

As mentioned above, in practice, major problems derive from the identification of a ship as a pirate ship in the sense of Article 103 UNCLOS. In the Gulf of Aden it is not uncommon for shipping crews to be armed and whether a fishing vessel has been converted into a pirate ship may not be readily discernible unless, the ship is actually engaged in a pirate attack at the time of encounter. It is estimated that around 700 suspects apprehended by European Union and NATO naval forces have been released between January and June 2010.[295] The principal reason cited for the

---

[295] United Nations, Secretary-General Report pursuant to S.C. Res. 1918, July 26, 2010, para. 20.

release of such a significant number of suspects is lack of evidence sufficient to support prosecution.[296] The first sentence of Article 103 UNCLOS does not specify when a ship may be considered to be intended by the persons in dominant control to be used for the purpose of committing an act of piracy, as defined in Article 101 UNCLOS. Thus, Articles 103 and 105 UNCLOS arguably leave law enforcement officials a certain margin of discretion in determining whether a ship qualifies as a pirate ship. However, on the level of adjudicative jurisdiction, when it comes to the prosecution of piracy suspects, higher evidential standards will apply and, unless caught in the midst of an ongoing attack, it may be difficult to prove beyond reasonable doubt that a defendant was engaged in an act of piracy.

bb) Ships Taken by Piracy and Under the Control of Pirates

According to the first sentence of Article 105 UNCLOS, enforcement measures may also be carried out against "a ship (…) taken by piracy and under the control of pirates." It is hardly conceivable that a ship could be taken by the acts described in Article 101(b) and (c) UNCLOS, which relate to acts of participation and incitement. Again, a more plausible reading is that the wording "a ship (…) taken by piracy and under the control of pirates" means a ship that has been the victim of the acts described in Article 101(a) UNCLOS and which has fallen under the control of the persons carrying out these acts, even though strictly speaking UNCLOS does not contain any definition of when an individual can be categorized as a pirate.

cc) Persons and Property on Board

Under Article 105 UNCLOS, persons encountered on either a pirate ship or a ship taken by piracy and under the control of pirates may be arrested. Likewise, property found on such ships may be seized. Article 105 UNCLOS is narrow in terms of place and physical ambit but wide in terms of the people against whom, and property against which, enforcement measures may be taken. It is narrow because the first sentence of Article 105 UNCLOS does not authorize any enforcement powers against persons or property encountered or found anywhere other than on board the specified categories of ships. Thus, Article 105 UNCLOS would not allow the arrest of a person who is known to have committed acts of piracy, but who is traveling on another (non-pirate) vessel as a regular passenger.

On the other hand, the personal scope of Article 105 UNCLOS is wide because, on the face of its wording, it authorizes the arrest of any person encountered on a pirate ship or on a ship taken by piracy and under the control of pirates, irrespective of whether the person has previously been engaged in piracy or not. Of course,

---

[296] *Id.*

without at least an initial suspicion that a person has engaged in any of the acts mentioned in Article 101 UNCLOS, a right to arrest could hardly be construed.

b) Geographical Scope of Enforcement Powers under Article 105 UNCLOS

In addition to the geographical limitation inherent in the definition of piracy in Article 101(a)(i) UNCLOS, Article 105 UNCLOS explicitly restricts States' right to exercise enforcement powers to the high seas or to any other place outside the jurisdiction of any State.[297] As stated above, the limitation to "places outside the jurisdiction of any State" can be ignored for the purposes of this analysis. The restriction of enforcement powers to the high seas, however, is highly relevant in the present context. It means that even if a ship clearly falls within the ambit of Article 101 UNCLOS read together with Article 103 UNCLOS and is thus within the definition of a pirate ship, the enforcement powers granted by the first sentence of Article 105 UNCLOS could not be exercised for as long as this ship remains within the territorial waters of a State.

What is more, even if initially encountered on the high seas, the enforcement powers granted to all States in international waters do not extend to pursuing pirate vessels into the territorial sea of any third State. Evidently, from the perspective of efficient law enforcement, such a right to so-called "reverse hot pursuit" (as opposed to conventional hot pursuit from within territorial waters onto the high seas) would be desirable.

Arguably, the most liberal and rather ambiguous position towards a right of "reverse hot pursuit" occurs in the United States Naval Commander's Handbook. After laying out that "every effort should be made to obtain the consent of the nation having sovereignty over the territorial sea, (...) to continue pursuit" and that "[t]he inviolability of the territorial integrity of sovereign nations makes the decision of a warship or military aircraft to continue pursuit into these areas without such consent a serious matter" the Handbook continues to stipulate that: "However, the international nature of the crime of piracy may allow continuation of pursuit if contact cannot be established in a timely manner with the coastal nation to obtain its consent. In such a case, pursuit must be broken off immediately upon request of the coastal nation and, in any event, the right to seize the pirate vessel or aircraft and to try the pirates devolves on the nation to which the territorial seas, archipelagic waters or airspace belong."[298]

---

[297] Art. 110(1)(a) UNCLOS, upon its wording, only applies to the high seas. It seems arguable, especially in view of the further reaching enforcement powers granted in the first sentence of Art. 105 UNCLOS, that the right of visit granted under Art. 110(1)(a) UNCLOS, applies to "any other place outside the jurisdiction of any State" as well as to the high seas.

[298] Moreover, it is provided that: "Pursuit of a pirate vessel or aircraft through or over international straits overlapped by territorial seas or through archipelagic sea lanes or air

However, a right to reverse hot pursuit is not anchored in any international treaty presently in force and there is no indication that such a right has developed by virtue of customary international law. Historically, proposals for a limited treaty-based right to pursue pirate ships from the high seas into territorial waters in the Harvard Draft Convention did not succeed.[299] The various treaties relating to issues that could possibly require a right to reverse hot pursuit, for example, treaties in the area of fisheries or anti-drug smuggling are all based on the assumption that foreign law enforcement activity within a State's territorial sea would require the coastal State's express consent. In particular, as far as piracy is concerned, the Djibouti Code of Conduct as well as the Regional Cooperation Agreement on Combating Piracy and Armed Robbery against Ships in Asia (ReCAAP) explicitly deny any right of foreign vessels to enter another State's territorial waters in order to counter piracy.[300] Thus, as with conventional hot pursuit, which is not comprised by the right of innocent passage,[301] pursuit of pirates must cease as soon as the pirate ship enters the territorial sea of another State.[302]

c) Types of Enforcement Measures Authorized under Article 105 UNCLOS

According to the first sentence of Article 105 UNCLOS, every State may seize a pirate ship or a ship taken and controlled by pirates and arrest the persons and seize the property on board.[303] UNCLOS does not explicitly allow for the sinking of

---

routes, may proceed with or without the consent of the coastal nation or nations, provided the pursuit is expeditious and direct and the transit passage or archipelagic sea lanes passage rights of others are not unreasonably constrained in the process." See The Commander's Handbook on the Law of Naval Operations, July 2007, Pursuit of Pirates Into Foreign Territorial Seas, Archipelagic Waters, or Airspace, Section 3.5.3.2, *available at* www.usnwc.edu/getattachment/a9b8e92d-2c8d-4779-9925-0defea93325c/1-14M_(Jul_2007)_(NWP) (last visited Aug. 30, 2010).

[299] ASIL-Commented Harvard Draft Convention on Piracy, pp. 745–746 and p. 873.

[300] Art. 15(j) Djibouti Code of Conduct; Art. 2(5) of the Regional Cooperation Agreement on Combating Piracy and Armed Robbery against Ships in Asia (ReCAAP).

[301] Art. 19(2)(l) UNCLOS.

[302] Art. 111(3) UNCLOS.

[303] Notably, as far as enforcement powers in relation to ships, namely, boarding provisions, are concerned, neither the SUA nor the Hostage Convention contains any such enforcement powers. Apart from a safeguard provision in Art. 9 SUA Convention, according to which the SUA Convention does not affect the competence of States to board ships not flying their flag, they contain neither a boarding provision nor any other enforcement power in relation to a foreign ship. The SUA Protocol 2005, which will upon its entry into force add an Art. 8*bis* to the SUA Convention (see note 404), only covers procedures to be followed if a State party desires to board a ship flying the flag of another State party, when there are reasonable grounds to suspect that the ship or a person on board the ship is, has been, or is about to be, involved in the commission of an offense under the Convention. Yet, the authorization and cooperation of the flag State generally is still required before such a boarding, see International Maritime Organization, Convention for the Suppression of Unlawful Acts Against the Safety of Maritime Navigation, 1988, *available at*

pirate ships, nor does it contain any explicit provision authorizing attacks on pirate ships by military means, nor more generally, the use of firearms in the pursuit of pirates.

Implicitly, however, the enforcement powers granted by the UNCLOS permit the use of such force as may be necessary to stop and seize a vessel and arrest persons on board. In *The M/V "Saiga" (No. 2) Case*, in which the use of force in the boarding, stopping and arresting of the *Saiga* was at issue, the International Tribunal for the Law of the Sea, while pointing out that "the use of force must be avoided as far as possible" clearly assumed that in certain instances the use of force may be justifiable. For example, the Tribunal referred to instances "where force is unavoidable."[304] Moreover, referring to the *I'm Alone* and *Red Crusader* cases,[305] the Tribunal went on to state that "[t]he normal practice used to stop a ship at sea is first to give an auditory or visual signal to stop, using internationally recognized signals. Where this does not succeed, a variety of actions may be taken, including the firing of shots across the bows of the ship. It is only after the appropriate actions fail that the pursuing vessel may, as a last resort, use force."[306] Similarly, Article 22(1)(f) of the Agreement for the Implementation of the Provisions of the United Nations Convention on the Law of the Sea of December 10, 1982, Relating to the Conservation and Management of Straddling Fish Stocks and Highly Migratory Fish Stocks, exceptionally provides for the use of force "when and to the degree necessary to ensure the safety of the inspectors and where the inspectors are obstructed in the execution of their duties."

Thus, in the pursuit of a pirate ship that has been clearly identified as such, *ultima ratio*, if all other methods to bring such ship to a halt have failed, using military means to render the ship unseaworthy and, thereby, immobilizing it, would be permissible under the UNCLOS. It would contradict the stated object and purpose of UNCLOS of repressing piracy and ensuring the safety of navigation if States, in pursuing a pirate ship, were not allowed to use all means necessary to effect arrests and seizures in such circumstances.

---

www.imo.org/Conventions/mainframe.asp?topic_id=259&doc_id=686 (last visited Aug. 30, 2010).

[304] International Tribunal for the Law of the Sea, *The M/V "Saiga" (No. 2) Case (Saint Vincent and the Grenadines v. Guinea)*, Judgment, July 1, 1999, para. 155.

[305] *Id.* at para. 157, citing the *S.S. "I'm Alone" Case* (Canada/United States, 1935), U.N.R.I.A.A., Vol. III, p. 1609, and the *The Red Crusader Case* (Commission of Enquiry, Denmark – United Kingdom, 1962), I.L.R., Vol. 35, p. 485.

[306] International Tribunal for the Law of the Sea, *The M/V "Saiga" (No. 2) Case (Saint Vincent and the Grenadines v. Guinea)*, Judgment, July 1, 1999, para. 156.

B. Extension of Enforcement Powers
through Security Council Resolution 1846

Against the background of these geographical limitations, the Security Council has chosen to expand the scope of enforcement powers under Security Council Resolutions 1816, 1846, 1851 and 1897, to allow for a more effective suppression of acts of piracy in the region.[307] Coincidentally, in the case of Somalia, the repercussions of the above-described geographical limitations inherent in UNCLOS' piracy definition could potentially be of particular impact. In 1972, Somalia adopted a national law, in deviation from the common rule according to which the territorial sea comprises 12 nautical miles,[308] declaring its territorial sea to expand over 200 nautical miles.[309] Apparently, this law was not repealed upon Somalia's unreserved ratification of UNCLOS in 1989 and it is not clear whether Somalia still maintains this claim.[310] It has been assumed that the various references to the Somali Transitional Federal Government's consent in the Security Council Resolutions may have been made in order to dispel any doubts that may arise in this regard.[311] However, under Article 3 UNCLOS, any claim exceeding 12 nautical miles is invalid. Therefore, whatever the domestic legal situation in Somalia may be, for purposes of international law and enforcement powers derived therefrom, it does not transform the area beyond 12 nautical miles into "territorial sea."[312]

In its attempt to enlarge the scope of enforcement powers under the UNCLOS so as to increase the effectiveness of counter-piracy operations in the area, the Security Council basically had two options: To draft a comprehensive and region-specific enforcement regime from scratch, tailored specifically towards the repression of the criminal phenomenon encountered in the Gulf of Aden, or to build upon the existing enforcement regime contained in UNCLOS and to remedy its shortcomings so as to better target piracy off Somalia's coast. The Security Council, understandably and without any realistic alternative, has chosen the latter option.[313]

---

[307] S.C. Res. 1838 also relates to piracy and armed robbery at sea but it merely calls for enhanced cooperation without authorizing specific enforcement powers.

[308] Art. 3 UNCLOS.

[309] Cited with further references in *Treves*, Piracy, Law of the Sea, and Use of Force: Developments off the Coast of Somalia, EJIL 20 (2009), 407.

[310] Apparently, the following nine African States still claim territorial seas extending beyond the 12 miles limit permitted under international law: Angola with 20 miles; Nigeria and Togo with 30 miles; Cameroon with 50 miles; and Benin, Congo, Liberia, Sierra Leone and Somalia with 200 miles; see www.un.org/Depts/los/LEGISLATIONAND TREATIES/africa.htm (last visited Aug. 30, 2010).

[311] *Treves*, Piracy, Law of the Sea, and Use of Force: Developments off the Coast of Somalia, EJIL 20 (2009), 407–408.

[312] *Dupuy/Vignes*, A Handbook on the New Law of the Sea, p. 1050.

[313] The respective paragraphs of S.C. Res. 1816 and S.C. Res. 1846 are largely identical. Given that S.C. Res. 1846 has superseded S.C. Res. 1816 and that its para. 10 was

Although the various Security Council Resolutions *de facto* remedy certain limitations inherent in the UNCLOS regime, *de jure*, they constitute a legal basis of their own, even where they cross-refer and explicitly draw on the UNCLOS enforcement regime.[314] These cross-references incorporate the content of Article 105 UNCLOS into the relevant Security Council Resolutions, rather than rendering Article 105 UNCLOS directly applicable within Somali territorial waters. Indeed, in Security Council Resolution 1846, the Security Council explicitly authorizes the use within the territorial waters of Somalia – in a manner consistent with such action permitted under relevant international law – of all necessary means to repress piracy. From the wording "consistent with" and the reference to relevant international law (i.e. UNCLOS)[315] it can be inferred that the Council did not in any way intend to extend the direct (geographical) application of UNCLOS to the territorial waters of a singular State, namely Somalia. This *modus operandi* is no novelty in the practice of the Security Council. Maritime interception operations aimed at combating transnational terrorism or the proliferation of weapons of mass destruction, for example, also derive their legal basis from Security Council Resolutions.[316]

1. Extension of the Personal Scope of Enforcement Powers

Unlike the first sentence of Article 105 UNCLOS, operative paragraph 6 of Security Council Resolution 1846 does not speak of "pirate ships" or "ships taken by piracy" and does not expressly designate the potential subjects of the enforcement powers which it authorizes. Rather, Security Council Resolution 1846 speaks far more generically of "the purpose of repressing acts of piracy and armed robbery at sea."[317] Intrinsically, this phrase could be understood to allow enforcement measures against anyone involved in either of these acts, irrespective of whether they are encountered on a "pirate ship."[318]

---

prolonged by virtue of S.C. Res. 1897, para. 7, the primary focus in this section is on S.C. Res. 1846.

[314] *Guilfoyle*, UN Security Council Resolution 1816 and IMO Regional Counter-Piracy Efforts, ICLQ 57 (2008), 696. But see also *Treves*, Piracy, Law of the Sea, and Use of Force: Developments off the Coast of Somalia, EJIL 20 (2009), 408.

[315] S.C. Res. 1846, preambular para. 7, for example, reads: "*Further reaffirming* that international law, as reflected in the United Nations Convention on the Law of the Sea of 10 December 1982 ("the Convention"), sets out the legal framework applicable to combating piracy and armed robbery at sea."

[316] *Heintschel von Heinegg*, The Proliferation Security Initiative – Security vs. Freedom of Navigation? Israel Yearbook on Human Rights 35 (2005), 181–203; *Schaller*, Die Unterbindung des Seetransports von Massenvernichtungswaffen – Völkerrechtliche Aspekte der "Proliferation Security Initiative," SWP-Studie 2004/17, *available at* www.swp-berlin.org/common/get_document.php?asset_id=1292 (last visited Aug. 30, 2010).

[317] S.C. Res. 1846, para. 10(a).

[318] On the definition of a pirate ship, see p. 59 *et seq.*

However, given that operative paragraph 10 of Security Council Resolution 1846 also speaks of enforcement action "consistent with such action permitted on the high seas with respect to piracy under relevant international law," it would seem more plausible to assume that the Resolution, by referring to acts of armed robbery at sea in addition to acts of piracy, aims to expand the somewhat limited definition of acts of piracy in Article 101 UNCLOS. Such a reading of operative paragraph 10 of Security Council Resolution 1846, firstly, requires that the notion of armed robbery at sea can be accorded a legal meaning independent of piracy, as understood in Article 101 UNCLOS and raises the question of how precisely armed robbery at sea is to be defined.

a) The Relationship between Piracy and Armed Robbery at Sea

It may be questioned whether the term armed robbery at sea is of any legal significance at all. The terminology of Security Council Resolutions 1816 and 1846 in relation to this phrase is highly inconsistent.[319] The variation in the wording could suggest that the expression describes a criminal phenomenon occurring off the coast of Somalia, rather than defining conduct with regard to which specific enforcement powers are conferred.

Indeed, one possible interpretation of the expression "piracy and armed robbery at sea" would be that it is no more than a convoluted reference to piracy, as defined in Article 101 UNCLOS and, thus, without any independent legal effect. Such a reading would be supported by the sentences in Security Council Resolutions 1816, 1838, 1846, 1851, 1897 and 1918, reaffirming "that international law, as reflected by the United Nations Convention on the Law of the Sea of 10 December, 1982 (UNCLOS), sets out the legal framework applicable to combating piracy *and* armed robbery at sea."[320] Since the concept of armed robbery at sea does not appear in the UNCLOS, it could only be understood as being comprised in the notion of piracy as defined in that treaty. However, given that the notion of armed robbery at sea is not only used in the preambles, but also in the operative paragraphs of the Security Council Resolutions on piracy, it appears more plausible to interpret it as an autonomous definition that triggers legal consequences similar to those resulting from acts of piracy.

---

[319] Various expressions are used in the counter-piracy Security Council Resolutions: "piracy and armed robbery" in S.C. Res. 1816, preambular para. 4 and paras. 7(b) and 11; "piracy and armed robbery at sea" in S.C. Res. 1816, para. 7(a), S.C. Res. 1851, paras. 2 and 3, and S.C. Res. 1897, para. 3; "piracy and armed robbery against vessels" in S.C. Res. 1816, preambular paras. 2, 9, 12 and para. 1, S.C. Res. 1851, para. 1, and S.C. Res. 1897, para. 1.

[320] S.C. Res. 1851, preambular para. 4 (emphasis added). The wording of the respective paragraphs of S.C. Res. 1816, S.C. Res. 1838, S.C. Res. 1846, and S.C. Res. 1897, is almost identical. S.C. Res. 1918, preambular para. 3, specifically mentions Articles 100, 101 and 105 UNCLOS.

Indeed, given that piracy can only be committed on the high seas, equating piracy and armed robbery at sea without any independent meaning of the latter, would limit the enforcement powers granted by Security Council Resolutions 1816 and 1846 to a mere right of "(hot) pursuit" into Somalia's territorial waters of people suspected of having engaged in piracy on the high seas. Thus, the above-cited reference to the UNCLOS, as reflecting the international "legal framework applicable to combating piracy *and* armed robbery at sea,"[321] should not be taken at face value and the notion of armed robbery at sea should be understood as being distinct from piracy, as defined in Article 101 UNCLOS.[322] It is, therefore, essential to have clarity as to how the offense of armed robbery at sea is defined.

b) The Definition of Armed Robbery at Sea

The definitional elements of armed robbery at sea are far from settled under international law.[323] A definition was not conferred by the Security Council Resolutions on piracy nor do soft-law instruments on the issue provide uniform definitions of armed robbery at sea. Thus, while there is fragmentation with regard to the various definitions of armed robbery at sea issued by different bodies, it can simultaneously be observed that these definitions all seek to bring a broad spectrum of acts (not to say a whole criminal phenomenon) under the umbrella of one neatly defined offense.

The Code of Practice for the Investigation of the Crimes of Piracy and Armed Robbery against Ships of the International Maritime Organization defines acts of armed robbery against ships broadly, but limits the offense geographically to areas under State jurisdiction, by stating that it encompasses "any unlawful act of violence or detention or any act of depredation, or threat thereof, other than an act of piracy, directed against a ship or against persons or property on board such a ship, within a State's jurisdiction over such offences." [324]

Even though the Djibouti Code of Conduct was also drafted with the involvement of the International Maritime Organization, the definition of armed robbery

---

[321] Emphasis added.

[322] That armed robbery at sea is conduct different from piracy is also suggested by the Investigation Code of Practice of the International Maritime Organization, where one of the definitional elements of "armed robbery against ships" is that they constitute acts "other than an act of piracy." See International Maritime Organization, Code of Practice for the Investigation of the Crimes of Piracy and Armed Robbery against Ships, IMO Doc. A22/Res.922 (Jan. 22, 2009).

[323] For an overview on various definitions of armed robbery at sea, see p. 249 *et seq.* of this book (Appendix).

[324] International Maritime Organization, Code of Practice for the Investigation of the Crimes of Piracy and Armed Robbery against Ships, IMO Doc. A22/Res.922 (Jan. 22, 2009).

against ships in its Article 1(2)(a) differs from the previous wording and encompasses "unlawful acts of violence or detention or any act of depredation, or threat thereof, other than an act of piracy, committed for private ends and directed against a ship or against persons or property on board such a ship, within a State's internal waters, archipelagic waters and territorial sea."

The Regional Cooperation Agreement on Combating Piracy and Armed Robbery against Ships in Asia (ReCAAP), in turn, defines armed robbery against ships in its Article 1 as "any illegal act of violence or detention, or any act of depredation, committed for private ends and directed against a ship, or against persons or property on board such ship, in a place within a Contracting Party's jurisdiction over such offences."

All of these definitions go well beyond pure property offenses in the sense of taking away moveable objects belonging to another person and may also include hijacking ships and holding persons on board hostage. Further, *ratione loci*, all three definitions require that the conduct occurs in a place under a State's jurisdiction and the Djibouti Code of Conduct explicitly states which geographical areas are encompassed. Thus, conduct taking place on the high seas, outside the jurisdiction of any State, cannot constitute armed robbery at sea, according to these definitions.

In contrast to the definitions provided by the International Maritime Organization and in the ReCAAP, Security Council Resolutions 1816 and 1846 are not entirely clear as to whether the main distinction between piracy and armed robbery at sea is indeed the *locus delicti*. These Security Council Resolutions use phrases such as "piracy and armed robbery in the territorial waters and on the high seas off the coast of Somalia."[325] Potentially, this wording could be read as eliminating the distinction between piracy and armed robbery, along the lines of whether the act is committed on the high seas or in the territorial waters and, thus, different from the definition of the International Maritime Organization and in the ReCAAP.[326] Leav-

---

[325] S.C. Res. 1816, para. 3; S.C. Res. 1846, para. 17. Also the wording of S.C. Res. 1816, para. 9, "to prevent and repress, within the provisions of international law, acts of piracy and armed robbery against vessels irrespective of where such acts occur" would speak against a separation of piracy and armed robbery at sea along the lines where the offense is committed, unless the words "within the provisions of international law" are understood as relating not only to the permitted powers but also to the definition of piracy and armed robbery at sea.

[326] The fragmentation with regard to the definition of the conduct in question as well as the concurrent application of various instruments (sometimes only covering partial aspects of the larger criminal phenomenon) is further illustrated by the statement in the Report of the Secretary-General on Oceans and the Law of the Sea, delivered to the General Assembly, UN Doc. A 63/63 (March 10, 2008), para. 58, according to which "[a]rmed robbery against ships also constitutes an offense under the 1988 Convention for the Suppression of Unlawful Acts against the Safety of Maritime Navigation (SUA Convention) and, in some cases, the 2000 United Nations Convention against Transnational Organized Crime."

ing aside linguistic irregularities within the text of the respective Security Council Resolutions, it is submitted that the reference to armed robbery at sea in the operative part of Security Council Resolution 1846 should be read as authorizing the use of enforcement measures against ships and persons and property aboard such ships that have engaged in violent acts directed against a ship within Somalia's territorial waters.

Still, another ambiguity inherent in the notion of armed robbery at sea is the question whether violent acts qualifying as armed robbery at sea need to be committed against another ship or whether violent acts on board a single ship (by a passenger or crew member) would, likewise, be comprised by the definition of armed robbery at sea. In other words, it is questionable whether armed robbery at sea, like piracy, entails a two-ship-requirement. On the one hand, the notion of armed robbery at sea could be regarded as an attempt to close down merely the geographical limitation inherent in the definition of acts of piracy, i.e. armed robbery at sea could be understood as comprising pirate-like acts of violence that differ from acts of piracy only in that they occur within territorial waters. On the other hand, the definitions inherent in the Code of Practice for the Investigation of the Crimes of Piracy and Armed Robbery against Ships of the International Maritime Organization, the Djibouti Code of Conduct and the ReCAAP all speak of acts that are "directed against *a ship* or against persons or property on board such a ship."[327] Conversely, Article 101(a) UNCLOS speaks of acts directed "against *another* ship."[328] The wording in the Code of Practice, the Djibouti Code of Conduct and the ReCAAP allows the conclusion that armed robbery at sea does not entail a two-ship-requirement and that violent acts on board a single ship suffice. In addition, the wording "any unlawful act of violence (...) other than an act of piracy" in these definitions would seem to support such a reading. In the absence of any conclusive guidance on the interpretation of the notion of armed robbery at sea, based on the similar wording adopted in the various definitions, it appears that the involvement of a single ship would be sufficient under the notion of armed robbery at sea.

Thus, by adding the offense of armed robbery at sea, the gap with regard to violence against ships taking place in areas under Somalia's jurisdiction was filled. Consequently, the concept of piracy, as used in the Security Council Resolutions, should be understood as referring to piracy as defined in Article 101 UNCLOS, while armed robbery at sea should be interpreted as encompassing acts of violence against a ship, committed in territorial waters.

---

[327] Emphasis added.
[328] Emphasis added.

2. Extension of the Geographical Scope of Enforcement Powers: Authorizing Enforcement Powers within Somalia's Territorial Waters

The Security Council has also remedied the territorial limitation contained in Article 105 UNCLOS, according to which enforcement measures may only be taken against vessels encountered on the high seas. Subject to cooperation with the Somali Transitional Federal Government and its advance notification to the Secretary-General of the United Nations, Security Council Resolution 1846 (similar to its predecessor Resolution 1816)[329] authorizes States and regional organizations for a period of 12 months to "[e]nter *into the territorial waters of Somalia* for the purpose of repressing acts of piracy and armed robbery at sea, in a manner consistent with such action permitted on the high seas with respect to piracy under relevant international law" and to "[u]se, *within the territorial waters* of Somalia, in a manner consistent with such action permitted on the high seas with respect to piracy under relevant international law, all necessary means to repress acts of piracy and armed robbery at sea."[330] This authorization contained in Security Council Resolution 1846, which was prolonged by Security Council 1897, has thus paved the way to exercise enforcement powers within Somalia's territorial waters.

3. Types of Enforcement Measures Authorized under Security Council Resolution 1846

In terms of the types of enforcement measures authorized, Security Council Resolution 1846 (as prolonged by Security Council Resolution 1897) allows no more and no less than the first sentence of Article 105 UNCLOS. Most importantly, despite the reference to the use of "all necessary means" in both Security Council Resolutions[331] (terminology which is commonly associated with a general authorization to use military force), neither Security Council Resolution authorizes means and measures beyond the enforcement regime of UNCLOS. In their respective operative paragraphs, both Security Council Resolutions contain a clear emphasis that any enforcement powers granted are to be carried out "in a manner consistent with action permitted on the high seas with respect to piracy under relevant international law."[332] This limitation restricts authorized action to pursuing, stopping and board-

---

[329] S.C. Res. 1816, para. 7, is almost identically worded.

[330] Emphasis added.

[331] S.C. Res. 1816, para. 7(b); S.C. Res. 1846, para. 10(b).

[332] *Id.* The fact that S.C. Res. 1816, preambular para. 5, speaks of "guiding principles including but *not limited* to boarding, searching, and seizing vessels engaged in or suspected of engaging in acts of piracy, and to apprehending persons engaged in such acts with a view to such persons being prosecuted" (emphasis added), has no effect on the explicit confinement of "all necessary means" in para. 7(b). Notably, S.C. Res. 1838, para. 3, referred to "*the necessary means*, in conformity with international law, as reflected in the Convention" (emphasis added).

ing vessels, to searching them, to seizing the vessel or the property on board, and to arresting persons aboard. Despite the martial wording "all necessary means," which was presumably chosen to symbolize the resolve of the Security Council members to repress piracy effectively, in terms of the types of enforcement measures authorized, Security Council Resolution 1846 does not surpass those granted under UNCLOS.

4. A Hypothetical: An Ideal Maritime Law Enforcement Regime for the Repression of Piracy

Hypothetically, the Security Council acting under Chapter VII of the United Nations Charter could simply have authorized States to intercept any vessel and to arrest any person who is suspected of having been engaged in acts of violence at sea, if encountered in Somalia's territorial waters or, more broadly, in the Gulf of Aden or any other meaningfully defined geographical area. Thereby, the Security Council could have ensured the application of a legally coherent and uniform enforcement regime, specifically designed to effectively repress violent acts at sea in the entire region. Proceeding in such a way could have avoided the various intricacies and ambiguities inherent in the enforcement regime of the UNCLOS, stemming in particular from the complex definitions of acts of piracy. Viewed exclusively from the perspective of effective law enforcement, such an approach would have been preferable, but would, in practice, not have been viable and was, therefore, never actually attempted.

Various member States of the Security Council already viewed the Council's tampering with an enforcement regime applicable exclusively within Somalia's territorial waters with skepticism. Security Council Resolution 1816 was the first Resolution to authorize enforcement measures within Somalia's territorial waters. Prior to the adoption of this Resolution, various delegations emphasized that the Resolution would only apply to the territorial waters of Somalia, that it solely addressed the specific situation of the coast off Somalia, that it was based upon that country's prior consent, that it was the situation in Somalia that constituted a threat to international peace and security but not piracy itself and, finally, that Security Council Resolution 1816 must respect UNCLOS, which remained the basis for cooperation among States on the issue of piracy.[333]

These concerns are explicitly acknowledged in the various Security Council Resolutions, all of which, presumably because of these explicit reservations, were

---

[333] See the statements provided by Indonesia, Vietnam, Libya, South Africa and China prior to the adoption of S.C. Res. 1816: United Nations, Department of Public Information, Security Council Condemns Acts of Piracy, Armed Robbery off Somalia's Coast, Authorizes for Six Months "All Necessary Means" to Repress Such Acts, Press Release, June 2, 2008, *available at* www.un.org/News/Press/docs/2008/sc9344.doc.htm (last visited Aug. 30, 2010).

adopted unanimously. Security Council Resolution 1897,[334] for example, expressly "affirms that the authorizations renewed in this resolution apply *only* with respect to the situation in Somalia and shall not affect the rights or obligations or responsibilities of Member States under international law, including any rights or obligations under the Convention [UNCLOS], with respect *to any other situation*, and stresses that this resolution shall not be considered as establishing customary international law, and further affirms that such authorizations have been renewed *only* following the receipt of the letters of 2 and 6 November 2009 conveying the consent of the TFG."

In light of the various competing interests at stake on the high seas, it seems unlikely that States would ever have designated the abstract phenomenon of piracy and armed robbery at sea, rather than the specific situation in Somalia, as a threat to the peace.[335]

Against this background, the Security Council chose to build its enforcement regime around UNCLOS, which has been ratified by no less than 160 States[336] and contains a definition of piracy as well as a counter-piracy enforcement regime that, despite its shortcomings, is widely accepted. The autonomous legal status of its Resolutions notwithstanding, the Security Council, taking UNCLOS as the starting point and primary frame of reference, aimed to remedy the UNCLOS' shortcomings illustrated above, in order to allow for more effective counter-piracy operations off Somalia's coast.

5. Conclusion

States authorized to act under Security Council Resolution 1846 (as prolonged by Security Council Resolution 1897) may intercept pirate ships not only on the high seas, as already authorized under Articles 110 and 105 UNCLOS, but also in Somalia's territorial waters. This authorization has remedied the geographical limitation contained in the first sentence of Article 105 UNCLOS, according to which enforcement powers can only be exercised on the high seas. In addition, if the interpretation suggested above that armed robbery at sea denotes violent acts directed against ships within a State's territorial waters, is accepted, Security Council

---

[334] S.C. Res. 1897, para. 8 (emphasis added); see also S.C. Res. 1816, para. 9; S.C. Res. 1846, para. 11; S.C. Res. 1918, preambular para. 4, which is "underscoring in particular that resolution 1897 shall not be considered as establishing customary law."

[335] See statement by South Africa in the Security Council: United Nations, Department of Public Information, Security Council Condemns Acts of Piracy, Armed Robbery off Somalia's Coast, Authorizes for Six Months "All Necessary Means" to Repress Such Acts, Press Release, June 2, 2008, *available at* www.un.org/News/Press/docs/2008/sc9344.doc. htm (last visited Aug. 30, 2010).

[336] In addition, the UNCLOS piracy regime is modeled upon the Convention on the High Seas, which enlarges the circle of States endorsing this model.

Resolution 1846 also partially closes the geographical gap inherent in the UNCLOS definition of acts of piracy. Thereby, Security Council Resolution 1846, unlike UNCLOS, grants enforcement powers not only against pirate ships but also against vessels that have committed armed robbery at sea.

A loophole remains, however, with regard to enforcement powers against vessels that have been engaged in armed robbery at sea (defined as violent acts in the territorial sea), which are subsequently encountered on the high seas. UNCLOS, in and of itself, does not authorize enforcement action against such vessels, since acts of armed robbery at sea do not fall within the ambit of UNCLOS' more narrow definition of piracy. Conversely, paragraph 10 of Security Council Resolution 1846 entails no authorization and has no influence on the exercise of enforcement powers on the high seas, since it only speaks of entering "into the territorial waters" and of taking enforcement measures "within the territorial waters of Somalia."[337] Security Council Resolution 1846 has nothing to say about the exercise of enforcement powers on the high seas, other than reconfirming the applicability of UNCLOS. The UNCLOS in turn does not confer any enforcement powers against ships that have engaged in armed robbery at sea in the territorial waters. Strictly speaking, no enforcement powers are authorized against ships that have been engaged in armed robbery at sea and are subsequently encountered on the high seas.

In practice, however, this "enforcement gap" should not be overstated, because, according to the first sentence of Article 103 UNCLOS, ships that have *not yet* been involved in acts of piracy but are *intended to be used* to commit an act of piracy, also qualify as pirate ships against which the first sentence of Article 105 UNCLOS grants enforcement powers. Arguably, any ship that is known to have been engaged in armed robbery at sea may be said to be a ship that is intended to be used to commit an act of piracy in the future. Evidently, in terms of legal certainty, such a "propensity argument" leaves much to be desired. However, given that it is far from clear under which circumstances a ship may be said to be intended to be used to commit an act of piracy in the sense of the first sentence of Article 103 UNCLOS, the argument appears to be maintainable. Indeed, if it is known that a ship has already been involved in pirate-like acts in territorial waters, this may be seen as a rather strong indicator that it may also be intended to be used for the commission of acts of piracy on the high seas. Irrespective thereof, as far as Somali ships are concerned, the consent of the Somali Transitional Federal Government to intercept vessels that have merely engaged in acts of armed robbery at sea, but are subsequently encountered on the high seas, may be presumed or is arguably implicitly entailed in the Transitional Federal Government's various requests to the Security Council for assistance in the repression of piracy and armed robbery at sea.

---

[337] S.C. Res. 1816, para. 7(a) and (b); S.C. Res. 1846, para. 10(a) and (b).

In conclusion, therefore, Security Council Resolution 1846 (like its predecessor Resolution 1816), which has been prolonged by virtue of Security Council Resolution 1897, has not changed the UNCLOS enforcement regime. As far as the high seas are concerned, enforcement powers derive exclusively from UNCLOS, namely Articles 101 and 105. Resolution 1846, however, has largely remedied the geographical limitation inherent in the UNCLOS enforcement regime. Resolution 1846 has extended the scope of enforcement powers *ratione loci* to Somalia's territorial sea. It follows, that pirate ships may be pursued and intercepted in Somalia's coastal waters. By introducing the concept of armed robbery at sea, Security Council Resolution 1846, in addition to the pursuit of vessels from the high seas into territorial waters, authorizes enforcement powers against ships involved in piracy-like attacks in the territorial waters themselves. Finally, as far as the types of enforcement measures authorized under Security Council Resolution 1846 are concerned, the Resolution allows no less and no more than Article 110 and the first sentence of Article 105 UNCLOS.

The enforcement regime set up under Security Council Resolution 1846 clearly amounts to a step towards more effective law enforcement operations against piracy off Somalia's coast. In terms of legal certainty, however, the Security Council's reversion to the ill-defined notion of armed robbery at sea raises some concerns. Moreover, in light of the differences between the UNCLOS' enforcement regime (confined to acts of piracy) and the 1846 enforcement powers (extended to also cover acts of armed robbery at sea), somewhat different legal regimes currently apply, depending on whether persons suspected of having been involved in violent acts at sea are pursued on the high seas or in Somalia's territorial waters. The enforcement regime contained in Security Council Resolution 1846, covering also acts of armed robbery at sea, is in its scope, therefore, more comprehensive than the enforcement regime laid out in UNCLOS, but it is confined to the narrow 12 miles zone of Somalia's territorial waters.

C. Extension of Enforcement Powers through Security Council Resolution 1851

The enforcement powers authorized by Security Council Resolution 1846 (as prolonged by Security Council Resolution 1897) are confined to Somalia's territorial sea. These Security Council Resolutions neither influenced the UNCLOS' enforcement regime with respect to the high seas, nor did they authorize any counter-piracy operations on the Somali mainland. Thus, in order to close down this last refuge, the Security Council adopted another Resolution under Chapter VII of the United Nations Charter, namely, Security Council Resolution 1851.

In addition, on the face of the wording of operative paragraph 2, it could possibly be argued that Resolution 1851 also created an additional enforcement power at sea and outside the regime of Article 105 UNCLOS. Operative paragraph 2 speaks of the "*disposition* of boats, vessels, arms and other related equipment used in the commission of piracy and armed robbery at sea off the coast of Somalia, or for which there are reasonable grounds for suspecting such use."[338] However, unlike in operative paragraph 6 where the Security Council "decides," in operative paragraph 2 it merely "calls upon" States. What is more, given that preambular paragraph 4 explicitly reaffirms that international law, as reflected in UNCLOS, sets out the legal framework applicable to combating piracy and armed robbery at sea and, in view of the explicit reference to counter-piracy activities consistent with Resolution 1846 in operative paragraph 2, it would seem more plausible to argue that Resolution 1851 did not create any additional enforcement powers with regard to counter-piracy operations at sea.

1. Extension of the Personal Scope of Enforcement Powers

Whereas Security Council Resolutions 1816 and 1846, being linked to the enforcement powers granted by the first sentence of Article 105 UNCLOS and, in keeping with this provision's approach, authorize enforcement powers only against certain ships and persons and property aboard such ships, the scope *ratione personae* of the enforcement regime established by Security Council 1851 is much broader. Without expressly designating the possible subjects of the enforcement measures authorized under operative paragraph 6, Security Council Resolution 1851 simply authorizes "all necessary measures that are *appropriate* in Somalia, for the purpose of suppressing acts of piracy and armed robbery at sea,"[339] thereby leaving States a wide margin of discretion in the choice of persons against whom such measures should be taken. It follows from Security Council Resolution 1851, that if deemed appropriate for purposes of suppressing acts of piracy and armed robbery at sea, measures may be taken against anyone on Somalia's mainland and are not restricted to persons who have (allegedly) been directly involved in acts of piracy or armed robbery at sea.

2. Extension of the Geographical Scope of Enforcement Powers: Paving the Way onto Somalia's Mainland

Security Council Resolution 1851, adopted two weeks after Security Council Resolution 1846, and now likewise prolonged by Security Council Resolution 1897, authorizes the exercise of enforcement powers on the mainland of Somalia. Specifically, operative paragraph 6 of Security Council Resolution 1851 authorizes States and regional organizations "to undertake all necessary measures that are

---

[338] S.C. Res. 1851, para. 2 (emphasis added).

[339] Emphasis added.

appropriate in Somalia, for the purpose of suppressing acts of piracy and armed robbery at sea."[340]

Unlike Security Council Resolutions 1816 and 1846, the enforcement powers under Security Council Resolution 1851 are not in any way linked to or confined by the UNCLOS regime applicable on the high seas. This is because operative paragraph 6 of Security Council Resolution 1851 only applies on the Somali mainland, which follows from the formulation "measures that are appropriate *in Somalia*."[341] Of course, the wording "in Somalia" could be understood to comprise not only Somalia's mainland but also its territorial waters. However, given that Security Council Resolution 1851 explicitly confirms the continuing relevance of Security Council Resolution 1846, which specifically deals with the exercise of enforcement powers in Somalia's territorial waters,[342] a more restrictive reading, under which Security Council Resolution 1851 only applies to the Somali mainland, appears more appropriate.[343] Indeed, Security Council Resolution 1851 in operative paragraph 2, explicitly requests States to adhere to the provisions of Security Council Resolution 1846 in the fight against piracy and armed robbery at sea off the coast of Somalia.[344] Thus, as far as the territorial sea is concerned, precedence is given to the regime of enforcement powers set up under Security Council Resolution 1846. In relation to Somalia's territorial waters and with respect to operations on the high seas, Security Council Resolution 1851 has not brought about any alterations in enforcement powers.

Some ambiguity has, arguably, remained with regard to the use of Somali airspace. During the drafting stages of Security Council Resolution 1851, there was debate whether to include an explicit reference to third State activities in Somali airspace. Concerns raised by some Council members led the United States to withdraw the relevant draft clause.[345] However, the United States have apparently continued to argue that the effect of the Security Council Resolution remains the same, despite the exclusion of the draft clause, with the result that the use of Somali airspace is also permitted. There is no doubt that the Security Council has the competency to authorize the use of Somalia's airspace under Articles 39 read together

---

[340] S.C. Res. 1851, para. 6.

[341] Emphasis added.

[342] S.C. Res. 1846, para. 10(a) and (b).

[343] Such a distinction between counter-piracy operations at sea and at land would seem to be in line with the fact that the Security Council did not qualify the incidents of piracy as such as a threat to international peace and security, but rather the crisis situation in Somalia: S.C. Res. 1846, preambular para. 14.

[344] S.C. Res. 1851, para. 2; similarly, preambular para. 4, reaffirms "that international law, as reflected in the United Nations Convention on the Law of the Sea of 10 December, 1982 (UNCLOS), sets out the legal framework applicable to combating piracy and armed robbery at *sea*" (emphasis added).

[345] See references cited by *Kontorovich*, International Legal Responses to Piracy off the Coast of Somalia, ASIL Insights (13) 2009.

with Article 42 of the United Nations Charter. Apart from the decision not to include an explicit reference to Somalia's airspace, nothing in the Security Council Resolutions indicates that activities in Somalia's airspace should be excluded. Land-based operations as envisaged by Security Council Resolution 1851 often depend on aerial support. In any case, should doubts remain as to whether Somalia's airspace may be used by States acting upon Security Council Resolution 1851, the required authorization could be obtained by way of specific consent of the Somali Transitional Federal Government.

3. Types of Enforcement Measures Authorized under Security Council Resolution 1851

Security Council Resolution 1851 also broadens the specific enforcement measures that may be taken in order to counter piracy. Whereas the explicit link to UNCLOS' enforcement regime in Security Council Resolutions 1816 and 1846 requires a restrictive reading of the phrase "all necessary means," the reference to "all necessary measures" in Security Council Resolution 1851 is not confined in any such way. Thus, in keeping with the common understanding of the term "all necessary measures" as authorizing a vast range of enforcement measures and taking into consideration the explicit reference in Security Council Resolution 1851 to the applicable international humanitarian law (the application of which would require the existence of an armed conflict),[346] the use of the wording "all necessary measures" in Security Council Resolution 1851 connotes its common meaning, authorizing the use of a broad range of measures, including military force.

4. Conclusion

Through Resolution 1851, the Security Council blocked another important escape route for persons involved in piracy and armed robbery at sea off Somalia's coast. However, at the time of writing, it appears that no land-based operations on the basis of Security Council Resolution 1851, adopted in December 2008, have been carried out.[347] The international community's unwillingness to become engaged on Somali mainland can be seen to have prevailed over its desire to repress piracy and armed robbery at sea. Of course, this could change in the near future. The authorization of operative paragraph 6 of Security Council Resolution 1851 (prolonged by Security Council Resolution 1897) goes far beyond the enforcement measures authorized within Somalia's territorial waters by virtue of Security Council Resolution 1846 and on the high seas under UNCLOS. Thus, as far as counter-

---

[346] On the applicability of international humanitarian law to counter-piracy operations, see p. 131 *et seq.*

[347] Regarding advance notification (the absence thereof) of the Somali Transitional Federal Government regarding land-based operations, see p. 16.

piracy operations in the Gulf of Aden region are concerned, a threefold legal regime applies, depending on whether persons involved in piracy and armed robbery
at sea are encountered on the high seas, within Somalia's territorial waters or on the
Somali mainland.

D. Authorization of Additional Enforcement Powers via Somalia's Specific Consent?

All of the aforementioned Security Council Resolutions have reaffirmed the sovereignty, territorial integrity, political independence and unity of Somalia.[348] These
Security Council Resolutions explicitly refer to the requests by, and the consent of,
the Somali Transitional Federal Government for States and regional organizations
to operate within Somalia's territorial waters and on its mainland. For example,
Security Council Resolution 1897 "affirms (…) that such authorizations have been
renewed only following the receipt of the letters dated 2 and 6 November 2009
conveying the consent of the TFG."[349] This is no novelty. The Security Council, for
a variety of reasons, has in the past cumulatively relied on its Chapter VII powers
and the explicit consent of concerned States.[350]

In the present context, at least in part, the "double" references to the Somali
Transitional Federal Government's consent and Chapter VII of the United Nations
Charter may be owed to the fact that some governments do not recognise the Tran-
sitonal Federal Government of Somalia and thus could not accept its consent as a
legal basis for enforcement operations.[351] Primarily, however, it seems that the references to Somalia's consent in addition to the invocation of Chapter VII powers
were intended to underline the continuous relevance of Somalia's oft-infringed
sovereign rights over its territorial waters and, in particular, its offshore natural

---

[348] S.C. Res. 1846, preambular para. 3; S.C. Res. 1851, preambular para. 3; S.C. Res. 1897,
preambular para. 3.

[349] S.C. Res. 1897, para. 8.

[350] *Frowein/Krisch*, in: Simma (ed.), UN-Charter, 754: In the case of Albania [S.C. Res.
1101, U.N. Doc. S/RES/1101 (March 28, 1997)], the Central African Republic [S.C. Res.
1125, U.N. Doc. S/RES/1125 (Aug. 6, 1997)], Sierra Leona [S.C. Res. 1270, U.N. Doc.
S/RES/1270 (Oct. 22, 1999) and S.C. Res. 1289, U.N. Doc. S/RES/1289 (Feb. 7, 2000)],
and of Bosnia after the Dayton Agreement, the Security Council authorized the use of
force for the protection of the troops on the ground and of the civilian population, although
the respective governments had already declared their consent or had expressly asked the
United Nations to intervene.

[351] *Dalton/Roach/Daley*, Introductory Note to United Nations Security Council: Piracy
and Armed Robbery at Sea – Resolutions 1816, 1846 & 1851, ILM 48 (2009), 130.

resources.[352] In addition, these references to the Somali Transitional Federal Government's consent forestall any doubts that could possibly arise as to the breadth of Somalia's territorial waters, or with regard to the legitimacy of the enforcement powers authorized by the Security Council under Chapter VII of the UN-Charter concerning conduct at sea, despite the Security Council Resolutions' explicit assertion that the threat to international peace and security in the region stems from the situation in Somalia, rather than from the acts of piracy themselves. Implicitly, the various references to the Somali Transitional Federal Government's consent also acknowledge the continuing legal significance and validity of the Transitional Federal Government's approval to third States law enforcement operations within Somalia, despite its undisputed inability to exert effective governmental control over its territory.

Thus, given that the Somali Transitional Federal Government is clearly recognized as the representative government that can validly consent to operations of third States on Somali territory, it follows that the Somali Transitional Federal Government could authorize further enforcement powers of specific States, on its own behalf, beyond and despite the regime of enforcement powers that has already been put in place in Somalia's territorial waters and mainland.[353] In view of the scope of enforcement powers currently authorized by virtue of Security Council Resolutions 1846 and 1851, as prolonged by Security Council Resolution 1897, the practical need for any additional authorizations appears to be limited. Nevertheless, with respect to certain issues such as the above-mentioned question whether Security Council Resolution 1851 implicitly authorizes counter-piracy operations within Somalia's airspace and the question whether Somali vessels suspected of having committed armed robbery at sea could be intercepted on the high seas, certainty could be achieved by obtaining the explicit consent of the Somali Transitional Federal Government. In this context, the embarkment of Somali law enforcement officials as so-called shipriders could facilitate the obtaining of the Somali Transitional Federal Government's consent on an *ad hoc* basis.

II. Shiprider Agreements

Security Council Resolutions 1851 and 1897 both invite States and regional organizations fighting piracy off the coast of Somalia to conclude so-called shiprider

---

[352] See S.C. Res. 1851, preambular para. 3; S.C. Res. 1897, para. 5.

[353] In the course of the *Ponant Affair* in April 2008, prior to the adoption of S.C. Res. 1851, the Somali Transitional Federal Government consented to French forces conducting a counter-piracy action on Somali territory: The New York Times, French Troops Seize Somali Pirates after Hostages are Freed, April 11, 2008, *available at* www.nytimes.com/2008/04/11/world/africa/11iht-yacht.4.11921315.html (last visited Aug. 30, 2010).

agreements with regional States, in order to embark law enforcement officials from the region on law enforcement vessels of patrolling naval States aiming to repress piracy in the area.[354] The Djibouti Code of Conduct also contains a provision on "embarked officers."[355]

The concept of shipriders, also referred to as "integrated cross-border maritime law enforcement"[356] or "joint policing," has a precedent in the fight against illegal fishing and in counter-drug operations at sea.[357] This explains why the idea of enlarging the range of tools in the fight against piracy by adding the shiprider mechanism originated from a proposal by the United Nations Office on Drugs and Crime.[358]

The exact content of existing shiprider agreements, for example, in the areas of illicit maritime drug trafficking or illegal fishing, varies. However, the existing shiprider agreements all share the common purpose of overcoming jurisdictional hurdles. Shiprider agreements typically broaden the law enforcement powers that may be exercised from a vessel not flying the flag of the coastal State by embarking officials of the coastal State. The embarked officials may legitimately take action in the territorial waters of their home State. Alternatively, embarked officials (shipriders) can authorize on-the-spot enforcement actions by the officials of the vessel on which they are embarked.[359] This ensures "seamless borders" with unin-

---

[354] S.C. Res. 1851, para. 3, and S.C. Res. 1897, para. 6; the wording of these two paragraphs is identical.

[355] Art. 7 Djibouti Code of Conduct.

[356] Terminology, which is, for instance, used in the Framework Agreement on Integrated Cross-Border Maritime Law Enforcement Operations Between the Government of the United States of America and the Government of Canada, *adopted* May 26, 2009, *available at* www.dhs.gov/xlibrary/assets/shiprider_agreement.pdf (last visited Aug. 30, 2010) [hereinafter: U.S.-Canadian Shiprider Agreement].

[357] Art. 1 U.S.-Canadian Shiprider Agreement, *supra* note 356, provides an idea for what type of criminality shipriders can be embarked: "The purpose of this Agreement is to provide the Parties additional means in shared waterways to prevent, detect, suppress, investigate, and prosecute criminal offenses or violations of law including, but not limited to, illicit drug trade, migrant smuggling, trafficking of firearms, the smuggling of counterfeit goods and money, and terrorism." In the Caribbean, shipriders have been used in counter-drug operations: United Nations, UNODC, Annual Report 2009, *available at* www.unodc.org/documents/about-unodc/AR09_LORES.pdf (last visited Aug. 30, 2010), p. 17. Shiprider agreements concluded for law enforcement measures against illicit drug traffic are based on Art. 17(9) of UN Convention against Illicit Traffic in Narcotic Drugs and Psychotropic Substances, *adopted* Dec. 20, 1988, 1582 U.N.T.S. 164 [hereinafter: UN Narcotic Convention].

[358] United Nations, UNODC, UNODC Proposes Measures to Stop Piracy in the Horn of Africa, Press Release, Dec. 16, 2008, *available at* www.unodc.org/unodc/en/press/releases/2008-12.16.html (last visited Aug. 30, 2010).

[359] The United States Model Maritime Agreement Concerning Cooperation to Suppress Illicit Traffic by Sea [hereinafter: United States Model Maritime Agreement] provides an example of a shiprider agreement in the field of counter-drug operations: reprinted in

terrupted continuity of law enforcement operations across territorial borders between the high seas and territorial waters.

A. Specificities of Counter-Piracy Shiprider Agreements

1. Common Rationale for the Use of Shipriders: Extending Enforcement Powers

The shiprider agreements called for by Security Council Resolutions 1851 and 1897 are somewhat different from previous joint policing models. In the counter-piracy context, joint law enforcement operations would not primarily take place in the territorial waters of one of the parties to the shiprider agreement.[360] Whereas a "common" shiprider agreement would have foreseen the embarkation of Somali law enforcement officials who could undertake or authorize law enforcement operations within Somalia's territorial waters, paragraph 3 of Security Council Resolution 1851 and paragraph 6 of Security Council Resolution 1897 refer to the embarkation of shipriders from "countries willing to take custody of pirates." This defies the common rationale for embarking shipriders, which is the authorization of law enforcement measures in the territorial waters of the coastal State. Further, irrespective of the use of any shipriders from "regional countries," Security Council Resolution 1846 already authorizes third States to exercise enforcement powers in the coastal waters of Somalia.[361] Thus, the conclusion of shiprider agreements in the context of the counter-piracy operations in the Gulf of Aden would not bring any additional enforcement powers in Somalia's territorial waters. Moreover, such agreements would not negate the requirement to obtain consent from Somalia to take police measures in its coastal waters, given that Security Council Resolution 1851 explicitly requires the "advance consent of the TFG" for the "exercise of third state jurisdiction by shipriders in Somali territorial waters."[362]

2. Context Specific Rationale for the Use of Shipriders: Facilitating Regional Criminal Prosecution of Pirates and Armed Robbers at Sea

Rather than facilitating law enforcement operations in Somalia's territorial waters, the shiprider agreements envisaged in Security Council Resolutions 1851

Kramek, Bilateral Maritime Counter-Drug and Immigrant Interdiction Agreements: Is This the World of the Future? Miami Inter-American Law Review 31 (2001), Appendix B.

[360] See for example Art. 3(1) and (2) of the United States-Canadian Shiprider Agreement, *supra* note 356, stating that integrated cross-border maritime law enforcement operations shall only take place in waterways shared between the United States and Canada or on their respective mainland.

[361] S.C. Res. 1846, para. 10(b).

[362] S.C. Res. 1851, para. 3.

and 1897 aim to bring pirates and armed robbers at sea directly within the jurisdiction of the shiprider's home State. In this way, the transfer or extradition of alleged
pirates upon their arrest to regional States willing to prosecute them becomes obsolete since they are already in the jurisdiction of such a State.

This rationale follows from the language used in Security Council Resolutions
1851 and 1897. Both Security Council Resolutions encourage the conclusion
of shiprider agreements "with countries willing to take custody of pirates in order
to embark law enforcement officials ('shipriders') from the latter countries, in
particular countries in the region, to facilitate the investigation and prosecution of
persons detained as a result of operations conducted under this resolution."[363]

The primary purpose of shiprider agreements in the fight against piracy and
armed robbery at sea in the Gulf of Aden region is not to enlarge enforcement
powers,[364] but rather a means for enabling the exercise of adjudicative jurisdiction
over pirates and armed robbers at sea. This also derives, quite plainly, from a
statement of the United Nations Office on Drugs and Crime: "Shiprider arrangements (...) would enable a law enforcement official from, for example, Djibouti,
Kenya, Tanzania or Yemen, to join a warship off the coast of Somalia as a 'shiprider,' arrest the pirates in the name of their country, and then have them sent to
their national court for trial."[365]

This purpose suggests the adoption of shiprider agreements similar to the United
States Model Maritime Agreement Concerning Cooperation to Suppress Illicit
Traffic by Sea.[366] This agreement foresees that shipriders take law enforcement
measures, such as search and seizure of property, detention of persons and use of
force, under the law of their *own* State.[367] If shiprider agreements concluded in the
fight against piracy stated that embarked officials apply and act under their *own*

---

[363] *Id.* and S.C. Res. 1897, para. 6.

[364] However, to combat armed robbery at sea in the territorial waters of States other
than Somalia (and thus not covered by the Security Council Resolutions on piracy and
armed robbery at sea), shipriders might be used to broaden enforcement powers.

[365] United Nations, UNODC, Annual Report 2009, *available at* www.unodc.org/
documents/about-unodc/AR09_LORES.pdf (last visited Aug. 30, 2010), p. 17. See also
United Nations, UNODC, UNODC Proposes Measures to Stop Piracy in the Horn of Africa, Press Release, Dec. 16, 2008, *available at* www.unodc.org/unodc/en/press/releases/
2008-12.16.html (last visited Aug. 30, 2010): "A third, and more realistic option, proposed
by UNODC is for the pirates to be tried in the region, having been arrested by local po-
licemen. "I encourage "ship riders" to be deployed on warships operating off the Horn of
Africa in order to arrest pirates and bring them to justice in neighboring countries," said
Mr. Costa [the Executive Director of United Nations Office on Drugs and Crime]."

[366] United States Model Maritime Agreement, *supra* note 359.

[367] Art. 5 United States Model Maritime Agreement, *supra* note 359 reads: "The Government of __ may designate qualified law enforcement officials to act as law enforcement
shipriders. Subject to __ law, these shipriders may in appropriate circumstances: (...) d.
enforce the laws of __ in __ waters or seaward therefrom in the exercise of the right of hot
pursuit or otherwise in accordance with international law (...)."

law, the alleged offender and the *corpus delicti* would, at no point, come under the jurisdiction of the host vessel (such as a military ship contributing to Operation Atalanta). Rather, alleged offenders would be detained and property would be seized exclusively, under the law and on behalf of the embarked official's State.[368]

3. A Further Rationale for the Use of Shipriders: Enhancing Policing Skills and Capacity Building

According to the Report of the Secretary-General pursuant to Security Council Resolution 1846, the locus of pirate activities has begun to shift from the Gulf of Aden to the Western Indian Ocean and, more recently, closer to the Seychelles. Hence, the naval operations seem to have had a "crowding-out effect."[369] In order to combat piracy and armed robbery at sea in these geographical areas, to which the enforcement powers granted under Security Council Resolutions 1846, 1851, and 1897 do not apply, shipriders might be used in their classical function, that is to overcome jurisdictional hurdles and to facilitate law enforcement operations in the territorial waters of third States. Thus, it is conceivable that law enforcement officials from, for example, the Seychelles, could be embarked on ships engaged in counter-piracy operations, in order to take enforcement measures in their respective territorial waters or to consent to *ad hoc* measures undertaken by flag State officials.

In the future, shipriders could also be used to increase the policing skills on board military ships. The crews of military vessels are members of the armed forces and, therefore, first and foremost trained and equipped for combat and other maritime military operations, but not for traditional police or forensic work. Thus, the initial and on-spot investigation of piracy cases – which is crucial for the gathering and collection of evidence for later criminal proceedings – has not always been carried out in an ideal manner. A potential lack of evidence resulting from such defective procedures may later inhibit prosecution on criminal charges or may lead to potentially unjustified acquittals. Embarking law enforcement officials, such as police officers as shipriders, could bring the necessary policing skills on board military vessels. Ideally, they would be familiar with the criminal procedure and evidentiary standards of the jurisdiction where criminal proceedings are later to be brought.[370]

---

[368] S.C. Res. 1851, para. 3, and S.C. Res. 1897, para. 6, inviting States and regional organizations to conclude agreements with third States, "in particular countries in the region."

[369] United Nations, Secretary-General Report on S.C. Res. 1846, Nov. 13, 2009, para. 6.

[370] *Petrig*, Counter-Piracy Operations in the Gulf of Aden, Expert Meeting on Multinational Law Enforcement & Sea Piracy held at the Max Planck Institute for Foreign and International Criminal Law, Press Release, Max Planck Society for the Advancement of Science, Jan. 15, 2010, *available at* www.mpg.de/english/illustrationsDocumentation/

Conversely, embarked officials can learn from the military crew of the host vessel. Since the deployment of multinational forces in piracy-prone areas is not likely
to be sustainable over a significant period of time and, therefore, does not constitute a long-term solution, the ultimate goal should be to enable regional coastal
States to secure their territorial waters on their own. Embarking law enforcement
officials from regional States on board military ships deployed in the Gulf of Aden
region, could enable them to become familiar with and trained for combating
piracy and armed robbery at sea. Thus, the use of shipriders could also serve for
training and capacity-building purposes as well as a means of preparing for the
eventual withdrawal of the multinational troops.[371]

B. Legal Problems Potentially Arising from the Use of Shipriders

1. "One Ship, One Law" Principle Put to Test

On the high seas, which are open to all nations,[372] the applicability of a specific
State law can only be established through the linkage of a ship to a specific State.
The flag of a ship makes this link; ships have the nationality of the State whose flag
they are entitled to fly.[373] Hence, the flag is the mechanism through which the applicability of municipal and international law on the high seas can be achieved and
ensured. It is thus the key for determining the applicable law on board a ship and
the law enforcement actions undertaken from or on board a warship or governmental ship are subject to the law of the flag State.[374]

Thereby, the law of the sea provides that "ships shall sail under the flag of one
State only."[375] The use of more than one flag would be problematic in that
"[d]ouble nationality may give raise to serious abuse by a ship using one or another
flag during the same voyage, according to its convenience."[376] Hence, it can be
concluded that on board vessels, the principle "one ship, one law" governs.

---

documentation/pressReleases/2010/pressRelease20100115/index.html (last visited Aug. 30,
2010).

[371] Issue discussed during the *Expert Meeting on Multinational Law Enforcement & Sea
Piracy* held at the Max Planck Institute for Foreign and International Criminal Law on
Nov. 27–28, 2009; notes on file with the author.

[372] Arts. 87 and 89 UNCLOS; see also Art. 2 Convention on the High Seas containing
the same idea as the two provisions of the UNCLOS read together.

[373] Art. 91 UNCLOS; see also Art. 5 Convention on the High Seas.

[374] Given that warships or government ships, which are the only vessels allowed to
carry out enforcement measures according to Art. 107 UNCLOS, are quasi representative
of the respective State, it seems logical that the respective State law is applicable on board.

[375] Art. 92(1) UNCLOS; see also Art. 6 Convention on the High Seas.

[376] United Nations, International Law Commission, Commentary on the Law of the Sea
Draft Convention, p. 280, Art. 31 reads: "A ship which sails under the flags of two or more

The use of shipriders challenges the assumption of "one ship, one law" because law enforcement actions are carried out under a legal order (that of the shiprider's home State), which is different from that of the ship's flag State. Alternatively, in case of mutual assistance between embarked and host vessel, law enforcement officials operate under two cumulatively and concurrently applicable legal regimes. If this is done in order to bring the offender under a jurisdiction other than that of the flag State, this practice comes close, in effect, to a prohibited change of flag during a voyage, i.e. using a flag according to convenience.[377] The potential ambiguity which this brings about would seem to defy the UNCLOS' objective of legal certainty in the exercise of enforcement powers at sea, which is the very rationale behind the "one ship, one law" principle.

Considering existing shiprider clauses, the application of a law different from the one of the flag State or the cumulative application of two laws on board a ship is a real concern. Thus, the United States Model Maritime Agreement envisages the possibility that crew members of the host vessel assist the shiprider in carrying out enforcement actions, if the latter expressly requests such assistance. Such requests may only be made, agreed and acted upon in accordance with the applicable laws and policies of *both* parties, except for the use of force in self-defense, which is only subject to the law and policies of the acting official's State.[378] Thus, under the United States Model Maritime Agreement constellations are potentially conceivable where, in contravention of the principle "one ship, one law", more than one legal order is applicable on board of a law enforcement vessel.

The same holds true for the Djibouti Code of Conduct. According to its Article 7(4), shipriders may assist the law enforcement officials of the host vessel[379] or

States, using them according to convenience, may not claim any of the nationalities in question with respect to any other State, and may be assimilated to a ship without nationality." Art. 92(2) UNCLOS and Art. 6(2) Convention on the High Seas, which sanction ships that are sailing under the flag of two or more States in assimilating them to stateless ships, are identical to Art. 31 of the Law of the Sea Draft Convention.

[377] Art. 92(2) UNCLOS; see also Art. 6(2) Convention on the High Seas.

[378] Art. 7 United States Model Maritime Agreement, *supra* note 359, reads: "When a shiprider is embarked on the other Party's vessel, and the enforcement action being carried out is pursuant to the shiprider's authority, any search and seizure of property, and detention of a person, and any use of force pursuant to this agreement whether or not involving weapons, shall be carried out by the shiprider except as follows: a. crew members of the other Party's vessel may assist in any such action if expressly requested to do so by the shiprider and only to the extent and in the manner requested. Such request may only be made, agreed to and acted upon in accordance with the *applicable laws and policies of both parties* (...)." (emphasis added).

[379] It is interesting to note, that while Art. 7 U.S. Model Maritime Agreement foresees that a request for assistance in carrying out enforcement measures is made by the shiprider, the Djibouti Code of Conduct reverses this role, in that the embarked officer may assist the host vessel, if expressly requested to do so by the host. This may be due to the specific use of shipriders in the counter-piracy context, where the shiprider is not acting in their own territorial waters, but in an area under Somalia's jurisdiction. In Somali waters, a shiprider

conduct operations from the host vessel "in a manner that is not prohibited by the *laws and policies of both participants*."[380] Thus, the Djibouti Code of Conduct also foresees the cumulative application of two laws (legal regimes) on board of one and the same law enforcement vessel. Yet, in spite of this affirmation, the clause provides no guidance on how these two laws are to be reconciled in case of conflicting commands or powers, for example regarding the permissibility of a certain measure. The shiprider clause in the Djibouti Code of Conduct gives no indication as to whether the balance should be struck in favor of greater protection of human rights and liberty or more permissive measures in order to attain the security goal.

2. A Challenge to the Rationale of Article 107 UNCLOS

Both the Convention on the High Seas[381] as well as the UNCLOS[382] grant enforcement powers vis-à-vis pirate ships only to a certain confined category of vessels. This restriction goes back to the International Law Commission,[383] which, in Article 45 of its 1956 draft,[384] proposed that only warships or military aircraft should be permitted to seize pirate ships. The International Law Commission explained its choice by stating that "State action against ships suspected of engaging in piracy should be exercised with great circumspection, so as to avoid friction between States. Hence, it is important that the right to take action should be confined to warships, since the use of other government ships does not provide the same safeguards against abuse."[385]

However, the diplomatic conference in 1958 perceived this proposal as too limiting and adopted Article 21 Convention on the High Seas, extending the authority to effect a seizure on account of piracy to other ships or aircraft on government service.[386] Compared to Article 21 of the Convention on the High Seas, additional

---

(for example from Kenya) has no better right or higher authority to act than the host vessel's officials. Rather, under the Djibouti Code of Conduct the shiprider is seen as a guest on the ship who is dependent on an invitation to act from his host ship master or captain.

[380] Art. 7(4) Djibouti Code of Conduct (emphasis added).

[381] Art. 21 Convention on the High Seas: "A seizure on account of piracy may only be carried out by warships or military aircraft, or other ships or aircraft on government service authorized to that effect."

[382] Art. 107 UNCLOS.

[383] Art. 12 ASIL-Commented Harvard Draft Convention on Piracy was less limiting in comparison and reads: "A seizure because of piracy may be made only on behalf of a state, and only by a person who has been authorized to act on its behalf."

[384] Art. 45 Law of the Sea Draft Convention reads: "A seizure on account of piracy may only be carried out by warships or military aircraft." See United Nations, International Law Commission, Commentary on the Law of the Sea Draft Convention, p. 283.

[385] *Id.*

[386] This extension goes back to a proposal submitted by Thailand: *Nandan*, in: Nordquist (ed.), UNCLOS-Commentary, Article 107, 221.

language was patched into Article 107 UNCLOS, apparently in order to further narrow down the scope for possible abuse.[387] According to Article 107 UNCLOS, enforcement measures can only be taken by warships and other vessels "clearly marked and identifiable as being on government service and authorized to that effect." The UNCLOS Commentary states that this limitation serves "to indicate the official character of these units and their personnel" and, in case of unjustified seizure, it "also helps in the allocation of responsibility and liability."[388] Consequently, the underlying rationale is legal certainty.

Ships engaged in the fight against piracy off the coast of Somalia are either warships or other ships clearly marked and identifiable as being on government service and, thus, formally meet the requirements of Article 107 UNCLOS. However, the use of shipriders belonging to a State different from the nationality displayed by the vessel undermines the rationale behind limiting the type of ships used for law enforcement, which is to decrease the risk of abuse of enforcement powers, to enhance transparency and, in case of unjustified or unlawful acts, to allocate responsibilities. Thus, the use of shipriders could potentially constitute a circumvention of Article 107 UNCLOS.

3. Risk of Circumventing Human Rights Obligations

Problems arise if, through the use of shipriders, a pirate or armed robber at sea is brought under the jurisdiction of a State to which a transfer or extradition would not be possible without violating the prohibition of *refoulement*. The outcome is the same whether a pirate or armed robber at sea is captured by a patrolling naval State and then transferred to a regional State in direct violation of the principle of *non-refoulement* or whether a shiprider from a regional State is employed in order to bring arrested offenders directly, without the necessity of subsequent transfer, into the regional State's jurisdiction. This would amount to a circumvention of the *non-refoulement* principle.

While the scope of the *non-refoulement* principle is analyzed below,[389] it should be pointed out that the Human Rights Committee held that States that have abolished the death penalty[390] must refrain from transferring persons to countries where they face its possible imposition, even in the absence of allegations of serious

---

[387] *Rubin*, Law of Piracy, p. 372.

[388] *Nandan*, in: Nordquist (ed.), UNCLOS-Commentary, Article 107, 222.

[389] On the principle of *non-refoulement* in the context of transfers, see p. 207 *et seq.*

[390] E.g. State parties to the Second Optional Protocol to the International Covenant on Civil and Political Rights, Aiming at the Abolition of the Death Penalty, *adopted* Dec. 15, 1989, 1642 U.N.T.S. 414 [hereinafter: 2nd Optional Protocol ICCPR].

shortcomings in the proceedings.[391] Thus, the use of shipriders from retentionist countries from the region[392] seems problematic.

C. Conclusion

Arguments in favor of the use of shipriders range from the "enhancement of operational effectiveness" to "removing policing barriers" and even to the "realization of seamless borders."[393] Shipriders, in contrast to members of private security and military companies that could potentially offer similar (security) services, have the advantage that they have the power and authority to take law enforcement measures such as arrest, seizure or even the use of (potentially deadly) force. Shipriders also have the benefit of bringing specific expertise on board (military) ships, such as skills in forensic investigation of criminal cases. Finally, avoiding casualties within one's own rank could be a further argument for using shipriders. It is, therefore, likely that the use of shipriders will increase in the near future, not only in the repression of piracy and armed robbery at sea, but also to counter other forms of criminal behavior at sea.

What originally was designed to be a valuable law enforcement mechanism in the context of counter-drug operations, might turn out to lower human rights protections, to circumvent the principle of *non-refoulement* and, overall, to run counter to legal certainty. Of course, much depends on how specific shiprider agreements are phrased and shaped. It seems, that in relation to the repression of piracy and armed robbery at sea off the coast of Somalia, shiprider agreements may not only be used to overcome jurisdictional and bureaucratic hurdles for the sake of effec-

---

[391] United Nations, Human Rights Committee, *Judge v. Canada* (communication no. 829/1998), U.N. Doc. CCPR/C/78/D/829/1998 (July 14-Aug. 28, 2003), para. 10(4): "For countries that have abolished the death penalty, there is an obligation not to expose a person to the real risk of its application. Thus, they may not remove, either by deportation or extradition, individuals from their jurisdiction if it may be reasonably anticipated that they will be sentenced to death, without ensuring that the death sentence would not be carried out." The Human Rights Committee, thereby, overruled its jurisprudence in *Kindler v. Canada* (communication no. 470/1991), U.N. Doc. CCPR/C/48/D/470/1991 (Nov. 11, 1993) and based itself on the dissenting opinions in *Kindler v. Canada*; this extension of the *non-refoulement* principle was based on Art. 6(1): *Nowak*, pp. 151–153 and p. 188. On the principle of *non-refoulement*, see also p. 207 *et seq.*

[392] While Somalia and Yemen are among the retentionist countries, Kenya and the United Republic of Tanzania retain death penalty as a sanction for ordinary crime, but are considered to be abolitionist in practice; the Seychelles abolished death penalty for all crimes: Amnesty International, Abolitionist and Retentionist Countries, *available at* www.amnesty.org/en/death-penalty/abolitionist-and-retentionist-countries (last visited Aug. 30, 2010).

[393] United Nations, UNODC, "Ship Riders": Tackling Somali Pirates at Sea, Press Release, Jan. 20, 2009, *available at* www.unodc.org/unodc/en/frontpage/ship-riders-tackling-somali-pirates-at-sea.html (last visited Aug. 30, 2010).

tive law enforcement, but may also be agreed upon to bypass one criminal jurisdiction and gain access to another, thereby, effectively enabling forum shopping.

The Security Council, perhaps in anticipation of potential abuses of shiprider agreements, introduced a safeguard clause in paragraph 3 of Security Council Resolution 1851 and paragraph 6 of Security Council Resolution 1897, providing that such agreements should "not prejudice the effective implementation of the SUA Convention." However, it is far from clear what this *caveat* means. Not prejudicing the effective implementation of the SUA Convention may be read as asserting that, if jurisdiction is conferred upon the shiprider's State, it must be ensured that this State will exercise its adjudicative jurisdiction. If a shiprider carries out an arrest, the individual will commonly not come within the jurisdiction of the patrolling naval State, but rather directly within the jurisdiction of the home State of the embarked official. Therefore, in the example under consideration, the patrolling naval State's duty under the SUA Convention to prosecute or extradite[394] will not usually be triggered. Considering the rationale behind the duty to prosecute or extradite, which is to avoid that the alleged offender escapes criminal prosecution, it could be argued that the Security Council meant that States party to the SUA Convention must ensure prosecution of the alleged offender even if he does not technically come within their jurisdiction. Otherwise the very rationale of the obligation to prosecute or extradite under the SUA Convention would possibly be bypassed by the use of shipriders.It is not clear, however, how the patrolling naval State could ever ensure with any degree of certainty that the home State of the embarked official does in fact instigate criminal proceedings.

III. Legal Constraints on Counter-Piracy Enforcement Powers

Thus far, rules constraining the exercise of enforcement powers in a maritime context have remained rudimentary. UNCLOS does not contain any explicit confines regarding the enforcement powers granted under Article 105 UNCLOS. Similarly, Security Council Resolutions 1846 (like predecessor Resolution 1816) makes no mention of any specific limitations in relation to the enforcement powers authorized therein.[395] The explicit references to human rights law in Security Council Resolution 1846 paragraph 14 (as well as in Security Council Resolution 1816 paragraph 11) relates to the exercise of adjudicative jurisdiction, i.e. the criminal

---

[394] On duty to prosecute or extradite under the SUA Convention, see p. 151.

[395] S.C. Res. 1816, para. 7(b), and S.C. Res. 1846, para. 10(b), merely call for consistency "with action permitted on the high seas with respect to piracy under international law," which, however, is to be interpreted as a mere reference to the UNCLOS regime and, therefore, does not add much clarity in terms of the applicable legal confines.

prosecution of suspected pirates and armed robbers at sea rather than to the exercise of enforcement powers. The same is true with regard to the references to human rights law in Security Council Resolution 1897.[396]

As far as constraints relating to enforcement powers are concerned, Security Council Resolution 1897 merely requests that "States take appropriate steps to ensure that the activities they undertake pursuant to the authorizations in paragraph 7 do not have the practical effect of denying or impairing *the right of innocent passage* to the ships of any third State."[397] The focus is thus clearly on the free flow of movement, rather than on individual rights of persons subjected to enforcement measures. Only Security Council Resolution 1851 refers to the "applicable humanitarian and human rights law" with regard to the exercise of enforcement powers.[398] Yet, in view of this general reference, merely to the *applicable* humanitarian and human rights law, the general conditions and requirements for applying either of these bodies of law in the context of the counter-piracy operations remain relevant. Against this background, an overview on general safeguards applicable to maritime interception operations is provided (A.). In a second step, the conditions of applicability of human rights and international humanitarian law are examined (B.).

A. General Safeguards Applicable to Maritime Interception Operations

Despite the absence of any explicit limitation on the enforcement powers granted under the first sentence of Article 105 UNCLOS, a graduation of enforcement powers can arguably be deduced from the structure of UNCLOS itself. According to Article 110(1)(a) UNCLOS, the right of visit is granted in order to verify a suspicion of the ship's engagement in piracy. Only once this suspicion has been ascertained, Article 105 UNCLOS, which on its wording requires positive knowledge that a ship is a pirate ship, provides for further enforcement powers, namely seizure and arrest.

1. Safeguards Developed in International Case Law

a) Safeguards Pertaining to Ship-to-Ship Operations

On the basis of rather limited case law pertaining to the legal confines of enforcement actions carried out at sea, it is commonly suggested that the use of force in maritime interception operations must be necessary, proportionate and should be

---

[396] S.C. Res. 1897, preambular paras. 9 and 11 and paras. 11 and 12.

[397] *Id.* at para. 10 (emphasis added).

[398] S.C. Res. 1851, para. 6.

preceded by warning shots if possible.[399] In *The M/V "Saiga" (No. 2) Case*, the International Tribunal for the Law of the Sea held that, in the absence of express provisions on the use of force in UNCLOS, general international law, applicable by virtue of Article 293(1) UNCLOS, as well as considerations of humanity, required that "the use of force must be avoided as far as possible and, where force is unavoidable, it must not go beyond what is reasonable and necessary in the circumstances."[400] Referring to the *I'm Alone* and *Red Crusader* cases,[401] the International Tribunal for the Law of the Sea in *The M/V "Saiga" (No. 2) Case* confirmed that these principles had been followed over the years in law enforcement operations at sea.[402] It went on to state that "all efforts should be made to ensure that life is not endangered."[403]

Similar language is employed in Article 8 SUA Protocol 2005 incorporating an Article 8*bis* in the SUA Convention,[404] which limits force to "the minimum degree (…) necessary and reasonable in the circumstances." Moreover, the formula that

---

[399] *Guilfoyle*, UN Security Council Resolution 1816 and IMO Regional Counter-Piracy Efforts, ICLQ 57 (2008), 696.

[400] International Tribunal for the Law of the Sea, *The M/V "Saiga" (No. 2) Case (Saint Vincent and the Grenadines v. Guinea)*, Judgment, July 1, 1999, para. 155.

[401] *Id.* at para. 157, citing the *S.S. "I'm Alone" Case* (Canada/United States, 1935), U.N.R.I.A.A., Vol. III, p. 1609, and the *The Red Crusader Case* (Commission of Enquiry, Denmark – United Kingdom, 1962), I.L.R., Vol. 35, p. 485.

[402] *Id.* at para. 156: "The normal practice used to stop a ship at sea is first to give an auditory or visual signal to stop, using internationally recognized signals. Where this does not succeed, a variety of actions may be taken, including the firing of shots across the bows of the ship. It is only after the appropriate actions fail that the pursuing vessel may, as a last resort, use force. Even then, appropriate warning must be issued to the ship and all efforts should be made to ensure that life is not endangered."

[403] *Id.* The prescription not to endanger the safety of life at sea can also be found in the following instruments: Art. 20(4) of the Agreement Concerning Co-Operation in Suppressing Illicit Maritime and Air Trafficking in Narcotic Drugs and Psychotropic Substances in the Caribbean Area, *available at* www.state.gov/s/l/2005/87198.htm (last visited Aug. 30, 2010) [hereinafter: Caribbean Regional Agreement]; Art. 8*bis*(10)(a) of the SUA Convention Protocol 2005; Art. 22(1) of the Agreement for the Implementation of the Provisions of the United Nations Convention on the Law of the Sea of December 10, 1982 relating to the Conservation and Management of Straddling Fish Stocks and Highly Migratory Fish Stocks, *adopted* Aug. 4, 1995, 2167 U.N.T.S. 3 [hereinafter: Fish Stock Agreement]; Art 9(1) of the Protocol against the Smuggling of Migrants by Land, Sea and Air, supplementing the United Nations Convention against Transnational Organized Crime, *adopted* Nov. 15, 2000, 2241 U.N.T.S. 480 [hereinafter: Migrant Smuggling Protocol]; Art. 17(5) of the UN Narcotic Convention.

[404] International Maritime Organization, Protocol of 2005 to the Convention for the Suppression of Unlawful Acts against the Safety of Maritime Navigation, Text Adopted by the International Conference on the Revision of the SUA Treaties, IMO Doc. LEG/CONF.15/21 (Nov. 1, 2005) [hereinafter: SUA Protocol 2005]. Excerpts of the SUA Protocol 2005 are reprinted on p. 243 *et seq.* of this book (Appendix).

force shall be "the minimum reasonably necessary" can also be found in almost every one of the United States' bilateral drug interdiction treaties.[405]

b) Safeguards Pertaining to Operations on Board of Intercepted Vessels

Notably, the International Tribunal for the Law of the Sea not only found use of excessive force before the boarding of the *Saiga* but, referring to the safety of the ship and the persons on board, also held that excessive force was used on board the ship.[406] This is in line with the reference of the International Tribunal for the Law of the Sea to Article 22(1)(f) of the Fish Stock Agreement, reaffirming the basic principle in relation to the use of force.[407] Article 22(1)(f) of the Fish Stock Agreement pertains to the use of force aboard an intercepted vessel and reads:

Art. 22(1)(f) Fish Stock Agreement – Basic Procedures for Boarding and Inspection Pursuant to Article 21

The inspecting State shall ensure that its duly authorized inspectors: avoid the use of force *except* when, and to the degree necessary, to ensure the safety of the inspectors and where the inspectors are obstructed in the execution of their duties. The degree of force used shall not exceed that reasonably required in the circumstances.[408]

2. Future Article 8*bis* of the SUA Convention

Indications regarding the restrictions on enforcement powers at sea may also be derived from Article 8 SUA Protocol 2005, which envisages the incorporation of a new Article 8*bis* in the SUA Convention.[409] The SUA Protocol 2005 was adopted at a diplomatic conference of the International Maritime Organization on October 14, 2005, but has not yet entered into force.[410] It has been described as an attempt to universalize Proliferation Security Initiative (PSI) activities.[411]

---

[405] See references in *Guilfoyle*, Shipping Interdiction, p. 281, note 64.

[406] International Tribunal for the Law of the Sea, *The M/V "Saiga" (No. 2) Case (Saint Vincent and the Grenadines v. Guinea)*, Judgment, July 1, 1999, para. 158.

[407] The Fish Stock Agreement came into force on December 11, 2001. To date, there are 77 parties to the agreement: United Nations, Treaty Collection, Status of Treaties, Chapter XXI, Law of the Sea, 7. Agreement for the Implementation of the Provisions of the United Nations Convention on the Law of the Sea of December 10, 1982, relating to the Conservation and Management of Straddling Fish Stocks and Highly Migratory Fish Stocks, *available at* http://treaties.un.org/Pages/ParticipationStatus.aspx (last visited Aug. 30, 2010). See generally *Barston*, United Nations Conference on Straddling and Highly Migratory Fish Stocks, Marine Policy 19 (1995).

[408] Emphasis added.

[409] Article 8 of the SUA Protocol 2005 is reprinted on p. 243 *et seq.* of this book (Appendix).

[410] SUA Protocol 2005.

[411] *Byers*, Policing the High Seas: The Proliferation Security Initiative, AJIL (98) 2004, 526–545.

The future Article 8*bis* will add a boarding provision to the SUA Convention. It was, *inter alia,* because of this boarding regime that negotiations of the SUA Protocol 2005 proved to be difficult.[412] In this context, Article 8*bis*(10) SUA Convention includes important safeguards in case a State party takes measures against another vessel, specifically when boarding another ship.[413] According to this provision, the use of force is to be avoided except when necessary to ensure the safety of officials and persons on board, or where the officials are obstructed in the execution of authorized actions.[414] Moreover, Article 8*bis* SUA Convention namely provides that the safety of life at sea is not to be endangered, that it is to be ensured that all persons on board are treated in a manner which preserves human dignity and is in keeping with human rights law, and that due account is taken of the safety and security of the ship and its cargo. There is no evident reason why conditions applicable to the conduct of enforcement operations on the basis of the SUA Convention and its 2005 Protocol should not also be applicable to similar operations on the basis of UNCLOS in the pursuance of pirates, since acts of piracy will typically also fulfill offenses described in Article 3 SUA Convention.

3. Caribbean Regional Agreement

On a regional level, further indications can be derived from Article 22 of the Agreement Concerning Co-Operation in Suppressing Illicit Maritime and Air Trafficking in Narcotic Drugs and Psychotropic Substances in the Caribbean Area, which resulted from negotiations between nineteen States including, not only the United States of America and Caribbean States, but also the United Kingdom, France and the Netherlands.[415] Article 22 of the Caribbean Regional Agreement provides:

Art. 22 Caribbean Regional Agreement – Use of Force

1. Force may only be used if no other feasible means of resolving the situation can be applied.

2. Any force used shall be proportional to the objective for which it is employed.

3. All use of force pursuant to this Agreement shall in all cases be the minimum reasonably necessary under the circumstances.

4. A warning shall be issued prior to any use of force except when force is being used in self-defense.

---

[412] International Maritime Organization, Report of the Legal Committee on the Work of its Nineteenth Session, IMO Doc. LEG 90/15 (May 9, 2005), paras. 30–31.

[413] The safeguards of Art. 8*bis*(10) SUA Protocol 2005 were largely drawn from Arts. 15 and 17(5) UN Narcotic Convention and Art. 9 Migrant Smuggling Protocol.

[414] See also explanations provided by the International Maritime Organization, *available at* www.imo.org (follow "legal" hyperlink, then follow "IMO Conventions" hyperlink, then follow "SUA" hyperlink) (last visited Aug. 30, 2010).

[415] *Guilfoyle*, Shipping Interdiction, p. 278.

5. In the event that the use of force is authorised and necessary in the waters of a Party, law enforcement officials shall respect the laws of that Party.

6. In the event that the use of force is authorised and necessary during a boarding and search seaward of the territorial sea of any Party, the law enforcement officials shall comply with their domestic laws and procedures and the directions of the flag State.

7. The discharge of firearms against or on a suspect vessel shall be reported as soon as practicable to the flag State Party.

8. Parties shall not use force against civil aircraft in flight.

9. The use of force in reprisal or as punishment is prohibited.

10. Nothing in this Agreement shall impair the exercise of the inherent right of self-defense by law enforcement or other officials of any Party.

Thus, force may only be used if no other feasible means of resolving a situation can be applied. The use of force must further be proportionate to the objective for which it is employed and it must be the minimum reasonably necessary under the circumstances.[416] Moreover, Article 22 of the Caribbean Regional Agreement requires that, generally, a warning shot shall be issued prior to any use of force and, that in the event that the use of force is authorized and necessary during a boarding, the law enforcement officials shall comply with their domestic laws and procedures and the directions of the flag State.

4. Towards a Minimum Safeguard Standard
for Maritime Interception Operations

Against this background, an "emerging consensus on minimum safeguard provisions" has been discerned, notably, in view of the SUA Protocol 2005, the Caribbean Regional Agreement, the Fish Stock Agreement and certain bilateral agreements concluded under the umbrella of the Proliferation Security Initiative (PSI).[417] Irrespective of whether the safeguards laid out in these instruments are reflective of pre-existing customary law or whether they only indicate emerging customary standards, calls to heed the safety of life at sea as well as abstract references to necessity and proportionality, remain vague and, arguably, only provide limited guidance for operations in practice. It is telling that in 2003, during the negotiations of the SUA Protocol 2005, the United States delegation still pointed out that "[s]imply put, there is almost no specific guidance regarding the use of force while conducting a boarding pursuant to treaty or customary international law."[418]

Indeed, the invocation of necessity as a veritable constraint inevitably begs the question: necessary for what? Similarly the relational decision and balancing of relative values required by the proportionality principle presupposes the existence

---

[416] Generally, see *Gilmore*, Caribbean Regional Agreement.

[417] *Guilfoyle*, Shipping Interdiction, p. 266.

[418] International Maritime Organization, United States of America Delegation, White Paper on Article 8*bis* of the SUA Convention (Dec. 22, 2003), para. 2(9)(2).

of readily identifiable legitimate aims. It has been asserted that the test must be that force has been used to secure a permitted goal, being an action either authorized directly by international law or an action falling within the scope of flag State authorization.[419] This is correct. Yet, neither UNCLOS nor the Security Council Resolutions on piracy and armed robbery at sea specify the authorized ends in any detail. The Security Council Resolutions proclaim the overall objective of suppressing and, as stipulated explicitly, fully and durably eradicating piracy and armed robbery at sea in the region. UNCLOS somewhat more precisely, in the first sentence of Article 105 UNCLOS, allows the arrest of persons and the seizure of property. Yet, the decision as to what degree of force is necessary and proportional in relation to these objectives in the specific circumstances is largely left to the discretion of the law enforcement officials carrying out the counter-piracy operations.

Safeguards found in the various international instruments are commonly aimed at the protection of ships, their cargo and, generally, the freedom of navigation rather than at the protection of individual rights of persons subject to law enforcement measures and criminal investigations. For example, the future Article 8*bis* of the SUA Convention, Article 20(4) of the Caribbean Regional Agreement as well as various bilateral Proliferation Security Initiative (PSI) agreements all require that undue delay of vessels be avoided.[420] Similarly, Security Council Resolution 1897 explicitly requests that States ensure that their counter-piracy activities do not have the practical effect of denying or impairing the right of innocent passage to the ships of any third State.[421] Provisions taking due account of individual rights, however, are not so readily discernible. What is more, abstract references to "keeping with human rights law" entailed only in the SUA Protocol 2005 and some bilateral Proliferation Security Initiative (PSI) agreements still require a more specific identification of the applicable human rights protections in a given case. Accordingly, it is appropriate at this stage of the analysis, to focus on the applicability of human rights in the context of maritime law enforcement operations.

B. Confines Derived From Human Rights Law

The exercise of enforcement jurisdiction against persons and ships allegedly engaged in acts of piracy and armed robbery at sea (such as arrest, police custody, transfer of alleged offenders or the seizure of boats and property aboard) interferes with rights and freedoms guaranteed either by domestic law or by regional and international human rights instruments. Yet, the applicability of human rights to

---

[419] *Guilfoyle*, Shipping Interdiction, p. 281.

[420] *Id.* at p. 266.

[421] S.C. Res. 1897, para. 10.

counter-piracy operations carried out in the Gulf of Aden region can be contested under various headings.

Firstly, the law enforcement actions undertaken in the region feature several extraterritorial elements, which could call into question the applicability of certain human rights instruments (1.). Secondly, the current enforcement operations, namely European Union Operation Atalanta, NATO Operation Ocean Shield and Coalition Task Force 151 are multinational in nature, involve international organizations such as the European Union and NATO, are authorized by Security Council Resolutions based on Chapter VII of the United Nations Charter and, at least formally, are conducted in collaboration with, and on the basis of, the consent of the Somali Transitional Federal Government. These various layers raise intricate questions regarding the attribution of possible human rights violations (2.). Thirdly, the reference to international humanitarian law in Security Council Resolution 1851 potentially could have repercussions on the applicable human rights protections. International humanitarian law, if applicable, as the *lex specialis*, could modify applicable human rights protections, especially where the use of force is concerned (3.).

1. Extraterritorial Application of Human Rights to Counter-Piracy Operations at Sea

The extraterritorial application of human rights at sea is becoming increasingly relevant in relation to the repression of drug and arms trafficking or smuggling at sea. This is true with regard to irregular migration by sea and maritime border control operations – for example, by *Frontex* or the United States Coast Guard[422] – and generally to law enforcement operations carried out at sea, whether counterterrorism or counter-piracy.[423] Indeed, the vast majority of enforcement measures against pirates operating off Somalia's coast are carried out by non-Somali law enforcement officials and in an area, which is either under Somalia's jurisdiction or on the high seas outside the jurisdiction of any State. In short, law enforcement officials involved in current counter-piracy operations off Somalia's coast typically act extraterritorially, i.e. outside their home State.

The extraterritorial application of human rights, despite persistent objections from some States,[424] has been firmly established in the jurisprudence of the Inter-

---

[422] Frontex is a European Union agency created as a specialized and independent body tasked to coordinate the operational cooperation between European Union member States in the field of border security, see www.frontex.europa.eu/ (last visited Aug. 30, 2010).

[423] Generally, see *Weinzierl/Lisson*, Border Management and Human Rights.

[424] See, for example, United Nations, Human Rights Committee, Replies of the Government of the Netherlands to the Concerns Expressed by the Human Rights Committee, UN Doc. CCPR/CO/72/NET/Add.1 (Apr. 29, 2003), para. 19; Second Periodic Report of Israel to the Human Rights Committee, UN Doc. CCPR/C/ISR/2001/2 (Dec. 4, 2001), para. 8; and Second and Third Periodic Reports of the United States of America, Consid-

national Court of Justice, regional human rights courts and pronouncements of the United Nations' Human Rights Committee.[425] Thus far, the jurisprudence on the matter has remained casuistic, which complicates the determination of the extraterritorial application of human rights law. It is one thing to assess, for example, the extraterritorial application of human rights law in a specific detention facility abroad,[426] but to evaluate the extraterritorial application of human rights to counter-piracy operations is more challenging. These operations may involve dynamic enforcement actions by different States and in a variety of different settings, locations and constellations, such as on board military vessels, in the pursuit of alleged pirate vessels and on board pirate or hijacked ships, within Somalia's territorial waters, its mainland and on the high seas. At the present juncture, especially in view of the casuistic jurisprudence, the identification of the applicable human rights law largely hinges on an *ex post* case-by-case assessment of whether factual control either over the person concerned or over the territory where the action took place was sufficiently established. This often leads to a piecemeal approach in the realm of human rights protection that may leave considerable gaps where the relevant degree of effective control cannot be clearly ascertained.

What is more, the criteria to define the extraterritorial applicability of human rights in the particular geographical context of the high seas have not yet been determined, except in some limited cases. Certainly, extraterritorial acts performed at sea may amount to an exercise of jurisdiction in the sense of the jurisdictional clauses of human rights treaties. But it is far from clear whether the common criterion of "effective control over territory" could be understood more broadly as "effective control over any given area" including the sea. Furthermore, it is unclear under what circumstances effective control over persons is established in law enforcement operations at sea.

---

eration of Reports Submitted by States Parties under Article 40 of the Covenant, Annex I: Territorial Scope of the Application of the Covenant, UN Doc. CCPR/C/USA/3 (Nov. 28, 2005). See also United Nations, Economic and Social Council, Second Periodic Report of Israel to the Committee on Economic, Social and Cultural Rights, UN Doc. E/1990/6/Add.32, (Oct. 16, 2001), para. 5. Finally, see United Nations, Committee against Torture, Conclusions and Recommendations on the United Kingdom, UN Doc. CAT/C/CR/33/3 (Dec. 10, 2004), para. 4(b), and, Summary Record of the 703rd meeting, UN Doc. CAT/C/SR.703 (May 12, 2006), para. 14.

[425] International Court of Justice, *Legal Consequences of the Construction of a Wall in the Occupied Palestinian Territory*, Advisory Opinion, July 9, 2004, I.C.J. Reports 2004, p. 180; *Case Concerning Armed Activities on the Territory of the Congo (Democratic Republic of the Congo v. Uganda)*, Judgement, Dec. 19, 2005, I.C.J. Reports 2005, p. 168; *Case Concerning Application of the International Convention on the Elimination of All Forms of Racial Discrimination (Georgia v. Russian Federation)*, Provisional Measure, Order, Oct. 15, 2008, I.C.J. Reports 2008. See also United Nations, Human Rights Committee, General Comment No. 31, para. 10.

[426] European Court of Human Rights, *Al-Saadoon and Mufdhi v. United Kingdom* (application no. 61498/08), Decision, June 30, 2009, para. 89.

In the following analysis, without intending to repeat the general debate on the extraterritorial application of human rights,[427] a tentative attempt is made to apply the common criteria of effective control over territory or individual persons to the different phases of counter-piracy law enforcement operations carried out at sea.

a) Application of Human Rights to Arrested Suspects Held on Military Ships

It is undisputed that where enforcement measures are carried out *on board* a military or government ship, such as the holding in custody of alleged pirates, the human rights obligations of the flag State are applicable.[428] However, there are several lines of argument on which this assertion can be founded. The application of human rights law on board a military ship may, arguably, be brought about by the flag State principle directly (aa.), by virtue of the ostensible "quasi-territoriality" of military and governmental ships (bb.) or in keeping with the common criteria determinative of the extraterritorial applicability of human rights, which is the effective control governmental agents exercise on board such a vessel (cc.).

aa) Application of Human Rights Directly Via the Flag State Principle

The most widely held view is that the applicability of human rights law follows directly from the flag State principle. According to this principle, a ship has the nationality of the State whose flag it is entitled to fly.[429] Against this background, the European Court of Human Rights has defined enforcement measures taken on board a ship or aircraft flying the flag of a State party to the European Convention on Human Rights[430] as an exercise of jurisdiction of that respective State and, therefore, requires that such measures be carried out in conformity with the standards set out in the European Convention on Human Rights.[431]

---

[427] For an overview on the case law of the European Court of Human Rights concerning the extraterritorial application of the European Convention on Human Rights, see *Dutt-wiler/Petrig*, Neue Aspekte der extraterritorialen Anwendbarkeit der EMRK, AJP (10) 2009.

[428] European Court of Human Rights, *Rigopoulos v. Spain* (application no. 37388/97), Decision, Jan. 12, 1999.

[429] Art. 91(1) UNCLOS; see also Art. 5(1) Convention on the High Seas.

[430] Convention for the Protection of Human Rights and Fundamental Freedoms as Amended by Protocol No. 11, *adopted* Nov. 4, 1950, 213 U.N.T.S. 222 [hereinafter: ECHR].

[431] European Court of Human Rights, *Banković v. Belgium et al.* (application no. 52207/99), Grand Chamber Decision, Dec. 12, 2001, para. 73: "Additionally, the Court notes that other recognized instances of the extra-territorial exercise of jurisdiction by a State include cases involving the activities (...) on board craft and vessels registered in, or flying the flag of, that State. In these specific situations, customary international law and treaty provisions have recognized the extra-territorial exercise of jurisdiction by the relevant State." See also, for example, European Court of Human Rights, *Al-Saadoon and Mufdhi v. United Kingdom* (application no. 61498/08), Decision June 30, 2009, para. 85.

bb) The "Quasi-Territoriality" of a Ship

As held by the Permanent Court of Justice in the *Lotus* case, a corollary of the flag principle is that any act occurring "on board a vessel on the high seas must be regarded as if it occurred on the territory of the State whose flag the ship flies."[432] Hence, the body of law in force in the respective State also governs situations on board vessels or aircraft flying the State's flag.[433] Thus, it has also been argued that every vessel flying a State's flag in fact constitutes part of the territory of that State, thereby rendering the State's human rights obligations applicable.[434]

cc) Effective Control Exercised on Military Ships

However, the fact that the flag State principle constitutes a basis for jurisdiction, as understood in general public international law (in other words as a basis for the jurisdiction to prescribe, to enforce and to adjudicate), does not automatically imply that it also satisfies the jurisdictional link required to render human rights law applicable extraterritorially. This jurisdictional link requires some form of factual control.[435] Similarly, the mere fact that a State has jurisdiction over its vessels in the general sense of public international law, conferred upon it via the flag, does not automatically render the ship part of the State's territory, as it was arguably implied in the *Lotus* case. This would amount to a confusion of territory and jurisdiction.[436]

Thus, rather than invoking the flag State principle or regarding ships as floating particles of their flag State's territory, the applicability of human rights law on a military or governmental vessel is better founded on the common effective control criterion. Thus, the jurisdictional link triggering the application of human rights law would be derived from the factual control exercised by the crew. This would be in keeping with the general criteria for the extraterritorial application of human rights. Military or governmental vessels in the sense of Article 107 UNCLOS are

---

[432] Permanent Court of International Justice, *The Case of the S.S. "Lotus"*, Judgment, Sept. 7, 1927, Collection of Judgments, Series A, No. 10, p. 25; *id.*, Dissenting Opinion Judge Nyholm, p. 62; United States of America, Supreme Court, *United States v. Flores*, 289 U.S. 137, 155 (1933); *id.*, *Lauritzen v. Larsen*, 345 U.S. 571, 585 (1953).

[433] This conclusion is based on the assumption that the law enforcement personnel on board of the vessel acts on behalf and under the authority and the law of the State whose flag the ship is flying. However, the use of shipriders may cause a rupture with the principle "one ship, one law" given that shipriders may carry out enforcement measures by applying their own law; see p. 90 *et seq.*

[434] United States of America, Supreme Court, *United States v. Flores*, 289 U.S. 137, 155 (1933); *id.*, *Lauritzen v. Larsen*, 345 U.S. 571, 585 (1953).

[435] *Milanovic*, From Compromise to Principle: Clarifying the Concept of State Jurisdiction in Human Rights Treaties, Human Rights Law Review (8) 2008, 417 *et seq.*

[436] *Jessup*, The Law of Territorial Waters and Maritime Jurisdiction, p. 191; *O'Connell/ Shearer*, The International Law of the Sea, p. 735.

largely made up of State agents, who have effective control over these vessels and, thereby, over any person that is held in custody on such a vessel.

Ultimately, the different lines of argument described above lead to the same result. Persons suspected of having engaged in piracy or armed robbery at sea, who are being *held* on a military or governmental vessel benefit from the human rights protections applicable to the flag State, irrespective of whether the said vessel is navigating on the high seas, within Somalia's territorial waters or within the coastal waters of any other State.

b) Application of Human Rights Law during the Interception-Phase

The lines of argumentation above, however, cannot readily be invoked as far as the interception-phase is concerned. Interception-phase here denotes the phase during which an alleged pirate ship is pursued, stopped and ultimately boarded. In other words, it denotes enforcement measures carried out not on board of the military vessel itself, but beyond its railings. For purposes of analysis, the interception-phase can be further divided, differentiating between the phase of pursuit, i.e. ship-to-ship operations prior to boarding, and the boarding phase, during which the alleged pirate ship is boarded and searched, and during which the crew may be arrested.

The flag State principle, at least in keeping with its common interpretation, merely pertains to measures taken *on board* military or governmental ships. The legal effects of this principle and any consequential human rights obligations do not apply beyond a ship's railing. Yet, irrespective of whether the flag State principle should perhaps be discarded altogether as a relevant jurisdictional link for purposes of extraterritorial human rights application, it certainly seems conceivable that a military or governmental ship, which in fact amounts to a floating "center of effective control," could exert effective control beyond its railings, i.e. beyond its exact nautical position.

Concordant with the common "effective control criteria," either over territory or over individual persons,[437] it could be argued that the effective control exercised on board a military ship is simply not confined to the ship itself. Modern military ships have "long arms" in that they are equipped with technology and weaponry, which give them the capability to exercise control over a wide area beyond their railings. It is, therefore arguable that military ships could be said to exert control over either a delimited geographical area at sea confined by the ship's operational radius analogous to the common "control over territory"-criterion (aa.), or over individual persons or vessels that come within the ship's operative range in application of the common "control over persons"-criterion (bb.).

---

[437] European Court of Human Rights, *Loizidou v. Turkey* (application no 15318/89), Judgment, March 23, 1995, paras. 62–64.

aa) Effective "Area" Control at Sea: The Operational Radius of Military Ships

A delimited radius of control at sea, beyond the exact nautical position of a law enforcement ship, seems generally conceivable. Given that the extraterritorial application of human rights law is established through the degree of factual control, it would not seem to matter whether such control is exercised over land or water, unless it was *per se* impossible to establish a sufficiently efficient degree of control at sea. However, in particular the jurisprudence of the European Court of Human Rights supports the proposition that establishing control at sea is possible. The pronouncements of the European Court of Human Rights do not constitute judicial precedents on the universal level; however, its case law may offer important indications valid beyond the regional scope of the European Convention of Human Rights.

The European Court of Human Rights, in relation to control over territory, in cases such as *Loizidou v. Turkey*,[438] *Cyprus v. Turkey*[439] and *Ilaşcu and Others v. Moldova and Russia*,[440] has held that effective control does not mean control over every act or part of a territory, but "effective overall control."[441] Also, merely temporary control only over a specific portion of an area suffices under the jurisprudence of the European Court of Human Rights. In *Issa*, for example, the European Court of Human Rights did not exclude the possibility that Turkey, as a consequence of its military action, could have been considered to have exercised, temporarily, effective overall control of a particular portion of the territory of northern Iraq.[442] In *Al-Saadoon*, the European Court of Human Rights further limited the geographical definition of jurisdiction and accepted jurisdiction over a specific place (the detention facility in which the applicants were kept), irrespective of control over the surrounding territory or over a wider geographical area.[443]

If, in light of *Issa* and *Al-Saadoon* temporary control over an (extremely) delimited area on land suffices to trigger human rights obligations, why should a

---

[438] *Id.* at para. 52.

[439] European Court of Human Rights, *Cyprus v. Turkey* (application no. 25781/94), Judgment, May 10, 2001, para. 77.

[440] European Court of Human Rights, *Ilaşcu v. Moldova and Russia* (application no. 48787/99), Judgment, July 8, 2004, para. 394.

[441] European Court of Human Rights, *Cyprus v. Turkey* (application no. 25781/94), Judgment, May 10, 2001, para. 78. The Court justified the effective control argument by saying that "any other finding would result in a regrettable vacuum in the system of human-rights protection in the territory in question by removing from individuals there the benefit of the Convention's fundamental safeguards and their right to call a High Contracting Party to account for violation of their rights in proceedings before the Court."

[442] European Court of Human Rights, *Issa et al. v. Turkey* (application no. 31821/96), Judgment, Nov. 16, 2004, para. 74.

[443] European Court of Human Rights, *Al-Saadoon and Mufdhi v. United Kingdom* (application no. 61498/08), Decision, June 30, 2009, para. 89.

difference be made between geographically limited control exercised over a portion of land and a portion of the sea? Admittedly, *Al-Saadoon* concerned specific premises, in a fixed location, whereas ships engaged in counter-piracy operations at sea are moving, thereby constantly altering their nautical position and operational radius. However, this does not necessarily challenge the assumption that they are capable of exercising a certain degree of factual control, sufficient to trigger human rights obligations within their (geographically changing) operational radius.

It seems that the *Öcalan*,[444] *Issa*, and *Al-Saadoon* decisions have rightly abandoned the unduly rigid *éspace juridique européen* restriction, which the European Court of Human Rights had introduced in *Banković*. Nevertheless, the flexibility and instability of the area control exercised by a military ship arguably resembles the factual *Banković* scenario.[445] The most persuasive interpretation of the *Banković* decision is that the European Court of Human Rights simply concluded that NATO airplanes did not have effective area control over territory of the Federal Republic of Yugoslavia. Against this background, the area control of military or government ships beyond their railing may not suffice to satisfy the criterion of effective overall control, in the sense of the European Court of Human Rights' jurisprudence. Still, *Banković* concerned the question whether effective overall control over territory could be exercised from airspace, whereas in the case at hand the question is raised whether a ship at sea can exercise effective area control over surrounding sea space. Overflight by a military plane certainly amounts to a less stable form of control than the presence of a battleship, in that battleships can resort to a far larger panoply of enforcement measures than are available to an airplane. A military ship could, for instance, dispatch smaller vessels or a helicopter to carry out specific tasks in the proximity of the "mother military ship," including the actual arrest of individual persons, a task that could never have been effected from a fighter plane, as in the *Banković* scenario.

Finally, shifting the perspective from the operational radius of an individual military ship, when considered cumulatively and viewed as a whole, the various vessels involved in the multinational enforcement operations in the Gulf of Aden could arguably be said to have established a net of effective overall control over their joint operational area. In fact, the Internationally Recommended Transit Corridor, which has been set up so as to ensure safe and unimpeded passage in the Gulf of Aden,[446] serves as a prime example, demonstrating that it is possible to cast a net of effective overall control through the employment of various vessels. Nevertheless, precise criteria determining effective area control at sea have not yet been estab-

---

[444] European Court of Human Rights, *Öcalan v. Turkey*, (no. 46221/99), Grand Chamber Judgment, 12 May 2005.

[445] European Court of Human Rights, *Banković v. Belgium et al.* (application no. 52207/99), Grand Chamber Decision, Dec. 12, 2001, para. 73.

[446] On the Internationally Recommended Transit Corridor, see p. 17 *et seq.*

lished. In other words, there is currently no jurisprudence confirming the application of the "control over territory"-criterion as an "area control"-criterion in constellations at sea.

bb) Effective Control Over Individuals: Individual Persons Within the Reach of a Military Ship

Alternatively, the jurisdictional link triggering the extraterritorial applicability of human rights protection during the interception-phase could potentially also be established via the "control over persons"-criterion. When exactly a person is under a State's authority and control, through its agents operating abroad, is not clearly established.[447] While "control over a person" is undisputed in cases of abduction, detention or ill-treatment, the use of firearms against an individual does not presuppose the same degree of control over a person, at least in the physical sense of the term.[448] It is precisely this combination of factors, which is at issue when it comes to the use of firearms and, generally, the use of potentially lethal force, by law enforcement officials in the pursuit of and during the boarding of an alleged pirate vessel.

The pursuit of a suspected pirate vessel only amounts to an initial step towards the gradual establishment of full control over the vessel and its crew. Certainly, at some point during the establishment of control, human rights protections become applicable, at the latest when the arrest of alleged pirates has actually been effected. At this point effective physical control over individual persons will undoubtedly have been fully established. The question at issue here is what the earliest point in time is, prior to the physical apprehension of a person, where "effective control over a person" can be said to have been established. It is helpful, in seeking to answer this question, to analyze enforcement operations at sea in two distinct phases: The first phase is ship-to-ship operations, during which a military ship pursues a suspected pirate ship and ultimately stops it (1). The second phase comprises the stopping and boarding of suspected pirate ships, as well as the searching and arresting of suspected persons on board (2).

---

[447] *Id.* at para. 71. The Inter-American Commission had to decide on killings of persons without their being "in the hands of the authorities." It condemned the assassination of Orlando Letelier in Washington and Carlos Prats in Buenos Aires by Chilean agents as a violation of the right to life: Inter-American Commission on Human Rights, *Case of Orlando Letelier del Solar*, Report on the Situation of Human Rights in Chile, OEA/Ser.L/V/II.66, Doc.17 (Sept. 9, 1985), paras. 81–91. Similarly, it condemned attacks of Surinamese citizens by Surinamese State agents in the Netherlands: Inter-American Commission on Human Rights, Second Report on the Human Rights Situation in Suriname, OEA/Ser.L/V/II.66, doc.21 rev. 1 (Oct. 2, 1985). See also United Kingdom, Sedley LJ, Court of Appeal, *R (Al-Skeini) v. Secretary of State for Defense* [2005] EWCA Civ 1609, para. 197.

[448] But see United Kingdom, Court of Appeal, *R (Al-Skeini) v. Secretary of State for Defence* [2005] EWCA Civ 1609, paras. 108 and 124.

(1) Ship-to-Ship Operations Prior to Boarding a Pirate Ship

During ship-to-ship operations, when an alleged pirate vessel is pursued and, ultimately, brought to a halt, the military ship exerts only a limited degree of control over the pursued vessel and its crew. The distance between the vessels involved may be considerable and while the military or government vessel will aim to establish full control over the alleged pirate vessel, the latter will most likely try to evade such control. The common perception seems to be that this particular phase is exclusively governed by general considerations of proportionality and necessity, as they have been established in sporadic international jurisprudence pertaining to enforcement activities at sea.[449] International jurisprudence has, however, occasionally interpreted the notion of control over persons broadly enough to also establish a jurisdictional link triggering the extraterritorial application of human rights law in situations akin to such ship-to-ship operations.

In the *Armando Alejandre v. Cuba* case, where the shooting down of two civilian aircraft by air-to-air missiles fired by military aircraft belonging to the Cuban Air force in international airspace was at issue, and where the relevant jurisdictional link (all of the deceased passengers of the civilian aircraft except one were United States citizens) could only have been established through the actual firing of the missiles, the Inter-American Commission for Human Rights found that the civilian pilots of the attacked plane were under Cuba's jurisdiction.[450]

Similarly, it seems that the European Court of Human Rights in its more recent case law has started to interpret the "control over persons"-criterion somewhat more broadly. In *Andreou,* the European Court of Human Rights stated that "[t]he opening of fire on the crowd from close range (...) was such that the applicant must be regarded as within [the] jurisdiction of Turkey."[451] Here the Court exclusively relied on the opening of fire without any consideration of whether control in the physical sense of the term had previously been established to any degree over the person concerned.[452] Similarly, in *Women on Waves*, the European Court of Human Rights endorsed a rather lenient understanding of the "control over persons"-criterion. In this case, the Court regarded the European Convention on Human Rights applicable simply on the basis that a Portuguese military vessel intercepted a Dutch vessel (the *Borndiep*) on the high seas off Portugal's coast (seemingly

---

[449] With regard to general confines applicable to maritime interception operations, see p. 96 *et seq.*

[450] Inter-Amercian Commission on Human Rights, *Armando Alejandre et al. v. Cuba*, Case 11.589, Report No. 86/99, OAS/Ser.L/V/II.104 Doc. 10 (1999), para. 25.

[451] European Court of Human Rights, *Andreou v. Turkey* (application no. 45653/99), Decision, June 3, 2008, para. A.3.c.

[452] *Id.*; the Court, however, included a *caveat* stating that "[u]nlike the applicants in the *Banković and Others* case she was accordingly within territory covered by the Convention," in order to maintain coherence with this judgment.

without boarding), so as to enforce a prohibition from entering Portugal's territorial waters that had previously been issued to the *Borndiep*.[453]

In light of these decisions, one could also assume "control over crew members" of a pursued pirate vessel even before the vessel has been stopped and boarded. This even more so given that in the context of counter-piracy operations off Somalia's coast, unlike for example in the Cuban case cited above, the establishment of full control over persons will be the very objective of any interception operation from the outset. Thus, it is arguable that fundamental human rights protections, particularly the right to life, should be accorded from the beginning of the operation. Otherwise, the same law enforcement operation would be guided by fundamentally different legal standards: Human rights law, including the fundamental right to life, would not apply up to the capture of a person, at which point a panoply of human rights obligations would be triggered. Understanding the notion of control over persons to encompass situations beyond immediate physical control over an individual person would also be in line with the teleological interpretation of Article 1 of the European Convention of Human Rights provided by the European Court of Human Rights in *Issa*, stating that the provision cannot be interpreted so as to allow a State party to perpetrate violations of the Convention abroad, which it could not perpetrate on its own territory.[454] But given that the cases cited here have thus far remained rather insular, it must be admitted that the only thing that may be said with certainty at the present juncture is that the extraterritorial application of human rights protections to ship-to-ship interception operations is far from established.

(2) Boarding and Searching a Pirate Ship and Arresting Persons on Board

The control over persons or control over vessels criterion is also at issue as far as the boarding of an alleged pirate vessel is concerned. Is control over crew members of such a vessel established as soon as the ship is boarded? As stated above, once a person has been apprehended, the physical control triggering the extraterritorial applicability of human rights protections is unquestionably established. Whether the arresting State subjectively perceives the arrest as a formal pre-trial or administrative detention or more colloquially as a temporary "holding" of the person has no impact on its jurisdiction over the person so held. Thus, in the German version of Council Joint Action Operation Atalanta – pertaining to enforcement operations against acts of piracy – the word "arrest" ("Festnahme") was officially changed to

---

[453] European Court of Human Rights, *Women on Waves et al. v. Portugal* (application no. 31276/05), Decision, Feb. 3, 2009, para. 23 (available only in French).

[454] European Court of Human Rights, *Issa et al. v. Turkey* (application no. 31821/96), Judgment, Nov. 16, 2004, para. 96.

"holding" ("Festhalten")[455] without any legal consequences. The "control over persons"-criterion hinges on an exclusively factual assessment, not on terminology.

Again, the more difficult question is whether during the boarding of an alleged pirate ship the applicability of human rights protections may be assumed from when boarding commences, prior to the actual arrest of crew members. Of course, if it were accepted (as has been alluded to above) that human rights law is already applicable during the entire interception-phase, *a fortiori*, human rights law would apply to the boarding and post-boarding phase. Irrespective of whether or not this is the case, in the specific context of the boarding of another vessel by law enforcement personnel a somewhat broadened interpretation of the notion "control over a person," going beyond requiring fully established physical control over individual persons, finds support in one of the few cases that specifically dealt with the application of the European Convention of Human Rights to a law enforcement operation on the high seas.

In *Medvedyev and others v. France* the European Court of Human Rights assumed that, from the point of interception of the *Winner* (the vessel that was intercepted) on June 13, 2002, until its arrival in Brest harbor on June 26, 2002, the vessel and its crew had been under the control of French military forces and, therefore, were within the jurisdiction of France for the purposes of Article 1 of the European Convention of Human Rights.[456] *Nota bene*, the Court relied on the "control over persons"-criterion but also invoked the jurisdiction based on control over the vessel (the *Winner*) as a whole.[457] In relation to the control over the vessel, the European Court of Human Rights did not make clear whether it relied on effective control over persons or effective control over territory.[458]

In *Al-Saadoon*, in which the Court asserted the United Kingdom's jurisdiction over a detention facility in Iraq, the European Court of Human Rights seemed to rely on the concept of control over territory. Irrespective of the specific control criterion, there is a notable parallel between the assumption of effective control over a vessel at sea and control over specific premises on land. It would appear that

---

[455] Berichtigung der Gemeinsamen Aktion 2008/851/GASP des Rates vom 10. November 2008 über die Militäroperation der Europäischen Union als Beitrag zur Abschreckung, Verhütung und Bekämpfung von seeräuberischen Handlungen und bewaffneten Raubüberfällen vor der Küste Somalias, 2009 Abl. (L 10) 35 (EU); this document is only available in German and was only published in the German Version of the Official Journal of the European Union. It is reprinted on p. 274 *et seq.* of this book (Appendix).

[456] European Court of Human Rights, *Medvedyev et al. v. France* (application no. 3394/03), Judgment, July 10, 2008, para. 50; see also *Rigopoulos v. Spain* (application no. 37388/97), Decision, Jan. 12, 1999.

[457] It seems, however, to follow from the context in European Court of Human Rights, *Medvedyev et al. v. France* (application no. 3394/03), Judgment, July 10, 2008, that the Court only considered the situation post-boarding by French forces.

[458] European Court of Human Rights, *Medvedyev et al. v. France* (application no. 3394/03), Judgment, July 10, 2008, para. 50.

once the crew has surrendered to the boarding law enforcement official, the re-quirement of (total) control in the sense of *Al-Saadoon* has been met.[459] But this is not the case during the actual boarding and up until the crew has surrendered and the entire ship has been secured.

However, an extended interpretation of the "control over persons"-criterion to cover the boarding of another vessel by law enforcement officials, could arguably be maintained in the specific context of operations at sea. Once a ship is boarded by law enforcement officials, while there may still be resistance defying total phys-ical control, suspects have no possibility of fleeing the ship. It is, therefore, argu-able that once the suspects are in an inescapable situation, they are already under effective control of the law enforcement officials on board. This line of argument finds support in the more recent jurisprudence of the European Court of Human Rights, which endorses a broader understanding of the "control over persons"-criterion, not necessarily requiring that a person has fallen into the hands of law enforcement officials in the physical sense.[460] Specifically, in *Isaak et al. v. Turkey* the Court assumed jurisdiction over a situation, which arose prior to the person's actual arrest, from which the person "could hardly have escaped the control of the security forces."[461]

c) Relevance of Somalia's Consent to Counter-Piracy Operations for the Applicability of Human Rights Law

In *Banković*, the European Court of Human Rights recognized the possibility of establishing the exercise of extra-territorial jurisdiction, irrespective of any territor-ial control, including when a State "through the consent, invitation or acquiescence of the Government of that territory, exercises all or some of the public powers normally to be exercised by that Government."[462] On this basis, States engaged in law enforcement operations to repress piracy within Somalia's territorial waters

---

[459] European Court of Human Rights, *Al-Saadoon and Mufdhi v. United Kingdom* (ap-plication no. 61498/08), Decision, June 30, 2009, para. 88 (emphasis added). In conclusion on the issue of jurisdiction, the Court considered that "given the *total and exclusive de facto*, and subsequently also *de jure*, control exercised by the United Kingdom authorities over the premises in question, the individuals detained there, including the applicants, were within the United Kingdom's jurisdiction." Surprisingly, the Court relied on the criteria of *de facto* and *de jure* control cumulatively and, what is more, it invoked the totality and exclusiveness of the *de facto* control.

[460] European Court of Human Rights, *Pad et al. v. Turkey* (application no. 60167/00), Decision, July 28, 2007, para. 54; *Andreou v. Turkey*, (application no. 45653/99), Decision, June 3, 2008, para. A.3.c.; *Medvedyev et al. v. France* (application no. 3394/03), Judg-ment, July 10, 2008, para. 50.

[461] European Court of Human Rights, *Isaak et al. v. Turkey* (application no. 44587/98), Judgment, June 24, 2008, para. 115.

[462] European Court of Human Rights, *Banković v. Belgium et al.* (application no. 52207/99), Grand Chamber Decision, Dec. 12, 2001, para. 71.

and on its mainland – an exercise of public powers that the Somali Transitional Federal Government is not able to effectively carry out but to which it has repeatedly consented[463] – could be said to exercise jurisdiction for the purposes of the extraterritorial application of human rights law. Arguably, this reasoning could be applied to any Somali vessel, irrespective of whether it is encountered in Somali territorial waters or on the high seas.

In fact, one of the few cases in which the European Court of Human Rights seems to have relied exclusively on the consent of another government in order to establish jurisdiction triggering the extraterritorial applicability of human rights law is similar to the situation under consideration here. In *Xhavara et al. v. Italy and Albania* an Italian military ship had carried out a risky maneuver against an Albanian ship 35 miles off the Italian coast. The Albanian vessel capsized and 58 people died in the incident. The European Court of Human Rights assumed jurisdiction in the sense of Article 1 of the European Convention of Human Rights, relying on an Italian-Albanian agreement, which authorized Italy to control Albanian vessels and generally vessels carrying Albanian nationals.[464]

However, in subsequent pronouncements, including most recently in *Al-Saadoon*,[465] the European Court of Human Rights has rarely relied exclusively on the consent of a government, independent of the question of whether control over territory or over a person had been established by the acting State. Thus, it is doubtful that the extraterritorial applicability of human rights law in relation to operations involving Somali ships and nationals could be established exclusively on the basis of Somalia's consent.

d) A Hypothetical: Towards a Coherent Human Rights Protection in Multinational Law Enforcement Operations

For the purpose of achieving legal certainty and to avoid the various protective gaps that derive from the piecemeal approach which currently exists towards the extraterritorial application of human rights, it would be desirable to identify the human rights law applicable in the event of an extraterritorial multinational law enforcement operation more coherently than is presently the case. The current case-

---

[463] S.C. Res. 1816, preambular para. 11; S.C. Res. 1846, para. 11; S.C. Res. 1851, para. 10; S.C. Res. 1897, preambular para. 6.

[464] European Court of Human Rights, *Xhavara et al. v. Italy and Albania* (application no. 39473/98), Decision, Jan. 11, 2001.

[465] European Court of Human Rights, *Al-Saadoon and Mufdhi v. United Kingdom* (application no. 61498/08), Decision June 30, 2009, paras. 19 and 87; Art. 1 of the Iraqi Council of Ministers Resolution 439/2008 (Dec. 16, 2008) states: "The forces of the United Kingdom and Northern Ireland are permitted to stay in Iraq to complete the tasks they are given." Of course, it must be noted that during the first months of the applicants' detention, the United Kingdom was still an occupying power in Iraq.

by-case approach – and the resulting uncertainty – is particularly incongruous in the context of a specific law enforcement operation, vested with a range of enforcement competencies and dispatched with the specific task of repressing and eradicating a criminal phenomenon such as piracy and armed robbery at sea. The authorization of "all necessary means" in the quest to eradicate piracy and armed robbery at sea should automatically be accompanied by the unequivocal and full application of all human rights protections that are relevant in the context of law enforcement operations (notably Articles 6, 7, 9 and 10 of the International Covenant on Civil and Political Rights), which should not be conditional on an unpredictable case-by-case assessment of whether the required degree of control over a territory or a person triggered the extraterritorial application of human rights law.

It has convincingly been shown that human rights jurisdictional clauses denote a sort of factual control and are not to be equated with the general notion of jurisdiction under public international law.[466] Indeed, if a State has effective control, human rights law will be applicable extraterritorially, irrespective of whether or not it also had enforcement jurisdiction within the meaning of general public international law. However, without challenging this assumption, is it inconceivable that, where specific enforcement powers are granted – and indeed acted upon through Security Council Resolutions – human rights protections should be applicable, irrespective of whether the required degree of effective control can be ascertained? From the perspective of a coherent and comprehensive human rights protection, it would seem desirable to maintain that any "pirate" off Somalia's coast against whom law enforcement measures are carried out, falls within the jurisdiction (in the sense of human rights jurisdictional clauses) of the State carrying out the operation.

A coherent application of human rights to extraterritorial law enforcement seems even more important given that multinational law enforcement operations, vested with specific mandates and elaborate enforcement competencies, are likely to increase in the future. The list of potential security threats of global reach is long. For example, in December 2009, the President of the Security Council issued a landmark statement in relation to international drug trafficking, underlining that illegal drug trade is increasingly a problem that requires an internationally coordinated response.[467] Concomitantly, the legitimacy and rule-of-law adherence of international law enforcement operations, which also affect their long-term effectiveness and credibility, will increasingly come under review. In this regard, the somewhat patchy human rights application brought about by an approach that is

---

[466] *Milanovic*, From Compromise to Principle: Clarifying the Concept of State Jurisdiction in Human Rights Treaties, Human Rights Law Review (8) 2008, 417 *et seq.*; *Thienel*, The Georgian Conflict, Racial Discrimination and the ICJ: The Order on Provisional Measures of 15 October 2008, Human Rights Law Review 9 (2009).

[467] United Nations, Security Council, Statement by the President of the Security Council, U.N. Doc. S/PRST/2009/32 (Dec. 8, 2009).

exclusively focused on effective control, ascertained by the European Court of Human Rights or the Inter-American Commission of Human Rights on a case-by-case basis, raises concerns. However, there is currently hardly any jurisprudential indication that would allow the conclusion that the mere fact that enforcement competencies are authorized and executed – irrespective of whether the relevant degree of factual control has been met – could suffice for the extraterritorial application of human rights law. Still, the *status quo*, where all that can be said with certainty is that apprehended piracy suspects and alleged armed robbers at sea benefit from human rights, whereas the application of human rights during the interception-phase and in the phase immediate prior to a suspects' capture (where the risk to life is typically the greatest) hinges on the specific circumstances, is hardly satisfying either. A middle-way out is a more lenient handling of the control criteria, as has arguably already been insinuated in a slowly growing list of judicial pronouncements by the European Court of Human Rights.

2. Multiple Layers in United Nations-Mandated (Multinational) Operations: The Attributability of Human Rights Violations

Having described the considerable complexities involved in the mere identification of applicable human rights protections and general safeguards applicable to maritime interception operations against the relatively broad and somewhat blurry range of enforcement powers granted to counter-piracy operations, yet another set of intricacies deserves mention: The question of attributability of human rights violations committed in the context of United Nations-mandated (multinational) counter-piracy operations in the Gulf of Aden.

a) The "Ultimate Authority and Control"-Test

In its much criticized *Behrami and Saramati* decision, the European Court of Human Rights held that actions of State armed forces acting pursuant to Chapter VII United Nations Charter based Security Council authorizations are attributable, not to the States themselves, but exclusively to the United Nations, if the latter has "ultimate authority and control."[468] The Strasbourg Court has continued to

---

[468] European Court of Human Rights, *Behrami v. France* (application no. 71412/01), *Saramati v. France*, Germany and Norway (application no. 78166/01) Joint Decision May 31, 2007, paras. 132–141. For a critique, see, for example, *Larsen,* Attribution of Conduct of Peace Operations: The "Ultimate Authority and Control" Test, EJIL 19 (2008), 509–531; *Milanovic/Papic,* As Bad As It Gets: The European Court of Human Rights Behrami and Saramati Decision and General International Law, ICLQ (58) 2009, 267–296; *Krieger,* A Credibility Gap: The Behrami and Saramati Decision of the European Court of Human Rights, Journal of International Peacekeeping 13 (2009), 159–180; *Bodeau-Livinec/Buzzini/ Villalpando,* Behrami & Bekir Behrami v. France; Ruzhdi Saramati v. France, Germany & Norway, AJIL 102 (2008), 325; *Bell,* Reassessing Multiple Attribution: The International

follow this reasoning also in *Kasumaj v. Greece*[469] and *Gajic v. Germany*,[470] where it declared that KFOR actions were "in principle attributable to the UN."[471] In *Berić v. Bosnia and Herzegovina*, the Court held that the impugned action by the high representative in Bosnia and Herzegovina was "in principle attributable to the UN."[472] In July 2008, in the case *Mothers of Srebrenica et al. v. State of the Netherlands and UN*, the District Court of The Hague also relied on *Behrami/Saramati*, holding that, based on the importance of non-interference with operations based on Chapter VII of the United Nations Charter as identified in *Behrami/Saramati*, "the contributing States [could] not be held liable before the Court for acts and omissions of their troops in missions covered by the UN Security Council resolutions and which occurred prior to or in the course of such missions."[473]

(European) States involved in counter-piracy operations off Somalia's coast could potentially invoke this reasoning to defer accountability for possible human rights violations to the United Nations, NATO or the European Union as the ostensible holders of "ultimate authority and control" over the counter-piracy operations in the Gulf of Aden. For example, in the United Kingdom's House of Lords *Al-Jedda* case, the facts of which were rather identical to those in *Saramati*, the United Kingdom argued that its actions in Iraq were attributable exclusively to the United Nations.[474]

In the joined *Behrami and Saramati* cases, the European Court of Human Rights analyzed whether certain acts and omissions of the NATO Kosovo Force (KFOR) and the United Nations Mission in Kosovo (UNMIK) constituted violations of the respective troop contributing nations' obligations under the European Convention

---

Law Commission and The Behrami and Saramati Decision, New York University Journal of International Law and Politics, 42 (2010), 501–548; *Van der Toorn*, Attribution of Conduct by State Armed Forces Participating in UN-Authorised Operations: The Impact of *Behrami* and *Al-Jedda*, Australian International Law Journal 15 (2008), 9–27.

[469] European Court of Human Rights, *Kasumaj v. Greece* (application no. 6974/05), Decision, July 5, 2007.

[470] European Court of Human Rights, *Gajic v. Germany* (application no. 31446/02), Decision, Aug. 28, 2007.

[471] See also European Court of Human Rights, *Stephens v. Cyprus, Turkey and the United Nations* (application no. 45267/06), Decision Dec. 11, 2008.

[472] European Court of Human Rights, *Berić v. Bosnia and Herzegovina* (application nos. 36357/04, 36360/04, 38346/04, 41705/04, 44790/04, 45578/04, 45579/04, 45580/04, 91/05, 97/05, 100/05, 101/05, 1121/05, 1123/05, 1125/05, 1129/05, 1132/05, 1133/05, 1169/05, 1172/05, 1175/05, 1177/05, 1180/05, 1185/05, 20793/05 and 25496/05), Decision, Oct. 16, 2007, para. 28 [hereinafter: European Court of Human Rights, *Berić v. Bosnia and Herzegovina*, Decision, Oct. 16, 2007].

[473] District Court of The Hague, *Mothers of Srebrenica v. Netherlands and United Nations*, July 10, 2008, De Rechtspraak BD6795.

[474] The House of Lords, however, avoided the Strasbourg Court's "ultimate authority and control" test; *Al-Jedda v. Secretary of State for Defence* [2007] UKHL 58, paras. 3 and 26–39; *Milanovic/Papic*, As Bad As It Gets: The European Court of Human Rights Behrami and Saramati Decision and General International Law, ICLQ (58) 2009, 289–293.

on Human Rights. The *Behrami* case concerned the alleged failure of French KFOR troops to mark and defuse undetonated cluster bomb units that subsequently exploded, thereby killing one child and severely injuring another.[475] The *Saramati* case concerned the arrest of a Kosovar (Mr. Saramati) by UNMIK police in April 2001 on suspicion of attempted murder and the repeated extension of the applicant's detention, who claimed that he had been subject to extrajudicial detention without access to a court.[476]

The European Court of Human Rights only briefly touched upon the issue of the European Convention on Human Rights's extraterritorial applicability, stating that Kosovo, where the incidents had taken place, "was under the effective control of the international presences which exercised the public powers normally exercised by the Government of the FRY."[477] Primarily, the Court focused on whether the impugned acts, i.e. the alleged failure to clear up the cluster bomb remnants in the *Behrami* case and the extended detention in the *Saramati* case, were attributable to the United Nations, NATO or the respective troop-contributing countries. It concluded that the acts were to be exclusively attributed to the United Nations. The Court invoked Draft Article 5 (now Draft Article 6) of the International Law Commission's Draft Articles on Responsibility of International Organizations, which reads:

Draft Art. 6 of the Draft Articles on Responsibility of International Organizations – Conduct of Organs or Agents Placed at the Disposal of an International Organization by a State or Another International Organization

The conduct of an organ of a State or an organ or agent of an international organization that is placed at the disposal of another international organization shall be considered under international law an act of the latter organization if the organization exercises *effective control* over that conduct.[478]

In spite of the explicit reference to "effective control" in the International Law Commission's Draft Article 6, the Strasbourg Court relied on "ultimate authority and control" as the relevant criterion determinative of the issue of attribution in a multinational, United Nations-mandated mission. Thus, it may be argued that the Court simply defined "effective control" as "ultimate authority and control."[479] But

---

[475] European Court of Human Rights, *Behrami v. France* (application no. 71412/01), *Saramati v. France*, Germany and Norway (application no. 78166/01), Joint Decision, May 31, 2007, paras. 5–7.

[476] *Saramati v. France*, Germany and Norway (application no. 78166/01), Joint Decision, May 31, 2007, paras. 8–17 and 62.

[477] *Id.* at para. 70.

[478] Emphasis added. The provision is reprinted in the United Nations, International Law Commission, Report of the International Law Commission on the Work of its 61st Session, 2009, p. 21.

[479] *Bell*, Reassessing Multiple Attribution: The International Law Commission and The Behrami and Saramati Decision, New York University Journal of International Law and Politics, 42 (2010), 530.

the Court never said explicitly that it is applying the Draft Article, which leaves it unclear whether it thought this rule to be applicable.[480]

The Court devised its "ultimate authority and control" test by linking the question of attribution to the mandates granted to UNMIK and KFOR and the delegation of Security Council powers. The Strasbourg Court affirmed "ultimate authority and control" of the United Nations, principally because UNMIK acted as a subsidiary organ of the United Nation's Security Council created under Chapter VII of the United Nations Charter and because KFOR exercised powers that had been lawfully delegated by the Security Council, namely by Resolution 1244.[481] Whereas the Court's finding with regard to UNMIK is in line with the United Nation's general position to assume responsibility for conduct during operations with the status of subsidiary organs,[482] the Court's reasoning regarding KFOR is more controversial.[483]

The Court's interpretation of Resolution 1244 was that the Security Council retained ultimate authority and control over KFOR, and that operation command was only delegated to NATO.[484] Specifically, the Court invoked five factors in its interpretation of Resolution 1244 to support the retention of "ultimate authority and control" by the Security Council: "In the first place, and as noted above, Chapter VII

---

[480] *Milanovic/Papic*, As Bad As It Gets: The European Court of Human Rights Behrami and Saramati Decision and General International Law, ICLQ (58) 2009, 283.

[481] The Court concluded that "KFOR was exercising lawfully delegated Chapter VII powers of the UNSC so that the impugned action was, in principle, attributable to the UN;" European Court of Human Rights, *Behrami v. France* (application no. 71412/01), *Saramati v. France*, Germany and Norway (application no. 78166/01) Joint Decision May 31, 2007, para. 141.

[482] In these operations a Special Representative of the Secretary-General is appointed to act as a co-coordinator and to have overall authority during the operation. See, for example, United Nations, Security Council, S. C. Res. 1542, U.N. Doc. S/RES/1542 (April 30, 2004), para. 3, on the establishment of MINUSTAH, which *"[r]equests* the Secretary General to appoint a Special Representative in Haiti who will have overall authority on the ground." Conversely, in S.C. Res. 1244, U.N. Doc. S/RES/1244 (June 10, 1999), para. 6, it was expressly stated that KFOR would not be controlled by a Special Representative. The International Law Commission before provisionally adopting Draft Article 6 of the Draft Articles on the Responsibility of International Organizations, considered the views of the United Nations as expressed by the United Nations Secretariat in a letter to the International Law Commission: "The principle of attribution of the conduct of a peacekeeping force to the United Nations is premised on the assumption that the operation in question is conducted under United Nations command and control, and thus has the legal status of a United Nations subsidiary organ;" International Law Commission, Responsibility of International Organizations: Comments and Observations Received from International Organizations, U.N. Doc. A/CN.4/545 (June 25, 2004).

[483] *Larsen*, Attribution of Conduct of Peace Operations: The "Ultimate Authority and Control" Test, EJIL 19 (2008), 520.

[484] European Court of Human Rights, *Behrami v. France* (application no. 71412/01), *Saramati v. France*, Germany and Norway (application no. 78166/01), Joint Decision, May 31, 2007, paras. 133 and 135.

allowed the UNSC to delegate to 'Member States and relevant international organisations'. Secondly, the relevant power was a delegable power. Thirdly, that delegation was neither presumed nor implicit, but rather prior and explicit in the Resolution itself. Fourthly, the Resolution put sufficiently defined limits on the delegation by fixing the mandate with adequate precision as it set out the objectives to be attained, the roles and responsibilities accorded as well as the means to be employed. The broad nature of certain provisions (...) could not be eliminated altogether given the constituent nature of such an instrument whose role was to fix broad objectives and goals and not to describe or interfere with the detail of operational implementation and choices. Fifthly, the leadership of the military presence was required by the Resolution to report to the UNSC so as to allow the UNSC to exercise its overall authority and control (consistently, the UNSC was to remain actively seized of the matter, Article 21 of the Resolution). The requirement that the SG present the KFOR report to the UNSC was an added safeguard since the SG is considered to represent the general interests of the UN."[485]

From this the Court inferred that "[a]ccordingly, UNSC Resolution 1244 gave rise to the following chain of command in the present cases. The UNSC was to retain ultimate authority and control over the security mission and it delegated to NATO (in consultation with non-NATO member states) the power to establish, as well as the operational command of, the international presence, KFOR."[486]

Thus, in essence, the Strasbourg Court found a Chapter VII of the United Nations Charter mandate vesting "ultimate authority and control" in the Security Council, despite the lack of any direct United Nations control over tactical operations on the ground.[487] The generalization of *Behrami/Saramati* may well be that a valid delegation of powers from the Security Council by virtue of Chapter VII means that the actions of the soldiers involved are attributable exclusively to the United Nations and not to the soldiers' State of nationality.[488] Evidently, this reasoning could likewise be invoked with regard to the current counter-piracy operations in the Gulf of Aden.

---

[485] *Saramati v. France*, Germany and Norway (application no. 78166/01), Joint Decision, May 31, 2007, para. 134.

[486] *Id.* at para. 135.

[487] *Guilfoyle*, Counter-Piracy Law Enforcement and Human Rights, ICLQ 59 (2010), 156.

[488] In *Berić v. Bosnia and Herzegovina* the ECtHR held: "Given that the UNSC had, as required, established a 'threat to international peace and security' within the meaning of Article 39 of the UN Charter, it had the power to authorise an international civil administration in Bosnia and Herzegovina and to delegate the implementation of that measure to specific member States, provided that it retained effective overall control;" European Court of Human Rights, *Berić v. Bosnia and Herzegovina*, Decision, Oct. 16, 2007, para. 27.

The five factors on which the Court relied in *Behrami/Saramati* in order to ascertain "ultimate authority and control" of the Security Council are rather abstract.[489] First of all, the Court's analysis involved assessing whether Chapter VII powers had been "lawfully delegated."[490] The counter-piracy Security Council Resolutions 1846 and 1851, like Security Council Resolution 1244 (deployment of international civil and security presences in Kosovo) and Resolution 1546 (the situation between Iraq and Kuwait; *Al-Jedda*), authorize the use of "all necessary means."[491] In the case of the counter-piracy operations it could thus well be argued that certain enforcement powers have been lawfully delegated by virtue of Resolutions 1846, 1851 and 1897.

Moreover, in determining "ultimate authority and control," the Strasbourg Court relied on factors relating to the supervision over the exercise of delegated powers, namely, that "the leadership of the military presence was required by the Resolution [1244] to report to the UNSC so as to allow the UNSC to exercise its overall authority and control (consistently, the UNSC was to remain actively seized of the matter, Article 21 of the Resolution)"[492] and held that "[t]he requirement that the SG present the KFOR report to the UNSC was an added safeguard since the SG is considered to represent the general interests of the UN."[493]

The reporting requirement in Resolutions 1846, 1851 and 1897 is less detailed than the reporting obligation in Resolution 1244. Resolution 1846 only requires the Secretary-General to present a general report to the Security Council on ways to ensure the long-term security of international navigation off the coast of Somalia, Resolution 1851 merely recalls this obligation and only Resolution 1897 entails somewhat more specific reporting requirements. According to Resolution 1897 States are required "to inform the Security Council and the Secretary-General within nine months of the progress of actions undertaken in the exercise of the authorizations provided"[494] and "[r]equests the Secretary-General to report to the Security

---

[489] *Id.* at paras. 27 and 28.

[490] European Court of Human Rights, *Behrami v. France* (application no. 71412/01), *Saramati v. France*, Germany and Norway (application no. 78166/01), Joint Decision, May 31, 2007, para. 141.

[491] With regard to the question whether S.C. Res. 1244 indeed granted a mandate to KFOR to issue detention orders, see *Milanovic/Papic*, As Bad As It Gets: The European Court of Human Rights Behrami and Saramati Decision and General International Law, ICLQ (58) 2009, 274 and 278.

[492] European Court of Human Rights, *Behrami v. France* (application no. 71412/01), *Saramati v. France*, Germany and Norway (application no. 78166/01), Joint Decision, May 31, 2007, para. 134.

[493] *Id.* at para. 134.

[494] S.C. Res. 1897, para. 16, "further requests all States contributing through the CGPCS to the fight against piracy off the coast of Somalia, including Somalia and other States in the region, to report by the same deadline on their efforts to establish jurisdiction and cooperation in the investigation and prosecution of piracy."

Council within 11 months of the adoption of this resolution on the implementation of this resolution and on the situation with respect to piracy and armed robbery at sea off the coast of Somalia."[495] Conversely, Resolution 1244 "[r]equests the Secretary-General to report to the Council at regular intervals on the implementation of this resolution, including reports from the leaderships of the international civil and security presences, the first reports to be submitted within 30 days of the adoption of this resolution."[496]

It seems that the Court regarded the specific reporting requirements in Resolution 1244 as indicative of "ultimate authority and control" rather than as a *conditio sine qua non* "for the establishement of ultimate authority and control." Notably, in *Berić*, where the Court likewise relied on the "ultimate authority and control" test, it merely invoked that "the High Representative was required by the Resolution [1031] to report to the UNSC, so as to allow the UNSC to exercise its overall control."[497] In light of the reasoning of the Strasbourg Court, the reporting requirement stipulated in Resolution 1897, would arguably suffice to establish "ultimate authority and control." Although, it should be pointed out that a reporting requirement for 30 days-intervals (1244) comes closer to a control mechanism than a summary report that is to be submitted after nine or eleven months (1897). Moreover, against the assumption of "ultimate authority and control" in the present context, it may still be said that the States that have deployed naval assets to the Gulf of Aden retain substantial powers over their troops, for example, jurisdiction in disciplinary, civil and criminal matters. The same, however, was true with respect to the home States of KFOR troops.[498]

In *Behrami/Saramati*, the European Court of Human Rights avoided analyzing whether the conduct of KFOR troops was attributable to NATO.[499] In subsequent cases, the Court likewise only ever invoked the "ultimate authority and control" test in relation to the United Nations. In light of the Court's reliance on the delegation of Chapter VII powers it is doubtful whether the Court would be ready to apply and affirm the "ultimate authority and control" test in relation to other international organizations such as NATO or the European Union in the current counter-

---

[495] S.C. Res. 1897, para. 17.

[496] S.C. Res. 1244, para. 20.

[497] European Court of Human Rights, *Berić v. Bosnia and Herzegovina*, Decision, Oct. 16, 2007, para. 28. S.C. Res. 1031, U.N. Doc. S/RES/1031 (Dec. 15, 1995), para. 32: "Requests the Secretary-General to submit to the Council reports from the High Representative, in accordance with Annex 10 of the Peace Agreement and the conclusions of the London Conference, on the implementation of the Peace Agreement."

[498] UNMIK Regulation 2007/47, Sections 2(4) and 6(2), *available at* www.unmik online.org/regulations/2000/reg47-00.htm (last visited Aug. 30, 2010). See also *Milanovic/ Papic*, *Milanovic/Papic*, As Bad As It Gets: The European Court of Human Rights Behrami and Saramati Decision and General International Law, ICLQ (58) 2009, 286.

[499] *Stein*, in: Tomuschat (ed.), Kosovo and the International Community: A Legal Assessment, p. 181 *et seq.*; *Pellet, id.*, p. 193 *et seq.*

piracy context.[500] Indeed, it has been discussed whether the real *ratio decidendi* in *Behrami/Saramati* was to create an exception for operations authorized by UN Chapter VII, in light of their importance for the maintenance of peace and security within the international community.[501]

Hypothetically, indicators for "ultimate authority and control" of, for example, the European Union over Operation Atalanta, could arguably be derived from the EU Council Joint Action Operation Atalanta which speaks of a "European Union military operation."[502] Moreover, it was the European Council that signed the Status of Forces Agreements (SOFAs) with Somalia, Djibouti and the Republic of Seychelles,[503] thereby, at least formally, declaring the European Union party to the agreements rather than the individual European Union member States.[504] What is more, European Union Operation Atalanta is based on a unified European Union command structure that reaches down from the EU Political and Security Committee via an EU Operation Commander and then a Force Commander to theatre-level operations.[505] However, in the realm of the European Union's Common Foreign and Security Policy (CFSP) and given that Operation Atalanta is not exclusively made up of European Union member States (it currently also involves Croatia,

---

[500] The European Union has not yet become a party to the European Convention on Human Rights. The Lisbon Treaty provides for the European Union's accession to the European Convention on Human Rights; see Art. 6 of the Treaty of Lisbon, Amendments to the Treaty on European Union and to the Treaty Establishing the European Community, 2007/C 306/01, 2007 O.J. (C 306) 1–329 (EU).

[501] *Larsen,* Attribution of Conduct of Peace Operations: The "Ultimate Authority and Control" Test, EJIL 19 (2008), 528. In *Behrami/Saramati* the Court held that: "[The] Convention cannot be interpreted in a manner which would subject the acts and omissions of Contracting Parties which are covered by UNSC Resolutions and occur prior to or in the course of [UN Chapter VII] missions, to the scrutiny of the court. To do so would be to interfere with the fulfilment [sic] of the UN's key mission in this field, including, as argued by certain parties, with the effective conduct of its operations. It would also be tantamount to imposing conditions on the implementation of a UNSC Resolution which were not provided for in the text of the Resolution itself." European Court of Human Rights, *Behrami v. France* (application no. 71412/01), *Saramati v. France*, Germany and Norway (application no. 78166/01), Joint Decision, May 31, 2007, para. 149.

[502] See, for example, the title of the EU Council Joint Action Operation Atalanta as well as its preambular para. 9.

[503] European Union, Council Decision, EU-Somalia SOFA, *supra* note 103; Council Decision, EU-Djibouti SOFA, *supra* note 103; and Council Decision, EU-Seychelles SOFA, *supra* note 104.

[504] This resorts, for example, from the wording of Art. 1 EU-Djibouti SOFA, *supra* note 103, reading: "The Agreement between the European Union and the Republic of Djibouti (…)" and Art. 2 stating "The President of the Council is hereby authorised to designate the person(s) empowered to sign the Agreement in order to bind the European Union." Articles 1 and 2 of the Council Decision, EU-Somalia SOFA, *supra* note 103, and Articles 1 and 2 of the Council Decision, EU-Seychelles SOFA, *supra* note 104, are similarly worded.

[505] Arts. 3 and 6 of the EU Council Joint Action Operation Atalanta. See *Guilfoyle,* Counter-Piracy Law Enforcement and Human Rights, ICLQ 59 (2010), 158.

Montenegro, Norway and the Ukraine) the assumption of either the European Union's "ultimate authority and control" or even "effective control" over the operation would seem rather far-fetched. In practice, for example, in the context of transfers of captured piracy suspects and alleged armed robbers at sea, the assent of both the national authorities of the capturing warship and the European Union Operating Commander is required; the European Union Operation Commander cannot decide alone.[506]

The "ultimate authority and control" test, especially the European Court of Human Rights' conflation of the issue of the delegation of powers and the attribution of conduct, has been widely criticized in the academic literature. The test bears no resemblance to the "effective control" test envisaged in Draft Article 6 (formerly Draft Article 5) of the International Law Commission's Draft Articles on Responsibility of International Organizations. According to the International Law Commission, "effective control" means "the factual control that is exercised over the *specific conduct* taken by the organ or agent placed at the receiving organization's disposal."[507] The "ultimate authority and control"-test finds no basis in either the Strasbourg Court's own jurisprudence, the jurisprudence of the International Court of Justice or in the International Law Commission's Draft Articles on State Responsibility or the Draft Articles on Responsibility of International Organizations. The European Court of Human Rights principally relied on doctrine.[508] Most importantly, the test is not linked with any direct control over a specific action or operation command and control. It has rightly been pointed out that according to general principles of public international law and the dominant view in legal literature, attribution derives from the exercise of "effective control" over an act; not from the ultimate source of legal authority for an act.[509] The question whether an organ of an international organization can lawfully empower some other entity, according to the rules of its own internal law, quite simply, has nothing to do with the secondary law of responsibility.[510]

---

[506] *Guilfoyle*, Counter-Piracy Law Enforcement and Human Rights, ICLQ 59 (2010), 158.

[507] United Nations, International Law Commission, Report of the International Law Commission on the Work of its 56th Session, 2004, p. 111, para. 3 (emphasis added).

[508] See *Sarooshi*, The Delegation by the UN Security Council of its Chapter VII Powers, pp. 163–166. For a critique, see *Milanovic/Papic*, As Bad As It Gets: The European Court of Human Rights Behrami and Saramati Decision and General International Law, ICLQ (58) 2009, 284–285; *Larsen*, Attribution of Conduct of Peace Operations: The "Ultimate Authority and Control" Test, EJIL 19 (2008), 521 and 522.

[509] *Guilfoyle*, Counter-Piracy Law Enforcement and Human Rights, ICLQ 59 (2010), 156; *Milanovic/Papic*, As Bad As It Gets: The European Court of Human Rights Behrami and Saramati Decision and General International Law, ICLQ (58) 2009, 282–286; *Larsen*, Attribution of Conduct of Peace Operations: The "Ultimate Authority and Control" Test, EJIL 19 (2008), 520–522, *Bodeau-Livinec/Buzzini/Villalpando*, Behrami & Bekir Behrami v. France; Ruzhdi Saramati v. France, Germany & Norway, AJIL 102 (2008), 328.

[510] *Milanovic/Papic*, As Bad As It Gets: The European Court of Human Rights Behrami and Saramati Decision and General International Law, ICLQ (58) 2009, 281.

In the 2009 revised Commentary of the Draft Articles on Responsibility of International Organizations, the International Law Commission points out that a finding of "operational" control meets the requirements of the "effective control" test much better than "ultimate" control. "Operational control" relates to the actual conduct in question whereas "ultimate" control hardly implies a role in the act in question.[511] More specifically, with regard to the decision in *Behrami/Saramati*, the International Law Commission emphasized that the "European Court did not apply the criterion of effective control in the way that had been envisaged by the International Law Commission."[512] The Special Rapporteur on the subject matter concluded that "had the Court applied the criterion of effective control set out by the Commission, it would have reached the different conclusion that the conduct of national contingents allocated to KFOR had to be attributed either to the sending State or to NATO."[513]

In a more recent case, *Stephens v. Cyprus, Turkey, and the UN*, the Court once more relied on its reasoning in *Behrami/Saramati* and invoked the "ultimate authority and control" test.[514] In this case, although the Court followed the *Behrami/Saramati* decision, it simultaneously applied the "effective control" and the "exclusive control" test and, unlike *Behrami/Saramati*, in addition to the responsibility of the United Nations also addressed the issue of State attribution. Whether this reflects an attempt by the Court to align its reasoning more closely with the International Law Commission's Draft Articles on Responsibility of International Organizations or if they are simply owed to the particular fact pattern in the *Stephens* case, remains unclear.[515] For the time being it may be concluded that the European Court of Human Rights continues to apply the "ultimate authority and control" test. On the basis of the rather vague factors raised by the Court to ascertain "ultimate authority and control" in *Behrami/Saramati* it could be argued that the United Nations Security Council also holds "ultimate authority and control" over the Chapter VII mandated counter-piracy operations in the Gulf of Aden. This would create a significant void in human rights protection. Irrespective of the extraterritorial application of the European Convention on Human Rights

---

[511] United Nations, International Law Commission, Report of the International Law Commission on the Work of its 61st Session, 2009, p. 67, note 102.

[512] *Id.* at p. 79.

[513] United Nations, International Law Commission, Second Report on Responsibility of International Organizations by Mr. Giorgio Gaja, Special Rapporteur, U.N. Doc. A/CN.4/541 (April 2, 2004), para. 26.

[514] European Court of Human Rights, *Stephens v. Cyprus, Turkey and the United Nations* (application no. 45267/06), Decision, Dec. 11, 2008.

[515] *Bell*, Reassessing Multiple Attribution: The International Law Commission and The Behrami and Saramati Decision, New York University Journal of International Law and Politics, 42 (2010), 539.

discussed above, European States could avoid their human rights obligations under the European Convention on Human Rights with regard to their troops engaged in United Nations-mandated Chapter VII operations.[516]

b) Dual or Multiple Attribution

The decisions in *Behrami and Saramati* skimmed over the possibility of dual or multiple attribution.[517] The Strasbourg Court, having attributed the conduct in question to the United Nations did not further examine the possibility of the additional attribution of conduct to NATO and/or troop-contributing countries. This unexplained omission has created confusion as it is not clear whether the Court regarded the law on multiple attributions to be too unclear and in flux to be applied at the time of the decision or whether it simply disagreed with affirmations of the possibility of multiple attributions as pronounced by the International Law Commission.[518]

Unlike the European Court of Human Rights, for purposes of attribution in multilateral constellations, the United Nations Human Rights Committee relies on the residual control of contributing States even when they are engaged in multinational operations.[519] The Committee has expressly affirmed that States party to the International Covenant on Civil and Political Rights[520] must respect and ensure the rights it entails to anyone within their power or effective control, "regardless of the circumstances in which such power or effective control was obtained, such as forces constituting a national contingent of a State Party assigned to an international peace-keeping or peace-enforcement operation."[521] Consequentially, the Human Rights Committee regularly requests specific information regarding the

---

[516] *Sari*, Jurisdiction and International Responsibility in Peace Support Operations: The *Behrami* and *Saramati* Cases, Human Rights Law Review 8 (2008), 167 and 168.

[517] See *Bell*, Reassessing Multiple Attribution: The International Law Commission and The Behrami and Saramati Decision, New York University Journal of International Law and Politics, 42 (2010), 503; *Bodeau-Livinec/Buzzini/Villalpando*, Behrami & Bekir Behrami v. France; Ruzhdi Saramati v. France, Germany & Norway, AJIL 102 (2008), 323 and 325.

[518] *Bell*, Reassessing Multiple Attribution: The International Law Commission and The Behrami and Saramati Decision, New York University Journal of International Law and Politics, 42 (2010), 520.

[519] See United Nations, Human Rights Committee, General Comment No. 31, para. 10; Concluding Observations: Belgium, UN Doc. CCPR/C/79/Add.99 (Nov. 19, 1998), para. 14; Concluding Observations: Netherlands, UN Doc. CCPR/CO/72/NET (Aug. 27, 2001), para. 8; Concluding Observations: Belgium, UN Doc. CCPR/CO/81/BEL (Aug. 12, 2004), para. 6.

[520] International Covenant on Civil and Political Rights, *adopted* Dec. 16, 1966, 999 U.N.T.S. 171 [hereinafter: ICCPR].

[521] United Nations, Human Rights Committee, General Comment No. 31, para. 10.

application of human rights instruments of States whose foreign military deployments are involved in multinational operations.[522]

The United Nations Secretariat has also not excluded the possibility of multiple attribution of responsibility in authorized Chapter VII operations.[523] Similarly, the Venice Commission[524] has concluded that "not all acts by KFOR troops which happen in the course of an operation 'under the unified command and control' (…) of a NATO Commander must be attributed in international law to NATO but they can *also* be attributed to their country of origin (…). Thus, acts by troops in the context of a NATO-led operation cannot simply all be attributed either to NATO or to the individual troop-contributing states. There may even be difficult intermediate cases, such as when soldiers are acting on the specific orders of their national commanders which are, however, themselves partly in execution of directives issued by the KFOR commander and partly within the exercise of their remaining scope of discretion."[525]

The Special Rapporteur for the Responsibility of International Organizations has stated that "conduct does not necessarily have to be attributed exclusively to one subject only."[526] Draft Article 6 of the International Law Commission's Draft

---

[522] *Zimmermann*, Extraterritoriale Staatenpflichten und internationale Friedensmissionen, Anhörung des Bundestagsausschusses für Menschenrechte und Humanitäre Hilfe, Dec. 17, 2008, *available at* www.bundestag.de/bundestag/ausschuesse/a17/anhoerungen/ Allg__Erkl__rung_MR__Extraterritoriale_Staatenpflichten/Prof__Dr__Andreas_Zimmerma nn__09_12_08.pdf (last visited Feb. 20, 2010), p. 16. See also United Nations, Human Rights Committee, Concluding Observations: Germany, UN Doc. CCPR/C/80/L/DEU (Nov. 26, 2003), para. 3; and Concluding Observations: Germany, UN Doc. CCPR/CO/80/ DEU (May 4, 2004), para. 11: "The Committee notes with concern that Germany has not yet taken a position regarding the applicability of the Convention to persons subject to its jurisdiction in situations where its troops or police forces operate abroad, in particular in the context of peace missions."

[523] *Bell*, Reassessing Multiple Attribution: The International Law Commission and The Behrami and Saramati Decision, New York University Journal of International Law and Politics, 42 (2010), 532.

[524] The European Commission for Democracy through Law, better known as the Venice Commission, is the Council of Europe's advisory body on constitutional matters; it was established in 1990: Council of Europe, Venice Commission, *available at* www.venice .coe.int/site/main/Presentation_E.asp (last visited Aug. 30, 2010).

[525] Council of Europe, European Commission for Democracy through Law (Venice Commission), Opinion on Human Rights in Kosovo: Possible Establishment of Review Mechanisms, adopted by the Venice Commission at its 60th plenary session, Strasbourg, Oct. 11, 2004, Opinion No. 280/2004, CDL-AD 2004(033), *available at* www.venice.coe.int/ docs/2004/CDL-AD%282004%29033-e.pdf (last visited Aug. 30, 2010), para. 79 (emphasis added).

[526] United Nations, International Law Commission, Second Report on Responsibility of International Organizations by Mr. Giorgio Gaja, Special Rapporteur, U.N. Doc. A/CN.4/ 541 (April 2, 2004), para. 6. In the same vein, the Special Rapporteur has stated in its Report at para. 48: "It should also be indicated that what matters is not exclusiveness of control, which for instance the United Nations never has over national contingents, but the

Articles on the Responsibility of International Organizations leaves open the possibility of attributing a single internationally wrongful act to more than one State or
international organization.[527] What is more, the introductory commentary to Chapter II of the Draft Articles on Responsibility of International Organizations, which,
inter alia, applies to Draft Article 6, stipulates that "[a]lthough it may not frequently occur in practice, *dual or even multiple attribution of conduct cannot be
excluded*. Thus, attribution of a certain conduct to an international organization
does not imply that the same conduct cannot be attributed to a State, nor does *vice
versa* attribution of conduct to a State rule out attribution of the same conduct to an
international organization."[528]

Admittedly, as of now, the law on multiple attribution remains in a certain state
of flux. Unfortunately, the International Law Commission, although it specifically
addressed the implications of *Behrami/Saramati* on the test to determine attribution, in its 2009 Annual Report, did not comment on the decisions' divergent implications for multiple attributions.[529] This may further exacerbate the uncertainty
created by the *Behrami/Saramati*.[530] Nonetheless, the practice cited above militates
strongly in favor of a rule of multiple attribution which could allow for a more effective distribution of international responsibility and could protect the United Nations from excessive unitary liability. In addition, if the State could also be held
liable, this would most likely provide the victim with more effective legal remedies, which it could enforce before domestic and potentially regional or international human rights bodies.[531] Moreover, in 2008, after *Behrami/Saramati* had
been decided by the European Court of Human Rights, the International Law
Commission adopted the following Draft Article:

---

extent of effective control. This would also leave the way open for dual attribution of certain conducts."

[527] Draft Article 6 of the Draft Articles on the Responsibility of International Organizations reads: "The conduct of an organ of a State or an organ or agent of an international
organization that is placed at the disposal of another international organization shall be
considered under international law an act of the latter organization if the organization exercises effective control over that conduct."

[528] United Nations, International Law Commission, Report of the International Law
Commission on the Work of its 56th Session, 2004, p. 101, para. 4 (emphasis added).

[529] United Nations, International Law Commission, Report of the International Law
Commission on the Work of its 61st Session, 2009, pp. 140–141; *Bell*, Reassessing Multiple Attribution: The International Law Commission and The Behrami and Saramati Decision, New York University Journal of International Law and Politics, 42 (2010), 512.

[530] *Bell*, Reassessing Multiple Attribution: The International Law Commission and The
Behrami and Saramati Decision, New York University Journal of International Law and
Politics, 42 (2010), 512.

[531] *Id.* at 547 and 548.

Draft Art. 47 of the Draft Articles on Responsibility of International Organizations – Plurality of Responsible States or International Organizations[532]

[1] Where an international organization and one or more States or other organizations are responsible for the same internationally wrongful act, the responsibility of each State or international organization may be invoked in relation to that act.

[...]

Thus, according to Article 47 of the Draft Articles on Responsibility of International Organizations, multiple entities may be responsible for a single wrongful act. Notably, the provision deals with multiple responsibility "for the same internationally wrongful act" rather than multiple attribution of that act. Implicitly, however, the provision reaffirms the International Law Commission's earlier position regarding multiple attribution of conduct because multiple attribution and multiple responsibility typically go hand-in-hand.[533] As the Special Rapporteur has pointed out, "[d]ual attribution of conduct normally leads to joint, or joint and several, responsibility."[534]

Indeed, multiple attribution would more adequately reflect that in international military missions control neither of the United Nations nor of NATO is ever exclusive given that decisive elements of control always remain with the Troop Contributing States.[535] Finally, multiple attribution would also seem to be more in line with

---

[532] The provision is reprinted in the United Nations, International Law Commission, Report of the International Law Commission on the Work of its 61st Session, 2009, p. 32.

[533] United Nations, International Law Commission, Report of the International Law Commission on the Work of its 60th Session, 2008, pp. 292–298; *Bell*, Reassessing Multiple Attribution: The International Law Commission and The Behrami and Saramati Decision, New York University Journal of International Law and Politics, 42 (2010), 517.

[534] United Nations, International Law Commission, Second Report on Responsibility of International Organizations by Mr. Giorgio Gaja, Special Rapporteur, U.N. Doc. A/CN.4/541 (April 2, 2004), para. 8. But there may be exceptions to the rule of parallel attribution of conduct and attribution of responsibility that are also comprised by Draft Article 47 of the Draft Articles on Responsibility of International Organizations. As the Special Rapporteur mentioned, joint or several responsibility does not necessarily depend on dual attribution. The example provided in the Special Rapporteur's Report relates to a scenario in which an international organization is jointly responsible for conduct that is attributable exclusively to a State; *id.* It has been pointed out that the reverse scenario, where a State may be jointly responsible for conduct attributed solely to an international organization, would likewise be conceivable; *Bell*, Reassessing Multiple Attribution: The International Law Commission and The Behrami and Saramati Decision, New York University Journal of International Law and Politics, 42 (2010), 517. Thus, even if the United Nations had effective control – *quid non* – over the counter-piracy operations in the Gulf of Aden region, enforcement measures taken by a war ship may breach an international obligation of the flag State.

[535] *Krieger*, A Credibility Gap: The Behrami and Saramati Decision of the European Court of Human Rights, Journal of International Peacekeeping 13 (2009), 171 and 172: For example, when German contingents are subordinated to the command of NATO – other NATO member States use similar models – individual soldiers act upon an instruction to co-operate, a so-called "Anweisung auf Zusammenarbeit." Soldiers receive an order from their superior to follow the orders of the foreign commander. The first order is limited in

earlier pronouncements of the European Court on Human Rights itself. For example, in *Waite and Kennedy*, the Court held that "where States establish international organizations (...) and where they attribute to these organizations certain competences and accord them immunities, there may be implications as to the protection of fundamental rights. It would be incompatible with the purpose and object of the convention, however, if the Contracting States were thereby absolved from their responsibility under the convention in relation to the field of activity covered by such attribution."[536] If multiple attribution is accepted, while the European Court of Human Rights would not have jurisdiction to determine the responsibility of the United Nations or NATO, as it correctly stated in *Behrami/Saramati*, its jurisdiction would extend to considerations of the State's possible joint responsibility.[537] Moreover, in the not so distant future the European Court of Human Rights' jurisdiction may extend to the European Union. Accession of the European Union to the European Convention for the Protection of Human Rights and Fundamental Freedoms is provided for in the Lisbon Treaty.[538] Protocol no. 14 to the European Convention on Human Rights, which provides the legal basis for the possibility of European Union accession to the Convention, has entered into force on June 1, 2010,[539] and on March 17, 2010, the Commission proposed negotiation Directives for the EU's accession to the Convention. Finally, on June 4, 2010, the European Union Justice Ministers gave the Commission the mandate to conduct the negotiations on their behalf.[540]

---

scope and remains revocable at any time; commonly, it does not contain any disciplinary powers. See also *Krieger*, Die Verantwortlichkeit Deutschlands nach der EMRK für seine Streitkräfte im Auslandseinsatz, Heidelberg Journal of International Law 62 (2002), 680 *et seq.*

[536] European Court of Human Rights, *Waite and Kennedy v. Germany* (application no. 26083/94), Judgment, Feb. 18, 1999, para. 67; see also *Matthews v. United Kingdom* (application no. 24833/94), Judgment, Feb. 18, 1999, para. 32, where the Court held: "[t]he convention does not exclude the transfer of competences to international organizations provided that Convention rights continue to be "secured." Member States' responsibility therefore continues even after such a transfer." See also *Bosphorus Hava Yollari Turizm ve Ticaret Anonim Sirketi v. Ireland* (application no. 45036/98), Grand Chamber Judgment, June 30, 2005, para. 154: "The State is considered to retain Convention liability in respect of treaty commitments subsequent to the entry into force of the Convention."

[537] *Bell*, Reassessing Multiple Attribution: The International Law Commission and The Behrami and Saramati Decision, New York University Journal of International Law and Politics, 42 (2010), 517.

[538] Art. 6(2) of the Treaty of Lisbon, Amendments to the Treaty on European Union and to the Treaty Establishing the European Community, 2007/C 306/01, 2007 O.J. (C 306) 1–329 (EU).

[539] Protocol No. 14 to the Convention for the Protection of Human Rights and Fundamental Freedoms, amending the control system of the Convention, Art. 17, *adopted* May 13, 2004, C.E.T.S. 194.

[540] Council of Europe, EU Accession to the European Convention on Human Rights, *available at* www.coe.int/t/dc/files/themes/eu_and_coe/default_EN.asp (last visited Aug. 30, 2010).

3. Application of International Humanitarian Law to Enforcement Operations against Piracy and Armed Robbery at Sea?

a) Reference to International Humanitarian Law in Security Council Resolution 1851

Security Council Resolution 1851 is the first and, so far, only Resolution that expressly refers to human rights law in relation to the exercise of enforcement powers against piracy and armed robbery at sea. Yet, the simultaneous reference to the "applicable" international humanitarian law could have repercussions to certain international human rights protections.[541] The continued application of human rights law during situations of armed conflict notwithstanding, more permissive international humanitarian law standards pertaining to the use of force, as the applicable *lex specialis,* could set aside certain human rights protections. Although Security Council Resolution 1851 expressly provides that measures undertaken pursuant to its operative paragraph 6 "shall be undertaken consistent with *applicable* international humanitarian and human rights law," this reference does not provide any clear-cut determination whether international humanitarian law does indeed apply.

Via Chapter VII of the United Nations Charter and in combination with its Article 103, the Security Council generally has the competence to derogate from (derogable) human rights protections up to the limit of *ius cogens.* It has done so in the past, namely, by declaring international humanitarian law applicable, for example, in the Western Sahara and Yugoslav conflicts, and in relation to terrorism.[542] In view of the far reaching legal implications of such a declaration, legal certainty requires an explicit stipulation with respect to the application of international humanitarian law. The existence of any such stipulation was already questionable in the Security Council Resolutions at issue in the *Al-Jedda* case on the applicable legal regime governing detention by the United Kingdom in Iraq[543] and it is clearly absent with respect to the current Security Council Resolutions on piracy and armed robbery at sea. It can thus safely be concluded that the Security Council did not declare international humanitarian law applicable to the counter-piracy operations in the Gulf of Aden region.

---

[541] S.C. Res. 1851, para. 6.

[542] *Nolte,* in: Lowe (ed.), Security Council and War, 529.

[543] United Nations, Security Council, S.C. Res. 1511, U.N. Doc. S/RES/1511 (Oct. 16, 2003); S.C. Res. 1546, U.N. Doc. S/RES/1546 (June 8, 2004); S.C. Res. 1637, U.N. Doc. S/RES/1637 (Nov. 8, 2005); S.C. Res. 1723, U.N. Doc. S/RES/1723 (Dec. 31, 2007).

b) Requirements for the Application of International Humanitarian Law

Yet, even though the Security Council has not declared international humanitarian law directly applicable, Security Council Resolution 1851 nevertheless implies the potential applicability of international humanitarian law. It is thus necessary to consider how the application of international humanitarian law could be construed in the present context. Security Council Resolution 1851 envisages operations in which external actors engage in law enforcement activities in the territory of a failed State where a non-international armed conflict is already ongoing.[544] In this context at least two interpretations seem possible.

On the one hand, in view of the ongoing non-international armed conflict in Somalia, third States cooperating with the Somali Transitional Federal Government,[545] as explicitly requested by Security Council Resolution 1851, could become parties to the existing conflict, simply by collaborating with an entity that is already party to an ongoing non-international armed conflict. On the other hand, Security Council Resolution 1851 could be read to mean that the counter-piracy operations in and of themselves, independent of the ongoing conflict in Somalia, could eventually reach the threshold of a non-international armed conflict, thereby triggering the application of international humanitarian law.

There is no indication that the Security Council took into consideration either of these constellations specifically during the discussions that led to the adoption of Security Council Resolution 1851.[546] It seems likely that the Security Council's general reference to the "applicable international humanitarian and human rights law" was simply intended to emphasize that, while authorizing the use of "all necessary measures," enforcement vis-à-vis pirates and armed robbers at sea is, nevertheless, subject to certain legal restraints, namely, the *applicable* international humanitarian or human rights law, as the case may be.

c) Law Enforcement Character of Current Counter-Piracy Operations

The Security Council's general allusion to international humanitarian law notwithstanding, for the time being, law enforcement and the repression of crime are the unequivocally stated objectives of the operations conducted on the basis of Security Council Resolutions 1846, 1851 and 1897. This is in line with the traditional

---

[544] With regard to the ongoing non-international armed conflict in Somalia, see, for example, S.C. Res. 1872.

[545] S.C. Res. 1851, para. 6.

[546] United Nations, Department of Public Information, Security Council Authorizes States to Use Land-Based Operations in Somalia, Press Release, Dec. 16, 2008, *available at* www.un.org/News/Press/docs/2008/sc9541.doc.htm (last visited Aug. 30, 2010).

concept of piracy as an offense over which universal jurisdiction should be exercised and the fight against piracy as an act of law enforcement.[547]

The mere fact that UNCLOS declares military ships competent to carry out enforcement measures does not alter this assessment.[548] The assignment of law enforcement tasks to military ships simply stems from the fact that military vessels navigate the high seas far more frequently than police vessels. Further, it serves legal certainty if vessels that are exceptionally authorized to interfere with free navigation on the high seas are clearly visible and readily identifiable as such.[549]

Moreover, the Security Council has repeatedly confirmed this law enforcement paradigm, for example, by referring to the overall aim of ensuring "the long-term security of international navigation off the coast of Somalia"[550] or the "purpose of suppressing acts of piracy and armed robbery at sea"[551] and by calling upon States "to effectively investigate and prosecute piracy and armed robbery at sea offences."[552] Security Council Resolution 1851 also calls for the implementation of the SUA Convention and Organized Crime Convention, hence, treaties on mutual cooperation in criminal matters.[553]

Even though the pirates and armed robbers at sea employ weapons of war, such as machine guns and portable rocket-launchers,[554] and despite a persistently high number of hostages,[555] significant fighting between those acting on the basis of these Security Council Resolutions and the pirates and armed robbers at sea has not been reported. Indeed, the actors involved in the repression of piracy off the coast of Somalia do not aim to overcome their "enemy" militarily – the legitimate aim underlying the rules of international humanitarian law relating to the conduct of hostilities. Rather, as Security Council Resolution 1846 explicitly confirms, the operation's aim is the "full eradication"[556] and the "rooting out" of piracy and armed

---

[547] S.C. Res. 1851, preambular para. 4.

[548] Art. 107 UNCLOS.

[549] On the limitation of the type of vessels allowed to engage in counter-piracy operations, see p. 92 *et seq.*

[550] S.C. Res. 1851, para. 4.

[551] *Id.* at para. 6.

[552] *Id.* at para. 5.

[553] *Id.*

[554] The type of weapons used is but one among various criteria potentially determinative of the existence of an armed conflict: International Criminal Tribunal for the former Yugoslavia, *Prosecutor v. Haradinaj*, Case No. IT-04-84-T, Judgment (Trial Chamber), April 3, 2008, paras. 49 and 60 *et seq.*

[555] Amnesty International, Somalia Pirates Hold 130 Hostages after Hijacking Nine Ships, Sept. 10, 2008, *available at* www.amnesty.org.uk/news_details.asp?NewsID=17875 (last visited Aug. 30, 2010).

[556] S.C. Res. 1846, preambular para. 10.

robbery at sea.[557] These are legitimate law enforcement objectives, which, in their comprehensiveness, however, cannot so readily be reconciled with international humanitarian law's military necessity-based "legitimate aim" to defeat the enemy militarily.

The repression and eradication of crime (especially if intended to be full, effective and durable) cannot make the distinction between civil and military which is central to international humanitarian law. Rather, law enforcement operations and measures need to aim at everyone involved in piracy and armed robbery at sea. If international humanitarian law's regime pertaining to the conduct of hostilities applied to pirates and armed robbers at sea as the enemy in this armed conflict, then pirates could be directly targeted simply for being pirates, without further proportionality considerations. Under human rights law, the proportionality of each and every enforcement measure would have to be ascertained on a case-by-case basis and the use of potentially lethal force would only be allowed *ultima ratio*.

Under international humanitarian law, piracy suspects could also be held in administrative detention for security reasons, without criminal charges being brought against them. In juxtaposition, under human rights law, pre-trial detention can only take place subject to rather stringent temporal limitations that may only very exceptionally be prolonged. The apprehension of pirates on the high seas could justify such an exception. The European Court of Human Rights in *Rigopoulos*, pointed out that a lapse of time (16 days in the case at hand) is, in principle, not compatible with the concept of being brought promptly before a judge as laid down in Article 5 of the European Convention of Human Rights. However, it held that "wholly exceptional circumstances" could justify such a period.[558] In the *Medvedyev* case, this was relied on and reaffirmed by the Court sitting as a Chamber in 2008[559] and as a Grand Chamber in 2010.[560] The exceptional circumstances taken into account in *Rigopoulos* included, *inter alia*, "the fact that the distance to be covered [to reach the closest investigating judge] was considerable" (the ship was more than 5'500 km from Spanish territory when it was intercepted) and that a delay of forty-three hours caused by the resistance put up by certain members of the crew could not be attributed to the Spanish authorities. The European Court of Human Rights accordingly considered "that it was therefore materially impossible to bring the

---

[557] S.C. Res. 1851, para. 6.

[558] European Court of Human Rights, *Rigopoulos v. Spain* (application no. 37388/97), Decision, Jan. 12, 1999, para 9.

[559] European Court of Human Rights, *Medvedyev et al. v. France* (application no. 3394/03), Judgment July 10, 2008, paras. 65 and 66.

[560] European Court of Human Rights, *Medvedyev et al. v. France* (application no. 3394/03), Grand Chamber Judgment, March 29, 2010, paras. 127–134.

applicant physically before the investigating judge any sooner."[561] This temporal exception notwithstanding, under human rights law, an apprehended piracy suspect or alleged armed robber at sea has nevertheless to be brought promptly before a judge, even if factual circumstances may bar an immediate appearance before an investigating judge. Conversely, under international humanitarian law, if it would apply, *quid non*, it would be maintainable to administratively detain piracy suspects for a significant period of time, i.e. as long as they constitute a security threat.

The character of a genuine law enforcement operation does not change simply because it is conducted *in lieu* of a disabled government and on a territory where an armed conflict is ongoing. In other words, the mere existence of an already elevated level of violence on the Somali mainland does not automatically convert each and every law enforcement operation conducted in this environment into an involvement in a non-international armed conflict, regulated by international humanitarian law. After all, even a government that is already undisputedly involved in a non-international armed conflict may still carry out regular law enforcement operations without any nexus to the armed conflict and subject merely to human rights law. Admittedly, the criteria for a delineation of law enforcement operations and military operations subject to international humanitarian law conduct of hostilities rules are not sufficiently clear. Yet, whether these are objective criteria similar to those employed in the determination of the existence of an armed conflict,[562] or subjective criteria related to the purpose of an operation, in the circumstances at hand, nothing but a law enforcement operation that is based exclusively on human rights law could be ascertained.

---

[561] European Court of Human Rights, *Medvedyev et al. v. France* (application no. 3394/03), Judgment July 10, 2008, para. 66; *Rigopoulos v. Spain* (application no. 37388/97), Decision, Jan. 12, 1999, para. 9.

[562] International Criminal Tribunal for the former Yugoslavia, *Prosecutor v. Haradinaj*, Case No. IT-04-84-T, Judgment (Trial Chamber), April 3, 2008, paras. 49 and 60 *et seq.*

Part 4

The Criminal Prosecution of Pirates and Armed Robbers at Sea

Instituting criminal proceedings against persons who have allegedly engaged in pirate attacks, besides preventing assaults and arresting suspected persons, constitutes an indispensable component in the quest for a "durable eradication of piracy and armed robbery at sea off the coast of Somalia."[563] So far, however, States which have captured suspected pirates and armed robbers at sea have frequently and for various reasons either been unable or unwilling to commence domestic criminal proceedings against alleged perpetrators. Rather, alleged offenders are generally transferred to regional States willing to prosecute them.

The root-causes of the reluctance to prosecute pirates and armed robbers at sea in domestic courts are only partly of a legal nature, such as a lack of jurisdiction or the absence of specific substantive criminal norms. Rather, the disinclination to commence domestic criminal proceedings seems to be based primarily on political, financial and logistical concerns. One of the more paradoxical arguments is that prosecution in Western States would fuel piracy in the Gulf of Aden[564] given the prospect of perpetrators receiving asylum status after serving their sentences.[565] Hence, it seems that a north-south divide of sufficient proportions could annul the deterrent effect of criminal law. Further, the high expense of the proceedings and the difficulties in collecting evidence and accessing witnesses are invoked as reasons against putting pirates and armed robbers at sea on trial in non-regional States. Finally, some statements reveal that during the initial phase of the counter-piracy operations the capture of pirates had not been considered to be very probable and, therefore, the scenario regarding the disposal and prosecution of arrested pirates had not been fully thought through.[566]

---

[563] S.C. Res. 1897, preambular para. 13.

[564] Financial Times, Piraten kommen nicht nach Deutschland, March 7, 2009, *available at* www.ftd.de/politik/international/:Festnahmen-am-Horn-von-Afrika-Deutscher-Haftbefehl-gegen-Piraten/483948.html (last visited Aug. 30, 2010)

[565] *Woolf,* The Sunday Times, Pirates Can Claim UK Asylum, April 13, 2008, *available at* www.timesonline.co.uk/tol/news/uk/article3736239.ece (last visited Aug. 30, 2010).

[566] *Richter/Höll,* Piratenjagd überfordert Bundesregierung, April 9, 2009, *available at* www.sueddeutsche.de/politik/987/464586/text/ (last visited Aug. 30, 2010): The Justice Minister from the German *Bundesland* Schleswig-Holstein, Uwe Döring, said that the Federal Government would not have clarified what would happen with captured persons before engaging in the European Union counter-piracy mission.

Thus, especially during the early stages of the mutual efforts to counter piracy in the Gulf of Aden, the "lack of capacity, domestic legislation, and clarity about how to dispose of pirates after their capture"[567] led on the one hand to a prolonged detention of pirates and armed robbers at sea aboard law enforcement vessels without legal action being taken. On the other hand, it led to a significant number of suspected pirates and armed robbers at sea being released without facing justice, regardless of whether there was "sufficient evidence to support prosecution."[568]

Meanwhile, various agreements have been concluded with regional States willing to receive piracy suspects with a view to their criminal prosecution. Currently, a considerable number of piracy suspects are undergoing criminal trials in regional States. The first convictions have already been issued and a number of persons are serving their sentences.

Against this background the legal framework for the criminal prosecution of pirates and armed robbers at sea is examined (I.). In a further step, possible venues for their criminal prosecution are presented (II.). Lastly, we turn to the issue of transfers of alleged pirates and armed robbers at sea to the jurisdiction where they are supposed to stand trial (III.).

I. Adjudicative Jurisdiction over Pirates and Armed Robbers at Sea

The criminal prosecution of acts referred to as piracy and armed robbery at sea in the Security Council Resolutions, requires the existence of a substantive criminal norm defining the prohibited conduct and threatening it with punishment. In the case of piracy, it is a controversial question whether such a norm exists under international law, namely, whether Article 101 UNCLOS constitutes an international crime on the basis of which a piracy suspect can be prosecuted in a domestic criminal court, or whether criminal norms on piracy have to be derived from municipal law. With regard to armed robbery at sea, no unified definition exists,[569] let alone, an international crime that could serve as a basis for a domestic prosecution. Thus offenses defined in other international treaties, such as the SUA or Hostage

---

[567] S.C. Res. 1851, preambular para. 9; S.C. Res. 1897, preambular para. 8, is somewhat more moderate in not speaking about a lack but of a *"continuing limited* capacity and domestic legislation to facilitate the custody and prosecution of suspected pirates after their capture" (emphasis added), which is of concern.

[568] *Id.*

[569] On the definition of armed robbery at sea, see p. 73 *et seq.*; for a set of definitions of armed robbery at sea under domestic and international law, see p. 249 *et seq.* of this book (Appendix).

Conventions, are analyzed as to whether they are relevant for the prosecution of conduct amounting to armed robbery at sea.

Secondly, criminal prosecutions of acts of piracy and armed robbery at sea require that a State has criminal jurisdiction over the offense in question. Given that piracy, by definition, takes place on the high seas and given the *de facto* absence of effective judicial structures in Somalia and its inability to prosecute armed robbery at sea occurring in its territorial waters, the exercise of *extraterritorial* jurisdiction by third States plays a crucial role in the fight against piracy and armed robbery at sea off Somalia's coast. It is commonly agreed that a State's authority to decide upon the extraterritorial reach of its penal power *(ius puniendi)* is limited by public international law, in particular by the principle of non-intervention.[570] Thus, whether a State may lawfully exercise extraterritorial jurisdiction over pirates and armed robbers at sea is a matter of international law. Piracy was among the first crimes for which international law ever granted States the permission to exercise extraterritorial jurisdiction.[571] By contrast, the recognition of an extraterritorial basis of jurisdiction over other offenses that are potentially relevant in connection with armed robbery at sea, such as those defined in the SUA or Hostage Conventions, has only been a component of the legislative counter-terrorism response during the last quarter of the 20th century.

It is not easy to determine which State(s) can exercise extraterritorial jurisdiction over piracy and armed robbery at sea, and on the basis of which substantive criminal norm(s) they may do so. A single pirate attack potentially fulfills several offense descriptions and generally affects a multitude of States, which could potentially claim criminal jurisdiction. In practice, it is not uncommon that the attacked vessel is flying the flag of one State but is owned by a company incorporated in another State. Quite often, the containerized cargo or bulk commodities on board such a ship are the property of corporations having their principal place of business in yet other States. The panoply of jurisdictions involved is further enlarged by the multinational composition of crews and passengers aboard and by the fact that the nationality of alleged offenders is usually different from that of their victims. Finally, yet another jurisdictional layer may be added when the respective law enforcement vessels are operating jointly with embarked law enforcement officials from third States. However, in practice States seem to be rather reluctant to prose-

---

[570] *Brownlie*, Principles of Public International Law, pp. 311–313; *Ambos*, Internationales Strafrecht, pp. 19–23; *Kamminga*, in: Wolfrum (ed.), EPIL-Extraterritoriality, para. 7.

[571] Art. 9 ASIL-Commented Harvard Draft Convention on Jurisdiction with Respect to Crime, p. 563 and p. 566; Art. 14 ASIL-Commented Harvard Draft Convention on Piracy, pp. 745–746; Privy Council, *In Re Piracy Iure Gentium*, also reported as: [1934] A.C. 586; Permanent Court of International Justice, *The Case of the S.S. "Lotus"*, Judgment, Dissenting Opinion of Judge Moore, Sept. 7, 1927, Collection of Judgments, Series A, No. 10, p. 70; United States of America, United States' Restatement (Third) of Foreign Relations Law, para. 404 (1987).

cute alleged pirates and armed robbers at sea and often decide not to exercise their criminal jurisdiction despite being competent. Hence, positive conflicts of competence generally do not occur.

Thirdly, besides the question pertaining to the existence of substantive criminal norms and jurisdictional bases to prosecute pirates and armed robbers at sea, it is discussed in the following whether States have a duty to prosecute or extradite seized suspects detained on board a warship, i.e. who are in their custody.

A. Prosecuting Piracy

1. Substantive Criminal Norms for Prosecuting Piracy

It is often asserted that Article 101 UNCLOS defining piracy establishes a crime under international law on which criminal prosecutions could be based. Yet, in fact there is little evidence to support such an assertion. The legal experts involved in the elaboration of the Harvard Draft Convention on Piracy thoroughly analyzed the debate on this issue as it stood in 1932 and concluded that only a minority of scholars assumed that piracy is an international crime.[572] The prevailing opinion at that time was that piracy constituted, not an international, but a *municipal* crime only.[573] Thus, the Harvard Draft Convention was built on the theory that "piracy is not a crime by the law of nations. It is the basis of an extraordinary jurisdiction in every state to seize and to prosecute and punish persons, and to seize and dispose of property, for factual offences which are committed outside the territorial and other ordinary jurisdiction of the prosecuting state."[574]

Consequentially, Article 14 Harvard Draft Convention on Piracy explicitly states that the crime of piracy derives from municipal law:

---

[572] ASIL-Commented Harvard Draft Convention on Piracy, pp. 751–752.

[573] *Id.* at 756–760 ; *Fauchille*, Traité de Droit International Public, Sec. 483, cited in the ASIL-Commented Harvard Draft Convention on Piracy, p. 759: "La piraterie est considérée comme un crime du droit des gens. Cela ne signifie pas que c'est un crime qui n'est pas spécial à chaque pays et que répriment toutes les nations, car à ce titre il y aurait beaucoup de crimes qui seraient des crimes du droit des gens: ainsi l'assassinat. Cela veut dire simplement que la piraterie *autorise certaines mesures de police et de juridiction* qui en général ne peuvent être prises par un Etat qu'à l'égard de ses nationaux et des navires portant son pavillon. Les pirates peuvent être poursuivis par les navires de tous les Etats et la juridiction du capteur est compétente pour les juger." (emphasis added). *Stiel*, Der Tatbestand der Piraterie, p. 62, cited in the ASIL-Commented Harvard Draft Convention on Piracy, p. 756: "*III. Die Piraterie ist ein Unternehmen gegen das Völkerrecht.* Der völkerrechtliche Tatbestand der Piraterie ist nicht deliktischer Natur. Wenn damit die gewöhnliche, hin und wieder auch bekämpfte Bezeichnung des Tatbestandes als eines Deliktes wider das Völkerrecht in sich hinfällig ist, so ergibt sich doch nur die ganz analoge Frage, ob man sie als ein Unternehmen gegen das Völkerrecht charakterisieren darf."

[574] ASIL-Commented Harvard Draft Convention on Piracy, p. 760.

Art. 14(1) and (2) Harvard Draft Convention on Piracy

1. A State which has lawful custody of a person suspected of piracy may prosecute and punish that person.

2. Subject to the provisions of this convention, *the law of the state which exercises such jurisdiction defines the crime*, governs the procedure and prescribes the penalty.[575]

The Harvard Draft Convention on Piracy and, therefore, the theory that piracy is not an international crime was the basis for the piracy provisions in the 1956 Draft Convention on the Law of the Sea of the International Law Commission.[576] This Draft and its definitions of piracy in turn entered into the Convention on the High Seas in 1958 and, subsequently, into the UNCLOS in 1982, without substantial changes.[577] In this way, the definitions of piracy in Article 15 of the Convention on the High Seas and in Article 101 UNCLOS can hardly be conceived as international crimes.[578] Such a major deviation from the theory of the draft conventions on which the Convention on the High Seas and the UNCLOS are based would certainly have been worth a mention in the records of the respective diplomatic conference, of which there is none.

An analysis of the content of Article 101 UNCLOS as well as Article 15 of the Convention on the High Seas also shows that they merely provide definitions of piracy, but not offense descriptions, i.e. criminal norms. Article 101 UNCLOS is entitled "definition of piracy" and, consequentially, stipulates what acts amount to piracy. However, the provision does not state that it is prohibited for an individual to engage in such conduct, nor does it threaten the commission of acts of piracy with punishment. A comparison with other treaties relating to conduct that constitutes an international crime supports this conclusion. Thus, for example, the Genocide Convention[579] states in its Article 1 that "[t]he Contracting Parties confirm that genocide, whether committed in time of peace or in time of war, *is a crime under*

---

[575] Emphasis added.

[576] *Rubin*, Law of Piracy, p. 360; *Lagoni*, in: Ipsen/Schmidt-Jortzig (eds.), Piracy, 512; United Nations, International Law Commission, Commentary on the Law of the Sea Draft Convention, p. 282.

[577] *Lagoni*, in: Ipsen/Schmidt-Jortzig (eds.), Piracy, 512. On the drafting of the UNCLOS, see p. 40 *et seq.*

[578] To what extent a crime of piracy exists under customary international law, goes beyond the scope of the present study. The matter is complex, as has been shown recently by the piracy cases before the United States of America Federal District Court of Virginia where the grand jury has returned two separate indictments in April 2010 charging 11 Somali men with, *inter alia*, engaging in piracy. The piracy charges have finally been dropped; it was argued by Judge Jackson that "the definition of piracy in the international community is unclear" and that "the court's reliance on these international sources as authoritative would not meet constitutional muster and must therefore be rejected." See *Schwartz*, The New York Times, Somalis No Longer Face Federal Piracy Charges, Aug. 17, 2010, *available at* www.nytimes.com/2010/08/18/us/18pirates.html?_r=1&ref=piracy_at_sea (last visited Aug. 30, 2010).

[579] Convention on the Prevention and Repression of the Crime of Genocide, adopted Dec. 9, 1948, 78 U.N.T.S. 277 [hereinafter: Genocide Convention].

international law which they undertake to prevent and to punish."[580] Article 2 of the Genocide Convention defines what constitutes genocide and is thus equivalent to Article 101 UNCLOS defining piracy. However, in contrast to UNCLOS, the Genocide Convention explicitly states in Article 3 what acts shall be punishable and specifies in Article 4 that persons committing any such act shall be punished. Regarding war crimes, it bears mentioning that Article 8(2) of the Rome Statute[581] defines the notion of war crimes. In addition, Article 8(1) of the Rome Statute stipulates that the International Criminal Court should have jurisdiction over these offenses, while Article 25 of the Rome Statute states that "[a] person who commits a crime within the jurisdiction of the Court shall be individually responsible and liable for punishment." From this it follows that war crimes are clearly international crimes.

Rather than constituting an international crime on which criminal prosecutions can directly be based, the definition of piracy in Article 101 UNCLOS is of a jurisdictional nature. It has, first and foremost, the function to set out the personal and material scope of application of the enforcement measures authorized under Article 105 UNCLOS. The same holds true for the definition of piracy contained in Article 15 of the Convention on the High Seas. It sets out the personal and material scope of application of the enforcement measures authorized under Article 19 of the Convention on the High Seas and clarifies against whom and against which conduct they can be taken. Thus, the definitions of piracy in Article 101 UNCLOS and Article 19 of the Convention on the High Seas are closely intertwined with the enforcement powers granted vis-à-vis pirate ships, in that they describe and delimit the conduct in relation to which enforcement measures can be taken under the first sentence of Article 105 UNCLOS.

Thus, it can be concluded that conduct by individuals fulfilling the international definition of piracy constitutes a violation of international law that justifies enforcement measures against these individuals and their ships, but neither Article 15 of the Convention on the High Seas nor Article 101 UNCLOS define substantive crimes of an international character on the basis of which a person seized in the Gulf of Aden region could be charged.[582] Hence, prosecution of alleged pirates must be based on domestic substantive criminal norms.[583]

---

[580] Emphasis added.

[581] Rome Statute of the International Criminal Court, *adopted* July 17, 1998, 2187 U.N.T.S. 3.

[582] *Rubin*, Law of Piracy, pp. 359–360 and pp. 391–393; *Lagoni*, in: Ipsen/Schmidt-Jortzig (eds.), Piracy, 513.

[583] Art. 14(2) ASIL- Commented Harvard Draft Convention on Piracy, p. 746; *Wille*, Die Verfolgung strafbarer Handlungen an Bord von Schiffen und Luftfahrzeugen, pp. 99–100; *Dahm*, Das materielle Völkerstrafrecht, p. 51; *Kreß*, Universal Jurisdiction over International Crimes and the Institut de Droit international, Journal of International Criminal Justice (4) 2006, 569; *Rubin*, Law of Piracy, p. 391 f.

States are, of course, free as to how they define piracy under their domestic criminal law. In this regard, some States have relied on Article 101 UNCLOS in order to define the conduct, which is threatened by punishment under their domestic criminal law. Thus, for example, in the United Kindgom, the Merchant Shipping and Maritime Security Act 1997, Section 26(1), states: "For the avoidance of doubt it is hereby declared that for the purposes of any proceedings before a court in the United Kingdom in respect of piracy, the provisions of the United Nations Convention on the Law of the Sea 1982 that are set out in Schedule 5 shall be treated as constituting part of the law of nations." Hence, judges are directed to construe piracy *jure gentium*[584] in line with UNCLOS. However, judges do not direcly apply Article 101 UNCLOS.

Others States have taken Article 101 UNCLOS merely as a starting point and go beyond its scope. The Kenyan Merchant Shipping Act defines piracy in Section 369 similarly to the UNCLOS but drops the limiting geographical element that the offense must be committed on the high seas. [585] In addition to the definition of piracy in Section 369, the Kenyan Merchant Shipping Act threatens piracy with punishment in Section 371 stating that "[a]ny person who (…) commits any act of piracy (…) shall be liable, upon conviction, to imprisonment for life." Thus, unlike UNCLOS which merely defines piracy without criminalizing it, the Kenyan Merchant Shipping Act threatens the defined conduct with punishment, which makes it a criminal norm. Similar to the Kenyan Merchant Shipping Act, the Crimes Act 1914 of the Commonwealth of Australia also defines piracy broader than in Article 101 UNCLOS, by stating in Section 51 that the act can likewise be committed in the territorial sea of Australia.[586] Besides Section 51 defining what constitutes an act of piracy, Section 52 explicitly prohibits committing an act of piracy and threatens the conduct with punishment in the following words: "A person must not perform an act of piracy. Penalty: Imprisonment for life."

In sum, Article 101 UNCLOS and Article 15 of the Convention on the High Seas both contain a definition of piracy merely for the purposes of defining the scope of enforcement powers. The provisions neither explicitly prohibit committing acts of piracy nor threaten their commission with punishment. Hence, in the light of the *nulla poena sine lege* principle, criminal charges should not be based on these treaty provisions. It is against this background that the Security Council stresses, in Resolution 1897, "the need for States to criminalize piracy under their domestic

---

[584] For the jurisdictional basis to prosecute pirates, see Privy Council, *In Re Piracy Iure Gentium*, also reported as: [1934] A.C. 586 UK.

[585] Kenyan Merchant Shipping Act (entry into force on Sept. 1, 2009), Part XVI – Maritime Security. Excerpts of the Kenyan Merchant Shipping Act are reprinted on p. 293 *et seq.* of this book (Appendix). With the Kenyan Merchant Shipping Act, the old criminal provision on piracy, i.e. Section 69 of the Kenyan Penal Code, was repealed.

[586] Section 51 of the Crimes Act 1914 of the Commonwealth of Australia.

law and to favorably consider the prosecution, in appropriate cases, of suspected pirates, consistent with applicable international law."[587]

2. Jurisdictional Bases for Prosecuting Piracy

a) Jurisdictional Basis Derived from Customary Law

aa) Piracy as the Paradigmatic Universal Jurisdiction Crime

It is well established that any nation may try pirates, even in the absence of a nexus between the pirate attack and the State claiming jurisdiction.[588] In the *Case Concerning the Arrest Warrant*, Judge Guillaume of the International Court of Justice stated that "international law knows only one true case of universal jurisdiction: piracy."[589] This statement is potentially misleading, since it is not clear what Judge Guillaume meant by referring to a "true case" of universal jurisdiction. Certainly, universal adjudicative jurisdiction exists over other crimes, namely genocide, war crimes and crimes against humanity.[590] Still, it seems safe to say that

---

[587] S.C. Res. 1897, preambular para. 8.

[588] The following cases state that universal jurisdiction over piracy consolidated into a customary international law norm: Permanent Court of International Justice, *The Case of the S.S. "Lotus"*, Judgment, Dissenting Opinion of Judge Moore, Sept. 7, 1927, Collection of Judgments, Series A, No. 10, p. 70; International Court of Justice, *Case Concerning the Arrest Warrant (Democratic Republic of the Congo v. Belgium)*, Judgment, Separate Opinion of President Guillaume, Feb. 14, 2002, I.C.J. Reports 2002, pp. 37–38; Privy Council, *In Re Piracy Iure Gentium*, also reported as: [1934] A.C. 586. For doctrine asserting the existence of a customary universality principle, see, for example, *Brierly*, The Law of Nations, p. 154, cited in the ASIL-Commented Harvard Draft Convention on Piracy, p. 758: "Any state may bring in pirates for trial by its own courts, on the ground that they are *hostes humanis generis.*" *Calvo*, Le Droit International, Sec. 485, cited in the ASIL-Commented Harvard Draft Convention on Piracy, p. 758: "Au nombre des crimes qui, par leur caractère spécial et la généralité des intérêts qu'ils affectent, rentrent dans le domaine du droit des gens, c'est-à-dire sont punissables partout sans relever directement et exclusivement de la juridiction d'un Etat plutôt que de celle d'un autre, on doit ranger la piraterie." *Wager Halleck*, International Law, p. 54, cited in the ASIL-Commented Harvard Draft Convention on Piracy, p. 852: "Certain offences against this law – as piracy, for example – wheresoever and by whomsoever committed, are within the cognizance of the judicial power of every State; for, being regarded as the common enemies of all mankind, any one may lawfully capture pirates upon the high seas, and the tribunals of any State, within whose territorial jurisdiction they may be brought, can try and punish them for the crimes." *Id.* at pp. 232–235, cited in the ASIL-Commented Harvard Draft Convention on Piracy, p. 759: "With respect to criminal matters the judicial power of the State extends, with certain qualifications: (...) [t]o the punishment of piracy, and other offences against the law of nations, by whomsoever and wheresoever committed." Further, see Art. 9 ASIL-Commented Harvard Draft Convention on Jurisdiction with Respect to Crime, p. 563.

[589] International Court of Justice, *Case Concerning the Arrest Warrant (Democratic Republic of the Congo v. Belgium)*, Judgment, Separate Opinion of President Guillaume, Feb. 14, 2002, I.C.J. Reports 2002, p. 42.

[590] *Werle*, Völkerstrafrecht, pp. 187–188.

piracy is not only the first, but also the paradigmatic universal jurisdiction crime as far as adjudicative jurisdiction is concerned.[591] In addition, regarding enforcement jurisdiction, it may well be argued that piracy is an exceptional case, since every State is competent to take enforcement measures against pirate ships.[592]

With regard to the scope of the universality principle, it should be noted that universal jurisdiction is only provided over conduct, which matches the piracy definition under international law. For acts defined as piracy under municipal law, which go beyond the definition of piracy under international law, the universality principle cannot be invoked. In this sense, the scope of universal jurisdiction over the municipal crime of piracy is limited by international law. This interpretation derives quite plainly from the Draft Convention on Jurisdiction with Respect to Crime and its provision on the universality principle and piracy:

Art. 9 Draft Convention on Jurisdiction with Respect to Crime – Universality-Piracy[593]

A State has jurisdiction with respect to any crime committed outside its territory by an alien which constitutes piracy by *international* law.

In the explanatory commentary of the Harvard Research Program on International Law on this provision, it is stated that "[s]uch a competence is recognized if the offence is one 'which constitutes piracy by international law.' It is essential that the competence should be so stated as to include only offences which constitute 'piracy by international law,' since many States denounce various offences as piracy by national law. Such national legislation is applicable, of course, only within the territory, upon national ships or aircraft, or in the prosecution of nationals."[594]

An example of a municipal law definition of piracy, deviating from the international definition of Article 101 UNCLOS, is the recently enacted Kenyan Merchant Shipping Act.[595] Section 369(1) of the Act does not confine piracy to the high seas. Rather, according to this provision, piracy can also be committed in places under Kenyan jurisdiction.[596] Hence, Kenyan criminal law appears to define acts

---

[591] Princeton University, Princeton Project on Universal Jurisdiction, The Princeton Principles on Universal Jurisdiction, 2001, *available at* http://lapa.princeton.edu/hosted docs/unive_jur.pdf (last visited Aug. 30, 2010), p. 45.

[592] On enforcement powers against pirate ships, see p. 55 *et seq.*

[593] Art. 9 ASIL-Commented Harvard Draft Convention on Jurisdiction with Respect to Crime, p. 563 (emphasis added).

[594] *Id.* at 566.

[595] See also the definition of piracy under the Crimes Act 1914 of the Commonwealth of Australia on p. 142.

[596] The old Kenyan criminal provision on piracy (Section 69 of the Kenyan Penal Code), which was repealed in 2009 with the entry into force of the Kenyan Merchant Shipping Act, also refrained from confining piracy to the high seas: "Any person who, in *territorial waters* or upon the high seas, commits any act of piracy *jure gentium* is guilty of the offence of piracy." (Emphasis added).

of piracy more broadly than they are defined under international law. For acts going beyond the international definition, Kenya cannot invoke the customary universality principle. Thus, criminal jurisdiction must be based on other grounds, such as the territoriality, nationality or flag principle.[597]

bb) Universal Jurisdiction Rationale in the Case of Piracy

(1) Heinousness of the Crime

Various rationales are invoked as to why piracy constitutes a universally cognizable crime. Quite commonly it is asserted that the extraordinary heinousness of the crime gave rise to the crime's unique jurisdictional status. Thus, judges Higgins, Kooijmans and Buergenthal of the International Court of Justice emphasized in the *Case Concerning the Arrest Warrant* that "[i]t is equally necessary that universal criminal jurisdiction be exercised only over those crimes regarded as the most heinous by the international community. Piracy is the classical example."[598] However, this statement provoked "a measure of astonishment," given that piracy commonly does not even come close to matching the "heinousness" of genocide or crimes against humanity. In terms of gravity, the offense of piracy is comparable to property offenses or hostage taking committed at land.[599]

Against invoking the gravity of the crime as a rationale for making piracy a universally cognizable crime, some authors refer to the practice of privateering. Historically, in times of war, armed robbery of civilian shipping, i.e. privateering, has been authorized or even encouraged by many maritime nations. The sole difference between piracy and privateering was that the privateers acted with State authorization embodied in letters of marque. The coexistence within the same legal order of lawful privateering and illegal piracy would undermine the theory that piracy, even though regarded as morally wrong, could be perceived as so heinous as to justify a universal response.[600] Yet, in turn it could be argued that privateering was first and

---

[597] Art. 9 ASIL-Commented Harvard Draft Convention on Jurisdiction with Respect to Crime, p. 566. How strict this "identity requirement" between the municipal crime of piracy and the international definition of piracy has to be interpreted seems to be an unsettled question; a possible avenue would be to treat it in a similar way as the "double criminality requirement" in the context of extradition law.

[598] See, for example, International Court of Justice, *Case Concerning the Arrest Warrant (Democratic Republic of the Congo v. Belgium)*, Judgment, Joint Separate Opinion of Judges Higgins, Kooijmans and Buergenthal, Feb. 14, 2002, I.C.J. Reports 2002, pp. 60–61.

[599] *Kreß*, Universal Jurisdiction over International Crimes and the Institut de Droit international, Journal of International Criminal Justice (4) 2006, 569.

[600] *Kontorovich*, The Piracy Analogy: Modern Universal Jurisdiction's Hollow Foundation, Harvard International Law Journal (45) 2004, 222–223; *Goodwin*, Universal Jurisdiction and the Pirate: Time for an Old Couple to Part, Vanderbilt Journal of Transnational Law 39 (2006), 981–982.

foremost a means and method of naval warfare. The same *actus reus* (such as taking a person's life) can be lawful in times of war, but may be unlawful and perceived as heinous in times of peace. Thus, from the mere fact that privateering constituted a lawful method of warfare, it cannot necessarily be concluded that the same conduct was also perceived as lawful and, therefore, not heinous in times of peace. Still, despite this flaw in the privateering analogy, heinousness seems not to be the rationale behind making piracy a universally cognizable crime, given that in terms of gravity, piracy simply does not stick out compared to other crimes.

(2) De-Nationalization of Pirates

Others explain universal jurisdiction over pirates by the "de-nationalization" of pirates and their ships and the jurisdictional gap that could result. While international law does not prescribe whether a pirate ship retains or loses its nationality, but leaves the decision to domestic law, the idea that pirates and their ships become "de-nationalized" as a legal consequence of piracy was not uncommon in earlier times.[601] Lorimer has aptly expressed this idea in the following words: "When [the law of nations] punishes pirates, it does not punish the citizens of the State to which the pirates belonged, but cosmopolitan criminals, whom it regards as having ceased to be State citizens altogether in consequence of their having broken the laws of humanity as a whole, and become enemies of the human race."[602]

If the "de-nationalization" theory is followed, the active personality principle (allowing a State to criminally prosecute his own nationals) would not be operable given that the alleged offender would no longer possess a nationality. Nor would the territoriality principle (allowing a State to criminally prosecute persons allegedly having committed an offense on its territory) work with regard to piracy, since the offense has, by definition, to be committed on the high seas. Thus, the need for universal jurisdiction (providing a State with criminal jurisdiction even if there is no link between the offender, the offense or the victim and the prosecuting State) is apparent since without this jurisdictional basis the prosecution of pirates could hardly be ensured. The fact that pirates are rarely perceived as "representing" or even acting on behalf of their State of origin may explain why the idea of exercising universal jurisdiction vis-à-vis alleged pirates has met with little resistance compared to "modern universal jurisdiction crimes," such as genocide or war crimes, where States often perceive universal jurisdiction as a potential interference in their internal affairs.

---

[601] Art. 5 Harvard Draft Convention on Piracy; see also commentary relating to Art. 5, ASIL-Commented Harvard Draft Convention on Piracy, p. 825.

[602] *Lorimer*, Institutes of the Law of Nations, p. 132, cited in the ASIL-Commented Harvard Draft Convention on Piracy, p. 828.

(3) Special *Locus Delicti* of Piracy

The most convincing explanation for the emergence of the jurisdictional pecu-
liarity that piracy can be prosecuted by every State, even in the absence of a link
to the offender, the offense or the victim, seems to be the special *locus delicti* of
piracy: the high seas, where every State has an interest in its own safety, but none
has jurisdiction.[603] A combination of factors was most probably the driving force
behind the rise of universal jurisdiction over piracy, namely that every State is a
potential victim of maritime depredations and that the interest in securing the free
flow of international trade has always been a shared interest of the international
community. The fact that the perpetrator's State might have turned a blind eye on
piracy when it suited its interests[604] might have further accentuated the perception
that every State – not only the pirate's "home State" – should be allowed to intervene.

This double rationale – the international interest combined with the home State's
inaction – does not seem to have lost its currency in the present day and is actually
apparent in the current situation in the Gulf of Aden. Here, "the lack of capacity of
the Transitional Federal Government (TFG) to secure the waters off the coast of
Somalia"[605] in conjunction with the "threat that piracy pose[s] to (…) international
navigation and the safety of commercial maritime routes"[606] seems to be the driving momentum behind the endeavors to set up a legal framework for combating
piracy.

While the rationale behind the universality principle over piracy is contested, it
can be said with certainty that customary international law allows every State,
whether it features a link with the concrete piracy offense or not, to prosecute the
offense. However, this only holds true for conduct that matches the definition of
piracy under international law, as contained in Article 101 UNCLOS, Article 15 of
the Convention on the High Seas and customary international law.

---

[603] Art. 9 ASIL-Commented Harvard Draft Convention on Jurisdiction with Respect to
Crime, p. 566: "Originating in a period when piratical depredations were a very real men-
ace to all water-borne commerce and traffic, the competence to prosecute and punish for
piracy was commonly explained by saying that the pirate who preyed upon all alike was
the enemy of all alike (…). The competence is perhaps better justified at the present time
upon the ground that the punishable acts are committed upon the seas where all have an
interest in the safety of commerce and where no state has territorial jurisdiction. Notwithstanding the more effective policing of the seas in modern times, the common interest and
mutual convenience which gave rise to the principle have conserved its vitality as a means
of preventing the recurrence of maritime depredations of a piratical character."

[604] *Kontorovich*, The Piracy Analogy: Modern Universal Jurisdiction's Hollow Foundation, Harvard International Law Journal (45) 2004, 192.

[605] S.C. Res. 1851, preambular para. 5; similar also S.C. Res. 1816, preambular para. 7.

[606] S.C. Res. 1846, preambular para. 2.

b) Jurisdictional Basis Conferred by Article 105 UNCLOS?

According to the Security Council, the UNCLOS sets out the primary legal framework for combating piracy off Somalia's coast.[607] The only reference to adjudicative jurisdiction over piracy in the UNCLOS is contained in the second sentence of Article 105:[608]

Art. 105 UNCLOS – Seizure of a Pirate Ship or Aircraft

[...] The courts of the State which carried out the seizure may decide upon the penalties to be imposed, and may also determine the action to be taken with regard to ship, aircraft or property, subject to rights of third parties acting in good faith.

The meaning of this statement on adjudicative criminal jurisdiction contained in Article 105 UNCLOS and Article 19 of the Convention on the High Seas, respectively, is not entirely clear.[609] While some authors assert that it embodies the universality principle, others maintain that the provision provides the competence to criminally prosecute exclusively to the seizing State (*forum deprehensionis*; limited universality principle). Alternatively, the norm could also be read as a conflict-of-law rule. Finally, as is our understanding, the second sentence of Article 105 UNCLOS could also be interpreted as simply reaffirming that prosecution of pirates takes place based on domestic criminal law. On the basis of this understanding, domestic criminal law defines the crime, procedure and sanction; while the universal competence to criminally prosecute pirates is provided under customary international law.

Neither the wording of Article 105 UNCLOS nor the sparse amount of drafting material provides a clear answer regarding the exact meaning of the provision. During the drafting process of the Convention on the High Seas, adjudication of pirates did not receive a great deal of attention. Besides requests for a complete deletion or a merger of the different articles on piracy,[610] no amendments were introduced specifically on the provision that became Article 19 Convention on the High Seas and

---

[607] S.C. Res. 1816, preambular para. 4; S.C. Res. 1838, at preambular para. 4; S.C. Res. 1846, preambular para. 4; S.C. Res. 1851, preambular para. 4; S.C. Res. 1897, preambular para. 4.

[608] While Art. 105 UNCLOS regulates enforcement powers and adjudication of pirates in a single provision, the ASIL-Commented Harvard Draft Convention on Piracy, pp. 744–745, separated these two forms of jurisdiction more neatly in that it devoted one set of articles to enforcement powers (Arts. 6 *et seq.* ASIL-Commented Harvard Draft Convention on Piracy) and another set of rules to the criminal prosecution of pirates (Arts. 13 *et seq.* ASIL-Commented Harvard Draft Convention on Piracy).

[609] For an explanation why the wording of Art. 19 Convention on the High Seas respectively Art. 105 UNCLOS is quite incomprehensible, see *Rubin*, Law of Piracy, pp. 359–360 and p. 393.

[610] On the little attention the legal regime on piracy received during the 1958 Conference on the Law of the Sea, see p. 39 *et seq.*

no (recorded) discussion took place.[611] Hence, the *travaux préparatoires* of Article 19 of the Convention on the High Seas do not further clarify the nature and content of the provision. Similarly, the official records of the diplomatic conference on the UNCLOS contain no substantial evidence on the meaning of Article 105 UNCLOS. Neither does doctrine provide a uniform interpretation of Article 19 Convention on the High Seas and UNCLOS; the different readings of these provisions are presented in the following.

aa) Article 105 UNCLOS: (Limited) Universality Principle?

Some scholars read the second sentence of Article 105 UNCLOS as referring to universal criminal jurisdiction.[612] However, it is difficult to see how the wording "the courts of the *State which carried out the seizure* may decide upon the penalties to be imposed"[613] can be equated to granting universal adjudicative jurisdiction in criminal matters, especially when contrasted with the universal enforcement jurisdiction so clearly expressed in the first sentence of Article 105 UNCLOS by the words "*every State* may seize a pirate ship (…) and arrest the persons."[614]

Other authors maintain that the provision contains a *limited* universality principle in that, under UNCLOS, not all States, but only the seizing State is competent to exercise its universal jurisdiction, in other words that the second sentence of Article 105 UNCLOS foresees a competence to adjudicate for the *forum deprehensionis*. Thus, Article 105 UNCLOS, in its entirety (comprising sentences one and two), would function as a funnel: At the outset every State has enforcement jurisdiction over pirates, but only the "successfully" enforcing State, i.e. the one arresting the pirates, is granted adjudicative criminal jurisdiction over the alleged offender under UNCLOS.[615]

---

[611] Art. 43 of the Law of the Sea Draft Convention became Art. 19 Convention on the High Seas; United Nations, Conference on the Law of the Sea, Feb. 24 – April 27, 1958, Official Records: Volume IV: Second Committee (High Seas: General Régime), U.N. Doc. A/CONF.13/40 (Feb. 24 to April 27, 1958), p. 78: "Article 43: The text of Article 43 submitted by the International Law Commission was adopted by 46 votes to 7, with 1 abstention;" United Nations Conference on the Law of the Sea, Feb. 24 – April 27, 1958, Official Records: Volume II: Plenary Meetings, U.N. Doc. A/CONF.13/38 (Feb. 24 – April 27, 1958), p. 97: "As there were no proposals relating to article 43, the International Law Commission text was put to the vote and adopted by 41 votes to 8, with one abstention."

[612] See, for example, *Shearer*, in: Wolfrum (ed.), EPIL-Piracy, para. 18: "The application to piracy of the universality principle of criminal jurisdiction is reflected in Art. 105 UN Convention on the Law of the Sea (…)."

[613] Second sentence of Art. 105 UNCLOS (emphasis added).

[614] First sentence of Art. 105 UNCLOS (emphasis added).

[615] E.g. *Lagoni*, in: Ipsen/Schmidt-Jortzig (eds.), Piracy, 521, stating that the exercise of universal jurisdiction is limited to the seizing State under Art. 19 Convention on the High Seas and Art. 105 UNCLOS; this, however, would be without prejudice to bases of jurisdiction recognized under general principles of law (and would merely clarify the factual

The proponents of the limited universality principle theory corroborate their thesis with the very short commentary of the International Law Commission on the almost identically worded draft provision of Article 19 of the Convention on the High Seas, which is in turn identical to the second sentence of Article 105 UNCLOS. The International Law Commissions' commentary to Draft Article 43, which later became Article 19 of the Convention on the High Seas, states: "This article gives any State the right to seize pirate ships (and ships seized by pirates) and to have them adjudicated upon by its courts. This right cannot be exercised at a place under the jurisdiction of another State. The Commission did not think it necessary to go into details concerning the penalties to be imposed and the other measures to be taken by courts."[616]

However, it is unclear whether the International Law Commission refers in its commentary to Draft Article 43 to the right to seize a pirate ship or the right to adjudicate in the second sentence of the commentary, leaving the question open to debate, whether it is the enforcement measure or adjudication that "cannot be exercised at a place under the jurisdiction of another State." A teleological interpretation, however, would suggest that the right to seize could not be exercised in a foreign jurisdiction, but that pirates can be adjudicated by any State, since the International Law Commission basically endorsed the Harvard Draft Convention on Piracy, which contains the idea that any State having lawful custody of a person suspected of piracy may prosecute and punish that person.[617]

Furthermore, against the background that under customary international law every State is competent to prosecute piracy, it is difficult to see why States would create such a specific adjudication basis for an issue already covered by customary law. Had such a significant narrowing down of the long-standing customary universality principle been intended, a word of explanation in the *travaux préparatoires* would certainly have been required all the more, as piracy is considered to be the paradigmatic universal jurisdiction crime. The drafting materials are silent in this regard, however, which implies that no such limitation was introduced in the second sentence of Article 105 UNCLOS.

---

advantage of the seizing State to bring alleged perpetrators to justice); *Münchau*, Terrorismus auf See, p. 170, stating that Art. 19 Convention on the High Seas and Art. 105 UNCLOS only allow criminal prosecution by the State that carried out the seizure of the pirate ship; accordingly, other States would not be allowed to exercise criminal jurisdiction (not even in the case of extradition), unless they are competent on other grounds of jurisdiction.

[616] United Nations, International Law Commission, Commentary on the Law of the Sea Draft Convention, p. 283, commenting Art. 43 of the Draft Convention.

[617] Art. 14 ASIL-Commented Harvard Draft Convention on Piracy. On the endorsement of the ASIL-Commented Harvard Draft Convention on Piracy by the International Law Commission, see note 204.

bb) Article 105 UNCLOS: Conflict-of-Law Rule?

Potentially, the second sentence of Article 105 UNCLOS could be read as having the effect of a mere conflict-of-law rule, to solve competing jurisdictional claims by according priority to the seizing State, without itself conferring a basis for the exercise of adjudicative jurisdiction. However, neither the drafting history of Article 105 UNCLOS nor analogous provisions preceding it, suggest that the provision amounts to a conflict-of-law rule.[618] If the drafters had understood the content of the second sentence of Article 105 UNCLOS as stating which State should be granted priority in case of competing jurisdictional claims, they would have drafted it similarly to Article 97 UNCLOS, which is unequivocally formulated as a conflict-of-law rule.[619]

cc) Article 105 UNCLOS: Reaffirming that Prosecution Is Based on Domestic Criminal Law and Procedure

It is submitted here that the second sentence of Article 105 UNCLOS should be read as simply reaffirming a cornerstone of customary international piracy law: That the prosecution of pirates takes place based on domestic criminal law, which defines the crime, procedure, and sanction. However, the jurisdictional basis for the prosecution of pirates is the universality principle as contained in customary international law, which allows every State to prosecute persons suspected of having committed acts of piracy as defined in Article 101 UNCLOS, which is reflective of customary international law, even absent a link to the offender, the victim or the offense.

This interpretation is backed by the UNCLOS Commentary stating that: "[t]he second sentence of Article 105 implies that the courts of the State which carried out the seizure will apply national law, including, where appropriate, the national rules governing the conflict of laws."[620]

3. Acts of Piracy: Duty to Extradite or Prosecute?

The Security Council, in its most recent Resolution on piracy, notes with concern that in some cases pirates were "released without facing justice, regardless of whether there is sufficient evidence to support prosecution."[621] This begs the

---

[618] On the drafting history of Art. 105 UNCLOS, see p. 40 *et seq.*

[619] Art. 97 UNCLOS.

[620] *Nandan*, in: Nordquist (ed.), UNCLOS-Commentary, Article 105, 216. The reference to domestic conflict-of-law rules contained in this commentary would be superfluous if Art. 105 UNCLOS would itself be a conflict-of-law rule.

[621] S.C. Res. 1897, preambular para. 8.

question whether States have a duty to prosecute or extradite piracy suspects or whether they are free to release them after apprehension.

Historically, customary international law did not oblige States to either prosecute or extradite persons suspected of having committed acts of piracy.[622] Consequentially, the Harvard Draft Convention on Piracy did not assert a definite duty of States to prosecute pirates. Rather, in Article 18, the Harvard Draft Convention on Piracy obliges States to discourage piracy by exercising their rights of prevention and punishment, as far as this is expedient.[623]

Article 105 UNCLOS and Article 19 of the Convention on the High Seas, respectively, state that the seizing State "may decide upon the penalties to be imposed." However, they do not entail a duty to prosecute or extradite alleged pirates by the State under whose control they are.[624] Neither can Article 100 UNCLOS, urging States to cooperate to the fullest possible extent in the repression of piracy, be read as an obligation to either prosecute or extradite piracy suspects. Compared with *aut dedere – aut iudicare* provisions contained in various other treaties, this clause is worded more generally.[625] It should also be noted that at the Diplomatic Conference on the Law of the Sea, a proposal by Malta was rejected which would have amended Article 100 UNCLOS to read "[a]ll States have the obligation to prevent and punish piracy and to fully cooperate in its repression."[626]

4. Conclusion

It can thus be concluded that neither Article 15 of the Convention on the High Seas nor Article 101 UNCLOS contains a substantive criminal provision on piracy. Thus, criminal prosecution of pirates has rather to be based on a *municipal* criminal law norm. Regarding the competence of a State to criminally prosecute an alleged pirate, it can be concluded that customary international law provides all States with criminal jurisdiction over acts of piracy, as far as the conduct in question matches the definition of piracy under international law, as reflected by Article 101 UNCLOS. While States have a general duty to cooperate in the repression of piracy, based on Article 100 UNCLOS, they are free to decide whether they want to prosecute or extradite piracy suspects who are in their hands given that the piracy law does not contain an *aut dedere – aut iudicare* clause.

---

[622] *Maierhöfer, aut dedere – aut iudicare*, pp. 113–114.
[623] ASIL-Commented Harvard Draft Convention on Piracy, p. 760.
[624] *Maierhöfer, aut dedere – aut iudicare*, pp. 179–180.
[625] See, for example, Art. 10 SUA Convention and Art. 8 Hostage Convention.
[626] *Nandan*, in: Nordquist (ed.), UNCLOS-Commentary, Article 100, 183.

B. Prosecuting Armed Robbery at Sea

Many violent acts against ships and persons on board take place in the territorial waters of littoral States of the larger Gulf of Aden region. Since the definition of piracy in Article 101 UNCLOS requires that the conduct takes place on the high seas, unlawful acts committed in the territorial waters cannot constitute piracy. However, these acts, which are referred to as armed robbery at sea in the Security Council Resolutions, may fall within the ambit of other treaties, namely the SUA or Hostage Conventions.[627] This section addresses the question to what extent these two treaties are relevant for the criminal prosecution of armed robbers at sea, namely, whether they contain relevant substantive criminal norms, jurisdictional bases and/or a duty to prosecute or extradite persons suspected of having committed armed robbery at sea. It bears mentioning, that the offenses defined in the SUA and Hostage Conventions may also be fulfilled by acts committed on the high seas, which potentially concurrently fulfill the definition of piracy.

1. Substantive Criminal Norms for Prosecuting Armed Robbery at Sea

a) SUA Convention

aa) Offenses Defined in Article 3 SUA Convention

Article 3 SUA Convention sets forth a long list of unlawful acts threatening the safety of maritime navigation. Since it was a terrorist act, which provided the impetus for the drafting of the SUA Convention, namely the *Achille Lauro* affair,[628] some offenses are clearly "terrorism-tailored"[629] and are, therefore, of little relevance in the context of pirate attacks. Nevertheless, various offenses listed in Article 3 SUA Convention may be fulfilled by pirates and armed robbers at sea.

---

[627] The phenomenon of piracy and armed robbery at sea extends far beyond acts carried out at sea. Even though the response of the international community has, thus far, primarily focused on these acts and actors, a sophisticated industry has started to evolve around piracy, which generally involves criminal conduct before the actual pirate attack (such as the procurement of arms) and after it (such as money laundering). Thus, for the sake of completeness, it should be noted that S.C. Res. 1851 also encourages the implementation of the Organized Crime Convention, which obliges State parties to criminalize, *inter alia*, the participation in an organized criminal group (Art. 5) and the laundering of proceeds of crime (Art. 6) as well as to establish jurisdiction over these offenses (Art. 15).

[628] On the drafting history of the SUA Convention, see p. 42 *et seq.* The *Achille Lauro* incident not only prompted the adoption of the SUA Convention, but also left its mark on the selection of the offenses in its Art. 3. Thus, Art. 3(1)(g) SUA Convention, for instance, goes back to the killing of a passenger on board the attacked cruiser; see *Plant*, in: Higgins/ Flory (eds.), Terrorism at Sea, 81, and *Halberstam*, Terrorism on High Seas: The Achille Lauro, Piracy and the IMO Convention on Maritime Safety, AJIL 82 (1988), 293–295.

[629] For instance Art. 3(d), (e) and (f) SUA Convention.

States are required to make all the various acts defined in Article 3 SUA Convention punishable under their domestic law.[630] Nevertheless, of all these, seizure and exercise of control over a ship[631] by force or intimidation, is of particular relevance.[632] Similarly of importance in the present context is the prohibition to perform an act of violence against a person on board a ship, if that act is likely to endanger the safe navigation of that ship.[633] Also the threat to perform such an act, if that threat is likely to endanger the safe navigation of the ship in question, may be of significance in the realm of pirate attacks.[634] The requirement that the acts have to be "likely to endanger the safe navigation" of the victim ship should exclude "acts involving isolated individuals which simply happen to be taking place on board a ship." It is, however, not necessary that the ship is put in danger of sinking or grounding or that the safety and lives of passengers and crew are threatened by the acts in question.[635] This requirement seems to be fulfilled by most piracy incidents. Also the offense of injuring or killing any person in connection with the (attempted) commission of any of the aforementioned offenses is likely to be fulfilled by pirates and armed robbers at sea.[636] Finally, also attempts to commit any of the offenses defined in Article 3 SUA Convention[637] as well

---

[630] Art. 5 SUA Convention.

[631] Art. 1 SUA Convention defines "ship," i.e. the vessel that can be the victim of an unlawful act, very broadly as a "vessel of any type whatsoever not permanently attached to the sea-bed, including dynamically supported craft, submersibles, or any other floating craft." This ship does not need to fly the flag of a State party to the SUA Convention (*Plant*, in: Higgins/Flory (eds.), Terrorism at Sea, 76). Neither must the victim ship be "in service". The draft convention submitted to the International Maritime Organization contained an "in service" limitation; however, the Preparatory Committee decided to omit this restrictive criteria altogether arguing that this restriction would potentially have excluded many situations from the Convention's ambit, such as for example cruise ships in port whose next voyage has not yet been set, ships temporarily in port for repairs, ships from which passengers have disembarked and which are cleaned and readied for the next trip (*Halberstam*, in: Bassiouni (ed.), International Maritime Navigation, 829–830). Hence, the SUA Convention also covers ships lying in port, such as hijacked ships hold in Somali ports. However, according to its Art. 2(1)(c), the SUA Convention does not apply to ships "withdrawn from navigation or laid up." Further, according to Art. 2(1)(a) and (b) SUA Convention, warships and ships owned and operated by a State when being used as a naval auxiliary or for police purposes do not fall within the ambit of the Convention. Thus, the attack in March 2009 against the German warship *Spessart* travelling in the Gulf of Aden and belonging to the European Union Operation Atalanta would not have been covered by the SUA Convention: Süddeutsche Zeitung, Piraten greifen erstmals deutsches Kriegsschiff an, March 30, 2009, *available at* www.sueddeutsche.de/panorama/817/463425/text/ (last visited Aug. 30, 2010).

[632] Art. 3(1)(a) SUA Convention.

[633] Art. 3(1)(b) SUA Convention.

[634] Art. 3(2)(c) SUA Convention.

[635] *Plant*, in: Higgins/Flory (eds.), Terrorism at Sea, 81.

[636] Art. 3(1)(g) SUA Convention.

[637] Art. 3(2)(a) SUA Convention.

as aiding and abetting in their commission constitute offenses under the SUA Convention.[638]

bb) Geographical Area in Which the SUA Offenses Can Take Place

While piracy, as defined in Article 101 UNCLOS, can only take place on the high seas, Article 3 SUA Convention does not contain such a geographical limitation. Rather, the scope of application *ratione loci* of the SUA Convention is defined very broadly. According to its Article 4(1), the SUA Convention applies "if the ship is navigating or is scheduled to navigate, through or from waters beyond the outer limit of the territorial sea of a single State, or the lateral limits of its territorial sea with adjacent States."[639] This provision has been criticized for not being carefully drafted and not fully expressing the intent of the drafters.[640]

Indeed, this rather confusing definition of the geographical scope of application in Article 4(1) of the SUA Convention encompasses all cases of navigation, actual or scheduled, except cases of short-range or local cabotage (i.e. ships navigating and scheduled to navigate only within the internal waters or territorial sea of a single State). Thus, the unlawful acts defined in Article 3 SUA Convention, can take place against a ship navigating (voluntarily or otherwise) in any waters, in as much as this is not limited to the territorial sea or internal waters of a single State. It suffices that such navigation was scheduled, even if that schedule ultimately cannot be followed due to an unlawful act as defined in Article 3 SUA Convention. Hence, according to Article 4(1) the locus of the unlawful act, as defined in Article 3 SUA Convention, can be either the high seas or the territorial sea of any State, so long as the scheduled or actual navigation is not limited to the territorial sea of that State. In addition, according to Article 4(2) SUA Convention, even in cases excluded under Article 4(1) SUA Convention, the treaty applies if the offender or alleged offender is found in the territory of a State other than the State in whose waters the cabotage was taking place.[641]

cc) Obligation to Enact Domestic Criminal Provisions

According to Article 5 SUA Convention, State parties are obliged to make the offenses set forth in Article 3 SUA Convention "punishable by appropriate

---

[638] Art. 3(2)(b) SUA Convention. However, aiding and abetting in the *attempted* commission of one of the offenses is not contained in the list of offenses of Art. 3 SUA Convention.

[639] Art. 4(1) SUA Convention.

[640] *Plant*, in: Higgins/Flory (eds.), Terrorism at Sea, 77.

[641] *Id.* 77–78.

penalties which take into account the grave nature of those offenses."[642] Thus, like Article 101 UNCLOS, the SUA Convention does not establish international crimes in the sense of a substantive criminal provision on which a domestic prosecution could be based. Rather, it obliges States to criminalize the acts set forth in Article 3 SUA Convention under their domestic criminal law. Whether conduct defined in Article 3 of the SUA Convention constitutes a crime can, thus, only be answered with regard to a specific national jurisdiction.

It should be noted that the Security Council urges States in its Resolutions 1846, 1851 and 1897[643] to fully implement their obligations under the SUA Convention, in particular to create the respective criminal offenses in their domestic legal order. Kenya, for instance, transposed the content of Article 3 SUA Convention into domestic criminal law by enacting the Kenyan Merchant Shipping Act in 2009.[644]

b) Hostage Convention

Under the Hostage Convention, State parties are obliged to incorporate into their domestic criminal law the offenses defined in the Convention, namely hostage taking,[645] attempts to commit an act of hostage taking[646] and participation as an accomplice in an act of hostage taking.[647] According to Article 2 Hostage Convention, State parties shall make these offenses "punishable by appropriate penalties which take into account the grave nature of those offenses."

Similar to the UNCLOS and SUA Conventions, the Hostage Convention does not establish an international crime in the sense of a substantive criminal norm on which prosecution can be based. Rather, once again the international treaty merely defines specific conduct, which State parties have to make punishable under their domestic criminal law.

2. Jurisdictional Bases for Prosecuting Armed Robbery at Sea

a) SUA Convention

Under the SUA Convention, which follows the model of other counter-terrorism treaties,[648] all those State parties featuring some connection with the crime (for

---

[642] Art. 5 SUA Convention.

[643] S.C. Res. 1846, para. 15; S.C. Res. 1851, preambular para. 9 and para. 5; S.C. Res. 1897, preambular para. 8 and para. 14.

[644] See Section 370 and 372 of the Kenyan Merchant Shipping Act.

[645] Art. 1(1) Hostage Convention.

[646] Art. 1(2)(a) Hostage Convention.

[647] Art. 1(2)(b) Hostage Convention.

[648] Such as the Convention for the Suppression of Unlawful Seizure of Aircraft, Art. 4(2), *adopted* Dec. 16, 1970, 860 U.N.T.S. 105 [hereinafter: Convention for the Sup-

example, if the offender or victim has its nationality or the attacked vessel flies its flag) are either obliged (mandatory primary jurisdiction)[649] or allowed (optional primary jurisdiction)[650] to establish their jurisdiction over the offenses.

Besides primary jurisdiction requiring a specific connection between the State and either the offense or the offender, the SUA Convention obliges any other State, irrespective of whether such a connection exists, to establish its jurisdiction in cases where the alleged offender is present on its territory and is not extradited.[651] This so-called secondary jurisdiction is analyzed in the context of the duty to prosecute or extradite.[652]

aa) Active Personality Principle

State parties to the SUA Convention are obliged to establish jurisdiction over offenses defined in Article 3 of the Convention if the offense is committed by their nationals.[653] Given that most of the attacks in the Gulf of Aden, Indian Ocean as well as the Red and Arabian Sea appear to be attributable to Somali nationals,[654] and given that Somalia is not a State party to the SUA Convention,[655] this ground of jurisdiction is of little relevance in the context at hand.

bb) Territoriality Principle

The SUA Convention further obliges States to establish jurisdiction over the offenses defined in Article 3 SUA Convention that occur on their territory or in their territorial sea.[656] Thus, the regional States of Kenya, the Seychelles, the United Republic of Tanzania, Djibouti, Yemen and Oman, which are all parties to

---

pression of Unlawful Seizure of Aircraft]; Convention for the Suppression of Unlawful Acts against the Safety of Civil Aviation, Art. 5(2), *adopted* Sept. 23, 1971, 974 U.N.T.S. 177 [hereinafter: Convention for the Suppression of Unlawful Acts against the Safety of Civil Aviation]; Convention on the Prevention and Punishment of Crimes against Internationally Protected Persons, Including Diplomatic Agents, Art. 3(2), *adopted* Dec. 14, 1973, 1035 U.N.T.S. 167 [hereinafter: Convention on the Prevention and Punishment of Crimes against Internationally Protected Persons, Including Diplomatic Agents]. *Wood*, The Convention on the Prevention and Punishment of Crimes against Internationally Protected Persons, Including Diplomats, ICLQ 23 (1974), 806.

[649] Art. 6(1) SUA Convention.

[650] Art. 6(2) SUA Convention.

[651] Art. 6(4) SUA Convention.

[652] This so-called secondary jurisdiction is analyzed in the context of the duty to prosecute or extradite; see p. 151 *et seq.*

[653] Art. 6(1)(c) SUA Convention.

[654] ICC-IMB, Piracy Report January-September 2009, pp. 6–7.

[655] See above note 224.

[656] Art. 6(1)(b) SUA Convention.

the SUA Convention, are under an obligation to establish jurisdiction over violent attacks occurring in their territorial sea.

The Security Council urged State parties to the SUA Convention to implement their obligations under the said Convention.[657] In addition, the Djibouti Code of Conduct (signed by all above mentioned States except Oman) calls for a review of national legislation in order to allow for the prosecution of armed robbery at sea.[658] Thus, those States are under an international obligation to establish criminal jurisdiction over criminal conduct as described in Article 3 SUA Convention, which occurs in their territorial waters.

cc) Flag State Principle

The SUA Convention further obliges State parties to establish jurisdiction if one of the catalog offenses in Article 3 is committed against or on board a ship flying their flag at the time the offense is committed.[659] Through the flag, the ship is moored to the State's jurisdiction. Its *ius puniendi* thus extends to acts occurring on board a vessel flying its flag. These acts are equated to conduct carried out on a State's territory.[660]

Under the SUA Convention, jurisdiction can only be based on the flag principle if the victim vessel matches the definition of "ship" contained in Article 1 read together with Article 2 SUA Convention.[661] Further, it is required that the offense was committed "against or on board a ship." This requirement is generally interpreted broadly, in that the jurisdiction of the flag State is not limited to acts carried out on board in the literal sense of the term. Rather, it extends to persons committing illegal activities on shore, such as the identification and location of potential targets and the provision of arms, as long as they work in furtherance of the offense committed against the vessel. Thereby, subordinate participants, such as aiders and abettors, would also fall within the ambit of the flag principle. Further, the flag State would also be competent to prosecute alleged offenders for attempts if the piracy-like attack, or planned attack, is defeated before its completion.[662]

Out of the total of 306 reported piracy attacks against ships worldwide in the first three quarters of 2009, the most represented flag State was Panama (52 ships), followed by Liberia (30 ships), Singapore (26 ships), Marshall Islands (21 ships),

---

[657] See for example S.C. Res. 1846, para. 15.

[658] Art. 11 Djibouti Code of Conduct.

[659] Art. 6(1)(a) SUA Convention.

[660] Council of Europe, Extraterritorial Criminal Jurisdiction, Criminal Law Forum 3 (1992), 449–450.

[661] On the definition of "ship" under the SUA Convention, see above note 631.

[662] Art. 4 ASIL-Commented Harvard Draft Convention on Jurisdiction with Respect to Crime; *Ambos*, Internationales Strafrecht, pp. 34–35.

Malta (19 ships) and Antigua and Barbuda (18 ships).[663] All these countries are State parties to the SUA Convention[664] and thus obliged to establish flag State jurisdiction in their national legal order. However, many of these States are known for having open registries, thereby, allowing vessels to register under a flag of convenience[665] and, for economic or political reasons, may not, in fact, commence criminal proceedings against persons allegedly having carried out attacks against ships flying their flag. Thus, the wider problem of flags of convenience impacts the effective prosecution of piracy suspects.

dd) Passive Personality Principle

Under the SUA Convention, State parties may establish jurisdiction if their nationals are seized, threatened, injured or killed during the commission of a SUA offense.[666] The exercise of jurisdiction based on the passive personality principle has traditionally been controversial[667] and scholars representing the Anglo-Saxon legal tradition have been particularly vocal in condemning its application.[668] However, this reluctance was dropped with regard to conventions negotiated at a regional or international level in response to transnational terrorist acts.[669]

Concerning the SUA Convention, the United States of America, which had traditionally been hostile towards recognizing the passive personality principle, had a particular and vital interest in providing jurisdiction to the State of the victim due to the fact that persons and interests of the United States of America have been prominent targets of terrorist attacks and given that the chances that the offender

---

[663] ICC-IMB, Piracy Report January-September 2009, pp. 18–19.

[664] International Maritime Organization, Status of Multilateral Conventions and Instruments in Respect of which the International Maritime Organization (IMO) or its Secretary-General Performs Depositary or Other Functions as at 31 December 2009, *available at* www.imo.org (follow "legal" hyperlink, then follow "IMO Conventions" hyperlink, then follow "Depositary Information on IMO Conventions" hyperlink) (last visited Aug. 30, 2010), pp. 385–387.

[665] For a definition of the term "flag of convenience," see *König*, in: Wolfrum (ed.), EPIL-Flag of Convenience, para. 1. According to the United Nations Conference on Trade and Development, the 10 major open and international registries are the following: Antigua and Barbuda, Bahamas, Bermuda, Cyprus, Isle of Man, Liberia, Malta, Marshall Islands, Panama, Saint Vincent and the Grenadines: United Nations, United Nations Conference on Trade and Development (UNCTAD), Review of Maritime Transport, 2009, Report by the UNCTAD Secretariat, *available at* www.unctad.org/en/docs/rmt2009_en.pdf (last visited Aug. 30, 2010), p. 207.

[666] Art. 6(2)(b) SUA Convention.

[667] In the ASIL-Commented Harvard Draft Convention on Jurisdiction with Respect to Crime, the passive personality principle was not yet included.

[668] *Freestone*, in: Higgins/Flory (eds.), Principles of Jurisdiction, 44–45.

[669] Council of Europe, European Committee on Crime Problems, Extraterritorial Criminal Jurisdiction, report reprinted in Criminal Law Forum 3 (1992), 450.

would have the nationality of the United States of America were perceived as marginal.[670] The controversial nature of the passive personality principle reverberates in the SUA Convention only in that its establishment is left optional.[671]

The passive personality principle, as foreseen in the SUA Convention, can only be invoked if the victim is a natural person. Thus, it cannot be applied if the victim of a piracy-like act is a legal person, such as a ship-owner company. Even though counter-terrorism treaties adopted earlier than the SUA Convention extended the application of the passive personality principle to moral persons,[672] this concept was defeated by an indicative vote at the SUA diplomatic conference in Rome in 1988.[673] However, since the SUA Convention "does not exclude any criminal jurisdiction exercised in accordance with national law,"[674] it seems that States are free to enact a passive personality principle under their domestic law, which extends to legal persons. This would allow prosecution by the State whose nationality the company operating the attacked ship possesses.

---

[670] *Halberstam*, Terrorism on High Seas: The Achille Lauro, Piracy and the IMO Convention on Maritime Safety, AJIL 82 (1988), 302. On the declining reluctance, see also United States of America, United States' Restatement (Third) of Foreign Relations Law, para. 402(g) (1987) stating that: "The principle has not been generally accepted for ordinary torts or crimes, but it is increasingly accepted as applied to terrorist and other organized attacks on a state's nationals by reason of their nationality, or to assassination of a state's diplomatic representatives or other officials."

[671] Other terrorism conventions also leave it optional for States to establish jurisdiction based on the passive personality principle; see, for example, International Convention for the Suppression of Terrorist Bombings, Art. 6(2)(a), *adopted* March 10, 1988, 1678 U.N.T.S. 304 or the Protocol for the Suppression of Unlawful Acts against the Safety of Fixed Platforms Located on the Continental Shelf, Art. 3(2)(b), *adopted* March 10, 1988, 1678 U.N.T.S. 201.

[672] According to Art. 4(1)(c) Convention for the Suppression of Unlawful Seizure of Aircraft, State Parties must establish jurisdiction "when the offence is committed on board an aircraft leased without crew to a lessee who has its principal place of business, or, if the lessee has no such place of business, his permanent residence, in that State." The Convention for the Suppression of Unlawful Acts against the Safety of Civil Aviation, Art. 5(1)(d), obliges State parties to establish jurisdiction if "the offence is committed against or on board an aircraft leased without crew to a lessee who has his principal place of business or, if the lessee has no such place of business, his permanent residence, in that State."

[673] The draft provision on jurisdiction in the SUA Convention provided that a State may establish jurisdiction over any of the SUA offenses when "the demise-charterer in possession of the ship concerned in the offence [is a national of that State and] has its principal place of business in that State:" International Maritime Organization, Draft Convention for the Suppression of Unlawful Acts against the Safety of Maritime Navigation, Art. 7(2)(d), IMO Doc. PCUA 2/5, Ann. 1 (June 2, 1987) (the brackets are in the draft Convention): cited in *Halberstam*, Terrorism on High Seas: The Achille Lauro, Piracy and the IMO Convention on Maritime Safety, AJIL 82 (1988), 295. Also the proposal by Iran to include the nationality or principal place of business of the "charterer of a bareboat chartered ship" was defeated by the diplomatic conference: IMO Doc. SUA/CONF/CW/WP.3 (March 1, 1988), cited in *Plant*, in: Higgins/Flory (eds.), Terrorism at Sea, 85.

[674] Art. 6(5) SUA Convention.

ee) Protective Principle

The SUA Convention further provides for jurisdiction based on the protective principle. The protective principle confers on States the right to try offenses threatening their security, institutions or other fundamental national interests. Given its vague definition, it allows a great deal of variation in implementation.[675] Under the SUA Convention, as for other counter-terrorism conventions, the protective principle provides a basis of jurisdiction to prosecute terrorist offenses that are committed in an attempt to coerce a particular State. However, this may generally not be the case regarding piracy. The driving force behind the commission of piracy and armed robbery at sea is not of a political character, but rather of a private and economic nature. In fact, political acts were traditionally excluded from the definition of piracy.[676] Further, the primary entities to compulsion (such as to pay ransom) are typically private shipping companies and not States. Hence, it seems that the SUA protective principle can generally not be invoked for piracy-like attacks.

However, the SUA Convention, as stated above, does not exclude any criminal jurisdiction exercised in accordance with municipal law.[677] Therefore, States may establish jurisdiction based on the protective principle for reasons other than the one stipulated in the SUA Convention (which is to coerce a State's will). The concept of "fundamental national interests," whose violation justifies the application of the protective principle, is being interpreted broadly by States and it is not rare that national shipping and certain industrial or commercial interests are considered "fundamental national interests" important enough to justify jurisdiction over acts violating these interests.[678]

b) Hostage Convention

State parties to the Hostage Convention are obliged to establish jurisdiction over the offense of hostage taking. Similar to the SUA Convention, the Hostage Convention also distinguishes between primary jurisdiction[679] and secondary jurisdiction.[680] Moreover, like the SUA Convention, the Hostage Convention also states

---

[675] Council of Europe, European Committee on Crime Problems, Extraterritorial Criminal Jurisdiction, report reprinted in Criminal Law Forum 3 (1992), 451.

[676] On the "private ends" requirements contained in the piracy definition of Article 101 UNCLOS, see p. 61 *et seq.*

[677] Art. 6(5) SUA Convention.

[678] Council of Europe, European Committee on Crime Problems, Extraterritorial Criminal Jurisdiction, report reprinted in Criminal Law Forum 3 (1992), 451.

[679] Art. 5(1) Hostage Convention.

[680] Art. 5(2) Hostage Convention. The issue of secondary jurisdiction is discussed in connection with the duty to prosecute or extradite persons allegedly having engaged in conduct referred to as armed robbery at sea, see p. 151 *et seq.*

that it "does not exclude any criminal jurisdiction exercised in accordance with internal law."[681]

In terms of primary jurisdiction, the Hostage Convention obliges States to establish jurisdiction over the offenses defined in the treaty, if they are committed in their territory (territoriality principle) or on board a ship[682] registered in that State (flag State principle).[683] States are, moreover, obliged to provide criminal jurisdiction if the crime is committed by one of its nationals (active personality principle).[684] Further, the Hostage Convention mandates States to foresee criminal jurisdiction if the crime of hostage taking is committed in order "to compel that State to do or abstain from doing any act" (protective principle).[685] While the establishment of these grounds of jurisdiction is mandatory, a State needs only to establish jurisdiction over acts of hostage taking against their nationals (passive personality principle) if "that State considers it appropriate."[686] Thus, despite the wording "shall (…) establish jurisdiction" used in Article 5(1) of the Hostage Convention, which suggests that all grounds of jurisdiction listed in the provision are mandatory, the clause "if that State considers it appropriate" gives States discretion as to whether they will apply the passive personality principle as a jurisdictional ground under their criminal law.[687]

Similar to the SUA Convention, the Hostage Convention, *prima facie*, provides a panoply of jurisdictional grounds to prosecute pirates and armed robbers at sea allegedly having committed hostage taking in the Gulf of Aden region. However, the territoriality and active personality principles often do not work in the present context, since Somalia is not a State party to the Hostage Convention.[688] As under the SUA Convention, the flag State principle may often not be activated since a high proportion of vessels attacked by pirates and armed robbers at sea are registered in States, which have an open registry. Since a genuine link between the victim ship

---

[681] Art. 5(3) Hostage Convention.

[682] The reach of the flag principle in Art. 5(1)(a) SUA Convention is described as "against or on board a ship" while Art. 5(1)(a) Hostage Convention limits the principle to acts committed "on board a ship." This seems appropriate since the SUA offenses (contrary to hostage taking) cannot only be committed physically on board a ship but also against it, namely, from distance. The SUA wording is identical to the Convention for the Suppression of Unlawful Acts against the Safety of Civil Aviation, Art. 5(1)(b), which was chosen in order to cover crimes that are committed against aircrafts from distance, such as plane bombings where the bomb is detonated from distance.

[683] Art. 5(1)(a) Hostage Convention.

[684] Art. 5(1)(b) Hostage Convention.

[685] Art. 5(1)(c) Hostage Convention.

[686] Art. 5(1)(d) Hostage Convention.

[687] A truly mandatory clause to establish jurisdiction based on the nationality of the victim is contained in Art. 3(1)(c) of the Convention on the Prevention and Punishment of Crimes against Internationally Protected Persons, Including Diplomatic Agents.

[688] On the status of ratification of the Hostage Convention, see note 229.

and the flag State (i.e. the State of registration) is generally missing in such cases, these States will rarely have a real interest in prosecuting alleged pirates.[689] In the context of piracy and armed robbery, the protective principle as stated in the Hostage Convention may not work either, since this jurisdictional ground is strongly terrorism-tailored by requiring that the offender coerced a State's will, which is rarely the case in piracy-like attacks.

3. Armed Robbery at Sea: Duty to Extradite or Prosecute?

As we have seen, primary jurisdictional grounds under the SUA and Hostage Conventions may only in few cases constitute a viable basis for commencing criminal proceedings against pirates and armed robbers at sea arrested during counter-piracy operations in the Gulf of Aden region. Thus, the duty to either prosecute or extradite and the related obligation to establish jurisdiction in cases where the alleged offender is present in the territory of a State and is not extradited, could be of major importance to bring alleged pirates and armed robbers at sea to justice.

The SUA and Hostage Convention both contain *aut dedere – aut iudicare* clauses,[690] which follow the so-called "Hague Model." According to this model, the obligation of the State of apprehension to prosecute is no longer dependent on a prior extradition request and its denial. Rather, the obligation applies in all cases of non-extradition.[691] In order to ensure that the *judex deprehensionis* (the courts of the State having custody over the alleged offender) is competent to exercise criminal jurisdiction, both treaties not only foresee the establishment of jurisdiction of States having some link to the crime (primary jurisdiction), but also oblige all other State parties to establish jurisdiction in cases where the alleged offender is present in their territory and not extradited (secondary jurisdiction).

Admittedly, the drafters of the wording "the State Party in the territory of which the alleged offender is found" in the *aut dedere – aut iudicare* clause of the SUA and Hostage Conventions most probably did not anticipate the scenario in which States have custody over pirates and armed robbers at sea as a result of law enforcement operations carried out on the high seas or in the territorial waters of a third State. Rather, and understandably, when considering the *raison d'être* of the SUA and Hostage Taking Conventions, the wording was aimed at preventing terrorists from fleeing the State of the *locus delicti* in order to find a safe haven in a

---

[689] On the flag principle and the problem of open registries, see p. 158 *et seq.*

[690] Art. 10 SUA Convention and Art. 8 Hostage Convention.

[691] The so-called "Hague Model" was enacted for the first time in Articles 4(2) and 7 of the Convention for the Suppression of Unlawful Seizure of Aircraft. See *Maierhöfer, aut dedere – aut iudicare*, pp. 338–349, for a detailed description of the "Hague Model." See also *Kreß*, in: Wolfrum (ed.), EPIL-International Criminal Law, para. 8; and *id.*, Universal Jurisdiction over International Crimes and the Institut de Droit international, Journal of International Criminal Justice (4) 2006, 567–568.

third State. However, the *aut dedere – aut iudicare* provision should also cover captured pirates and armed robbers at sea detained on board of a warship. Firstly because the underlying rationale of the clause – not letting alleged offenders escape trial and if guilty punishment, which in the interest of the international community as a whole – should equally apply to the situation at hand. Secondly, it is a well-established principle that ships are factually equated with territory regarding jurisdictional questions.[692] Thirdly, if the duty to prosecute or extradite is incumbent on a State when an alleged perpetrator enters its territory without the will of that particular State, it should *a forteriori* apply to situations where the specific State takes action, which results in the alleged offender coming within its jurisdiction. For these various reasons, it should be enough that an alleged offender is within a State's jurisdiction, even if detained outside that State's territory, to trigger the duty to extradite or prosecute.

Hence, it must be concluded that State parties to the SUA or Hostage Conventions, which capture alleged pirates or armed robbers at sea are under an obligation to either prosecute[693] (based on primary or secondary jurisdiction) or to extradite the alleged offender to a third State if the act falls within the ambit of one of the conventions. These obligations to either extradite or prosecute do not leave any room for a third alternative, such as the release of alleged offenders. Thus, State parties to the SUA or Hostage Conventions that release alleged pirates suspected of having engaged in conduct as defined in Article 3 SUA Convention or Article 1 Hostage Convention do so in violation of their obligations under the SUA or Hostage Conventions, the very rationale of which is to avoid alleged offenders evading criminal prosecution.

4. Conclusion

Given that international law neither contains a well-settled definition nor an international crime of armed robbery at sea, other offenses partially covering conduct referred to as armed robbery at sea in the Security Council Resolutions on piracy have to be applied. Specifically, conduct defined in Article 3 SUA Convention and Article 1 Hostage Convention is relevant for armed robbery at sea. However, these provisions do not constitute international crimes on which domestic prosecutions can be based. Rather, State parties are obliged to criminalize the conduct so defined under their domestic criminal law. Further, the SUA and Hostage Conventions provide various bases to establish criminal jurisdiction over the respective conduct. However, for the various reasons laid out above, many of the jurisdictional bases

---

[692] On the equivalence of criminal acts occurring on board a vessel to criminal conduct occurring on a State's territory for jurisdictional purposes, see the explanations on the flag State principle p. 158 *et seq.*

[693] On what the obligation to prosecute entails see *Maierhöfer, aut dedere – aut iudicare*, pp. 372–398.

are not operable in the context at hand. Against this background, the obligation of State parties to establish jurisdiction in cases where the alleged offender is within their jurisdiction and not extradited is of considerable importance.

C. Impact of Security Council Resolutions 1846, 1851 and 1897 on the Criminal Prosecution of Pirates and Armed Robbers at Sea

Having described the current legal framework pertaining to criminal prosecution of pirates and armed robbers at sea, the question arises whether the various Security Council Resolutions on piracy impacted the legal regime. In particular it needs to be discussed: whether Security Council Resolutions 1846, 1851, and 1897 provide States with further jurisdictional bases to prosecute crimes committed in the Gulf of Aden region (1.); whether they create a general duty to prosecute or extradite pirates and armed robbers at sea (2.) or whether they amount to a mere call for enhanced interstate cooperation in criminal matters (3.).

1. Conferring a Jurisdictional Basis?

While there is universal jurisdiction under customary international law for the crime of piracy, the jurisdictional net for the prosecution of criminal conduct in the territorial waters of a State (such as Somalia), referred to as armed robbery at sea, is less densely knotted with the result that jurisdictional *lacunae* may occur in some situations. The Security Council Resolutions on piracy did not remedy the situation, since they do not provide a new or general jurisdictional basis to bring pirates and armed robbers at sea to trial.

The authorization in Security Council Resolution 1846 (as prolonged by Security Council Resolution 1897) to use "all necessary means to repress acts of piracy and armed robbery at sea"[694] can hardly be interpreted as providing adjudicative jurisdiction to States carrying out arrests of piracy suspects and alleged armed robbers at sea. Firstly, the wording "*enter into* the territorial waters of Somalia *for the purpose* of repressing acts of piracy and armed robbery at sea"[695] of Security Council Resolution 1846, points towards an authorization to take immediate action once entering the territorial waters and authorizes policing rather than criminal prosecutions against pirates and armed robbers at sea.

Further, the text of Security Council Resolution 1846 (as prolonged by Security Council Resolution 1897) to "*use, within the territorial waters* (...) all necessary

---

[694] S.C. Res. 1846, para. 10, read together with S.C. Res. 1897, para. 7.
[695] S.C. Res. 1846, para. 10(a) (emphasis added), read together with S.C. Res. 1897, para. 7.

means"[696] suggests that measures authorized are to be taken in that geographical area. Hence, this provision cannot be interpreted as allowing adjudication in a third State. This geographical scope argument also holds true with regard to the authorization in Security Council Resolution 1851 (as prolonged by Security Council Resolution 1897) to "undertake all necessary measures that are appropriate *in Somalia*."[697] This wording clearly limits the authorization to measures taken on the Somali mainland and, therefore, cannot include criminal proceedings in third States.

What is more, the authorizations to use all necessary means or to undertake all necessary measures in Security Council Resolutions 1846 and 1851 (compared to the remainder of the Resolutions) are limited in time. Security Council Resolution 1897 renewed the validity of these specific authorizations only for a period of twelve months, until November 2010.[698] These temporal limitations likewise suggest that the authorization clauses do not provide a basis for criminal prosecution of pirates and armed robbers at sea. Any such authorization would need to be available for a significant time after November 2010.

Lastly, as can be seen, the piracy definition was not extended to the territorial sea by Security Council Resolution 1846. Rather, the Security Council introduced the ill-defined concept of armed robbery at sea to designate violent acts directed against ships and persons on board, committed in territorial seas.[699] Therefore, it can hardly be maintained that the universality principle, which only exists over acts constituting piracy under international law, has been extended, *qua* Security Council Resolutions, to crimes committed in the territorial seas.

2. Establishing a Duty to Prosecute or Extradite?

As has been shown, parties to the SUA and Hostage Conventions are under an obligation to either extradite or prosecute an alleged offender if he is found on their territory. However, theses treaties have not (yet) been universally ratified. Furthermore, no similar obligation exists, *per se*, with regard to the crime of piracy. Since it is not uncommon for the Security Council to oblige States to prosecute or extradite suspects on specific charges under Chapter VII-based Resolutions,[700] it is appropriate, at this stage, to consider whether the Security Council Resolutions on piracy contain an *aut dedere – aut iudicare* obligation.

---

[696] S.C. Res. 1846, para. 10(b) (emphasis added), read together with S.C. Res. 1897, para. 7.

[697] S.C. Res. 1851, para. 6 (emphasis added), read together with S.C. Res. 1897, para. 7.

[698] S.C. Res. 1897, para.7.

[699] On the notion of armed robbery at sea, see p. 73 *et seq.*

[700] For an overview on Chapter VII-based (Art. 41 United Nations Charter) Security Council Resolutions containing an explicit or implicit duty to prosecute or extradite, see *Maierhöfer, aut dedere – aut iudicare*, pp. 329–335.

The post 9/11 Security Council Resolution 1373,[701] for instance, stipulates an obligation to either prosecute or extradite alleged terrorists.[702] However, the wording of Security Council Resolutions 1846[703] and 1897[704] on piracy is much more discretionary, in that the Security Council only "calls upon all States (...) to cooperate in determining jurisdiction, and in the investigation and prosecution of persons responsible for acts of armed robbery and piracy (...) by providing disposition and logistics assistance." This contrasts with the wording of Security Council Resolution 1373 according to which "States shall (...) [e]nsure that any person who participates in the financing, planning, preparation or perpetration of terrorist acts (...) is brought to justice."[705] Hence, the statement in Security Council Resolution 1846 amounts to a restatement of the general obligation to cooperate in the repression of piracy contained in Article 100 UNCLOS rather than to a specific obligation to prosecute or extradite.

While Security Council Resolutions 1846 and 1897 do not stipulate a duty to prosecute or extradite persons allegedly having committed piracy or armed robbery at sea, State parties to the SUA and/or Hostage Conventions are, nevertheless under an obligation to prosecute or extradite *qua* treaty law, as long as these acts constitute conduct as defined in Article 3 SUA Convention or Article 1 Hostage Convention. Thus, by pursuing a catch-and-release approach regarding persons having engaged in conduct as defined in the SUA and Hostage Conventions, they would violate this obligation. However, for conduct not matching an offense of the SUA and/or Hostage Conventions or if a State is not party to them, no general obligation to either prosecute or extradite has been conferred by the Security Council Resolutions.

3. A Mere Call for Enhanced Interstate Cooperation in Criminal Matters

Security Council Resolutions 1846, 1851 and 1897 neither provide an additional basis for jurisdiction nor do they generally oblige States to prosecute or extradite alleged pirates and armed robbers at sea. However, the Security Council Resolutions are not entirely mute on aspects of adjudicative jurisdiction either. For

---

[701] S.C. Res. 1373.

[702] *Frowein*, Der Terrorismus als Herausforderung für das Völkerrecht, Heidelberg Journal of International Law 62 (2002), 897; *Maierhöfer, aut dedere – aut iudicare*, p. 330.

[703] S.C. Res. 1846, para. 14.

[704] S.C. Res. 1897, para. 12.

[705] S.C. Res. 1373, para. 2(e): "Acting under Chapter VII of the Charter of the United Nations [the Security Council] (...) [d]ecides also that all States shall: (...) (e) Ensure that any person who participates in the financing, planning, preparation or perpetration of terrorist acts or in supporting terrorist acts is brought to justice and ensure that, in addition to any other measures against them, such terrorist acts are established as serious criminal offences in domestic laws and regulations and that the punishment duly reflects the seriousness of such terrorist acts."

instance, the Security Council invites States to adopt shiprider agreements in order to bring pirates and armed robbers at sea *ab initio* under the jurisdiction of a State "willing to take custody of pirates" and to sit in judgment over alleged offenders.[706] Further, it urges States to implement international legal instruments, such as the "SUA Convention, the UN Convention against Transnational Organized Crime and other relevant instruments to which States in the region are party" in order to effectively investigate and prosecute piracy and armed robbery at sea.[707] Interestingly, the Security Council does not explicitly refer to the Hostage Convention. Nonetheless, the reference to "other relevant instruments to which States in the region are party"[708] clearly includes this treaty, which is of major importance given the current scale of hostage takings in the region. The Security Council does not urge States to sign and ratify these conventions but simply calls upon States already party to them to implement the arising obligations.

While the Security Council Resolutions have had a considerable impact on the scope of enforcement powers, they did not alter the current legal framework pertaining to the criminal prosecution of pirates and armed robbers at sea. Hence, regarding adjudicative jurisdiction, the Security Council Resolutions on piracy are nothing more than a call for enhanced interstate cooperation in criminal matters. Prosecutions of pirates and armed robbers at sea thus remain governed by the existing treaty patchwork, with all its *lacunae* and overlaps, despite the legal regime on piracy and armed robbery at sea set up by the Security Council.

II. Possible Venues for the Criminal Prosecution of Piracy Suspects

While initial catch-and-release practices have now decreased, the reluctance of various States participating in the maritime operations in the Gulf of Aden region to prosecute pirates within their own criminal justice system has remained. The Security Council explicitly affirms "that the failure to prosecute persons responsible for acts of piracy and armed robbery at sea off the coast of Somalia undermines anti-piracy efforts of the international community."[709] Hence, the search for adequate judicial fora to prosecute piracy suspects has been a predominant feature

---

[706] S.C. Res. 1851, para. 3; on the definition and use of shipriders, see p. 85 *et seq.*

[707] See, for example, S.C. Res. 1846, para. 15, urging States party to the SUA Convention to fully implement their obligations under said Convention and S.C. Res. 1851, preambular para. 9 and para. 5, reiterating the obligations of States party to the SUA Convention; see also S.C. Res. 1897, para. 14.

[708] S.C. Res. 1851, para. 5.

[709] S.C. Res. 1918, para. 1.

of the international debate over the effective repression of piracy in the Gulf of Aden region.

Various options for the criminal prosecution of piracy suspects and alleged armed robbers at sea have been put forward, but two rather general alternatives can be discerned from the discussion: prosecuting persons suspected of having committed acts of piracy in domestic courts in the region ("the regional approach") or seeking justice on the international level ("the international approach"). Discussions continue as the number of apprehended piracy suspects awaiting trial constantly rises.[710] In Resolution 1918, the Security Council, therefore, requested the Secretary-General to present a report on possible options to further the aim of prosecuting and imprisoning persons responsible for acts of piracy and armed robbery at sea off the coast of Somalia.[711]

The Secretary-General in his report of July 26, 2010, pursuant to Security Council Resolution 1918, has identified seven options for consideration by the Security Council.[712] Yet, for the time being, in practice, preference is accorded to the domestic prosecution of pirates in the affected region. Captured piracy suspects and alleged armed robbers at sea are handed over to regional States willing and able to commence criminal proceedings, often on the basis of specific transfer agreements.[713] Prosecutions of acts of piracy are currently ongoing in Kenya, the Seychelles, Somalia (however, only in the Somaliland and Puntland regions), Maldives and Yemen.[714] Out of these States, the main burden-carriers are presently Puntland (Somalia), where by May 2010, a total of 208 prosecutions were ongoing,[715] and Kenya,[716] where 123 prosecutions following arrest by patrolling naval States were under way. In Somaliland, the number of prosecutions amounts to 100, in the Seychelles to 31 and in Yemen, it is estimated that currently 60 prosecutions are ongoing.[717] The United Republic of Tanzania, Mauritius and Maldives are, likewise,

---

[710] United Nations, Secretary-General Report pursuant to S.C. Res. 1918, July 26, 2010, para. 29.

[711] S.C. Res. 1918, para. 4.

[712] United Nations, Secretary-General Report pursuant to S.C. Res. 1918, July 26, 2010.

[713] On transfer agreements concluded between the European Union and regional States, see p. 33 *et seq.* and p. 198 *et seq.*

[714] United Nations, Secretary-General Report pursuant to S.C. Res. 1918, July 26, 2010, para. 19. Notably, in Kenya there were no prosecutions following arrest by Kenyan forces. According to an earlier report, by the end of October 2009, over 100 piracy suspects were undergoing trial; United Nations, Secretary-General Report on S.C. Res. 1846, Nov. 13, 2009, para. 46.

[715] Out of the total number of 208 prosecutions, 60 are following arrest by patrolling naval States and 148 prosecutions are following arrest by Puntland's own forces: United Nations, Secretary-General Report pursuant to S.C. Res. 1918, July 26, 2010, para. 19.

[716] S.C. Res. 1918, preambular para. 8.

[717] United Nations, Secretary-General Report pursuant to S.C. Res. 1918, July 26, 2010, para. 19.

considering undertaking piracy prosecutions. In March 2010, the Council of the European Union authorized the High Representative to open neogiations with Mauritius, Mozambique, South Africa, Tanzania and Uganda with, a view to concluding transfer agreements in the framework of the European Union counter-piracy Operation Atalanta.[718]

The United Nations Office on Drugs and Crime estimates that if Kenya, Seychelles, the United Republic of Tanzania and Mauritius all engage in piracy prosecutions and, provided they are fully supported by the international community, their capacity to prosecute piracy suspects could reach 600 to 800 suspects per year.[719] There are currently only around 40 prosecutions taking place outside the region, namely, in the Netherlands, United States of America, France, Spain and Germany.[720]

Against this background, the analysis now turns to an overview on the various regional options to prosecute piracy suspects and alleged armed robbers at sea. As a practical example we shall consider the ongoing piracy trials in Kenya (A.). The various international(ized) models that are currently under discussion are then examined (B.), before we turn to general questions arising in relation to the criminal prosecution of pirates irrespective of the institutional venue chosen (C.).

A. The Regional Approach

1. Regional Options to Further the Prosecution and Imprisoning of Persons Responsible for Acts of Piracy and Armed Robbery at Sea

a) Prosecution in Regular Domestic Courts of Regional States

The first option for the furtherance of prosecutions of piracy suspects mentioned in the Secretary-General's report refers to the enhancement of United Nations assistance to regional States. This is the model that is currently being followed. The United Nations Office on Drugs and Crime, in particular, provides targeted support to regional countries, namely, Kenya and the Seychelles, but also to the Puntland and Somaliland regions of Somalia.[721] Unlike the various other options invoked in

---

[718] European Union, Council of the European Union, Press Release, Foreign Affairs, 3005th Council Meeting, 7828/1/10 REV 1 (Presse 73), March 22, 2010, *available at* www.consilium.europa.eu/uedocs/cms_data/docs/pressdata/EN/foraff/113482.pdf (last visited Aug. 30, 2010).

[719] United Nations, Secretary-General Report pursuant to S.C. Res. 1918, July 26, 2010, paras. 19 and 27.

[720] *Id.* at paras. 19 and 22.

[721] United Nations, UNODC, UNODC and Piracy, *available at* www.unodc.org/easternafrica/en/piracy/index.html?ref=menuside%20and (last visited Aug. 30, 2010).

the Secretary-General's Report, this option is already ongoing and has demonstrated that it can be effective.[722]

The Report points out that trials in regional States have been relatively rapid and cost-effective. Regional proximity is an additional advantage of this approach. The costs of assistance to national trials and prison facilities are relatively modest compared to the establishment of a genuinely new (international) mechanism. What is more, assistance to national jurisdictions benefits the criminal justice system of the State as a whole. Thus, in the long run, enhanced assistance to regional States, including Somalia, will build the capacity of regional States to prosecute and imprison persons responsible for acts of piracy and armed robbery at sea.[723]

The Report is drafted in a relatively neutral manner and does not provide an explicit recommendation for any of the seven options identified. Implicitly, however, the Report appears to favor pursuing the current regional approach. Apart from highlighting that the current model has already proved to have some success, regional prosecution is the only option for which the Report provides suggestions for conrete steps to be taken by the Security Council.[724] Moreover, the only disadvantage the Report mentions with regard to the prosecution in regional States is that patrolling naval States may not know at the time of apprehending piracy suspects whether they will be able to transfer them to a prosecuting State.[725] However, it is pointed out that this disadvantage would likewise apply to the various other options laid out in the Report.[726]

Continuing prosecutions in regional States and further enhancing international and United Nation's assistance to these States appears to be the most realistic option. In addition to the various advantages laid out above, prosecutions in regional States avoid the difficult jurisdictional and definitional issues that the setting up of an international tribunal would bring about and that would presumably lead to prolonged negotiations among States. What is more, domestic prosecutions of piracy

---

[722] United Nations, Secretary-General Report pursuant to S.C. Res. 1918, July 26, 2010, para. 56.

[723] Id.

[724] The Secretary-General in its Report pursuant to S.C. Res. 1918, July 26, 2010, para. 61, inter alia, commends Kenya, the Seychelles and other States engaged in prosecutions for their role; commends the work of the United Nations Office on Drugs and Crime in assisting States prosecuting alleged pirates and armed robbers at sea and imprisoning convicted person; urges regional States to accept the transfer of suspects from patrolling naval States for prosecution; calls upon all States to ensure that they have the relevant jurisdiction, offences and procedures to enable them to prosecute acts of piracy off the coast of Somalia; and encourages States and the international shipping industry to financially contribute to the International Trust Fund.

[725] United Nations, Secretary-General Report pursuant to S.C. Res. 1918, July 26, 2010, para. 57.

[726] Id.

suspects are in line with the traditional model as it is envisaged in the UNCLOS.[727] National criminal legislation in various key regional States has already been reviewed by the United Nations Office on Drugs and Crime and, where necessary, been up-dated. Building on the various existing judicial systems in the region, having already defined the respective crimes and having established jurisdiction over them, arguably provides the most realistic way to deal with the current and future case-load. It is estimated that by the end of 2011 prosecutions might amount to 2,000 persons.[728]

b) The "Lockerbie Model" – A Somali Court Sitting in the Territory of a Third State

In addition to, or potentially even as an alternative to, the model currently being pursued of prosecuting piracy suspects in various regional States, the Report also contemplates the establishment of a Somali court sitting in the territory of a third State in the region, possibly with or without United Nations assistance. This option is modeled upon the so-called Lockerbie court, a specially convened Scottish Court in the Netherlands set up under Scottish law following the terrorist bombing of PanAm Flight 103.[729] The national jurisdiction would be that of Somalia, not the host State, which would only be providing a secure environment for trials to take place under Somali law. However, as is pointed out in the Secretary-General's Report, serious concerns regarding the adequacy of Somalia's piracy laws and the capacity of Somalia's judicial system militate against this option. In the words of the report "it may not be a possibility at present."[730] This conclusion is also supported by the findings of the assessment mission to the region of Working Group 1 of the Contact Group on Piracy off the coast of Somalia.[731]

c) Specialized Piracy Chambers in the Domestic Courts of Regional States

The Report also invokes the option to establish a special chamber within the national court structure of a regional State or States, respectively with or without

---

[727] Art. 105 UNCLOS; see p. 148 *et seq.*

[728] United Nations, Secretary-General Report pursuant to S.C. Res. 1918, July 26, 2010, para. 29.

[729] *Aust*, Lockerbie: The Other Case, ICLQ 49 (2000), 278–296; United Nations, Secretary-General Report pursuant to S.C. Res. 1918, July 26, 2010, para. 24.

[730] United Nations, Secretary-General Report pursuant to S.C. Res. 1918, July 26, 2010, para. 65.

[731] *Id.* at para. 65, referring to an unpublished report of Working Group 1 of the Contact Group entitled "Regional Counter-Piracy Capability Development Needs Assessment and Prioritization Mission to East Africa and the Gulf of Aden," Oct. 20, 2009, p. 12.

United Nations participation.[732] At present, none of the regional States conducting prosecutions has a special chamber to deal with piracy and armed robbery at sea. The newly opened courtroom in Shimo-La-Tewa, Mombasa, Kenya, which will be used for piracy trials as well as for trials of other crimes, does not constitute a special chamber, but only a modernized premise to hold high-profile criminal trials.

Whether or not the establishment of a special chamber (with or without United Nations participation in the form of United Nations selected judges or prosecutors) would indeed be feasible, depends on a case-by-case evaluation of the situation in each respective State. Given that the courts in the Puntland and Somaliland regions currently handle piracy cases more regularly than other States, the establishment of a special chamber that could bundle the expertise in dealing with cases of piracy and armed robbery at sea, may be most feasible in those regions. However, as far as Puntland is concerned, the Monitoring Group on Somalia is rather concerned about State support for acts of piracy. In its most recent Report, the Monitoring Group held that "[i]n contrast with central Somalia, where piracy may be accurately described as a product of statelessness and warlordism, in north-eastern Somalia [Puntland] it benefits from the patronage and protection of State institutions."[733]

The option of instituting a special chamber potentially carries the risk of drawing resources and expertise from the criminal justice system in the respective country and could lead to a form of "two-tier justice" if the standards of fairness and efficiency in the special chamber exceed those of the national criminal system.[734] Whether or not this option should be pursued in certain countries will ultimately depend on the caseload and whether currently ongoing prosecutions evidence a need for a further bundling of judicial expertise with respect to piracy trials.

Kenya is one of the regional States where criminal prosecutions of persons suspected of having committed acts of piracy or armed robbery at sea are currently ongoing. In fact, Kenya received the highest numbers of suspects from patrolling naval States. Thus, before turning to the "international approach," in the following the piracy trials in Kenya are explained in greater detail.

---

[732] *Id.* at paras. 68 and 73.

[733] United Nations, Monitoring Group on Somalia, Report, March 10, 2010, para. 137. The Report goes on to state: "After 12 years of relatively positive evolution in Puntland, the newly established administration of Abdirahman Mohamed 'Faroole' is nudging Puntland in the direction of becoming a criminal State. Monitoring Group investigations, (...) have confirmed that senior Puntland officials, including President Faroole and members of his Cabinet, notably the Minister of the Interior, General Abdullahi Ahmed Jama 'Ilka-jiir'and the Minister for Internal Security, General Abdillahi Sa'iid Samatar, have received proceeds from piracy and/or kidnapping."

[734] United Nations, Secretary-General Report pursuant to S.C. Res. 1918, July 26, 2010, para. 71.

2. A Practical Example: Piracy Trials in Kenya

For the Kenyan State, conducting a growing number of piracy trials means putting an additional strain on the already notoriously congested criminal justice system.[735] If piracy trials were to be conducted with extra speed and caution, thereby
discriminating in favor of alleged pirates and armed robbers at sea as "first class
suspects," other trials would be significantly delayed by the additional caseload
being given priority. Evidently, growing numbers of persons prosecuted for acts of
piracy or armed robbery at sea will, in due course, also put an increasing burden on
the Kenyan prison system.

a) The Human Rights Situation in the Judicial and Penitentiary System in Kenya

Criminal proceedings in Kenya are potentially problematic from a human rights
perspective. Even though the Kenyan Constitution confers upon the accused a panoply of fair trial rights[736] and in spite of the fact that the EU-Kenya Transfer
Agreement obliges Kenya to treat transferred persons "humanely and in accordance
with international human rights obligations (...) and in accordance with the requirement to have a fair trial,"[737] recent country reports on the human rights situation in Kenya point to structural problems in the Kenyan justice system. The
United Nations Committee against Torture, for example, stated in its report on
Kenya released in January 2009, that steps taken in view of ensuring the integrity,
efficiency and transparency of Kenya's justice system have not been comprehensive enough and that reform measures would still be necessary.[738] The Human
Rights Report on Kenya issued by the State Department of the United States of
America further observes a lack of independence in the judiciary, with undue ex-
ecutive influence on judicial matters.[739]

---

[735] *Wambua*, in: Petrig (ed.), Sea Piracy Law – Droit de la piraterie maritime, Section III.B.

[736] See Section 77 of the Kenyan Constitution, stipulating the following rights of defendants: the right to a fair trial within a reasonable time and before an independent and impartial tribunal; the right to be presumed innocent until proven guilty; the right to be informed as reasonably as practical in a language that he understands and in detail, of the
nature of the offense with which he is charged; the right to be given adequate time and
facilities for the preparation of his defense; the right to defend himself before the court in
person or by a legal representative of his choice; the right to examine witnesses called by the
prosecution; the right to an interpreter where he cannot follow the proceedings in the language
of the court; and the right to be present in court during the course of the criminal trial.

[737] Art. 2(c) EU-Kenya Transfer Agreement states this general obligation, which is
detailed in Art. 3 EU-Kenya Transfer Agreement.

[738] United Nations, Committee against Torture, Consideration of Reports Submitted by
States Parties Under Article 19 of the Convention, Concluding Observations of the Committee against Torture, Kenya, U.N. Doc. CAT/C/KEN/CO/1 (Jan. 19, 2009), para. 9.

[739] United States of America, Department of State, Bureau of Democracy, Human
Rights, and Labor, 2008 Human Rights Report: Kenya, Feb. 25, 2009, *available at*

Another problem raised in the State Department's Report is that the "vast majority of defendants could not afford representation and were tried without legal counsel. Indigent defendants do not have the right to government-provided legal counsel except in capital cases. The lack of a formal legal aid system seriously hampered the ability of many poor defendants to mount an adequate defense. Legal aid was available only in major cities where some human rights organizations – notably, the Federation of Women Lawyers – provided it."[740] The Committee against Torture commends the establishment of a national legal aid scheme and an awareness program, but remains concerned about the persistent problem of access to justice, particularly by those without economic resources. It explicitly urges Kenya to take all necessary measures to ensure that the lack of resources is not an obstacle to accessing justice, in particular by establishing a national legal aid scheme, which could be accompanied by the setting up of an Office of Public Defender.[741]

The Committee against Torture also "notes with deep concern the numerous and consistent allegations of widespread use of torture and ill-treatment of suspects in police custody."[742] A further ground for concern was the "dire conditions of detention in Kenyan prisons, particularly the overcrowding, lack of appropriate health services and high levels of violence inside the prisons, including inter-prisoner violence," which do not live up to the United Nations Standard Minimum Rules for the Treatment of Prisoners.[743]

That said, especially with regard to the piracy trials, a number of rather positive developments have taken place in Kenya. Generally speaking, the piracy trials have international observers and, as far as can be seen, significant government interference in these trials has not been reported. Kenya benefits from assistance provided

---

www.state.gov/g/drl/rls/hrrpt/2008/af/119007.htm (last visited Aug. 30, 2010), Section 1, lit. e.

[740] *Id.*

[741] United Nations, Committee against Torture, Consideration of Reports Submitted by States Parties Under Article 19 of the Convention, Concluding Observations of the Committee against Torture, Kenya, U.N. Doc. CAT/C/KEN/CO/1 (Jan. 19, 2009), para. 10.

[742] *Id.* at para. 13. See also United States of America, Department of State, Bureau of Democracy, Human Rights, and Labor, 2008 Human Rights Report: Kenya, Feb. 25, 2009, *available at* www.state.gov/g/drl/rls/hrrpt/2008/af/119007.htm (last visited Aug. 30, 2010), Section 1, lit. c. stating: "The constitution and law prohibit such practices; however, police frequently used violence and torture during interrogations and as punishment of pretrial detainees and convicted prisoners."

[743] U.N. Standard Minimum Rules for the Treatment of Prisoners, adopted by the First United Nations Congress on the Prevention of Crime and the Treatment of Offenders, held at Geneva in 1955, and approved by the Economic and Social Council by its resolutions 663 C (XXIV) of July 31, 1957 and 2076 (LXII) of May 13, 1977, *available at* www2.ohchr.org/english/law/pdf/treatmentprisoners.pdf (last visited Aug. 30, 2010); United Nations, Committee against Torture, Consideration of Reports Submitted by States Parties Under Article 19 of the Convention, Concluding Observations of the Committee against Torture, Kenya, U.N. Doc. CAT/C/KEN/CO/1 (Jan. 19, 2009), para. 15.

by the European Union as well as the States that have concluded transfer agreements with it.[744] Simultaneously, the United Nations Office on Drugs and Crime is providing targeted support and capacity building to Kenya to ensure that the trials and detention are fair, humane and efficient and take place within the rule of a sound legal framework.[745] According to information provided by the United Nations Office on Drugs and Crime, since the inception in May 2009 of its Counter-Piracy Programme, it has, *inter alia*, completed reviews of the legal framework of Kenya, supported prosecutors through office improvements, the provision of evidence handover routines and training in the law of the sea and lent support to the Kenyan police. Moreover, the United Nations Office on Drugs and Crime has developed and improved court facilities, provided interpreters, defence services,[746] online legal resources and supplied technical equipment.[747] In June 2010, a high-security courtroom opened its doors at Shimo-La-Tewa; Mombasa, which was built by the United Nations Office on Drugs and Crime with contributions from Australia, Canada, the European Union, France, Germany and the United States.[748]

As far as the material conditions of detention are concerned, piracy suspects awaiting trial in Kenya are currently held at Shimo-La-Tewa prison, which has reportedly been raised through the United Nations Office on Drugs and Crime efforts to at least international minimum standards. In particular, the United Nations Office on Drugs and Crime has helped to reduce overcrowding, doubled sanitation and water supply capacity, procured mattresses and blankets, painted facilities and provided extra prison medical services at Shimo-La-Tewa prison, Mombasa.[749] Ultimately, these developments could have positive repercussions on the criminal justice and the corrections system in Kenya at large.

---

[744] United Nations, Secretary-General Report pursuant to S.C. Res. 1918, July 26, 2010, para. 25.

[745] United Nations, UNODC, UNODC and Piracy, *available at* www.unodc.org/eastern africa/en/piracy/index.html?ref=menuside%20and (last visited Aug. 30, 2010).

[746] Provision of defence lawyers is granted only where the United Nations Office on Drugs and Crime is requested to do so by the court and where no other defence assistance is in place. In November 2009 this applied to two cases, see United Nations, UNODC, Counter Piracy Programme, November 2009, *available at* www.unodc.org/documents/ easternafrica//piracy/UNODC_Counter_Piracy_Programme.pdf (last visited Aug. 30, 2010), p. 4.

[747] United Nations, UNODC, UNODC and Piracy, *available at* www.unodc.org/eastern africa/en/piracy/index.html?ref=menuside%20and (last visited Aug. 30, 2010).

[748] *Stemple*, Jurist, UN Announces Opening of New Kenya Courtroom for Piracy Trials, June 25, 2010, *available at* http://jurist.org/paperchase/2010/06/un-announces-opening-of-new-kenya-courtroom-for-piracy-trials.php (last visited Aug. 30, 2010); United Nations, News Centre, UN Opens New Courtroom to Try Pirate Suspects in Kenyan Port, June 25, 2010, *available at* www.un.org/apps/news/story.asp?NewsID=35156&Cr=UNODC&Cr1= (last visited Aug. 30, 2010).

[749] *Id.*

b) Kenyan Criminal Law – Hurdles to Overcome

Initial piracy trials held in Kenya demonstrated that significant hurdles in Kenyan criminal law[750] had to be overcome to pave the way for an effective prosecution of pirates and armed robbers at sea. Against this background, in 2009, the Kenyan legislature enacted a new criminal provision pertaining to piracy and armed robbery at sea, namely, the Kenyan Merchant Shipping Act.[751] The Kenyan Merchant Shipping Act defines the crime of piracy more comprehensively than the old norm of the Kenyan Penal Code. Moreover, under the Kenyan Merchant Shipping Act, the jurisdiction of the Kenyan courts has been extended to cover acts of piracy committed by non-Kenyan nationals.

Prior to the enactment of the Kenyan Merchant Shipping Act, the offense of piracy was included in Section 69 of the Kenyan Penal Code. With the entry into force of the Kenyan Merchant Shipping Act in 2009, this old piracy norm was repealed and, thereby, ceased to exist.[752] This was done despite the fact that pending piracy cases had already been commenced under this (now repealed) criminal provision. In this context, it has been argued that since the norm on which the charges are based ceased to exist, a conviction thereupon would no longer be possible. At the same time, the prohibition of retroactive application of a criminal law as stipulated in the Kenyan Constitution[753] would prohibit the conviction of a defendant based on the Kenyan Merchant Shipping Act, which was not yet in force at the time of the commission of the offense. According to this view conviction in those piracy cases, which were pending at the time the Kenyan Merchant Shipping Act came into force, can neither be based on this new law nor on the repealed old piracy provision contained in Section 69 of the Kenyan Penal Code. It is argued that this regrettable situation should have been avoided by inclusion of a "sunset clause" providing that the repeal of Section 69 of the Kenyan Penal Code would not affect the power of the court to try, convict and sentence accused persons then already charged under Section 69.[754] However, it could also be argued that the repeal of Section 69 of the Kenyan Penal Code was not (explicitly) retrospective and the repeal of this criminal norm without a "sunset clause" does not affect criminal liability for acts committed before the date of the repeal. Kenyan courts also seem

---

[750] Kenyan laws are *available at* www.kenyalaw.org/kenyalaw/klr_home/ (last visited Aug. 30, 2010).

[751] See Section 369 and 371 of the Kenyan Merchant Shipping Act.

[752] See Section 454(1) of the Kenyan Merchant Shipping Act.

[753] Section 77(4) of the Kenyan Constitution provides: "No person shall be held to be guilty of a criminal offence on account of an act or omission that did not, at the time it took place, constitute such an offence, and no penalty shall be imposed for such a criminal offence that is severer in degree or prescription than the maximum penalty that might have been imposed for that offence at the time it was committed."

[754] *Wambua*, in: Petrig (ed.), Sea Piracy Law – Droit de la piraterie maritime, Section III.A.1.

to share this view and continue to conduct trials, the underlying acts of which predate the repeal of Section 69 of the Kenyan Penal Code. Another problem derives
from the fact that Kenyan law contains contradictory statements as to which court
has jurisdiction over acts of piracy. The Kenyan Criminal Procedure Code[755] vests
jurisdiction in either the High Court or in subordinate courts. However, this contra-
dicts the Judicature Act,[756] which vests exclusive jurisdiction in the High Court.
Given that a lack of jurisdiction results in nullity of the judgment, clarification on
this question is essential.[757]

In addition, Kenya's Evidence Act[758] contains certain elements which may hamper the expediency of piracy trials. Among them is, firstly, the requirement to obtain direct oral evidence to prove a given fact[759] and, secondly, a restriction on the
admissibility of photographic evidence.[760] Thus, it appears to be mandatory that
witnesses – namely, the arresting naval officers or crew members of attacked merchant ships – personally attend the court proceedings in Kenya to give testimony,
since the use of a video link or other techniques to hear a witness from distance are
not permitted.[761]

Trials in regional States such as Kenya certainly have their benefits, namely, the
closeness to the *locus delicti*, which ensures that the criminal act can be dealt with
in the region where it occurred and that sentences can be enforced in States that are
as close as possible to the convicted person's home State. Nevertheless, certain
drawbacks of the regional approach as currently pursued are apparent. It is against

---

[755] Section 4 read together with Schedule 1 of the Kenyan Criminal Procedure Code.

[756] Section 4 of the Kenyan Judicature Act.

[757] *Wambua*, in: Petrig (ed.), Sea Piracy Law – Droit de la piraterie maritime, Section
III.A.1.

[758] The Kenyan Evidence Act entered into force on December 10, 1963 and is based on
the colonial Indian Evidence Act; it has been amended several times but still does not provide a suitable framework for the trial of modern offenses like piracy, terrorism and other
related crimes of an international character: *Wambua*, in: Petrig (ed.), Sea Piracy Law –
Droit de la piraterie maritime, Section III.C.

[759] Section 62 of the Kenyan Evidence Act provides that: "All facts, except the contents
of documents, may be proved by oral evidence." Section 63 Evidence Act stipulates: "(1)
Oral evidence must in all cases be direct evidence. (2) For the purposes of subsection (1)
"direct evidence" means – (a) with reference to a fact which could be seen, the evidence of
a witness who says he saw it; (b) with reference to a fact which could be heard, the evidence of a witness who says he heard it; (c) with reference to a fact which could be perceived by any other sense or in any other manner, the evidence of a witness who says he
perceived it by that sense or in that manner; (…)"

[760] Section 78 of the Kenyan Evidence Act provides that photographic evidence may
only be tendered in criminal proceedings by an officer appointed by the Attorney General
and in the prescribed form and who shall "have prepared the photographic print or photographic enlargement from exposed film submitted to him."

[761] *Wambua*, in: Petrig (ed.), Sea Piracy Law – Droit de la piraterie maritime, Section
III.C.

this background that namely the Netherlands,[762] Germany[763] and Russia[764] have proposed the creation of an international piracy tribunal. In April 2010, the Security Council unanimously adopted Resolution 1918 requesting the Secretary-General to present a report on possible options to further the aim of prosecuting and imprisoning pirates.[765] The Report submitted three months later identifies, among other options, a range of international venues for the prosecution of piracy suspects and alleged armed robbers at sea.[766] It is thus appropriate here to sketch out and weigh up the potential of the suggested international models.

B. International Venues under Discussion

Regarding possible international venues for the prosecution of pirates and armed robbers at sea, the Secretary-General in his Report pursuant to Security Council Resolution 1918 contemplates the establishment of an international tribunal by virtue of a Security Council Resolution under Chapter VII of the Charter of the United Nations (1.),[767] the setting up of a regional piracy tribunal on the basis of a multilateral agreement among regional States with United Nations participation (2.),[768] and the possibility of an international tribunal on the basis of an agreement between a State in the region and the United Nations (3.)[769] What is also under discussion is the possibility to prosecute pirates and armed robbers at sea in existing international fora, such as the International Criminal Court or the International Tribunal for the Law of the Sea (4.).

Whether the idea of establishing a (permanent) international piracy court is viable, however, appears questionable. Piracy has traditionally been prosecuted on the national level, on the basis of domestic criminal law. There are currently no

---

[762] Agence France Press/Expatica, Netherlands Proposes International Anti-Piracy Tribunal, May 30, 2009, *available at* www.expatica.com/nl/news/dutch-news/Netherlands-proposes-international-anti_piracy-tribunal_53106.html (last visited Aug. 30, 2010).

[763] Deutscher Bundestag, 16. Wahlperiode, Antwort der Bundesregierung auf die Kleine Anfrage der Abgeordneten Birgit Homburger, Dr. Rainer Stinner, Elke Hoff, weiterer Abgeordneter und der Fraktion der FDP, Beteiligung deutscher Soldaten am geplanten EU-Einsatz "Atalanta," Drucksache 16/11088, 12.12.2008, p. 8.

[764] Radio Netherlands Worldwide, Medvedev Calls for Piracy Tribunal, Nov. 20, 2009, *available at* www.rnw.nl/international-justice/article/medvedev-calls-piracy-tribunal (last visited Aug. 30, 2010).

[765] S.C. Res. 1918, para. 4.

[766] United Nations, Secretary-General Report pursuant to S.C. Res. 1918, July 26, 2010.

[767] Option 7 out of the seven options for the criminal prosecution of pirates and armed robbers at sea as identified in: *id.* at paras. 97 *et seq.*

[768] Option 5 out of the seven options for the criminal prosecution of pirates and armed robbers at sea as identified in: *id.* at paras. 80 *et seq.*

[769] Option 6 out of the seven options for the criminal prosecution of pirates and armed robbers at sea as identified in: *id.* at paras. 90 *et seq.*

indications whatsoever that a majority of States are willing to deviate from this established practice. Indeed, notwithstanding the particularities of the present case, which involves a failed State unable to instigate criminal proceedings at a national level, it is not clear that there would be any general, genuine need to set up an international venue.

1. International Piracy Tribunal Established by Virtue
of a Chapter VII-Based Security Council Resolution

Evidently, an *ad hoc* tribunal based on a Chapter VII Resolution of the Security Council, similar to the International Criminal Tribunals for the former Yugoslavia (ICTY)[770] and Rwanda (ICTR)[771] could help to overcome Somalia's inability to prosecute alleged pirates and armed robbers at sea. However, the criminal phenomenon of piracy as such, has not thus far been accepted as constituting a threat to international peace and security, which is the prerequisite for the adoption of a Chapter VII-based measure.[772] Thus, the tribunal's competence, *ratione loci*, could not be universal and would be restricted to occurrences within Somalia and its territorial waters, from where the threat to the peace currently emanates. Acts of piracy, however, which by definition can only occur on the high seas, as well as armed robbery at sea committed in the territorial waters of States other than Somalia, would not constitute a threat to international peace or security and would thus fall outside the competence of a tribunal established on a Chapter VII-based Security Council Resolution.

What is more, while the creation of the *ad hoc* tribunals for Rwanda and former Yugoslavia was seen as a contribution to the restoration and maintenance of peace,[773] a piracy tribunal would not necessarily be comparably conducive towards a solution to the situation in Somalia. Whereas the commission of crimes was central to the situations in the former Yugoslavia and Rwanda, piracy is just one (particularly recent) element out of many contributing to the overall situation in Somalia. This is evidenced by the statement in the Security Council Resolution that "piracy and armed robbery at sea off the coast of Somalia *exacerbate* the situation in Somalia, which continues to constitute a threat to international peace and security in the region."[774]

---

[770] United Nations, Security Council, S.C. Res. 827, U.N. Doc. S/RES/827 (May 25, 1993) [hereinafter: S.C. Res. 827].

[771] United Nations, Security Council, S.C. Res. 955, U.N. Doc. S/RES/955 (Nov. 8, 1994).

[772] United Nations, Secretary-General Report pursuant to S.C. Res. 1918, July 26, 2010, para. 97.

[773] S.C. Res. 827, preambular para. 6: "Convinced that in the particular circumstances of the former Yugoslavia the establishment as an ad hoc measure by the Council of an international tribunal (…) would contribute to the restoration and maintenance of peace."

[774] S.C. Res. 1897, preambular para. 14 (emphasis added).

An international piracy tribunal would primarily be dealing with ongoing and future criminal activity and the time lapse until a new judicial mechanism could be fully functioning would thus need to be covered by other options.[775] Experience with other tribunals, such as the International Criminal Tribunals for the former Yugoslavia and Rwanda, the Special Court for Sierra Leone and the Extraordinary Chambers in the Courts of Cambodia, has shown that the establishment of any new judicial tribunal is usually a matter of years.[776] In view of the ongoing criminal activity, a newly established judicial mechanism would face a significant caseload and it would seem impossible to anticipate a completion date. Irrespective of these considerations, it may also be reckoned with that the current political climate and a certain tribunal fatigue may hardly be favorable to the creation of another *ad hoc* tribunal via the Security Council. Finally, the Secretary-General's Report points out that an international tribunal established by virtue of a Security Council Resolution is not likely to be among the most cost-effective alternatives.[777]

2. A Regional Piracy Tribunal Set Up on the Basis of a Multilateral Agreement among Regional States

As far as the establishment of a regional tribunal on the basis of a multilateral agreement among regional States is concerned, the Secretary-General's Report, while acknowledging the advantage of regional proximity and capacity-building in the region, also points out a number of disadvantages.[778] Most importantly, a newly established regional tribunal would not have a pre-existing territorial jurisdiction and negotiating the limits of such jurisdiction would most likely be an arduous process in view of the various interests involved. If the tribunal's jurisdiction were to include crimes of financing and organization of piracy, definitions would need to be negotiated among the participating States. The same holds true with regard to armed robbery at sea for which no accepted definition exists under international law. Moreover, such a tribunal would need to draw judges and prosecutors from regional jurisdictions at the risk of depleting the expertise that has been built up, for example, in Kenya and Seychelles.[779] As would be the case with any newly established judicial mechanism, a regional tribunal would most likely incur considerable costs that a special chamber within an existing national jurisdiction, for example, would not have.[780]

---

[775] United Nations, Secretary-General Report pursuant to S.C. Res. 1918, July 26, 2010, para. 110.

[776] *Id.* at para. 28.

[777] *Id.* at para. 101.

[778] *Id.* at para. 82.

[779] *Id.* at paras. 83–85.

[780] *Id.* at para. 86.

3. International UN-Assisted Piracy Tribunal Based on an Agreement between the United Nations and a Regional State(s)

The Report of the Secretary-General also discusses the establishment of an international United Nations-assisted tribunal on the basis of an agreement between a regional State and the United Nations, similar to the Special Court for Sierra Leone and the Special Tribunal for Lebanon.[781] Although Somalia, from where the piracy problem originates, would be the obvious choice, the Report from the outset dismisses the idea of setting up such a tribunal in Somalia because of the considerable problems concerning Somali judicial and prosecutorial capacity. Choosing a singular State among the various regional States affected by piracy may prove problematic and, if the agreement is not concluded with Somalia, it may be difficult to establish jurisdiction over offences committed within Somalia's territorial sea.[782]

4. Prosecuting Piracy in Existing International Judicial Fora

Adding the crime of piracy to the Rome Statute and, thereby, providing the International Criminal Court (ICC) with jurisdiction over persons arrested in the counter-piracy operations in the Gulf of Aden region, has likewise been contemplated as a possible way to implement the idea of an international venue to prosecute piracy.[783] However, according to the Rome Statute, the jurisdiction of the International Criminal Court "shall be limited to the most serious crimes of concern to the international community as a whole,"[784] defined as crimes that "threaten the peace, security and well-being of the world."[785] Most instances of piracy are below the threshold of gravity inherent in the crimes for which the International Criminal Court is competent, namely, war crimes, crimes against humanity and genocide. In fact, in terms of gravity, piracy does not differ from other forms of (organized) crime, such that any endeavor towards an international prosecution of crimes relating to piracy raises the question why similar avenues are not sought for other equally grave or arguably worse forms of (organized) criminal conduct. A possible amendment of the Rome Statute of the International Criminal Court with a view to include the crime of piracy was not taken up by the states parties at the first review conference, which took place in June 2010, in Kampala.[786]

The International Tribunal for the Law of the Sea (ITLOS) is another institutional framework that has been mentioned in the discussion on the creation of an

---

[781] *Id.* at para. 90.

[782] *Id.* at paras. 91–94.

[783] *Id.* at para. 105.

[784] Art. 1 Rome Statute.

[785] *Id.* at preambular para. 3.

[786] United Nations, Secretary-General Report pursuant to S.C. Res. 1918, July 26, 2010, p. 5.

international piracy tribunal.[787] However, creating a specialized chamber for piracy within the International Tribunal for the Law of the Sea seems unlikely, because it would entail amending the UNCLOS, which would not only be a time consuming undertaking, but as alluded to above, States would be more than reluctant to open this instrument to renewed discussion with a view to its reform. A way to get around the resistance to re-opening of the UNCLOS would be to negotiate and adopt a protocol to the main treaty. However, notwithstanding the treaty-making technique chosen, the International Tribunal for the Law of the Sea is not a tribunal specialized in deciding on individual criminal responsibility, but rather on disputes between States.[788] This renders the International Tribunal for the Law of the Sea a rather inappropriate venue for the criminal prosecution of pirates and armed robbers at sea.

Finally, amending the statute of the African Court on Human and Peoples' Rights has also been raised as an option, according to the Secretary-General's Report. This, however, would require substantial modifications of the Court's jurisdiction which is concerned with African Union States' compliance with the African Charter on Human and Peoples' Rights rather than individual criminal responsibility. There is currently no evidence that African Union States' are discussing or seriously considering this option.[789]

C. General Questions Relating to International(ized) Prosecution of Pirates and Armed Robbers at Sea

Irrespective of the institutional venue chosen, the international adjudication of pirates and armed robbers at sea raises a number of general questions. Whatever the venue chosen, competencies *ratione loci* and *ratione personae* of the adjudicative body would have to be clarified. Should jurisdiction be limited to pirate attacks committed in a specific geographical area, such as the Gulf of Aden, or should it be a world court for piracy in the true sense? Furthermore, *ratione materiae*, the crimes falling within the jurisdiction of the court would have to be identified. Jurisdiction could simply be limited to piracy. However, it could theoretically comprise piracy and armed robbery at sea, or even more broadly, it could also encompass related criminal behavior, such as money laundering.

---

[787] *Id.* at para. 106. See also *Fischer-Lescano*, Bundesmarine als Polizei der Weltmeere? Zeitschrift für öffentliches Recht in Norddeutschland 12 (2009), 47.

[788] Art. 287 and 288 UNCLOS as well as Art. 20 and 21 of Annex VI to the UNCLOS containing the Statute of the International Tribunal for the Law of the Sea.

[789] United Nations, Secretary-General Report pursuant to S.C. Res. 1918, July 26, 2010, para. 107.

What is more, if conduct amounting to piracy or armed robbery at sea should no longer be prosecuted based on national criminal law, international offenses would have to be enacted. Although the definition of acts of piracy laid out in Article 101 UNCLOS is well agreed upon, as shown above, this provision entails numerous significant ambiguities[790] and, as such, we submit, does not constitute a substantive criminal norm on which criminal charges can be based. In terms of remedying current ambiguity, agreement may be possible on the accepted definition of piracy. The challenge would arguably be greater in relation to armed robbery at sea, which takes place in the territorial waters and thus within the sovereign domain of States. As we have seen, the definitional elements of armed robbery at sea are far from settled under international law.[791]

In addition, the relationship to other jurisdictions also potentially competent to adjudicate would have to be clarified. Thus, it would have to be determined as to whether the piracy tribunal would be a complementary mechanism or whether it would have priority over other courts.

Finally, the question of enforcement of sentences should not be ignored. Even if an international(ized) piracy court were to be established, the enforcement of prison sentences would have to take place on a national level. It remains doubtful whether the will of States to enforce sentences against pirates and armed robbers at sea would be any greater than the faint will to pronounce them.

D. Conclusion

It seems that the most viable alternative to purely domestic prosecution in regional States is the creation of specialized piracy chambers within the domestic criminal justice systems of regional States willing and able to prosecute pirates and armed robbers at sea, as has been proposed by the Contact Group on Piracy off the Coast of Somalia.[792] Such specialized chambers could feature international elements ranging from, for instance, financial support to international experts assisting local judicial personnel. However, for the time being it is not clear whether the establishment of special chambers would significantly contribute to the prosecution of persons responsible for acts of piracy and armed robbery at sea. It may well be that the continuation of the currently pursued model, i.e. international assistance to national jurisdictions, is the most efficient way to prosecute persons suspected of

---

[790] On the definition of piracy, see p. 59 *et seq.*

[791] On the definition of armed robbery at sea, see p. 73 *et seq.*

[792] Norway, Mission to the United Nations, Communiqué: The Contact Group on Piracy off the Coast of Somalia, Jan. 29, 2010, *available at* www.norway-un.org/NorwayandUN/ Selected_Topics/Regional-Issues/Somalia/COMMUNIQUE-Contact-Group-on-Piracy-off-the-Coast-of-Somalia/ (last visited Aug. 30, 2010).

having committed acts of piracy and armed robbery at sea. In any case, the current model does not preclude the setting up of special chambers in States where this is deemed to be conducive.

The assistance provided to national jurisdictions over the past months increasingly appears to be yielding fruit. A number of transfer agreements have been concluded between patrolling naval States and regional States; others are under negotiation. Moreover, national legislations have been reviewed and up-dated in a number of regional States,[793] many of which are able and willing to deal with a considerable amount of piracy cases. Security Council Resolution 1918 accordingly "notes with appreciation the assistance being provided by UNODC and other international organizations and donors, to enhance the capacity of the judicial and the corrections systems in Somalia, Kenya, Seychelles and other States in the region."[794] At the same time, Resolution 1918 notes "with concern (…) that the domestic law of a number of States lacks provisions criminalizing piracy and/or procedural provisions for effective criminal prosecution of suspected pirates."[795] This of course could be remedied in due course, as it has already been the case in a number of regional States, such as Kenya and the Seychelles.

Notably, the Secretary-General's Report does not explain in any detail what is not functioning with regard to ongoing domestic prosecutions in the region nor does it show any exigency to resort to an international model. Merely Security Council Resolution 1918 had stressed, in a rather abstract manner, "the need to address the problems caused by the limited capacity of the judicial system of Somalia and other States in the region to effectively prosecute suspected pirates."[796] But, this appeal is clearly being heeded by the model currently pursued.

Another main concern of the Security Council was that a number of persons suspected of piracy and armed robbery at sea are still being released without facing justice.[797] This particular problem, however, is only remotely related – if at all – to (ostensible) deficiencies in regional judicial systems. Rather, the principal reason for the release of piracy suspects and alleged armed robbers at sea is today often a lack of evidence sufficient to support prosecution.[798] Furthermore, at least in the initial phase of the counter-piracy operations in the Gulf of Aden, the release of suspects by apprehending States was due to the fact that they were unwilling to

---

[793] S.C. Res. 1918, preambular para. 13, commends "those States that have amended their domestic law in order to criminalize piracy and facilitate the prosecution of suspected pirates in their national courts."

[794] S.C. Res. 1918, preambular para. 6.

[795] *Id.* preambular para. 14.

[796] *Id.* preambular para. 5.

[797] *Id.* preambular para. 18.

[798] United Nations, Secretary-General Report pursuant to S.C. Res. 1918, July 26, 2010, para. 20.

commence prosecutions themselves, but did not know where to transfer the arrested persons. Thus, despite the various options laid out in the Secretary-General's Report, the best option "to further the aim of prosecuting and imprisoning persons responsible for acts of piracy and armed robbery at sea off the coast of Somalia"[799] may well be to maintain the current model and possibly to increase the assistance that is provided to regional States.

As the number of regional prosecutions rises, the assistance will increasingly have to focus on imprisonment arrangements in the region.[800] It is estimated that by the end of 2011 the imprisonment requirement may be as high as 2,000 persons. The sentences to be served by those convicted may be lengthy – in Kenya, sentences of 8 and 20 years have been imposed – and thus will burden the respective States for a significant number of years.[801] Finally, the current model of assistance to regional States also appears to have the best long-term prospects. Tellingly, the Secretary-General's Report concludes that "whichever of the options may be favoured by the Security Council, assisting Somalia and its regions in the longer term to develop the capacity to prosecute and imprison to international standards will be essential in sustaining results in the fight against impunity for those responsible for acts of piracy and armed robbery at sea off the coast of Somalia."[802]

III. Transfers of Suspects of Piracy or Armed Robbery at Sea

A. Transfers as a Means to Bring a Suspect within another Jurisdiction for Criminal Prosecution

1. The Necessity for Transfers: Seizing States Rarely Prosecute

Thus far, patrolling naval States carrying out the seizure of alleged pirates and armed robbers at sea have only rarely instigated criminal proceedings against the arrested suspects. Rather, alleged pirates and armed robbers at sea are commonly prosecuted either in the victim State, i.e. the State whose nationals or vessels were attacked, or (far more frequently) in a regional State.[803] Prosecution in a State other than the seizing State implies that seized suspects have to be brought from the cus-

---

[799] S.C. Res. 1918, para. 4.

[800] United Nations, Secretary-General Report pursuant to S.C. Res. 1918, July 26, 2010, para. 107.

[801] *Id.* at para. 29.

[802] *Id.* at para. 111.

[803] On the reluctance of the patrolling naval States to criminally prosecute seized suspects, see p. 29 *et seq.* On the regional approach currently pursued with regard to the prosecution of piracy suspects and armed robbers at sea, see p. 170 *et seq.*

tody of the seizing State into the custody of the prosecuting State. Such a change of jurisdiction is obtained by different means in the counter-piracy context, each raising an array of specific legal questions.

2. How a Change in Jurisdiction Is Obtained

a) Extradition

One possibility of bringing a criminal suspect within the jurisdiction of a State willing and able to prosecute him is extradition. Extradition is commonly defined as the "official surrender of an alleged criminal by one state or nation to another having jurisdiction over the crime charged."[804] Although UNCLOS is silent on the matter, certain other treaties relevant for the prosecution of behavior amounting to acts of piracy and armed robbery at sea, namely the SUA and Hostage Conventions, contain a so-called "extradite or prosecute" *(aut dedere – aut iudicare)* clause. Thus, under both treaties a State has free choice whether to extradite an alleged offender to another State or "to submit the case without delay to its competent authorities for the purpose of prosecution."[805] It has been submitted that the *aut dedere – aut iudicare* provisions of the SUA and Hostage Conventions are not limited to cases where the alleged offender is present on the territory of a State (as the wording of the provisions may suggest) but also comprises the situation where suspects are detained on a warship of the seizing State and thus in its custody and under its control.[806]

Despite these conventional "extradite or prosecute" clauses in the SUA and Hostage Conventions, extradition currently plays a negligible role in the piracy context. Thus far, only the Netherlands and Germany have requested extradition of alleged pirates and armed robbers at sea. Despite the significant number of persons currently being handed over to regional States for prosecution, these handovers do not qualify as extradition in the legal sense. These handovers are generally conducted in a rather informal manner that does not fulfill the more formal requirements of an extradition.

b) Art. 8 SUA Deliveries

Besides the option to extradite a piracy suspect,[807] the SUA Convention foresees another mechanism to bring arrested persons within a third State's jurisdiction.

---

[804] *Garner*, Black's Law Dictionary, Extradition, 623.

[805] Art. 10 SUA Convention; Art. 8 Hostage Convention is similarily worded, except for not mentioning that the case should be submitted "without delay."

[806] On our understanding of the extradite or prosecute clause contained in the SUA and Hostage Conventions, see p. 163 *et seq.*

[807] Art. 10 SUA Convention.

According to Article 8 SUA Convention, the master of a ship of a State Party to the Convention can deliver a person suspected of having committed any of the offenses defined in Article 3 SUA Convention to the authorities of any other State Party.[808] Article 8 SUA Convention states that the receiving State is under an obligation to accept the delivery of a suspect, except if it has grounds to consider that the Convention is not applicable to the acts giving rise to the delivery. Such a refusal must be accompanied by a statement providing the reasons for the refusal.[809]

The Security Council refers to Article 8 SUA Convention deliveries in its various counter-piracy Resolutions. In Resolution 1846, for example, the Security Council "*[n]otes* that the 1988 Convention for the Suppression of Unlawful Acts Against the Safety of Maritime Navigation ('SUA Convention') provides for parties to (…) accept delivery of persons responsible for or suspected of seizing or exercising control over a ship by force or threat thereof or any other form of intimidation."[810] Resolutions 1851 and 1897 reiterate this obligation.[811] Also the Djibouti Code of Conduct recalls the obligation to accept deliveries of piracy suspects in its preamble.[812]

The question arising in the present context is whether Article 8 SUA Convention only allows deliveries carried out by masters of a victim ship or whether it also permits deliveries from seizing warships or other types of law enforcement vessels to a State party to the SUA Convention. One view held in legal doctrine is that Article 8 SUA Convention does not preclude the master of a ship other than the ship attacked relying on this provision. Proponents of this view argue that even though Article 2 SUA Convention states that the SUA Convention does not apply to warships, "this provision [Article 2 SUA Convention] was intended to prevent the Convention covering offences against military discipline. Neither the actual language used nor the intent behind it prevents this provision being *applied by* a warship."[813] Hence, according to this view, in addition to the master of a ship that has been the victim of a pirate attack, the captain of a law enforcement vessel (i.e. a

---

[808] Art. 8(1) SUA Convention.

[809] Art. 8(4) SUA Convention. According to Art. 8(5) SUA Convention, the receiving State, i.e. the State having accepted the delivery of a person in accordance with Art. 8(3) SUA Convention, may in turn, "request the flag State to accept the delivery of that person." However, it is not clear whether "flag State" means the flag State of the attacked vessel or the flag State of the vessel having delivered the suspect. It is argued that common sense would suggest that the former is intended, but that the wording of Art. 8(1) SUA Convention, defining the delivering State as the "flag State," would suggest the latter: *Guilfoyle*, Treaty Jurisdiction over Pirates: A Compilation of Legal Texts with Introductory Notes, Prepared for the 3rd Meeting of Working Group 2 on Legal Issues, Copenhagen, August 26–27, 2009, p. 18, para. 45.

[810] S.C. Res. 1846, para. 15.

[811] S.C. Res. 1851, preambular para. 9, and S.C. Res. 1897, preambular para. 8.

[812] Preambular para. 10 of the Djibouti Code of Conduct.

[813] *Guilfoyle*, Counter-Piracy Law Enforcement and Human Rights, ICLQ 59 (2010), 149.

warship deployed in the Gulf of Aden) could also carry out deliveries of seized piracy suspects based on Article 8 SUA Convention.[814] We, however, submit that Article 8 SUA Convention only covers deliveries by masters of private ships (victim ships and others) but not by officials of warships or law enforcement vessels.

It is true that the wording of Article 8(1) SUA Convention provides the power of delivery to "the master of a ship of a State party" without limiting this power to the master of the attacked ship. Regarding the person subject to delivery, Article 8(1) SUA Convention provides the power of delivery over "any person who [the master of a ship] has reasonable grounds to believe has committed one of the offences set forth in article 3." Hence, the wording of Article 8 SUA Convention does not limit the power of delivery to the master of the *attacked* private ship but allows deliveries by the master of *any* private ship, for so long as it flies the flag of a State party.[815]

However, the term "master of a ship" cannot be read as encompassing law enforcement officials or warship captains. This follows from the definition of ship as contained in Article 1 SUA Convention read together with Article 2 SUA Convention. This definition excludes warships and law enforcement vessels from the Convention's scope of application. To limit the power of delivery to masters of private ships is consistent with the subject matter of the SUA Convention, which is not law enforcement, but rather international cooperation in criminal matters. The SUA Protocol 2005 will (upon its entry into force) add a law enforcement component to the SUA Convention, namely by adding a new boarding provision (Article 8*bis*). This boarding provision, which will be included after Article 8 SUA Convention on deliveries, explicitly states that it applies despite Article 2 SUA Convention. From this explicit statement it may be inferred that absent such an explicit *caveat*, provisions of the SUA Convention do not apply to warships and law enforcement vessels:

Art. 8*bis*(10)(d) SUA Convention *(not yet in force)*

Any measure taken pursuant to this article shall be carried out by law enforcement or other authorized officials from warships or military aircraft, or from other ships or aircraft clearly marked and identifiable as being on government service and authorized to that effect and, notwithstanding articles 2 and 2bis, the provisions of this article shall apply.

---

[814] *Guilfoyle*, Treaty Jurisdiction over Pirates: A Compilation of Legal Texts with Introductory Notes, Prepared for the 3rd Meeting of Working Group 2 on Legal Issues, Copenhagen, August 26–27, 2009, p. 18, para. 42.

[815] Art. 9 Tokyo Convention, which stood model for the delivery provision in the SUA Convention, limits the power of delivery to the commander of the aircraft on board which an offense was committed: "The aircraft commander may deliver to the competent authorities of any Contracting State in the territory of which the aircraft lands any person who he has reasonable grounds to believe has committed on board the aircraft an act which, in his opinion, is a serious offence according to the penal law of the State registration of the aircraft."

Furthermore, in Article 8*bis* the term "master of a ship" occurs several times,[816] but is clearly used as a term being different from "law enforcement or other authorized officials", which is defined in the very same provision as follows:

Art. 8*bis*(10)(e) SUA Convention *(not yet in force)*

For the purposes of this article "law enforcement or other authorized officials" means uniformed or otherwise clearly identifiable members of law enforcement or other government authorities duly authorized by their government. For the specific purpose of law enforcement under this Convention, law enforcement or other authorized officials shall provide appropriate government-issued identification documents for examination by the master of the ship upon boarding.

From the SUA Protocol 2005 adding an Article 8*bis* to the SUA Convention upon its entry into force, it thus follows quite plainly that the term "master of a ship" cannot encompass law enforcement officials. That the term would have a different meaning in the preceding Article 8 SUA Convention on deliveries does not appear to be maintainable.

Also the drafting history of Article 8 SUA Convention suggests that the "master of a ship" is a person acting in his private capacity. Deliveries of alleged offenders to third States by the captain of a private ship were introduced in the SUA Convention "out of a desire to avoid masters of ships which are far from or which never call at home ports (most notably flag of convenience or land-locked State ships) having to detain alleged offenders on board for long periods – a situation for which few ships are equipped."[817] Moreover, it should also be born in mind that Article 8 SUA Convention on deliveries is modeled upon Articles 9, 13 and 14 of the Tokyo Convention,[818] which is more explicit in its wording and expressly limits the power of delivery to the aircraft commander on board whose aircraft a serious offense was committed.[819]

Finally, the argument that the Security Council has provided an authoritative interpretation of Article 8 SUA Convention in the sense that the term "master of a ship" encompasses captains of warships and other law enforcement vessels must be

---

[816] Art. 8*bis*(10)(a)(viii), (d) and (e) SUA Convention (not yet in force).

[817] *Plant*, in: Higgins/Flory (eds.), Terrorism and International Law, 86. Consequently, one of the major disadvantages of the delivery provision is seen in the fact that a private person is making a "forum choice," which may not only be politically sensitive but also having far reaching consequences for the person subject to delivery.

[818] *Id.* Convention on Offences and Certain Other Acts Committed on Board Aircraft, *adopted* Sept. 14, 1963, 1969 U.N.T.S. 219 [hereinafter: Tokyo Convention].

[819] See, for example, the wording of Art. 9(1) Tokyo Convention; see also *Boyle/ Pulsifer*, The Tokyo Convention on Offenses and Certain Other Acts Committed on Board Aircraft, Journal of Air Law and Commerce 30 (1964), 342–343 (on Article 9 Tokyo Convention) and pp. 347–350 (on Articles 13 and 14 Tokyo Convention). Art. 6 Tokyo Convention describes the powers of the aircraft commander over persons on board his aircraft, among which figures delivery of persons.

rejected.[820] The Security Council has done nothing more than recalling the obligation of States party to the SUA Convention, which besides creating the respective criminal offenses under domestic law and establishing jurisdiction over them, is to "accept delivery of persons responsible for or suspected of seizing or exercising control over a ship by force or threat thereof or any other form of intimidation."[821] While the obligation of the receiving State is stressed, nothing is said about who has the power of delivery and thus it cannot be maintained that the Security Council provided a different interpretation of Article 8 SUA Convention.

Against this background, the handover of piracy suspects and alleged armed robbers at sea from naval States patrolling in the Gulf of Aden to regional States willing to prosecute them, cannot be qualified as "delivieries" in the sense of Article 8 SUA Convention.

c) Transfers and Handovers

As we have seen, extradition is a method rarely used to bring piracy suspects within the jurisdiction of a State willing to prosecute. And deliveries in the sense of Article 8 SUA Convention seem only possible from a ship other than a military ship or law enforcement vessel to a State party to the SUA Convention. Hence, rather than being "extradited" or "delivered" to a third State, piracy suspects are brought within the jurisdiction of States willing and able to prosecute by means of so-called "transfers"[822] or "handovers."[823] The two terms are synonymous and will be used interchangeably in the following.

The form and modalities of such transfers vary considerably, reaching from simple and factual *ad hoc* physical handovers by law enforcement officials of one State to those of another, to more institutionalized and legally framed transfers, such as those based on the Memoranda of Understanding signed between the European Union and Kenya[824] or between the European Union and the Seychelles.[825] Transfers or handovers currently constitute the common *modus operandi* in the Gulf of Aden in order to bring seized alleged offenders within the jurisdicition of regional States willing to prosecute them. They will be analyzed in detail in the following section.

---

[820] *Guilfoyle*, Treaty Jurisdiction over Pirates: A Compilation of Legal Texts with Introductory Notes, Prepared for the 3rd Meeting of Working Group 2 on Legal Issues, Copenhagen, August 26–27, 2009, p. 18, footnote 42.

[821] S.C. Res. 1846, para. 15; S.C. Res. 1851, preambular para. 9; and S.C. Res. 1897, preambular para. 8.

[822] Terminology used in Art. 12 EU Council Joint Action Operation Atalanta.

[823] Terminology used in Art. 11 Djibouti Code of Conduct.

[824] EU-Kenya Transfer Agreement.

[825] EU-Seychelles Transfer Agreement.

B. Characteristics and Forms of Transfers
in the Counter-Piracy Context

1. Main Characteristics of Transfers

The notion of transfer or handover is not of a technical nature. Rather, the term "transfers" is commonly used to describe a variety of techniques to move a person from one jurisdiction to another. Transfers do not occur only in the sea piracy context, but also in the context of other law enforcement operations, such as counter-terrorism,[826] or in situations of armed conflict,[827] for example, in Afghanistan. Transfers are undertaken for different purposes, such as to facilitate the obtaining of intelligence or evidence,[828] to criminally prosecute in the receiving State or to repatriate persons detained in an armed conflict. In short, "transfers" is an umbrella term and a clear-cut, universally accepted legal definition of what is meant by the notion of "transfer" currently does not exist. Still, a range of characteristic elements regarding the transfers of piracy suspects can be discerned.

First of all, in the piracy context the change in custody is not brought about by the formal means of extradition.[829] Even though extradition proceedings vary according to domestic law, they feature common elements. They usually arise under a bi- or multilateral treaty and begin with a request addressed from State A (the receiving State) to State B (the extraditing State) for the transfer of a named individual, who is present on the territory of State B. The request is followed by a proceeding determining whether the individual is extraditable, which generally requires, *inter alia*, that the offense is covered by a valid extradition treaty and is criminalized in both jurisdictions, as well as a certain degree of evidence that the offense was committed. In addition, no ground for refusing extradition, either stated in the extradition treaty (e.g. a political offense exception) or arising from human rights law (e.g. a violation of the *non-refoulement* principle) must exist.

---

[826] In the context of counter-terrorism, the term "rendition" rather than "transfer" is used: *Satterthwaite*, The Legal Regime Governing Transfer of Persons in the Fight Against Terrorism, May 2010, *available at* http://ssrn.com/abstract=1157583 (last visited Aug. 30, 2010), 3 and 9.

[827] For an overview, see e.g. *Droege*, Transfer of Detainees: Legal Framework, *non-refoulement*, and Contemporary Challenges, IRRC 90 (2008).

[828] See, for example, The Committee on International Human Rights of the Association of the Bar of the City of New York and The Center for Human Rights and Global Justice, New York University School of Law, Torture by Proxy: International and Domestic Law Applicable to "Extraordinary Renditions," 2004, *available at* www.chrgj.org/docs/TortureByProxy.pdf (last visited Aug. 30, 2010).

[829] *Guilfoyle*, Counter-Piracy Law Enforcement and Human Rights, ICLQ 59 (2010), 161. This holds also true for transfers, i.e. renditions in the context of counter-terrorism operations: *Satterthwaite*, The Legal Regime Governing Transfer of Persons in the Fight Against Terrorism, May 2010, *available at* http://ssrn.com/abstract=1157583 (last visited Aug. 30, 2010), pp. 5–6.

This proceeding is generally followed or preceded by a decision of the executive, whether to extradite the individual or not.[830]

Transfers of piracy suspects do not feature these main characteristics of extraditions. First of all, the request for a transfer does not come from the State to which the alleged offender shall be handed over; rather it is the State or international organization having custody over the alleged "pirate" that requests a third State to take over a person for purposes of criminal prosecution.[831] Another difference to extradition is that transfer decisions are generally not reached in a formalized procedure consisting of an admissibility proceeding (which grants the transferee a preventive effective remedy against a possible transfer) combined with a decision of the executive whether or not to extradite an alleged offender.[832]

Transfers in the piracy context do not fulfill the characteristics of deportations or exclusions, i.e. those legal processes which countries use to expel an individual who has entered its territory (deportation) or to prevent a person from entering its territory from the outset (exclusion). These proceedings are regulated by national immigration law. If deportation is used with the aim of bringing a person into a specific jurisdiction in order to prosecute him or her, this is often referred to as "disguised extradition."[833] Transfers in the piracy context are obviously not based on immigration law and do not fulfill the definitions of deportation or expulsion.

In sum, transfers in the piracy context can best be described negatively as a change of custody brought about by means other than extradition or deportation. Transfers of piracy suspects share the common feature that they are undertaken for the purpose of criminal prosecution of the transferred individual in the receiving State.[834] Another specific characteristic is that these transfers commonly take place

---

[830] *Id.* at pp. 6–7.

[831] See, for example, Art. 2(a) EU-Kenya Transfer Agreement where Kenya undertakes to receive piracy suspects for their criminal prosecution upon request of the EUNAVFOR, i.e. the transferring entity.

[832] Some transfers involve a decision by an administrative and/or an executive body, which are similar to extradition proceedings. Thus, in Germany a body consisting of representatives of various federal ministries took the decision that the persons suspected of having attacked the German flagged ship Courier are transferred to Kenya rather than being brought before a German criminal tribunal; this body was set up specifically for this case.

[833] *Satterthwaite*, The Legal Regime Governing Transfer of Persons in the Fight Against Terrorism, May 2010, *available at* http://ssrn.com/abstract=1157583 (last visited July 6, 2010), pp. 7–8.

[834] The object of this Chapter are only transfers with a view to criminal prosecution. In the piracy context, however, transfers in order to enforce a criminal sentence will increasingly play a role. Thus far, sentences pronounced against pirates and armed robbers at sea are enforced in prosecuting State. However, Kenya appealed to other States to take over convicted persons. The United Nations Office on Drugs and Crime is also investigating the possibility of transfer agreements between prosecuting States and Somalia to allow convicted pirates and armed robbers at sea to serve their sentence in their home State: United Nations, Secretary-General Report pursuant to S.C. Res. 1918, July 26, 2010, para. 31; United

on an involuntary basis, i.e. they amount to a forced movement of individuals from the custody of one State or international organization to the custody of a State willing to instigate criminal proceedings.

2. Entities Deciding About Transfers of Piracy Suspects

The phase between the capture of alleged pirates and armed robbers at sea and their release, respectively their transfer to a State competent and willing to prosecute them, is often referred to as "disposition."[835] The Security Council in its counter-piracy Resolutions calls upon States to cooperate during this phase.[836] What procedures are followed and who takes the necessary decisions during this disposition phase, in particular, with regard to the decision whether to transfer the captured persons, varies according to the entity that carryied out the seizure of the alleged offender.

a) EUNAVFOR

The EUNAVFOR is one of the entities transferring alleged pirates and armed robbers at sea to third States for their criminal prosecution, namely, to Kenya and the Seychelles, with whom the European Union has concluded transfer agreements.[837]

Article 12 of the EU Council Joint Action Operation Atalanta addresses the question of transfers of persons arrested by the European Union Naval Force. However, it neither specifies the procedure nor does it state by whom the transfer decision is to be taken. Neither do the existing transfer agreements with Kenya and the Seychelles, which are required by Article 12(2) Council Joint Action Operation Atalanta in order to carry out transfers to States not participating in the EUNAVFOR mission, specify these procedural points. The EU-Kenya Transfer Agreement, for example, simply states that "Kenya will accept, upon the request of EUNAVFOR, the transfer of persons detained by EUNAVFOR in connection with piracy (…) and will submit such persons and property to its competent authorities for the purpose of investigation and prosecution"[838] and that "EUNAVFOR will,

---

Nations, UNODC, Counter Piracy Programme, November 2009, *available at* www.unodc. org/documents/easternafrica//piracy/UNODC_Counter_Piracy_Programme.pdf (last visited Aug. 30, 2010), p. 9.

[835] *Guilfoyle*, Counter-Piracy Law Enforcement and Human Rights, ICLQ 59 (2010), 151, footnote 86.

[836] S.C. Res. 1897, para. 12; S.C. Res. 1846, para. 14, contains similar language.

[837] United Nations, Secretary-General Report pursuant to S. C. Res. 1918, July 26, 2010, para. 23.

[838] Art. 2(a) EU-Kenya Transfer Agreement.

when acting under this Exchange of Letters, transfer persons (…) only to competent Kenyan law enforcement authorities."[839]

For the purposes of the EU-Kenya Transfer Agreement, EUNAVFOR means "EU military headquarters and national contingents contributing to the EU operation 'Atalanta', their ships, aircrafts and assets."[840] Since this definition of EUNAVFOR encompasses a European as well as a national component, it seems that authorities from both levels are cumulatively involved in the decision to transfer a person. Thus, transfers occurring under the EU-Kenya Transfer Agreement require both the assent of the European Union Operation Commander as well as the national authorities of the capturing warship. Hence, it seems to be a joint decision making process, where both the international organization and the contributing State would have the power to prevent a specific transfer from taking place.[841]

b) NATO

NATO is another entity engaged in law enforcement operations in the Gulf of Aden. However, unlike the European Union, NATO has not concluded any transfer agreements with regional States. Rather, for the seizure and arrest of pirates, vessels contributing to NATO Operation Ocean Shield revert back to national control. Thus, disposition and potential transfer proceedings and decisions are within the responsibility of the State whose flag the seizing warship flies.[842]

c) National Contingents

In addition to multinational missions, many States contribute independently to the counter-piracy efforts in the Gulf of Aden region. Transfers that are carried out by these individual States are (within the limits of public international law) governed by national law and principles.

As we have seen, national law and principles are also relevant for transfers occurring in the context of multinational missions, such as EUNAVFOR Operation Atalanta where transfers require a national decision in addition to the assent of the European Union. National law and principles also govern transfers occurring within the framework of NATO Operation Ocean Shield where ships revert back to national control for the seizure and, therefore, the arrested piracy suspect is within the custody of the respective seizing State.

---

[839] Art. 2(b) EU-Kenya Transfer Agreement.

[840] Art. 1(a) EU-Kenya Transfer Agreement.

[841] *Guilfoyle*, Counter-Piracy Law Enforcement and Human Rights, ICLQ 59 (2010), 158. On the attribution of human rights violations in cases where a State and an international organization are acting jointly, see p. 116 *et seq.*

[842] *Id.*

Hence, currently every transfer occurring in the counter-piracy context features a national component and is thus at least partly governed by national law or practices. These national transfer frameworks and practices vary considerably from State to State. It is reported that some transfers are of a purely factual nature, i.e. piracy suspects are handed over to coast guards of a third State without any legal proceedings held before the transfer. At the other end of the spectrum, some States subject transfers to close judicial review. Thus, for example, Italy brought alleged offenders intercepted by its frigate *Maestrale*, which contributes to the EUNAVFOR, before an Italian investigating judge by video conference in order to determine to which State the seized persons should be brought for prosecution.[843]

3. Receiving Entity

As of May 2010, over 200 piracy suspects have been transferred from patrolling naval States to so-called regional States for criminal prosecution. Kenya is the regional State that has received the highest numbers of piracy suspects (123 persons) from patrolling naval States. It is followed by the two Somali entities of Puntland (60 persons) and Somaliland (20 persons). Also the Seychelles accepted piracy suspects for investigation and prosecution, namely based on the Exchange of Letters with the European Union (11 persons).[844]

C. The Normative Framework Pertaining to Transfers

The normative framework pertaining to transfers of piracy suspects is rather complex and subject to a variety of rules, deriving in particular from the law of the sea, specific transfer agreements and human rights law. First of all, we rebut the contention that Article 105 UNCLOS prohibits the transfer of piracy suspects to a State other than the seizing State (1.). Secondly, in the present context specific legal instruments exclusively pertaining to the transfer of piracy suspects, namely, the so-called transfer agreements must be observed (2.). Thirdly, given that these instruments only partially regulate the proceedings and substantive criteria relating to transfers, especially the rights of the transferees, recourse to general human rights law and, in particular, the principle of *non-refoulement*, is necessary (3.).

---

[843] *Id.* at 164.

[844] United Nations, Secretary-General Report pursuant to S.C. Res. 1918, July 26, 2010, para. 19.

1. Law of the Sea: Does 105 UNCLOS Allow for Transfers to Third States?

Some scholars maintain that the second sentence of Article 105 UNCLOS provides the competence to criminally prosecute piracy suspects *exclusively* to the
seizing State, i.e. that only the State arresting the pirates would be granted adjudicative jurisdiction over the alleged offenders. If Article 105 UNCLOS is understood
as limiting the competence to prosecute alleged pirates to the *forum deprehensionis*, the provision would not allow for transfers of pirates to any other State.
However, for various reasons already discussed earlier, we oppose a reading of
Article 105 UNCLOS as containing a limited universality principle.[845]

The practice of States and international organizations participating in the counter-piracy missions in the Gulf of Aden region also does not suggest a reading of
Article 105 UNCLOS whereby only the seizing State has a right to criminally
prosecute the arrested suspects. Patrolling naval States regularly transfer piracy
suspects to regional States. This practice seems to be in line with the Security
Council's call to cooperate in determining jurisdiction with a view to the criminal
prosecution of piracy suspects.[846]

Even if Article 105 UNCLOS is read as limiting the competence to prosecute to
the seizing State, all those attacks against vessels and their crews occurring in
States' territorial waters (so-called armed robberies at sea)[847] would not be subject
to this provision, which only relates to piracy. Legal instruments covering, *inter
alia*, incidents in the territorial waters, namely the SUA and Hostage Conventions,
do not prohibit the transfer of alleged offenders to another State's custody for investigation and prosecution. On the contrary, the SUA and Hostage Conventions
both contain *aut dedere – aut iudicare* clauses,[848] while the SUA Convention even
foresees so-called deliveries of suspects by the master of private ships to third
States.[849]

Public international law does not generally oppose transfers to third States. However, it contains rules governing the conditions and modalities of transfers, which
may bar a concrete transfer or subject it to certain limitations. These are, on the one
hand, rules specifically drafted with regard to transfers occurring in the Somali
counter-piracy operations context, such as the various transfer agreements (2.).
Plus, on the other hand, rules that flow from general human rights law, specifically
from the principle of *non-refoulement* (3.).

---

[845] On the various interpretations of Art. 105 UNCLOS, see p. 148 *et seq.*

[846] S.C. Res. 1816, para. 11; S.C. Res. 1846, para. 14; S.C. Res. 1897, para. 12.

[847] On the definition of armed robbery at sea, see p. 73 *et seq.*

[848] On the extradition or prosecution clause in the SUA and Hostage Conventions, see p.
163 *et seq.*

[849] On deliveries according to Art. 8 SUA Convention, see p. 187 *et seq.*

2. Transfer Agreements: Specific Rules on Transfers
in the Somali Counter-Piracy Context

Several States as well as the European Union have concluded transfer agreements with regional States, in which the latter agree to receive piracy suspects for criminal prosecution and in which modalities and conditions for the transfers are laid down.

a) Transfer Agreements Concluded Among States

Several States have bilaterally concluded transfer agreements with Kenya and the Seychelles, in which the two countries agreed to take over piracy suspects for criminal prosecution.

The United Kingdom, for example, signed a Memorandum of Understanding with Kenya on December 11, 2009, pertaining to the transfer of suspects from the custody of United Kingdom forces to Kenyan authorities. On July 27, 2009, the United Kingdom signed another bilateral Memorandum of Understanding with the government of the Seychelles in which the latter accepts the handover of piracy suspects.[850] These Memoranda of Understanding are not publicly available and their exact content is thus unknown. However, the Memorandum of Understanding between the United Kingdom and Kenya seems to be similar in content to the EU-Kenya Transfer Agreement, which is public.[851]

The United States of America also concluded transfer agreements with Kenya on January 16, 2009[852] and the Seychelles in July 2010.[853] The content of these trans-

---

[850] United Kingdom, Foreign & Commonwealth Office, Prisoner Transfer Agreements, www.fco.gov.uk/en/global-issues/conflict-prevention/piracy/prisoners (last visited Aug. 30, 2010).

[851] This conclusion is drawn from the answer of the United Kingdom's Foreign & Commonwealth Office to a Freedom of Information Act Request filed by the authors, in which disclosure of the Memoranda of Understanding between the United Kingdom and Kenya was requested: "Whilst we realise that there is a public interest in knowing the details of how we are combating piracy off the coast of Somalia, in this case, should we act contrary to the stated wishes of the Kenyan government it would adversely affect our ability to combat piracy in the Gulf of Aden and in the seas off the east coast of Africa and damage the wider UK-Kenya relationship. However, you may find it useful to look at the Exchange of Letters between the European Union and Kenya on the transfer of persons suspected of having committed acts of piracy [Internet link omitted]. It is similar in content to the agreement between the UK and Kenya and is available to the public." United Kingdom, Foreign & Commonwealth Office, Answer to a Freedom of Information Request filed by Anna Petrig, 21 April 2009 (on file with author).

[852] *Morgan*, Reuters, Kenya Agrees to Prosecute U.S.-Held Pirates: Pentagon, Jan. 29, 2009, *available at* www.reuters.com/article/worldNews/idUSTRE50S4ZZ20090129 (last visited Aug. 30, 2010).

[853] African Press Organization, Seychelles and the USA Sign Piracy Agreement, July 14, 2010, *available at* http://appablog.wordpress.com/2010/07/14/seychelles-and-the-usa-sign-piracy-agreement/ (last visited Aug. 30, 2010).

fer agreements was so far not disclosed to the public. This is also true of the agreements concluded between Kenya and Canada, China and Denmark respectively.[854]

b) EU Transfer Agreements

In contrast to the transfer agreements concluded between individual States, the transfer agreements concluded by the European Union are publicly available. Those transfer agreements are based on Article 12 EU Council Joint Action Operation Atalanta, which requires such agreements in order to transfer persons to third States not participating in the European Union Operation Atalanta. Accordingly, Article 12 EU Council Joint Action Operation Atalanta requires closer scrutiny.

aa) Legal Basis: Article 12 Council Joint Action Operation Atalanta

The following provision deals with the transfer of persons arrested and detained by the EUNAVFOR to third States for their criminal prosecution:

Art. 12 EU Council Joint Action Operation Atalanta – Transfer of Persons Arrested and Detained with a View to Their Prosecution

1. On the basis of Somalia's acceptance of the exercise of jurisdiction by Member States or by third States, on the one hand, and Article 105 of the United Nations Convention on the Law of the Sea, on the other hand, persons having committed, or suspected of having committed, acts of piracy or armed robbery in Somali territorial waters or on the high seas, who are arrested and detained, with a view to their prosecution, and property used to carry out such acts, shall be transferred:

– to the competent authorities of the Member State or of the third State participating in the operation, of which the vessel which took them captive flies the flag, or

– if this State cannot, or does not wish to, exercise its jurisdiction, to a Member State or any third State which wishes to exercise its jurisdiction over the aforementioned persons and property.

2. No persons referred to in paragraphs 1 and 2[855] may be transferred to a third State unless the conditions for the transfer have been agreed with that third State in a manner consistent with relevant international law, notably international law on human rights, in order to guarantee in particular that no one shall be subjected to the death penalty, to torture or to any cruel, inhuman or degrading treatment.

It follows that Article 12(1) Council Joint Action Operation Atalanta covers two types of transfer. The first bullet point refers to the situation where the alleged offender is physically taken from the vessel of the seizing State to the competent

---

[854] United Nations, Secretary-General Report pursuant to S.C. Res. 1918, July 26, 2010, para. 23.

[855] The German texts only refer to paragraph 1 of Article 12 EU Council Joint Action, which seems to be the correct scope: "Die in Absatz 1 genannten Personen (...);" see 2008 Abl. (L 301) 36 (EU). The same holds true for the French text: "Aucune des personnes mentionnées au paragraphe 1 (...);" see 2008 J.O. (L 301) 36 (EU).

authorities on the mainland of that same State. To date, the only seizing State contributing to EUNAVOR bringing seized suspects before its own domestic authorities seems to have been Spain in the case of the *Alakrana*.[856]

The second bullet point of Article 12(1) Council Joint Action Operation Atalanta, however, deals with a far more problematic circumstance, namely, the transfer from the seizing State to a third State. Adherence to the principle of *non-refoulement* is of utmost importance here. Therefore, according to Article 12(2) Council Joint Action Operation Atalanta, these transfers to a third State[857] can only take place if the conditions for the transfer have been agreed with the receiving State and are consistent with relevant international law, notably, human rights law, embodying the principle of *non-refoulement*.[858] On the basis of this provision, the European Union concluded its transfer agreements with Kenya and the Seychelles.

bb)   Existing Transfer Agreements – A Closer Look

(1) EU-Kenya Transfer Agreement

In March 2009, an Exchange of Letters between the European Union and Kenya concerning the conditions and modalities for the transfer of piracy suspects and seized property took place and was approved by the Council of the European Union. In the following, the personal scope of application as well as the main content of this agreement will be analyzed.

(i) Scope of Application: "Transferred Persons"

The scope of application of the EU-Kenya Transfer Agreement is somewhat astonishingly defined. On the one hand it is very narrow and on the other hand quite broad. According to Article 1(h) EU-Kenya Transfer Agreement, the term "transferred person" is defined as "any person suspected of intending to commit, committing, or having committed, acts of piracy transferred by EUNAVFOR to Kenya under this Exchange of Letters." The notion of "piracy" under Article 1(g) EU-Kenya Transfer Agreement is "as defined in Article 101 UNCLOS."

---

[856] On the fact that States carrying out the seizure of alleged pirates and armed robbers at sea have only rarely instigated criminal proceedings against them, see p. 29 *et seq.*

[857] In Art. 12 EU-Kenya Transfer Agreement the notion of "third States" refers to States which are neither European Union member States nor participating in the Operation Atalanta; the conditions for transfers from European Union member States to non-European Union member States participating in the Operation Atalanta are, according to Art. 10(6) EU Council Joint Action Operation Atalanta, laid down in the participation agreements foreseen in Art. 10(3) EU Council Joint Action Operation Atalanta.

[858] Art. 12(2) EU Council Joint Action Operation Atalanta.

On the one hand, the scope seems wide, given that the term "transferred person" encompasses persons solely "intending to commit" an act of piracy. Thus, it seems that having the necessary *mens rea* to commit piracy, without having fulfilled any element of the *actus reus*, suffices to fall under the EU-Kenya Transfer Agreement. Given the considerable impact a transfer usually has for the transferee, the mere intention to commit an act of piracy can hardly be sufficient to justify a person's transfer into another State's jurisdiction. There should be at least some overt act manifesting the individual's intention to engage in piracy.

On the other hand, the scope of application of the EU-Kenya Transfer Agreement is very narrow, as it is confined to persons having engaged in acts of piracy as defined in Article 101 UNCLOS. Hence, persons who have allegedly committed violent acts against ships and persons on board in the territorial waters of Somalia, which is referred to as armed robbery at sea in the counter-piracy Security Council Resolutions, are not covered by the EU-Kenya Transfer Agreement. In practice, however, this awkward definition of the scope of the EU-Kenya Transfer Agreement[859] does not seem to inhibit transfers of persons having committed armed robbery at sea and generally violent acts against ships and persons other than piracy, as defined in Article 101 UNCLOS.

(ii) Main Content

The EU-Kenya Transfer Agreement states the principle that "Kenya will accept, upon the request of the EUNAVFOR, the transfer of persons detained by EUNAVFOR in connection with piracy (...) and will submit such persons and property to its competent authorities for the purpose of investigation and prosecution."[860] It also provides that the EUNAVFOR will "transfer persons or property only to the competent Kenyan law enforcement authorities."[861] It is further stipulated that transfers for the purpose of investigation or prosecution from Kenya to any other State is subject to prior written consent from EUNAVFOR.[862]

The core of the transfer agreement is dedicated to the post-transfer phase. On the one hand, substantive rights of transferred persons, such as their humane treatment upon transfer and fair trial rights, are laid down.[863] Most importantly, the agree-

---

[859] The personal scope of application of Art. 12(1) EU Council Joint Action Operation Atalanta is more appropriately defined in that it refers to "persons having committed, or suspected of having committed, acts of piracy or armed robbery in Somali territorial waters or on the high seas." Thus, it does not mention the "intention to commit" acts of piracy while it includes alleged armed robbers at sea.

[860] Art. 2(a) EU-Kenya Transfer Agreement.

[861] Art. 2(b) EU-Kenya Transfer Agreement.

[862] Art. 3(h) EU-Kenya Transfer Agreement.

[863] Art. 3(a) EU-Kenya Transfer Agreement stipulates that transferred persons must be treated humanely; Art. 3(b) provides the right to be brought promptly before a judge decid-

ment stipulates that "[n]o transferred person will be liable to suffer the death sentence." On the other hand, the agreement contains procedural requirements for the post-transfer phase. It requires that Kenya keeps an accurate account of all transferred persons, for example about their physical condition, place of detention and any decisions taken with regard to the transferred person and that these records are available to representatives of the European Union or EUNAVFOR.[864] Kenya is further under an obligation to notify EUNAVFOR about any specific issue that may arise, such as an alleged improper treatment of the transferred person.[865] The agreement further foresees that representatives of the European Union and EUNAVFOR have access to transferred persons and that they are entitled to question them.[866] In addition, national and international humanitarian agencies are allowed to visit transferred persons.[867] Finally, the transfer agreement obliges EUNAVFOR to provide, within its means and capabilities, all assistance to Kenya with a view to the investigation and prosecution of transferred persons.[868]

While the post-transfer phase is quite extensively covered by the transfer agreement, the phase leading to a transfer, i.e. the criteria and proceedings regarding a transfer, is hardly regulated at all. The only statements regarding the formal requirements that have to be observed when transferring a person to Kenya can be found in Article 5 EU-Kenya Transfer Agreement. It stipulates, on the one hand, that any transfer will be the subject of an "appropriate document" signed by a representative of the EUNAVFOR (which is defined as "EU military headquarters and national contingents contributing to the EU operation 'Atalanta'")[869] and the competent Kenyan law enforcement authority respectively.[870] On the other hand, it obliges the EUNAVFOR to provide detention records to Kenya with regard to any transferred person stating, *inter alia*, the time of transfer to the Kenyan authorities, the reasons for a person's detention as well as the time and place of the commencement of the detention.[871]

Thus, neither Article 12 EU Council Joint Action Operation Atalanta nor the EU-Kenya Transfer Agreement based thereupon lay down the procedure that is to be followed in order to reach a transfer decision. These instruments neither grant any rights to transferees similar to procedural safeguards generally accorded in extradi-

---

ing about the lawfulness of the detention; Art. 3(c) states that the transferred person is entitled to a trial within reasonable time; Art. 3(d) to (f) stipulate fair trial rights; and Art. 3(g) provides the right to appeal.

[864] Art. 5(c) and (d) EU-Kenya Transfer Agreement.

[865] Art. 5(e) EU-Kenya Transfer Agreement.

[866] Art. 5(e) EU-Kenya Transfer Agreement.

[867] Art. 5(f) EU-Kenya Transfer Agreement.

[868] Art. 6 EU-Kenya Transfer Agreement.

[869] Art. 1(a) EU-Kenya Transfer Agreement.

[870] Art. 5(a) EU-Kenya Transfer Agreement.

[871] Art. 5(b) EU-Kenya Transfer Agreement.

tion proceedings, such as the right to be heard on the arguments invoked against the extradition, to have access to the file, to have the assistance of a lawyer and an interpreter or to have the extradition decision reviewed by an independent body.[872] The instruments neither specify the material criteria, which would have to be fulfilled in order to allow a transfer, nor do they list specific circumstances precluding a transfer. The EU-Kenya Transfer Agreement simply states in a quite general manner that the person to be transferred must be treated humanely and in accordance with international human rights law prior to and following the transfer.[873] However, the agreement does not oblige the parties to the transfer to make an assessment in the specific and individual case whether the conditions for the transfer are fulfilled and if Kenya is able to discharge its post-transfer responsibilities regarding a specific person.

Given that the EU-Kenya Transfer Agreement leaves open some important questions regarding the procedural and substantive requirements of transfer decisions, these gaps have to be filled by recourse to general human rights law, in particular the *non-refoulement* principle.

(iii) Transfers Based on the Agreement

In Kenya, there have been fourteen prosecutions involving 123 accused since 2006. Nine prosecutions concerned piracy suspects transferred to Kenya by EUNAVFOR based on the EU-Kenya Transfer Agreement.[874] In April 2010, Kenya announced that it was unwilling to receive any more piracy suspects for prosecution in its courts and that it was considering terminating the agreement. According to the Foreign Affairs Minister of Kenya, the international community had not lived up to its promises to help Kenya with the burden to prosecute and some countries had failed to provide adequate financial support to Kenya's already strained justice system.[875] The fact that Kenya declined to accept arrested pirates for a couple of weeks (before reassuming to receive and adjudicate suspects in May 2010)

---

[872] See, for example, Council of Europe, Extradition, pp. 97–104.

[873] Art. 2(c) EU-Kenya Transfer Agreement. The determination of the applicable human rights law in the situation at hand is quite complex given that States and international organizations are acting extraterritorially and jointly in a maritime context and based on a Chapter VII Resolution of the United Nations' Security Council; on the applicability of human rights and the attribution of human rights violations in the context of the counter-piracy operations in the Gulf of Aden region, see p. 116 *et seq.*

[874] United Nations, Secretary-General Report pursuant to S. C. Res. 1918, July 26, 2010, para. 21; *Stemple*, Jurist, UN Announces Opening of New Kenya Courtroom for Piracy Trials, June 25, 2010, *available at* http://jurist.org/paperchase/2010/06/un-announces-opening-of-new-kenya-courtroom-for-piracy-trials.php (last visited Aug. 30, 2010).

[875] BBC News, Kenya Ends Somali Pirate Trials, April 1, 2010, *available at* http://news.bbc.co.uk/2/hi/africa/8599347.stm (last visited Aug. 30, 2010); BBC News, Q&A: What Do You Do With a Captured Pirate? June 24, 2010, *available at* http://news.bbc.co.uk/2/hi/africa/8664623.stm (last visited Aug. 30, 2010).

spurred the international community into action. In June 2010, for example, a high-security courtroom in the Kenyan port town Mombasa opened its doors; it was built by the Counter Piracy Programme of the United Nations Office on Drugs and Crime with contributions from Australia, Canada, the European Union, France, Germany and the United States.[876]

(2) Exchange of Letters between the Seychelles and European Union

Since October 2009, an increasing number of attacks have been observed in the Western Indian Ocean and towards the Seychelles. This led to an Exchange of Letters between the European Union and the Republic of Seychelles on the transfer of piracy suspects to the Seychelles for the purpose of prosecution. The agreement reached under this Exchange of Letters applies only "on a transitional basis, pending the conclusion of a mutually acceptable transfer agreement."[877] Based on this Exchange of Letters, the EUNAVFOR has reportedly transferred 31 suspects to the Seychelles to date.[878]

(i) Scope of Application

The category of persons who can be transferred based on the Exchange of Letters between the European Union and the Seychelles is different from the EU-Kenya Transfer Agreement. Whereas Kenya has accepted the transfer of any person detained by EUNAVFOR in connection with piracy, the transfer agreement between the European Union and the Republic of Seychelles only pertains to a specific category of arrested person.

The Government of Seychelles "may authorize the EUNAVFOR to transfer suspected pirates and armed robbers captured in the course of its operations in the exclusive economic zone, territorial sea, archipelagic waters and internal waters of the Republic of Seychelles. This authorization is extended to the protection of Seychelles flagged vessels and Seychellois Citizens on a non-Seychelles flagged vessel beyond the limit aforementioned and in other circumstances on the high seas at the

---

[876] *Stemple*, Jurist, UN Announces Opening of New Kenya Courtroom for Piracy Trials, June 25, 2010, *available at* http://jurist.org/paperchase/2010/06/un-announces-opening-of-new-kenya-courtroom-for-piracy-trials.php (last visited Aug. 30, 2010); United Nations, News Centre, UN Opens New Courtroom to Try Pirate Suspects in Kenyan Port, June 25, 2010, *available at* www.un.org/apps/news/story.asp?NewsID=35156&Cr=UNODC&Cr1= (last visited Aug. 30, 2010).

[877] EU-Seychelles Transfer Agreement, last paragraph of the letter from the European Union to the Republic of the Seychelles.

[878] United Nations, News Centre, UN Opens New Courtroom to Try Pirate Suspects in Kenyan Port, June 25, 2010, *available at* www.un.org/apps/news/story.asp?NewsID=35156&Cr=UNODC&Cr1= (last visited Aug. 30, 2010).

discretion of the Republic of the Seychelles."[879] Thus, the Seychelles has from the outset limited transfers to those persons who have allegedly committed crimes in *its* waters or against *its* interests, i.e. its nationals or vessels. This may first and foremost be due to a realistic assessment of the limited judicial capacities of the island. Although, transfers in cases where no Seychellois interests are involved would seem to be encompassed by the formulation "in other circumstances on the high seas," in this case the authorization is expressly conditioned upon the discretion of the Republic of the Seychelles.

(ii) Main Content

The Exchange of Letters between the European Union and the Seychelles differs from the EU-Kenya Transfer Agreement in another aspect in that it exclusively relates to the post-transfer phase. *Inter alia*, it stipulates that the transferee must be treated humanely,[880] that he must be brought promptly before a judge deciding on the lawfulness of his detention and that he is entitled to a trial within a reasonable time. In addition, fair trial rights of the piracy suspects and the right to appeal the conviction and sentence are guaranteed.[881]

While the EU-Kenya Transfer Agreement contains some rules of a procedural nature pertaining to the phase prior to the transfer (e.g. that transfers must be documented[882] or what kind of documents EUNAVFOR must hand over to the receiving State[883]) the letter from the Seychelles to the European Union is silent in this regard.

Moreover, provisions relating to the tracing and post-transfer monitoring of the piracy suspects handed over to the Seychelles are not included in the letter from the Seychelles as accepted by the European Union. Rather, they are contained in a separate, so-called "Declaration by the European Union on the Occasion of the Signature of the Exchange of Letters between the European Union and the Republic of Seychelles." In this Declaration, the European Union "notes that representatives of the EU and EUNAVFOR will be granted access to any person transferred" and "be entitled to question them."[884] Further, the European Union notes that national and

---

[879] EU-Seychelles Transfer Agreement.

[880] In juxtaposition to the EU-Kenya Transfer Agreement, the EU-Seychelles Transfer Agreement does not state that the person must be treated humanely *"prior* to and *following* transfer"* (emphasis added).

[881] EU-Seychelles Transfer Agreement.

[882] Art. 5(a) EU-Kenya Transfer Agreement.

[883] Art. 5(b) EU-Kenya Transfer Agreement.

[884] Declaration by the European Union on the Occasion of the Signature of the Exchange of Letteres between the European Union and the Republic of Seychelles on the Conditions and Modalities for the Transfer of Supected Pirates and Armed Robbers from

humanitarian agencies will be allowed to visit the transferees.[885] To what extent these declarations of the European Union are (meant to be) binding upon the Seychelles seems questionable. Differing from the Exchange of Letters, there is no indication that the Seychelles has accepted this Declaration as a binding instrument.

Unlike Kenya, the Seychelles has abolished the death penalty. This made the inclusion of diplomatic assurances regarding the non-imposition of the death penalty upon convicted pirates dispensable.

In general, compared with the EU-Kenya Transfer Agreement, the Exchange of Letters with the Seychelles expresses the self-interests, discretion and limited capacities of the receiving State to a greater extent. In that vein, the Exchange of Letters even contains a clause which foresees that if the Seychelles' Attorney General concludes that there is insufficient evidence to prosecute, the "EUNAVFOR shall take the full responsibility, including the financial costs, of transferring the suspected pirates and armed robbers back to their country of origin within 10 days of EUNAVFOR having been notified of such a decision."[886] The category of persons potentially received by the Seychelles is also limited from the outset by requiring some link of the transferee to the Seychelles; absent such a link, the transfer is at the discretion of the Seychelles. The Seychelles has further expressed its reluctance to enforce sentences of convicted pirates;[887] thus the Exchange of Letter stipulates that the European Union shall provide the Seychelles "with such full financial, human resource, material, logistical and infrastructural assistance for detention, incarceration maintenance, investigation, prosecution, trial and *repatriation* of suspected or convicted pirates and armed robbers."[888]

cc) Ongoing Negotiations

Since the scourge of piracy extends to an expanding geographical area and given that the number of captured pirates is constantly rising while the absorption capacities of regional States is limited, the Council of the European Union authorized its High Representative, in March 2010, to open negotiations regarding the conclusion

---

EUNAVFOR to the Republic of Seychelles and for their Treatment after Such Transfer, 2009 O.J. (L 315) 43 (EU), para. 1.

[885] *Id.* at para. 4.

[886] EU-Seychelles Transfer Agreement.

[887] United Nations, Department of Public Information, Piracy off Somali Coast Not Only Criminal, But Very Successful, Security Council Hears, Cautioned There Could Be No Peace at Sea Without Stability on Land, Press Release, Nov. 18, 2009, statement by Ronald Jumeau (Seychelles), *available at* www.un.org/News/Press/docs/2009/sc9793.doc.htm (last visited Aug. 30, 2010).

[888] EU-Seychelles Transfer Agreement (emphasis added).

of transfer agreements with further States in the region. Among them are Mauritius, Mozambique, South Africa, Tanzania and Uganda.[889]

3. The Principle of *Non-Refoulement* in the Piracy Context

The various transfer agreements do not regulate transfers exhaustively; in particular they do not cover the transfer procedure and the applicable procedural safeguards. What is more, agreements pertaining to transfers of suspects of piracy and armed robbery at sea exist thus far only with regard to the regional States of Kenya and the Seychelles. However, to date no such agreement has been concluded with Somalia (respectively the entities of Puntland and Somaliland) to which the second highest number of alleged offenders have been transferred. It is thus by having recourse to general human rights law and, specifically, to the principle of *non-refoulement*, that important limitations regarding the transfer of suspects of piracy and armed robbery at sea can be derived.

The principle of *non-refoulement* can be found in various areas of international law, namely, refugee law, international humanitarian law and international human rights law. Generally speaking, the principle prohibits bringing a person within a jurisdiction where he or she is at risk of certain human rights violations. However, the scope of the principle is different in each of the three areas of law. In particular, differences exist with regard to the persons it protects as well as the nature of the risk that a person must face upon transfer and the probability of the risk's realization in order to trigger the application of the principle of *non-refoulement*. Indeed, even if the prohibition of *refoulement* is considered exclusively within the context of human rights law, its content differs under the Convention against Torture, the European Convention of Human Rights and the International Covenant of Civilian and Political Rights.

a) Refugee Law

The principle of *non-refoulement* is most commonly associated with refugee law. Indeed, the Refugee Convention[890] states the prohibition of *refoulement* explicitly in its Article 33(1). The provision prohibits to "expel or return ('refouler') a refugee in any manner whatsoever to the frontiers of territories where his life or freedom would be threatened on account of his race, religion, nationality, membership of a particular social group or political opinion." Under the Refugee Convention

---

[889] European Union, Council of the European Union, Press Release, Foreign Affairs, 3005th Council Meeting, 7828/1/10 REV 1 (Presse 73), March 22, 2010, *available at* www.consilium.europa.eu/uedocs/cms_data/docs/pressdata/EN/foraff/113482.pdf (last visited Aug. 30, 2010), p. 16.

[890] Convention relating to the Status of Refugees, *adopted* July 28, 1951, 189 U.N.T.S. 137 [hereinafter: Refugee Convention].

and its Protocol of 1967, the term "refugee" applies to any person who is, owing to well-founded fear of being persecuted for reasons of race, religion, nationality, membership of a particular social group or political opinion, outside the country of his nationality. The person must be unable or, owing to such fear, unwilling to avail himself or herself of the protection of his or her country of nationality.[891]

The first question arising is thus, whether piracy suspects can be considered refugees under the Refugee Convention's definition. While piracy suspects are, when being held on a warship after their arrest, outside their country of origin or habitual residence,[892] they generally do not fulfill the requirement that they have quit their country out of a well-founded fear of persecution resulting from one or more of the grounds listed in the definition (race, religion, nationality, membership of a particular social group, or political opinion). Rather, the pirates, who reportedly mainly originate from Puntland (north-eastern Somalia) and from central Somalia near Xarardheere and Hobyo,[893] leave their country in order to commit a crime, i.e. they are driven by economic reasons and often extremely dire living conditions, rather than on persecutory grounds.

In addition, the Refugee Convention does not apply to persons with respect to whom there are serious reasons for considering that they have committed a serious non-political crime outside the country of refuge prior to the admission to that country as a refugee.[894] Some scholars suggest that Somali pirates are excluded from the Refugee Convention's protection already based on this provision.[895]

---

[891] Article I(A)2 Refugee Convention, as amended by Article I(2) of the Protocol relating to the Status of Refugees, *adopted* Jan. 31, 1967, 606 U.N.T.S. 267

[892] Even if Somali pirates are arrested within Somali territorial waters, they are in the custody and under the control of the seizing State and should thus be considered outside their territory of origin or habitual residence.

[893] United Nations, Monitoring Group on Somalia, Report, March 10, 2010, para. 126, stating that "[p]iracy operations continue to be anchored in two principal locations: the coast of Puntland and the central Somalia littoral east of Xarardheere and Hobyo" and para. 131, stating that "the Monitoring Group identified two major piracy networks operating along the Somali coastline: one from Puntland (north-eastern Somalia) and one from central Somalia near Xarardheere and Hobyo." See also *Middleton*, Piracy in Somalia, Threatening Global Trade, Feeding Local War, Chatham House, Africa Programme, Briefing Paper, London, Oct. 2008, pp. 4–5, *available at* www.chathamhouse.org.uk/files/12203_1008piracysomalia.pdf (last visited Aug. 30, 2010).

[894] Art. I(F)(b) Refugee Convention. Art. 33(2) Refugee Convention states that a person, who, having been convicted by final judgment of a particularly serious crime, constitutes a danger to the community of that country, cannot claim the protection of the *non-refoulement* principle. However, piracy suspects being held on a warship are not yet convicted for the crime of piracy and Art. 33(2) Refugee Convention could only be invoked for a final conviction for another crime. However, to determine this on board a warship seems difficult, especially against the background of absent state structures in Somalia that would be able to provide such information.

[895] *Guilfoyle*, Counter-Piracy Law Enforcement and Human Rights, ICLQ 59 (2010), 153.

Even if a specific piracy suspect would qualify as a refugee under the Refugee Convention's refugee definition, the principle of *non-refoulement*, as contained in Article 33(1) of the Convention, is only triggered if the person is sent to a territory where his life or freedom would be threatened because of his race, religion, nationality, membership of a particular social group or political opinion. Persecution for these specific reasons seems unlikely in those States, which are currently prosecuting pirates.

b) International Humanitarian Law

The principle of *non-refoulement* is also contained in international humanitarian law.[896] However, the current counter-piracy operations amount to law enforcement operations rather than to conduct of hostilities in the context of an armed conflict. Thus, the requirements for the application of international humanitarian law in the context of counter-piracy operations off the coast of Somalia and in the Gulf of Aden region are clearly not fulfilled despite an ongoing non-international armed conflict on the Somali mainland.[897]

c) International Human Rights Law

International law does not generally prohibit the transfer of piracy suspects to third States. However, the principle of *non-refoulement* as embodied in international human rights law could bar a specific transfer if, generally speaking, the transferee risks certain human rights violations in the receiving State. A rough overview on the scope and content of the prohibition of *refoulement* under the Convention against Torture, the European Convention of Human Rights and the International Covenant of Civilian and Political Rights respectively will be provided.[898]

---

[896] *Droege*, Transfer of Detainees: Legal Framework, *non-refoulement*, and Contemporary Challenges, IRRC 90 (2008), 674–676.

[897] On the qualification of the current counter-piracy operations as law enforcement operations, see p. 131 *et seq.*

[898] The principle of *non-refoulement* is also contained in other human rights treaties, for example in Art. 22(8) of the American Convention on Human Rights, *adopted* Nov. 22, 1969, 1144 U.N.T.S. 143 or in Art. 19(2) of the Charter of Fundamental Rights of the European Union, 2000/C 364/01, 2000 O.J. (C 364) 1–22, which has become a legally binding instrument with the entry into force of the Treaty of Lisbon: Art. 6(1) of the Treaty of Lisbon, Amendments to the Treaty on European Union and to the Treaty Establishing the European Community, 2007/C 306/01, 2007 O.J. (C 306) 1–329.

aa) The Scope of the Principle of *Non-Refoulement*

(1) Convention against Torture

The Convention against Torture states the prohibition of *refoulement* as follows:

Art. 3 Convention against Torture

1. No State Party shall expel, return ("refouler") or extradite a person to another State where there are substantial grounds for believing that he would be in danger of being subjected to torture.

2. For the purpose of determining whether there are such grounds, the competent authorities shall take into account all relevant considerations including, where applicable, the existence in the State concerned of a consistent pattern of gross, flagrant or mass violations of human rights.

The provision applies to any method of moving a person to another State, i.e. Article 3 of the Convention against Torture protects any person against any form of "obligatory departure" to another State.[899] Thus, not only extraditions, which play a very minor role in the counter piracy context, but also so-called transfers and generally any form of a handover of piracy suspects would be subject to the *non-refoulement* provision of the Convention against Torture.

The personal scope of the provision is wider compared to the *non-refoulement* provision of the Refugee Convention in that Article 3 of the Convention against Torture protects every person notwithstanding his or her status (e.g. as refugee). Given the absolute nature of the provision, it does not contain any exclusion or derogation clause. Thus even the most dangerous criminal and, *a forteriori*, a piracy suspect, cannot be excluded from its protective ambit.[900]

According to Article 3 of the Convention against Torture, States not only violate the absolute prohibition of torture if their own authorities subject a person to torture, but also if their authorities send a person to another State where there are substantial grounds for believing that the person would be in danger of being subjected to torture, as defined in Article 1 of the Convention against Torture.[901] The scope of the *refoulement* prohibition under the Convention against Torture is limited to torture and does not extend to cruel, inhuman or degrading treatment as defined in Article 16 of the Convention against Torture.[902]

The *non-refoulement* provision of the Convention against Torture can thus only be applied to such forms of corporal and capital punishment (which some States were piracy suspects are transferred still retain, namely, also for the specific crime

---

[899] *Nowak/McArthur*, Convention Against Torture Commentary, pp. 195–196, para. 173.

[900] See Arts. I(F)(b) and 33(2) Refugee Convention. *Nowak/McArthur*, Convention Against Torture Commentary, pp. 148–149, paras. 70, 73 and 75, and p. 195, para. 171.

[901] *Id.* at p. 127, para. 1.

[902] *Id.* p. 165, para. 116, and p. 200, para. 183.

of piracy)[903] that are to be considered torture in the sense of Article 1 Convention against Torture. This requires that the pain or suffering inflicted by the punishment reaches the level of being "severe."[904]

Article 3 of the Convention against Torture requires that there are substantial grounds for believing that the person to be transferred would be in danger of being subjected to torture in the receiving State. Regarding the proof of this risk, the Committee against Torture stressed in its General Comment No. 1 that the transferee must establish a *prima facie* case by providing substantial grounds that go beyond mere theory or suspicion that torture is objectively practiced in the receiving State and that he runs a personal risk of being tortured upon return. However, if there exists a consistent pattern of gross, flagrant or mass violations of human rights,[905] it is up to the government of the host State to provide evidence why the applicant would not be at risk of torture. If the transferee subtantiated the risk in the way described, the burden of proof shifts to the State party, who has then the responsibility to gather relevant information and evidence and to carry out a proper risk asessement.[906]

The principle of *non-refoulement* of Article 3 of the Convention against Torture also contains a procedural aspect. Given that in the present context, the publicly available transfer agreements are virtually silent on the procedure to reach a transfer decision and that for a number of transfers no such instrument exists, the due process aspects guaranteed under the *refoulement* prohibition of the Convention against Torture are quite important. The Committee against Torture for instance has held that a State party should always assess its *non-refoulement* obligations "on an individual basis and provide, in practice, all procedural guarantees to the person expelled, returned or extradited."[907] Further, State parties "should take measures to

---

[903] On retentionist regional States prosecuting pirates and armed robbers at sea, see note 392. Yemen pronounced the death penalty against six Somali pirates: *Miley*, Jurist, Yemen Court Sentences 6 Somali Pirates to Death, May 18, 2010, *available at* http://jurist.org/paperchase/2010/05/yemen-court-sentences-12-pirates-6-to-death.php (last visited Aug. 30, 2010).

[904] *Nowak/McArthur*, Convention Against Torture Commentary, pp. 218–219, para. 215.

[905] In the case of *Elmi v. Australia* (communication no. 120/1998), U.N. Doc. CAT/C/22/D/120/1998 (May 14, 1999), para. 6(6), the Committee against Torture found that in Somalia such a consistent pattern of gross, flagrant or mass violations of human rights exsited; see also *Nowak/McArthur*, Convention Against Torture Commentary, p. 227, para. 234.

[906] United Nations, Committee against Torture, General Comment No. 01, paras. 5–7; *Nowak/McArthur*, Convention Against Torture Commentary, pp. 129–130, paras. 6–7, and pp. 219–224, paras. 217–227.

[907] United Nations, Committee Against Torture, Considerations of Reports Submitted by States Parties under Article 19 of the Convention, Conclusion and Recommendations of the Committee against Torture, Estonia, UN Doc. CAT/C/EST/CO/4 (Feb. 19, 2008), para. 12.

ensure that individuals subject to removal have access to all existing remedies."[908] Moreover, the transferee should always have the possibility to challenge the *re-foulement* decision. This judicial review or appeal should be effective, independent and impartial and have suspensive effect.[909] As noted above, transfer procedures vary considerably among the various States participating in the counter-piracy operations in terms of judicial oversight and procedural safeguards granted to the transferee. While some States seem to fulfill the procedural requirements flowing from the *non-refoulement* principle, others may not live up to the procedural obligations of Article 3 Convention against Torture.

Finally, it should be noted that threats of torture by non-state actors without the consent or acquiescence of the government are not covered by Article 3 of the Convention against Torture.[910] However, in the situation of a failed State, specifically with regard to Somalia, the Committee against Torture has made an exception holding that in such a scenario the risk of being subjected to torture by a non-state actor may also prevent a person from being returned.[911] However, three years later the Committee against Torture stated that Somalia possessed a State authority in the form of the Transitional National Government and, despite doubts about its territorial authority and sustainability, acts of non-state actors in Somalia would no longer be covered by the *non-refoulement* provision.[912]

In the present context quite a number of piracy suspects have been transferred to Puntland and Somaliland. These entities have declared their independence from Somalia but are not recognized as States by the international community.[913] With regard to the application of Article 3 Convention against Torture, it could be ar-

---

[908] United Nations, Committee against Torture, Considerations of Reports Submitted by States Parties under Article 19 of the Convention, Conclusion and Recommendations of the Committee against Torture, France, UN Doc. CAT/C/FRA/CO/3 (April 3, 2006), para. 7.

[909] United Nations, Committee against Torture, Considerations of Reports Submitted by States Parties under Article 19 of the Convention, Conclusion and Recommendations of the Committee against Torture, United States of America, UN Doc. CAT/C/USA/CO/2 (July 25, 2006), para. 20; Considerations of Reports Submitted by States Parties under Article 19 of the Convention, Conclusion and Recommendations of the Committee against Torture, France, UN Doc. CCPR/CO/84/THA (July 8, 2005), para. 17; Considerations of Reports Submitted by States Parties under Article 19 of the Convention, Conclusion and Recommendations of the Committee against Torture, France, UN Doc. CAT/C/FRA/CO/3 (April 3, 2006), para. 7; Considerations of Reports Submitted by States Parties under Article 19 of the Convention, Conclusion and Recommendations of the Committee against Torture, Bosnia and Herzegovina, UN Doc. CAT/C/BIH/CO/1 (Dec. 15, 2005), para. 12.

[910] Art. 1 Convention against Torture.

[911] *Nowak/McArthur*, Convention Against Torture Commentary, pp. 165–166, para. 118, and p. 201, para. 185, citing *Elmi v. Australia* (communication no. 120/1998), U.N. Doc. CAT/C/22/D/120/1998 (May 14, 1999).

[912] *Id.* pp. 165–166, para. 118, and p. 201, para. 185, citing *H.M.H.I. v. Australia* (communication no. 177/2001), U.N. Doc. A/57/44 at 166 (2002).

[913] On the semi-autonomous entities of Somaliland and Puntland, see p. 13 *et seq.*

gued that these semi-autonomous entities are quasi-States and the members of their authorities "public officials" in the sense of Article 1 Convention against Torture. Alternatively, it could also be argued that although they are not independent States, they constitute entities of Somalia and that persons acting on behalf of an authority in Puntland or Somaliland can be considered to be Somali public officials. In view of the number of transfers to these entities (reportedly 60 to Puntland and 20 to Somaliland) it would be unacceptable if States could circumvent their undisputed *non-refoulement* obligation vis-à-vis Somalia by transferring suspects to Puntland or Somaliland.

(2) International Covenant on Civilian and Political Rights

Under the International Covenant on Civil and Political Rights, the principle of *non-refoulement* is derived from Article 7 (prohibition of torture) and Article 6 (right to life).

In its second General Comment on Article 7, the Human Rights Committee stated that "States parties must not expose individuals to the danger of torture or cruel, inhuman or degrading treatment or punishment upon return to another country by way of their extradition, expulsion or refoulement."[914] Thus, in contrast to the Convention against Torture under which the principle of *non-refoulement* only applies to torture, the *refoulement* prohibition of the International Covenant on Civilian and Political Rights also covers cruel, inhuman or degrading treatment or punishment.[915]

Without analyzing in depth what kind of treatment constitutes a violation of the prohibition of Article 7 of the Covenant, it should be noted that some forms of corporal[916] or capital punishment amount to cruel, inhuman or degrading treatment or punishment.[917] Also harsh conditions of detention can constitute inhuman[918] or degrading[919] treatment.[920] A general statement on the conditions of detention of piracy suspects or convicts is hardly possible because the detention standards in the various countries receiving pirates vary considerably. In addition to this, as assessment of even an individual State may be difficult given that piracy suspects are often held in specific prisons, which are "above average." For those prisons,

---

[914] United Nations, Human Rights Committee, General Comment No. 20, para. 9, contained in: Compilation of General Comments and General Recommendations Adopted by Human Rights Treaty Bodies, U.N. Doc. HRI/GEN/1/Rev.1 (May 12, 2004), p. 152.

[915] *Nowak/McArthur*, Convention Against Torture Commentary, pp. 128–129, para. 3.

[916] *Nowak*, ICCPR Commentary, pp. 167–168, paras. 17–19.

[917] *Id.* pp. 168–169, paras. 19–23.

[918] *Id.* p. 165, para. 13.

[919] *Id.* pp. 165–166, paras. 14–15.

[920] *Id.* pp. 172–175, paras. 24–28.

general reports on the detention conditions in the specific country as issued, for example, by human rights bodies or organizations, may not be accurate. Thus, for example, most piracy suspects transferred to Kenya are detained in the Shimo-La-Tewa prison.[921] This prison was subject to major reforms within the framework of the Counter Piracy Program of the United Nations Office on Drugs and Crime, which can hardly be compared with an average Kenyan prison.[922]

With regard to the principle of *non-refoulement* as derived from the right of life as guaranteed in Article 6 of the Covenant, the obligations of transferring States differ between retentionist and abolitionist States.[923]

Retentionist State parties to the Covenant have the obligation to carefully assess the probability that the death penalty is imposed or executed upon the transferee in the receiving State. If a real risk exists that the death penalty is imposed or executed, the transferring State must assess whether the limitations contained in Article 6(2), (4) and (5) will be respected in the receiving State. If not, a transfer would be prohibited.[924]

One such limitation is contained in Article 6(2) of the International Covenant on Civil and Political Rights according to which the death sentence may only be imposed for the most serious crimes according to a law in force at the time the crime was committed. If this limitation is not respected in the receiving State, a transfer would be prohibited by the principle of *non-refoulement* as derived from the right to life. In the piracy context, the prohibition to apply a criminal law retroactively deserves special mention given that many States only introduced or revised criminal norms on piracy and armed robbery at sea once the problem became acute in the Gulf of Aden region.

Article 6(2) of the International Covenant on Civil and Political Rights contains another limitation on the imposition of the death penalty, stating that it can only be carried out pursuant to a final judgment rendered by a competent court. It further states that a sentence of death may not be imposed contrary to the provisions of the Covenant. Hence, the principle of *non-refoulement* prohibits transferring a piracy suspect to a State where there exists a real risk that the death penalty is imposed in a criminal proceeding not fulfilling the minimum fair trial guarantees of the Cove-

---

[921] United Nations, UNODC, Promoting Health, Security and Justice, Cutting the Threads of Drugs, Crime and Terrorism, 2010 Report, *available at* www.unodc.org/documents/frontpage/UNODC_Annual_Report_2010_LowRes.pdf (last visited Aug. 30, 2010), p. 29.

[922] United Nations, UNODC, Counter Piracy Programme, November 2009, *available at* www.unodc.org/documents/easternafrica//piracy/UNODC_Counter_Piracy_Programme.pdf (last visited Aug. 30, 2010).

[923] *Nowak*, ICCPR Commentary, p. 151, para. 53.

[924] *Id.* pp. 150–151, para. 52.

nant, such as stated in Articles 14 and 15.[925] Some countries, to which pirates are transferred still retain the death penalty, such as Yemen or Puntland (Somalia) that have already pronounced capital punishment in piracy cases.[926] If there is a real risk that the capital punishment will be imposed following a trial not fulfilling the standard as required by Article 6(2) of the Covenant, the prohibition of *refoulement* would bar such a transfer.

Further limitations on the imposition of a death sentence is contained in Article 6(3) of the Covenant, requiring that "[a]nyone sentenced to death shall have the right to seek pardon or commutation of the sentence" and Article 6(5) of the Covenant stating that the "[s]entence of death shall not be imposed for crimes committed by persons below eighteen years of age." These are additional considerations to take into account when deciding upon a transfer of a piracy suspect.

As far as abolitionist States are concerned the *non-refoulement* obligations under Article 6 go even further. In the landmark case of *Judge v. Canada*, the Human Rights Committee ruled that abolitionist States are prevented by Art. 6(1) of the Covenant from extraditing or deporting a person to a retentionist State, where that person faces a real risk of being subjected to the death penalty in all cases, i.e. regardless of whether the requirements of Article 6(2) to (5) as described above are respected in the receiving State. In particular, the Human Rights Committee held: "For countries that *have* abolished the death penalty, there is an obligation not to expose a person to a real risk of its application. Thus, they [abolitionist countries] may not remove, either by *deportation* or *extradition*, individuals from their jurisdiction if it may be reasonably anticipated that they will be sentenced to death, without ensuring that the death sentence would not be carried out."[927] From this it can be inferred that States having abolished the death penalty[928] must also refrain from *transferring* piracy suspects to States where they face the possible imposition and execution of the death penalty, since the principle of *non-refoulement* applies to all forms of involuntary handovers.[929]

---

[925] *Id.* pp. 138–141, paras. 31–35, and pp. 142–144, paras. 38–41.

[926] *Miley*, Jurist, Yemen Court Sentences 6 Somali Pirates to Death, May 18, 2010, *available at* http://jurist.org/paperchase/2010/05/yemen-court-sentences-12-pirates-6-to-death.php (last visited Aug. 30, 2010). Puntland State of Somalia, Puntland Marines Stormed a Dubai Flagged Ship, Current Issues, April 25, 2010, www.puntlandgovt.com/en/currentissues/information/current_issues_more.php?id=734 (last visited August 30. 2010).

[927] *Nowak*, ICCPR Commentary, p. 188, para. 50, citing United Nations, Human Rights Committee, *Judge v. Canada* (communication no. 829/1998), U.N. Doc. CCPR/C/78/D/829/1998 (July 14-Aug. 28, 2003), para. 10(4) (emphasis added).

[928] For example State parties to the 2nd Optional Protocol ICCPR.

[929] See above note 392 on retentionist and abolitionist countries in the region.

(3) European Convention on Human Rights

In the European Convention on Human Rights, the principle of *non-refoulement* is derived from Article 3. According to the Strasbourg Court's case law, the decision to bring a person within another jurisdiction raises an issue under Article 3 of the Convention "where substantial grounds have been shown for believing that the person concerned (…) faces a real risk of being subjected to torture or to inhuman or degrading treatment or punishment" in the receiving State.[930] Those risks must not necessarily emanate from State authorities or organs, but can also be posed by non-state actors.[931]

If the human rights violation should materialize in the receiving State upon transfer, an irreparable harm may result from it. Therefore granting a remedy which may prevent a transfer is of utmost importance. It could be argued that transferring a person without granting any review procedure prior to the implementation of the transfer decision, which has suspensive effect, would violate the transferee's right to an effective remedy as stipulated in Article 13 of the European Convention on Human Rights.[932] According to the case law of the European Court of Human Rights, the authority before which an effective remedy must be available does not necessarily have to be a judicial authority, but can be another body whose effectiveness is namely measured by its powers and the procedural guarantees it affords.[933]

The judicial control provided to piracy suspects on board warships regarding their transfer decision, if it exists at all, varies in its form. Italy, for example, brought alleged offenders held on its frigate, *Maestrale*, which was contributing to the EUNAVFOR, before an Italian investigating judge by video conference. The Netherlands seem to apply their extradition standards and embark besides law enforcement officials also assistant-district attorneys on board.[934] Other States, such as the United Kingdom, have no such judicial monitoring mechanism for transfer-

---

[930] European Court of Human Rights, *Cruz Varas and Others v. Sweden* (application no. 15576/89), Judgment March 20, 1991, paras. 69–70; *Vilvarajah and Others v. United Kindgom* (application no. 13163/87, 13164/87, 13165/87, 13447/87, 13448/87), Judgment Oct. 30, 1991, para. 103. See also *Van Dijk et al.*, Theory and Practice of the European Convention on Human Rights, pp. 434–435.

[931] *Frowein/Peukert*, EMRK-Kommentar, p. 56, para. 22.

[932] *Guilfoyle*, Counter-Piracy Law Enforcement and Human Rights, ICLQ 59 (2010), 167.

[933] *Van Dijk et al.*, Theory and Practice of the European Convention on Human Rights, p. 1006.

[934] Meijers Committee, Standing Committee of Experts on International Immigration, Refugee and Criminal Law, Comment on the Agreement Between the EU and Kenya on the Transfer of Persons Suspected of Piracy to Kenya, *available at* www.commissie-meijers.nl/commissiemeijers/pagina.asp?pagkey=92379 (follow "Comments on the Agreement Between the EU and Kenya on Piracy" hyperlink) (last visited Aug. 30, 2010).

ees in place on board their ships.[935] Thus, some transfer practices occurring in the context of the counter-piracy operations off the coast of Somalia and in the larger Gulf of Aden region may violate the right to an effective remedy as guaranteed under the European Convention on Human Rights in connection with the prohibition of *refoulement*.

bb) Diplomatic Assurances in the Context of Counter-Piracy Operations

States, especially European States, often rely on so-called diplomatic assurances, i.e. bilateral assurances by one government to another guaranteeing that certain fundamental human rights prescriptions will be complied with, when handing over a person to another State.[936] Diplomatic assurances in this sense are also used in the context of transfers of piracy suspects to regional States. The EU-Kenya Transfer Agreement, for example, contains the assurance that "[no] transferred person will be liable to suffer the death sentence. Kenya will (…) take steps to ensure that any death sentence is commuted to a sentence of imprisonment."[937] Moreover, the Agreement – under the rubric "Treatment, prosecution and trial of transferred persons" provides, inter alia, that "[a]ny transferred person will be treated humanely and will not be subjected to torture or cruel, inhuman or degrading treatment or punishment, will receive adequate accommodation and nourishment, access to medical treatment and will be able to carry out religious observance."[938] Provisions contained in Article 3(b) to (g) of the EU-Kenya Transfer Agreement lay out detailed fair trial provisions.

In the EU-Seychelles Transfer Agreement, the government of the Republic of the Seychelles confirms that "[a]ny transferred person will be treated humanely and will not be subjected to torture or cruel, inhuman or degrading treatment or punishment, will receive adequate accommodation and nourishment, access to medical treatment and will be able to carry out religious observance." In addition, the Agreement provides a number of fair trial rights.[939]

---

[935] *Guilfoyle*, Counter-Piracy Law Enforcement and Human Rights, ICLQ 59 (2010), 164.

[936] Amnesty International, Dangerous Deals – Europe's Reliance on "Diplomatic Assurances" Against Torture, 2010, *available at* www.amnesty.org/en/library/asset/EUR01/012/2010/en/608f128b-9eac-4e2f-b73b-6d747a8cbaed/eur010122010en.pdf (last visited Aug. 30, 2010); Human Rights Watch, Not the Way Forward – The UK's Dangerous Reliance on Diplomatic Assurances, Oct. 22, 2008, *available at* www.hrw.org/en/node/75603/section/1 (last visited Aug. 30, 2010).

[937] Art. 6 EU-Kenya Transfer Agreement.

[938] Art. 3(a) EU-Kenya Transfer Agreement.

[939] EU-Seychelles Transfer Agreement.

Diplomatic assurances have widely been criticized as a means to circumvent the absolute nature of the principle of *non-refoulement*.[940] In 2009, a report of the Eminent Jurists Panel of the International Commission of Jurists urged States "not to rely on diplomatic assurances or other forms of non-binding agreements to transfer individuals when there is a real risk of serious human rights violations."[941] In 2010, Amnesty International released a report showing that diplomatic assurances do not provide an effective safeguard against torture or other cruel, inhuman and degrading treatment and punishment and called "on all governments to halt the use of unreliable diplomatic assurances against torture and other ill-treatment to forcibly return persons to places where they are at risk of such violations."[942] The European Court of Human Rights, in a number of recent cases, namely in *Saadi v. Italy*,[943] *Ismoilov v. Russia*,[944] *Ryabikin v. Russia*,[945] *Ben Khemais v. Italy*[946] and *Klein v. Russia*,[947] ruled decisively that the diplomatic assurances received by the sending states were insufficient to safeguard against abuse upon return to the receiving country. Indeed, the Strasbourg Court explicitly "cautioned against reliance on diplomatic assurances against torture from a state where torture is endemic or persistent."[948] In particular, the Court held that "[d]iplomatic assurances are not in themselves sufficient to ensure adequate protection against the risk of ill-treatment where reliable sources have reported practices resorted to or tolerated by the authorities which are manifestly contrary to the principles of the Convention."[949]

---

[940] United Nations, Human Rights Council, Report of the Special Rapporteur on Torture and Other Cruel, Inhuman and Degrading Treatment or Punishment, UN Doc A/HRC/13/39 (Feb. 9, 2010), p. 18, para. 67.

[941] International Commission of Jurists, Assessing Damage, Urging Action – Report of the Eminent Jurists Panel on Terrorism, Counter-Terrorism and Human Rights, May 4, 2009, *available at* www.icj.org (follow "Publications" hyperlink, then follow "Panel Series" hyperlink) (last visited Aug. 30, 2010), p. 167.

[942] Amnesty International, Dangerous Deals – Europe's Reliance on "Diplomatic Assurances" Against Torture, 2010, *available at* www.amnesty.org/en/library/asset/EUR01/012/2010/en/608f128b-9eac-4e2f-b73b-6d747a8cbaed/eur010122010en.pdf (last visited Aug. 30, 2010), p. 32.

[943] European Court of Human Rights, *Ismoilov v. Russia* (application no. 2947/06), April 24, 2008.

[944] European Court of Human Rights, *Saadi v. Italy* (application no. 37201/06), Feb. 28, 2009.

[945] European Court of Human Rights, *Ryabikin v. Russia* (application no. 8320/04), June 19, 2008.

[946] European Court of Human Rights, *Ben Khemais v. Italy* (application no. 246/07), Feb. 24, 2009.

[947] European Court of Human Rights, *Klein v. Russia* (application no. 24268/08), April 1, 2010.

[948] European Court of Human Rights, *Ismoilov v. Russia* (application no. 2947/06), April 24, 2008, para. 127.

[949] European Court of Human Rights, *Ryabikin v. Russia* (application no. 8320/04), June 19, 2008, para. 119.

To date, however, the European Court of Human Rights has not held that the transfer of persons on the basis of diplomatic assurances against torture and other ill-treatment violates Article 3 of the European Convention on Human Rights *per se*. Rather, as the Court pointed out explicitly in *Saadi v. Italy*, it carries out a case-by-case assessment of whether the "practical application" of such a diplomatic assurance provides a sufficient guarantee of protection. Thus, what matters is not so much the specific formulation of a given assurance but its protective effects when applied in practice.[950] Notably, the Committee against Torture pursues a similar approach. It likewise assesses the sufficiency of any diplomatic assurances on a case-by-case basis. Thus, for example, in its 2006 conclusions and recommendations on the United States of America periodic report, the Committee declined to rule out the use of diplomatic assurances entirely, but recommended that the United States of America should "establish and implement clear procedures for obtaining such assurances, with adequate judicial mechanisms for review, and effective post-return monitoring arrangements."[951] However, specifically with regard to torture, the Committee suggests that diplomatic assurances from States known for their practice of torture are generally unreliable and ineffective and should thus not be resorted to. Compliance with assurances not to resort to torture – in comparison to diplomatic assurances not to impose or enforce the death penalty – could hardly be monitored and enforced, namely, because torture is commonly surrounded by secrecy. The government issuing diplomatic assurances not to resort to torture often lacks the factual power to stop practices prohibited by the Convention against Torture.[952]

From this it follows that diplomatic assurances against the death penalty are to be assessed not on the basis of their formulation but in view of their effects in practice and on a case-by-case basis. In this regard, the threshold set by international jurisprudence is quite high. While there are random examples where undertakings by a receiving State not to impose or execute the death penalty have been accepted as sufficient to deny the existence of a risk, which would preclude a transfer,[953] the European Court of Human Rights in particular, has, in its recent jurisprudence, been rather strict in the assessment of diplomatic assurances.

---

[950] European Court of Human Rights, *Saadi v. Italy* (application no. 37201/06), Feb. 28, 2009, para. 148; *Ben Khemais v. Italy* (application no. 246/07), Feb. 24, 2009, paras. 4–5. See also *Ismoilov v. Russia* (application no. 2947/06), April 24, 2008, para. 127, and *Ryabikin v. Russia* (application no. 8320/04), June 19, 2008, para. 119.

[951] United Nations, Committee against Torture, Considerations of Reports Submitted by States Parties under Article 19 of the Convention, Conclusion and Recommendations of the Committee against Torture, United States of America, U.N. Doc. CAT/C/USA/CO/2 (May 18, 2006), para. 21.

[952] *Id.* at pp. 212–217, paras. 205–212.

[953] United Nations, Human Rights Committee, *Judge v. Canada* (communication no. 829/1998), U.N. Doc. CCPR/C/78/D/829/1998 (July 14–Aug. 28, 2003), para. 10(4).

With regard to transfers based on diplomatic assurances that occurred in the context of the counter-piracy missions in the Gulf of Aden region – as far as can be seen – in the example of Kenya, there have not been any reports of human rights violations of the transferees. As far as post-return monitoring mechanisms are concerned, the EU-Kenya Transfer Agreement provides, *inter alia*, that "Kenya will be responsible for keeping an accurate account of all transferred persons, including, but not limited to (…) the person's physical condition, the location of their places of detention, any charges against him and any significant decisions taken in the course of his prosecution and trial."[954] Moreover, the Agreement explicitly states that "[t]hese records will be available to representatives of the EU and EUNAVFOR upon request in writing to the Kenyan Ministry of Foreign Affairs."[955] "(…) Kenya will notify EUNAVFOR of the place of detention of any person transferred under this Exchange of Letters, any deterioration of his physical condition and of any allegations of alleged improper treatment. Representatives of the EU and EUNAVFOR will have access to any persons transferred under this Exchange of Letters as long as such persons are in custody and will be entitled to question them."[956] Finally, the EU-Kenya Transfer Agreement stipulates that "[n]ational and international humanitarian agencies will, at their request, be allowed to visit persons transferred under this Exchange of Letters."[957] In view of the European Court of Human Rights'jurisprudence on the matter, the assessment of these provisions will depend first and foremost on their practical application.

D. Conclusion

Transfers of piracy suspects into the jurisdiction of third States, particularly regional States, constitute a common feature of counter-piracy operations in the Gulf of Aden. The current practice evidences that such transfers can indeed contribute towards the effective repression of piracy in the region by facilitating the instigation of criminal proceedings. International law neither endorses nor prohibits such transfers. However, it is clear that certain limitations and safeguards apply whenever a change in jurisdiction over a piracy suspect is brought about. In this regard it is irrelevant whether such a change in jurisdiction qualifies as an extradition in the legal sense or whether it simply amounts to a physical handover of the person concerned. The principle of *non-refoulement* is absolute; it applies irrespective of such legal technicalities.

---

[954] Art. 5(c) EU-Kenya Transfer Agreement.
[955] Art. 5(d) EU-Kenya Transfer Agreement.
[956] Art. 5(e) EU-Kenya Transfer Agreement.
[957] Art. 5(f) EU-Kenya Transfer Agreement.

Conclusion

Some years ago, Alfred Rubin concluded that the treaty rules on piracy are "incomprehensible and therefore codify nothing."[958] Indeed, contrary to what seems to be a widespread perception, the UNCLOS rules neither define an international crime on which criminal prosecutions could be based nor were they ever specifically designed to vest States with the necessary jurisdiction to enforce or to adjudicate. The slipshod and partially faulty craftsmanship of UNCLOS' piracy regime is largely due to the fact that in 1982 the drafters of the UNCLOS perceived piracy as an outdated 18th century phenomenon, not requiring renewed elaboration for purposes of a 20th century codification of the law of the sea. Moreover, the primary interest underlying Articles 100 to 107 UNCLOS was to ensure the freedom of the high seas, as laid out in Article 87 UNCLOS, rather than enabling efficient law enforcement and criminal investigations vis-à-vis individual suspects. This is the reason why UNCLOS' enforcement powers, laid out in Articles 110 and 105 UNCLOS, are directed against suspected pirate ships and their entire crew, rather than against individual persons (pirates) or the underlying criminal structures.

The Security Council Resolutions 1816, 1846, 1851, 1897 and 1918 set out to remedy some of the well-known deficiencies inherent in these rules. Acting under Chapter VII United Nations Charter and upon the explicit request of the Somali Transitional Federal Government, the Security Council removed the oft-lamented geographical limitations inherent in the enforcement regime of the UNCLOS. Most importantly, the Security Council has successfully authorized counter-piracy operations in Somalia's territorial waters and paved their way onto its mainland.

But the Security Council could not so easily brush aside the sovereign interests of its member States. Piracy is a worldwide phenomenon. Any more general regulation going beyond the particular context of Somalia could have had repercussions in various parts of the world, potentially impairing free navigation and opening access into the territorial waters of other States whose coastal waters are likewise affected by piracy and armed robbery at sea. Against this background, the Security Council relied on the specific situation in Somalia as the threat to world peace justifying its various Chapter VII-based Resolutions rather than the abstract phenomenon of piracy and armed robbery at sea. In particular, tampering with UNCLOS itself, such as by way of reforming the UNCLOS piracy regime, was not an option. Already in the context of the very first counter-piracy Resolution, Security Council

---

[958] *Rubin*, Law of Piracy, p. 373 and p. 393.

Resolution 1816 of June 2008, various member States of the Security Council had voiced their strongest opposition against any alteration to UNCLOS. This may partly be due to the fact that despite the seriousness of the problem of piracy, it is not this aspect of UNCLOS which currently most concerns member States. Present preoccupations of greater priority include the competing continental shelf claims to the North Pole.

Ultimately, this resulted in the setting up of a threefold legal enforcement regime depending on whether pirates are pursued on the high seas, within Somalia's territorial waters or on its mainland.[959] Firstly, with regard to enforcement operations on the high seas nothing has changed. These operations remain exclusively governed by the UNCLOS.

Secondly, within Somalia's territorial waters, Security Council Resolutions 1816, 1846 and 1897 have somewhat expanded the range of enforcement competencies by including the notion of armed robbery at sea. On the one hand, this is to be welcomed as an attempt to comprehensively grasp a larger criminal phenomenon that goes beyond UNCLOS' limited definition of piracy and so enable more effective enforcement operations. On the other hand, in terms of legal certainty, the inclusion of the ill-defined notion of armed robbery at sea raises concerns. In the backyard of a failed State, with explicit safeguards not to create a legal precedent and in light of a persistent threat to a universally endorsed interest (namely, the free flow of international trade), consensus on the inclusion of this concept could nevertheless readily be reached. Security Council Resolutions 1816, 1846, 1851 as well as 1897 were all adopted unanimously.

Thirdly, as far as operations on Somalia's mainland are concerned, the Security Council has put in place a broad range of enforcement powers, leaving States a wide margin of discretion in pursuit of their far-reaching objective to fully and durably eradicate piracy and armed robbery at sea off Somalia's coast. Security Council Resolution 1851 authorizes "all necessary measures that are appropriate in Somalia, for the purpose of suppressing acts of piracy and armed robbery at sea."[960] The contrast is conspicuous: By far the most comprehensive enforcement regime against piracy, *nota bene* the traditional definition of which confines acts of piracy to the high seas, has now been set up on Somali mainland rather than on the high seas.

This graduation of ever wider enforcement powers from the UNCLOS-governed high seas, where enforcement powers have remained confined as before, via Somalia's territorial waters, where their scope has been extended and onto the territory

---

[959] In fact, yet another dimension is added if enforcement operations were to be carried out in the coastal waters of littoral States, which would require the consent of the States concerned.

[960] S.C. Res. 1851, para. 6.

of a consenting failed State, where – it seems – third States could freely pursue anyone remotely suspected of having been involved in piracy with "all necessary means," confirms the conclusion that in framing the enforcement competencies of the counter-piracy operations in the Gulf of Aden, States' sovereign interests have played a rather significant role, albeit partially at the expense of a more coherent law enforcement regime.[961]

The Security Council Resolutions evidence yet another differentiation with respect to the theatres of land and sea: Security Council Resolution 1851, applicable to counter-piracy operations on land, contains an explicit reference, albeit in the most generic manner, to the "applicable human rights law." Security Council Resolution 1846, pertaining to the repression of piracy at sea, is, however, conspicuously silent on human rights. Despite the ambiguity evoked by this discrepancy, it is worth emphasizing that the extraterritorial application of human rights law at sea is certainly possible. It has been affirmed by a growing corpus of judicial pronouncements, sporadically seemingly going so far as to cover ship-to-ship operations where effective control is least manifest.

Admittedly, many of the ambiguities inherent in UNCLOS' definition of acts of piracy or in relation to the concept of armed robbery at sea, could simply be discarded as being chiefly of an academic interest. In the current practice of law enforcement operations, many of these ambiguities have no immediate practical relevance and they do not hamper effective law enforcement operations. However, the long-term success of counter-piracy efforts in the region will depend, not only on effective enforcement operations, but also on credible prosecutions. In other words, current law enforcement activities must not be viewed in isolation from adjudication, which is likewise key to a lasting repression of piracy. In this respect, many of the ambiguities pertaining to the identification of pirates and pirate ships, the ill-defined notion of armed robbery at sea, as well as the question of the applicable human rights standards, combined with the fact that many of the military personnel carrying out current enforcement operations are often not properly trained in crime scene investigation, could come back to haunt subsequent efforts to achieve appropriate criminal convictions against piracy suspects in court proceedings.

---

[961] See, for example, the explanations of vote after the adoption of S.C. Res. 1816 delivered by South Africa, Vietnam, Libya, and China: United Nations, Department of Public Information, Security Council Condemns Acts of Piracy, Armed Robbery off Somalia's Coast, Authorizes for Six Months "All Necessary Means" to Repress Such Acts, Press Release, June 2, 2008, *available at* www.un.org/News/Press/docs/2008/sc9344.doc.htm (last visited Aug. 30, 2010). See also the explanation of vote delivered by the Russian Federation upon the adoption of S.C. Res. 1851: United Nations, Department of Public Information, Security Council Authorizes States to Use Land-Based Operations in Somalia, Press Release, Dec. 16, 2008, *available at* www.un.org/News/Press/docs/2008/sc9541 .doc.htm (last visited Aug. 30, 2010).

Whereas the Security Council has considerably expanded the range of enforce-ment powers, as far as the level of adjudicative jurisdiction is concerned the coun-ter-piracy Security Council Resolutions do not go beyond calling for enhanced cooperation in criminal matters and a solemn invocation of a meshwork of inter-national treaties pertaining to crimes committed at sea. This approach is mirrored in practice, where States involved in counter-piracy missions have been rather reluc-tant to administer criminal justice and to commence proceedings against persons suspected of having committed acts of piracy and armed robbery at sea within their domestic jurisdictions. In order to overcome the evident problems arising from (ini-tial) catch-and-release practices, legal mechanisms have been devised to bring sus-pects within the criminal jurisdiction of States willing to commence criminal pro-ceedings against pirates and armed robbers at sea. Transfer agreements that envisage the handover of suspected pirates and alleged armed robbers at sea to jur-isdictions willing to prosecute them, have been concluded with regional States. Shiprider agreements could potentially also be used in order to bring alleged pirates directly within the jurisdiction of third States willing to initiate criminal proceed-ings. These instruments, which allow bringing alleged offenders within a jurisdic-tion willing to institgate criminal proceedings against them, are not *per se* illegal. However, they must be designed and used in a way that ensures the respect of hu-man rights, especially the principle of *non-refoulement*. In this regard, the lesson learned in the fight against international terrorism, should be heeded also when aiming to sustainably repress piracy in the Gulf of Aden, namely that unambiguous rule-of-law adherence is, in the long run, the best way to success in the repression of a criminal phenomenon.

Piracy is not Somalia's biggest problem. Yet, piracy is symptomatic of Somalia's biggest problems and like the unstable situation on Somali mainland, at the time of writing, the problem of piracy persists in the Gulf of Aden and even extends to the Western Indian Ocean. There are no quick-fix solutions to such complex problems. It may well be that efforts to successfully counter piracy and to create the condi-tions for a durable repression of piracy and armed robbery at sea, as has been the case with so many force deployments abroad, will take much longer than initially expected. As experienced in almost all troop deployments of the past, legitimacy and rule-of-law adherence will be increasingly vital to the success and the percep-tion of the entire mission. The Security Council's proclaimed objective of "full eradication of piracy," in its totality and without a resolute readiness to address the root causes, is probably as unattainable a goal as the full eradication of any crime in any given country, least of all in a failed State and off its shores. Perhaps, in view of present operations, "securing free navigation in the Gulf of Aden," would be a more realistic objective. For the time being, the absence of any significant practice in relation to Security Council Resolution 1851 certainly evidences that the readiness to become engaged in law enforcement operations on Somalia's main-land, although indisputably a prerequisite for any long-term solution, remains as remote as ever. The Security Council, by virtue of a number of Chapter VII-based Resolutions, has left no doubt that it is firmly resolved to act against piracy and armed robbery at sea in the Gulf of Aden. What must be done now is to show equal resolve to ensure the long-term success of the fight against piracy and armed robbery at sea in the Gulf of Aden. Inevitably, this will require a stronger focus on the situation in Somalia.

Appendix

Contents

Harvard Draft Convention on Piracy[1]

Piracy

Article 1

As the terms are used in this convention:

1. The term "jurisdiction" means the jurisdiction of a state under international law as distinguished from municipal law.

2. The term "territorial jurisdiction" means the jurisdiction of a state under international law over its land, its territorial waters and the air above its land and territorial waters. The term does not include the jurisdiction of a state over its ships outside its territory.

3. The term "territorial sea" means that part of the sea which is included in the territorial waters of a state.

4. The term "high sea" means that part of the sea which is not included in the territorial waters of any state.

5. The term "ship" means any water craft or air craft of whatever size.

Article 2

Every state has jurisdiction to prevent piracy and to seize and punish person and to seize and dispose of property because of piracy. This jurisdiction is defined and limited by this convention.

Article 3

Piracy is any of the following acts, committed in a place not within the territorial jurisdiction of any state:

1. Any act of violence or of depredation committed with intent to rob, rape, wound, enslave, imprison or kill a person or with intent to steal or destroy property, for private ends without bona fide purpose of asserting a claim of right, provided that the act is connected with an attack on or from the sea or in or from the air. If the act is connected with an attack which starts from on board ship, either that ship or another ship which is involved must be a pirate ship or a ship without national character.

2. Any act of voluntary participation in the operation of a ship with knowledge of facts which make it a pirate ship.

3. Any act of instigation or of an intentional facilitation of an act described in paragraph 1 or paragraph 2 of this article.

---

[1] The Draft Convention on Piracy, Supplement: Research in International Law, Part IV – Piracy, 26 American Journal of International Law 739–747 (1932).

Article 4

1. A ship is a pirate ship when it is devoted by the persons in dominant control to the purpose of committing an act described in the first sentence of paragraph 1 of Article 3, or to the purpose of committing any similar act within the territory of a state by descent from the high sea, provided in either case that the purposes of the persons in dominant control are not definitely limited to committing such acts against ships or territory subject to the jurisdiction of the state to which the ship belongs.

2. A ship does not cease to be a pirate ship after the commission of an act described in paragraph 1 of Article 3, or after the commission of any similar act within the territory of a state by descent from the high sea, as long as it continues under the same control.

Article 5

A ship may retain its national character although it has become a pirate ship. The retention or loss of national character is determined by the law of the state from which it was derived.

Article 6

In a place not within the territorial jurisdiction of another state, a state may seize a pirate ship or a ship taken by piracy and possessed by pirates, and things or persons on board.

Article 7

1. In a place within the territorial jurisdiction of another state, a state may not pursue or seize a pirate ship or a ship taken by piracy and possessed by pirates; except that if pursuit of such a ship is commenced by a state within its own territorial jurisdiction or in a place not within the territorial jurisdiction of any state, the pursuit may be continued into or over the territorial sea of another state and seizure may be made there, unless prohibited by the other state.

2. If a seizure is made within the territorial jurisdiction of another state in accordance with the provisions of paragraph 1 of this article, the state making the seizure shall give prompt notice to the other state, and shall tender possession of the ship and other things seized and the custody of persons seized.

3. If the tender provided for in paragraph 2 of this article is not accepted, the state making the seizure may proceed as if the seizure had been made on the high sea.

Article 8

If a pursuit is continued or a seizure is made within the territorial jurisdiction of another state in accordance with the provisions of paragraph 1 of Article 7, the state continuing the pursuit or making the seizure is liable to the other state for any damage done by the pursuing ship, other than damage done to the pirate ship or the ship possessed by pirates, or to persons and things on board.

Article 9

If a seizure because of piracy is made by a state in violation of the jurisdiction of another state, the state making the seizure shall, upon the demand of the other state, surrender or release the ship, things and persons seized, and shall make appropriate reparation.

Article 10

If a ship seized on suspicion of piracy outside the territorial jurisdiction of the state making the seizure, is neither a pirate ship nor a ship taken by piracy and possessed by pirates, and if the ship is not subject to seizure on other grounds, the state making the seizure shall be liable to the state to which the ship belongs for any damage caused by the seizure.

Article 11

1. In a place not within the territorial jurisdiction of any state, a foreign ship may be approached and on reasonable suspicion that it is a pirate ship or a ship taken by piracy and possessed by pirates, it may be stopped and questioned to ascertain its character.

2. If the ship is neither a pirate ship nor a ship taken by piracy and possessed by pirates, and if it is not subject to such interference on other grounds, the state making the interference shall be liable to the state to which the ship belongs for any damage caused by the interference.

Article 12

A seizure because of piracy may be made only on behalf a state, and only by a person who has been authorized to act on its behalf.

Article 13

1. A state, in accordance with its law, may dispose of ships and other property lawfully seized because of piracy.

2. The law of the state must conform to the following principles:

(a) The interests of innocent persons are not affected by the piratical possession or use of property, nor by seizure because of such possession or use.

(b) Claimants of any interest in the property are entitled to a reasonable opportunity to prove their claims.

(c) A claimant who establishes the validity of his claim is entitled to receive the property or compensation therefor, subject to a fair charge for salvage and expenses of administration.

Article 14

1. A state which has lawful custody of a person suspected of piracy may prosecute and punish that person.

2. Subject to the provisions of this convention, the law of the state which exercises such jurisdiction defines the crime, governs the procedure and prescribes the penalty.

3. The law of the state must, however, assure protection to accused aliens as follows:

(a) The accused person must be given a fair trial before an impartial tribunal without unreasonable delay.

(b) The accused person must be given humane treatment during his confinement pending trial.

(c) No cruel and unusual punishment may be inflicted.

(d) No discrimination may be made against the nationals of any state.

4. A state may intercede diplomatically to assure this protection to one of its nationals who is accused in another state.

Article 15

A state may not prosecute an alien for an act of piracy for which he has been charged and convicted or acquitted in a prosecution in another state.

Article 16

The provisions of this convention do not diminish a state's right under international law to take measures for the protection of its nationals, its ships and its commerce against interference on or over the high sea, when such measures are not based upon jurisdiction over piracy.

Article 17

1. The provisions of this convention shall supersede any inconsistent provisions relating to piracy in treaties in force among parties to this convention, except that such inconsistent provisions shall not be superseded in so far as they affect only the interests of the parties to such treaties *inter se*.

2. The provisions of this convention shall not prevent a party from entering into an agreement concerning piracy containing provisions inconsistent with this convention which affect only the interests of the parties to that agreement *inter se*.

Article 18

The parties to this convention agree to make every expedient use of their powers to prevent piracy, separately and in co-operation.

Article 19

1. If there should arise between the High Contracting Parties a dispute of any kind relating to the interpretation or application of the present convention, and if such dispute cannot be satisfactorily settled by diplomacy, it shall be settled in accordance with any applicable agreements in force between the parties to the dispute providing for the settlement of international disputes.

2. In case there is no such agreement in force between the parties to the dispute, the dispute shall be referred to the arbitration or judicial settlement. In the absence of agreement on the choice of another tribunal, the dispute shall, at the request of any one of the parties to the dispute, be referred to the Permanent Court of International Justice, if all the parties to the dispute are parties to the Protocol of December 16, 1920, relating to the Statute of that Court; and if any of the parties to the dispute is not a party to the Protocol of December 16, 1920, to an arbitral tribunal constituted in accordance with the provisions of the Convention for the Pacific Settlement of International Disputes, signed at The Hague, October 18, 1907.

Convention on the High Seas[2] (excerpts)

Article 14

All States shall cooperate to the fullest possible extent in the repression of piracy on the high seas or in any other place outside the jurisdiction of any State.

Article 15

Piracy consists of any of the following acts:

(1) Any illegal acts of violence, detention or any act of depredation, committed for private ends by the crew or the passengers of a private ship or a private aircraft, and directed:

(a) On the high seas, against another ship or aircraft, or against persons or property on board such ship or aircraft;

(b) Against a ship, aircraft, persons or property in a place outside the jurisdiction of any State;

(2) Any act of voluntary participation in the operation of a ship or of an aircraft with knowledge of facts making it a pirate ship or aircraft;

(3) Any act of inciting or of intentionally facilitating an act described in subparagraph 1 or subparagraph 2 of this article.

Article 16

The acts of piracy, as defined in article 15, committed by a warship, government ship or government aircraft whose crew has mutinied and taken control of the ship or aircraft are assimilated to acts committed by a private ship.

Article 17

A ship or aircraft is considered a pirate ship or aircraft if it is intended by the persons in dominant control to be used for the purpose of committing one of the acts referred to in article 15. The same applies if the ship or aircraft has been used to commit any such act, so long as it remains under the control of the persons guilty of that act.

Article 18

A ship or aircraft may retain its nationality although it has become a pirate ship or aircraft. The retention or loss of nationality is determined by the law of the State from which such nationality was derived.

---

[2] Convention on the High Seas, *adopted* April 29, 1958, 450 U.N.T.S. 11.

Article 19

On the high seas, or in any other place outside the jurisdiction of any State, every State may seize a pirate ship or aircraft, or a ship taken by piracy and under the control of pirates, and arrest the persons and seize the property on board. The courts of the State which carried out the seizure may decide upon the penalties to be imposed, and may also determine the action to be taken with regard to the ships, aircraft or property, subject to the rights of third parties acting in good faith.

Article 20

Where the seizure of a ship or aircraft on suspicion of piracy has been effected without adequate grounds, the State making the seizure shall be liable to the State the nationality of which is possessed by the ship or aircraft, for any loss or damage caused by the seizure.

Article 21

A seizure on account of piracy may only be carried out by warships or military aircraft, or other ships or aircraft on government service authorized to that effect.

UNCLOS[3] (excerpts)

Article 3 – Breadth of the territorial sea

Every State has the right to establish the breadth of its territorial sea up to a limit not exceeding 12 nautical miles, measured from baselines determined in accordance with this Convention.

Article 87 – Freedom of the high seas

1. The high seas are open to all States, whether coastal or land-locked. Freedom of the high seas is exercised under the conditions laid down by this Convention and by other rules of international law. It comprises, *inter alia*, both for coastal and land-locked States:

(a) freedom of navigation;

(b) freedom of overflight;

(c) freedom to lay submarine cables and pipelines, subject to Part VI;

(d) freedom to construct artificial islands and other installations permitted under international law, subject to Part VI;

(e) freedom of fishing, subject to the conditions laid down in section 2;

(f) freedom of scientific research, subject to Parts VI and XIII.

2. These freedoms shall be exercised by all States with due regard for the interests of other States in their exercise of the freedom of the high seas, and also with due regard for the rights under this Convention with respect to activities in the Area.

Article 89 – Invalidity of claims of sovereignty over the high seas

No State may validly purport to subject any part of the high seas to its sovereignty.

Article 91 – Nationality of ships

1. Every State shall fix the conditions for the grant of its nationality to ships, for the registration of ships in its territory, and for the right to fly its flag. Ships have the nationality of the State whose flag they are entitled to fly. There must exist a genuine link between the State and the ship.

2. Every State shall issue to ships to which it has granted the right to fly its flag documents to that effect.

---

[3] United Nations Convention on the Law of the Sea, *adopted* Dec. 10, 1982, 1883 U.N.T.S. 3.

Article 92 – Status of ships

1.   Ships shall sail under the flag of one State only and, save in exceptional cases expressly provided for in international treaties or in this Convention, shall be subject to its exclusive jurisdiction on the high seas. A ship may not change its flag during a voyage or while in a port of call, save in the case of a real transfer of ownership or change of registry.

2.   A ship which sails under the flags of two or more States, using them according to convenience, may not claim any of the nationalities in question with respect to any other State, and may be assimilated to a ship without nationality.

Article 97 – Penal jurisdiction in matters of collision
or any other incident of navigation

1.   In the event of a collision or any other incident of navigation concerning a ship on the high seas, involving the penal or disciplinary responsibility of the master or of any other person in the service of the ship, no penal or disciplinary proceedings may be instituted against such person except before the judicial or administrative authorities either of the flag State or of the State of which such person is a national.

2.   In disciplinary matters, the State which has issued a master's certificate or a certificate of competence or licence shall alone be competent, after due legal process, to pronounce the withdrawal of such certificates, even if the holder is not a national of the State which issued them.

3.   No arrest or detention of the ship, even as a measure of investigation, shall be ordered by any authorities other than those of the flag State.

Article 100 – Duty to cooperate in the repression of piracy

All States shall cooperate to the fullest possible extent in the repression of piracy on the high seas or in any other place outside the jurisdiction of any State.

Article 101 – Definition of piracy

Piracy consists of any of the following acts:

(a) any illegal acts of violence or detention, or any act of depredation, committed for private ends by the crew or the passengers of a private ship or a private aircraft, and directed:

  (i) on the high seas, against another ship or aircraft, or against persons or property on board such ship or aircraft;

  (ii) against a ship, aircraft, persons or property in a place outside the jurisdiction of any State;

(b) any act of voluntary participation in the operation of a ship or of an aircraft with knowledge of facts making it a pirate ship or aircraft;

(c) any act of inciting or of intentionally facilitating an act described in subparagraph (a) or (b).

Article 102 – Piracy by a warship, government ship
or government aircraft whose crew has mutinied

The acts of piracy, as defined in article 101, committed by a warship, government ship or government aircraft whose crew has mutinied and taken control of the ship or aircraft are assimilated to acts committed by a private ship or aircraft.

Article 103 – Definition of a pirate ship or aircraft

A ship or aircraft is considered a pirate ship or aircraft if it is intended by the persons in dominant control to be used for the purpose of committing one of the acts referred to in article 101. The same applies if the ship or aircraft has been used to commit any such act, so long as it remains under the control of the persons guilty of that act.

Article 104 – Retention or loss of the nationality of a pirate ship or aircraft

A ship or aircraft may retain its nationality although it has become a pirate ship or aircraft. The retention or loss of nationality is determined by the law of the State from which such nationality was derived.

Article 105 – Seizure of a pirate ship or aircraft

On the high seas, or in any other place outside the jurisdiction of any State, every State may seize a pirate ship or aircraft, or a ship or aircraft taken by piracy and under the control of pirates, and arrest the persons and seize the property on board. The courts of the State which carried out the seizure may decide upon the penalties to be imposed, and may also determine the action to be taken with regard to the ships, aircraft or property, subject to the rights of third parties acting in good faith.

Article 106 – Liability for seizure without adequate grounds

Where the seizure of a ship or aircraft on suspicion of piracy has been effected without adequate grounds, the State making the seizure shall be liable to the State the nationality of which is possessed by the ship or aircraft for any loss or damage caused by the seizure.

Article 107 – Ships and aircraft which are entitled to seize on account of piracy

A seizure on account of piracy may be carried out only by warships or military aircraft, or other ships or aircraft clearly marked and identifiable as being on government service and authorized to that effect.

Article 110 – Right of visit

1. Except where acts of interference derive from powers conferred by treaty, a warship which encounters on the high seas a foreign ship, other than a ship entitled to complete immunity in accordance with articles 95 and 96, is not justified in boarding it unless there is reasonable ground for suspecting that:

(a) the ship is engaged in piracy;

(b) the ship is engaged in the slave trade;

(c) the ship is engaged in unauthorized broadcasting and the flag State of the warship has jurisdiction under article 109;

(d) the ship is without nationality; or

(e) though flying a foreign flag or refusing to show its flag, the ship is, in reality, of the same nationality as the warship.

2. In the cases provided for in paragraph 1, the warship may proceed to verify the ship's right to fly its flag. To this end, it may send a boat under the command of an officer to the suspected ship. If suspicion remains after the documents have been checked, it may proceed to a further examination on board the ship, which must be carried out with all possible consideration.

3. If the suspicions prove to be unfounded, and provided that the ship boarded has not committed any act justifying them, it shall be compensated for any loss or damage that may have been sustained.

4. These provisions apply *mutatis mutandis* to military aircraft.

5. These provisions also apply to any other duly authorized ships or aircraft clearly marked and identifiable as being on government service.

SUA Convention[4] (excerpts)

Article 1

For the purposes of this Convention, "ship" means a vessel of any type whatsoever not permanently attached to the sea-bed, including dynamically supported craft, submersibles, or any other floating craft.

Article 2

1. This Convention does not apply to:

(a) a warship; or

(b) a ship owned or operated by a State when being used as a naval auxiliary or for customs or police purposes; or

(c) a ship which has been withdrawn from navigation or laid up.

2. Nothing in this Convention affects the immunities of warships and other government ships operated for non-commercial purposes.

Article 3

1. Any person commits an offence if that person unlawfully and intentionally:

(a) seizes or exercises control over a ship by force or threat thereof or any other form of intimidation; or

(b) performs an act of violence against a person on board a ship if that act is likely to endanger the safe navigation of that ship; or

(c) destroys a ship or causes damage to a ship or to its cargo which is likely to endanger the safe navigation of that ship; or

(d) places or causes to be placed on a ship, by any means whatsoever, a device or substance which is likely to destroy that ship, or cause damage to that ship or its cargo which endangers or is likely to endanger the safe navigation of that ship; or

(e) destroys or seriously damages maritime navigational facilities or seriously interferes with their operation, if any such act is likely to endanger the safe navigation of a ship; or

(f) communicates information which he knows to be false, thereby endangering the safe navigation of a ship; or

(g) injures or kills any person, in connection with the commission or the attempted commission of any of the offences set forth in subparagraphs (a) to (f).

2. Any person also commits an offence if that person:

(a) attempts to commit any of the offences set forth in paragraph 1; or

---

[4] Convention for the Suppression of Unlawful Acts against the Safety of Maritime Navigation, *adopted* March 10, 1988, 1678 U.N.T.S. 221.

(b) abets the commission of any of the offences set forth in paragraph 1 perpetrated by any person or is otherwise an accomplice of a person who commits such an offence; or

(c) threatens, with or without a condition, as is provided for under national law, aimed at compelling a physical or juridical person to do or refrain from doing any act, to commit any of the offences set forth in paragraph 1, subparagraphs (b), (c) and (e), if that threat is likely to endanger the safe navigation of the ship in question.

Article 4

1. This Convention applies if the ship is navigating or is scheduled to navigate into, through or from waters beyond the outer limit of the territorial sea of a single State, or the lateral limits of its territorial sea with adjacent States.

2. In cases where the Convention does not apply pursuant to paragraph 1, it nevertheless applies when the offender or the alleged offender is found in the territory of a State Party other than the State referred to in paragraph 1.

Article 5

Each State Party shall make the offences set forth in article 3 punishable by appropriate penalties which take into account the grave nature of those offences.

Article 6

1. Each State Party shall take such measures as may be necessary to establish its jurisdiction over the offences set forth in article 3 when the offence is committed:

(a) against or on board a ship flying the flag of the State at the time the offence is committed; or

(b) in the territory of that State, including its territorial sea; or

(c) by a national of that State.

2. A State Party may also establish its jurisdiction over any such offence when:

(a) it is committed by a stateless person whose habitual residence is in that State; or

(b) during its commission a national of that State is seized, threatened, injured or killed; or

(c) it is committed in an attempt to compel that State to do or abstain from doing any act.

3. Any State Party which has established jurisdiction mentioned in paragraph 2 shall notify the Secretary-General of the International Maritime Organization (hereinafter referred to as "the Secretary-General"). If such State Party subsequently rescinds that jurisdiction, it shall notify the Secretary-General.

4. Each State Party shall take such measures as may be necessary to establish its jurisdiction over the offences set forth in article 3 in cases where the alleged offender is present in its territory and it does not extradite him to any of the States Parties which have established their jurisdiction in accordance with paragraphs 1 and 2 of this article.

5. This Convention does not exclude any criminal jurisdiction exercised in accordance with national law.

Article 7

1. Upon being satisfied that the circumstances so warrant, any State Party in the territory of which the offender or the alleged offender is present shall, in accordance with its law,

take him into custody or take other measures to ensure his presence for such time as is necessary to enable any criminal or extradition proceedings to be instituted.

2. Such State shall immediately make a preliminary inquiry into the facts, in accordance with its own legislation.

3. Any person regarding whom the measures referred to in paragraph 1 are being taken shall be entitled to:

(a) communicate without delay with the nearest appropriate representative of the State of which he is a national or which is otherwise entitled to establish such communication or, if he is a stateless person, the State in the territory of which he has his habitual residence;

(b) be visited by a representative of that State.

4. The rights referred to in paragraph 3 shall be exercised in conformity with the laws and regulations of the State in the territory of which the offender or the alleged offender is present, subject to the proviso that the said laws and regulations must enable full effect to be given to the purposes for which the rights accorded under paragraph 3 are intended.

5. When a State Party, pursuant to this article, has taken a person into custody, it shall immediately notify the States which have established jurisdiction in accordance with article 6, paragraph 1 and, if it considers it advisable, any other interested States, of the fact that such person is in custody and of the circumstances which warrant his detention. The State which makes the preliminary inquiry contemplated in paragraph 2 of this article shall promptly report its findings to the said States and shall indicate whether it intends to exercise jurisdiction.

Article 8

1. The master of a ship of a State Party (the "flag State") may deliver to the authorities of any other State Party (the "receiving State") any person who he has reasonable grounds to believe has committed one of the offences set forth in article 3.

2. The flag State shall ensure that the master of its ship is obliged, whenever practicable, and if possible before entering the territorial sea of the receiving State carrying on board any person whom the master intends to deliver in accordance with paragraph 1, to give notification to the authorities of the receiving State of his intention to deliver such person and the reasons therefor.

3. The receiving State shall accept the delivery, except where it has grounds to consider that the Convention is not applicable to the acts giving rise to the delivery, and shall proceed in accordance with the provisions of article 7. Any refusal to accept a delivery shall be accompanied by a statement of the reasons for refusal.

4. The flag State shall ensure that the master of its ship is obliged to furnish the authorities of the receiving State with the evidence in the master's possession which pertains to the alleged offence.

5. A receiving State which has accepted the delivery of a person in accordance with paragraph 3 may, in turn, request the flag State to accept delivery of that person. The flag State shall consider any such request, and if it accedes to the request it shall proceed in accordance with article 7. If the flag State declines a request, it shall furnish the receiving State with a statement of the reasons therefor.

Article 9

Nothing in this Convention shall affect in any way the rules of international law pertaining to the competence of States to exercise investigative or enforcement jurisdiction on board ships not flying their flag.

Article 10

1. The State Party in the territory of which the offender or the alleged offender is found shall, in cases to which article 6 applies, if it does not extradite him, be obliged, without exception whatsoever and whether or not the offence was committed in its territory, to submit the case without delay to its competent authorities for the purpose of prosecution, through proceedings in accordance with the laws of that State. Those authorities shall take their decision in the same manner as in the case of any other offence of a grave nature under the law of that State.

2. Any person regarding whom proceedings are being carried out in connection with any of the offences set forth in article 3 shall be guaranteed fair treatment at all stages of the proceedings, including enjoyment of all the rights and guarantees provided for such proceedings by the law of the State in the territory of which he is present.

SUA Protocol 2005[5] (excerpts)

Art. 8(2)

The following text is added as article 8*bis* of the Convention:

Article 8bis

1. States Parties shall co-operate to the fullest extent possible to prevent and suppress unlawful acts covered by this Convention, in conformity with international law, and shall respond to requests pursuant to this article as expeditiously as possible.

2. Each request pursuant to this article should, if possible, contain the name of the suspect ship, the IMO ship identification number, the port of registry, the ports of origin and destination, and any other relevant information. If a request is conveyed orally, the requesting Party shall confirm the request in writing as soon as possible. The requested Party shall acknowledge its receipt of any written or oral request immediately.

3. States Parties shall take into account the dangers and difficulties involved in boarding a ship at sea and searching its cargo, and give consideration to whether other appropriate measures agreed between the States concerned could be more safely taken in the next port of call or elsewhere.

4. A State Party that has reasonable grounds to suspect that an offence set forth in article 3, 3*bis*, 3*ter* or 3*quater* has been, is being or is about to be committed involving a ship flying its flag, may request the assistance of other States Parties in preventing or suppressing that offence. The States Parties so requested shall use their best endeavours to render such assistance within the means available to them.

5. Whenever law enforcement or other authorized officials of a State Party ("the requesting Party") encounter a ship flying the flag or displaying marks of registry of another State Party ("the first Party") located seaward of any State's territorial sea, and the requesting Party has reasonable grounds to suspect that the ship or a person on board the ship has been, is or is about to be involved in the commission of an offence set forth in article 3, 3*bis*, 3*ter* or 3*quater*, and the requesting Party desires to board,

    (a) it shall request, in accordance with paragraphs 1 and 2 that the first Party confirm the claim of nationality, and

    (b) if nationality is confirmed, the requesting Party shall ask the first Party (hereinafter referred to as "the flag State") for authorization to board and to take appropriate measures with regard to that ship which may include stopping, boarding and searching the ship, its cargo and persons on board, and questioning the persons on board in order to determine if an offence set forth in article 3, 3*bis*, 3*ter* or 3*quater* has been, is being or is about to be committed, and

---

[5] International Maritime Organization (IMO), *Protocol of 2005 to the Convention for the Suppression of Unlawful Acts against the Safety of Maritime Navigation*, Text Adopted by the International Conference on the Revision of the SUA Treaties, IMO Doc. LEG/CONF.15/21 (Nov. 1, 2005).

(c) the flag State shall either:

   (i)   authorize the requesting Party to board and to take appropriate measures set out in subparagraph (b), subject to any conditions it may impose in accordance with paragraph 7; or

   (ii)   conduct the boarding and search with its own law enforcement or other officials; or

   (iii) conduct the boarding and search together with the requesting Party, subject to any conditions it may impose in accordance with paragraph 7; or

   (iv) decline to authorize a boarding and search.

The requesting Party shall not board the ship or take measures set out in subparagraph (b) without the express authorization of the flag State.

(d) Upon or after depositing its instrument of ratification, acceptance, approval or accession, a State Party may notify the Secretary-General that, with respect to ships flying its flag or displaying its mark of registry, the requesting Party is granted authorization to board and search the ship, its cargo and persons on board, and to question the persons on board in order to locate and examine documentation of its nationality and determine if an offence set forth in article 3, 3*bis*, 3*ter* or 3*quater* has been, is being or is about to be committed, if there is no response from the first Party within four hours of acknowledgement of receipt of a request to confirm nationality.

(e) Upon or after depositing its instrument of ratification, acceptance, approval or accession, a State Party may notify the Secretary-General that, with respect to ships flying its flag or displaying its mark of registry, the requesting Party is authorized to board and search a ship, its cargo and persons on board, and to question the persons on board in order to determine if an offence set forth in article 3, 3*bis*, 3*ter* or 3*quater* has been, is being or is about to be committed.

The notifications made pursuant to this paragraph can be withdrawn at any time.

6. When evidence of conduct described in article 3, 3*bis*, 3*ter* or 3*quater* is found as the result of any boarding conducted pursuant to this article, the flag State may authorize the requesting Party to detain the ship, cargo and persons on board pending receipt of disposition instructions from the flag State. The requesting Party shall promptly inform the flag State of the results of a boarding, search, and detention conducted pursuant to this article. The requesting Party shall also promptly inform the flag State of the discovery of evidence of illegal conduct that is not subject to this Convention.

7. The flag State, consistent with the other provisions of this Convention, may subject its authorization under paragraph 5 or 6 to conditions, including obtaining additional information from the requesting Party, and conditions relating to responsibility for and the extent of measures to be taken. No additional measures may be taken without the express authorization of the flag State, except when necessary to relieve imminent danger to the lives of persons or where those measures derive from relevant bilateral or multilateral agreements.

8. For all boardings pursuant to this article, the flag State has the right to exercise jurisdiction over a detained ship, cargo or other items and persons on board, including seizure, forfeiture, arrest and prosecution. However, the flag State may, subject to its constitution and laws, consent to the exercise of jurisdiction by another State having jurisdiction under article 6.

9. When carrying out the authorized actions under this article, the use of force shall be avoided except when necessary to ensure the safety of its officials and persons on board, or where the officials are obstructed in the execution of the authorized actions. Any use of force pursuant to this article shall not exceed the minimum degree of force which is necessary and reasonable in the circumstances.

10. Safeguards:

(a) Where a State Party takes measures against a ship in accordance with this article, it shall:

    (i)   take due account of the need not to endanger the safety of life at sea;

    (ii) ensure that all persons on board are treated in a manner which preserves their basic human dignity, and in compliance with the applicable provisions of international law, including international human rights law;

    (iii) ensure that a boarding and search pursuant to this article shall be conducted in accordance with applicable international law;

    (iv) take due account of the safety and security of the ship and its cargo;

    (v)   take due account of the need not to prejudice the commercial or legal interests of the flag State;

    (vi) ensure, within available means, that any measure taken with regard to the ship or its cargo is environmentally sound under the circumstances;

    (vii) ensure that persons on board against whom proceedings may be commenced in connection with any of the offences set forth in article 3, 3*bis*, 3*ter* or 3*quater* are afforded the protections of paragraph 2 of article 10, regardless of location;

    (viii) ensure that the master of a ship is advised of its intention to board, and is, or has been, afforded the opportunity to contact the ship's owner and the flag State at the earliest opportunity; and

    (ix) take reasonable efforts to avoid a ship being unduly detained or delayed.

(b) Provided that authorization to board by a flag State shall not *per se* give rise to its liability, States Parties shall be liable for any damage, harm or loss attributable to them arising from measures taken pursuant to this article when:

    (i)   the grounds for such measures prove to be unfounded, provided that the ship has not committed any act justifying the measures taken; or

    (ii) such measures are unlawful or exceed those reasonably required in light of available information to implement the provisions of this article.

States Parties shall provide effective recourse in respect of such damage, harm or loss.

(c) Where a State Party takes measures against a ship in accordance with this Convention, it shall take due account of the need not to interfere with or to affect:

    (i)   the rights and obligations and the exercise of jurisdiction of coastal States in accordance with the international law of the sea; or

    (ii) the authority of the flag State to exercise jurisdiction and control in administrative, technical and social matters involving the ship.

(d) Any measure taken pursuant to this article shall be carried out by law enforcement or other authorized officials from warships or military aircraft, or from other ships or aircraft clearly marked and identifiable as being on government service and authorized to that effect and, notwithstanding articles 2 and 2*bis*, the provisions of this article shall apply.

(e) For the purposes of this article "law enforcement or other authorized officials" means uniformed or otherwise clearly identifiable members of law enforcement or other government authorities duly authorized by their government. For the specific purpose of law enforcement under this Convention, law enforcement or other authorized officials shall provide appropriate government-issued identification documents for examination by the master of the ship upon boarding.

11. This article does not apply to or limit boarding of ships conducted by any State Party in accordance with international law, seaward of any State's territorial sea, including

boardings based upon the right of visit, the rendering of assistance to persons, ships and property in distress or peril, or an authorization from the flag State to take law enforcement or other action.

12. States Parties are encouraged to develop standard operating procedures for joint operations pursuant to this article and consult, as appropriate, with other States Parties with a view to harmonizing such standard operating procedures for the conduct of operations.

13. States Parties may conclude agreements or arrangements between them to facilitate law enforcement operations carried out in accordance with this article.

14. Each State Party shall take appropriate measures to ensure that its law enforcement or other authorized officials, and law enforcement or other authorized officials of other States Parties acting on its behalf, are empowered to act pursuant to this article.

15. Upon or after depositing its instrument of ratification, acceptance, approval or accession, each State Party shall designate the authority, or, where necessary, authorities to receive and respond to requests for assistance, for confirmation of nationality, and for authorization to take appropriate measures. Such designation, including contact information, shall be notified to the Secretary-General within one month of becoming a Party, who shall inform all other States Parties within one month of the designation. Each State Party is responsible for providing prompt notice through the Secretary-General of any changes in the designation or contact information.

Hostage Convention[6] (excerpts)

Article 1

1. Any person who seizes or detains and threatens to kill, to injure or to continue to detain another person (hereinafter referred to as the "hostage") in order to compel a third party, namely, a State, an international intergovernmental organization, a natural or juridical person, or a group of persons, to do or abstain from doing any act as an explicit or implicit condition for the release of the hostage commits the offence of taking of hostages ("hostage-taking") within the meaning of this Convention.

2. Any person who:

(a) Attempts to commit an act of hostage-taking, or

(b) Participates as an accomplice of anyone who commits or attempts to commit an act of hostage-taking

likewise commits an offence for the purposes of this Convention.

Article 2

Each State Party shall make the offences set forth in article 1 punishable by appropriate penalties which take into account the grave nature of those offences.

Article 5

1. Each State Party shall take such measures as may be necessary to establish its jurisdiction over any of the offences set forth in article 1 which are committed:

(a) In its territory or on board a ship or aircraft registered in that State;

(b) By any of its nationals or, if that State considers it appropriate, by those stateless persons who have their habitual residence in its territory;

(c) In order to compel that State to do or abstain from doing any act; or

(d) With respect to a hostage who is a national of that State, if that State considers it appropriate.

2. Each State Party shall likewise take such measures as may be necessary to establish its jurisdiction over the offences set forth in article 1 in cases where the alleged offender is present in its territory and it does not extradite him to any of the States mentioned in paragraph 1 of this article.

3. This Convention does not exclude any criminal jurisdiction exercised in accordance with internal law.

Article 6

1. Upon being satisfied that the circumstances so warrant, any State Party in the territory of which the alleged offender is present shall, in accordance with its laws, take him into

---

[6] International Convention against the Taking of Hostages, *adopted* Dec. 18, 1979, 1316 U.N.T.S. 205.

custody or take other measures to ensure his presence for such time as is necessary to enable any criminal or extradition proceedings to be instituted. That State Party shall immediately make a preliminary inquiry into the facts.

2. The custody or other measures referred to in paragraph 1 of this article shall be notified without delay directly or through the Secretary-General of the United Nations to:

(a) The State where the offence was committed;

(b) The State against which compulsion has been directed or attempted;

(c) The State of which the natural or juridical person against whom compulsion has been directed or attempted is a national;

(d) The State of which the hostage is a national or in the territory of which he has his habitual residence;

(e) The State of which the alleged offender is a national or, if he is a stateless person, in the territory of which he has his habitual residence;

(f) The international intergovernmental organization against which compulsion has been directed or attempted;

(g) All other States concerned.

3. Any person regarding whom the measures referred to in paragraph 1 of this article are being taken shall be entitled:

(a) To communicate without delay with the nearest appropriate representative of the State of which he is a national or which is otherwise entitled to establish such communication or, if he is a stateless person, the State in the territory of which he has his habitual residence;

(b) To be visited by a representative of that State.

4. The rights referred to in paragraph 3 of this article shall be exercised in conformity with the laws and regulations of the State in the territory of which the alleged offender is present subject to the proviso, however, that the said laws and regulations must enable full effect to be given to the purposes for which the rights accorded under paragraph 3 of this article are intended.

5. The provisions of paragraphs 3 and 4 of this article shall be without prejudice to the right of any State Party having a claim to jurisdiction in accordance with paragraph 1(b) of article 5 to invite the International Committee of the Red Cross to communicate with and visit the alleged offender.

6. The State which makes the preliminary inquiry contemplated in paragraph 1 of this article shall promptly report its findings to the States or organization referred to in paragraph 2 of this article and indicate whether it intends to exercise jurisdiction.

Article 8

1. The State Party in the territory of which the alleged offender is found shall, if it does not extradite him, be obliged, without exception whatsoever and whether or not the offence was committed in its territory, to submit the case to its competent authorities for the purpose of prosecution, through proceedings in accordance with the laws of that State. Those authorities shall take their decision in the same manner as in the case of any ordinary offence of a grave nature under the law of that State.

2. Any person regarding whom proceedings are being carried out in connexion with any of the offences set forth in article 1 shall be guaranteed fair treatment at all stages of the proceedings, including enjoyment of all the rights and guarantees provided by the law of the State in the territory of which he is present.

Definition of "Armed Robbery at Sea"

IMO Code of Practice for the Investigation of the Crimes of Piracy and Armed Robbery against Ships[7]

Art. 2.2

"Armed robbery against ships" means any unlawful act of violence or detention or any act of depredation, or threat thereof, other than an act of piracy, directed against a ship or against persons or property on board such a ship, within a State's jurisdiction over such offences.

Regional Cooperation Agreement on Combating Piracy and Armed Robbery against Ships in Asia (ReCAAP)[8]

Art. 1(2) – Definitions

For the purposes of this Agreement, "armed robbery against ships" means any of the following acts:

(a) any illegal act of violence or detention, or any act of depredation, committed for private ends and directed against a ship, or against persons or property on board such ship, in a place within a Contracting Party's jurisdiction over such offences;

(b) any act of voluntary participation in the operation of a ship with knowledge of facts making it a ship for armed robbery against ships;

(c) any act of inciting or of intentionally facilitating an act described in subparagraph (a) or (b).

Djibouti Code of Conduct[9]

Art. 1(2) – Definitions

2. *"Armed robbery against ships"* consists of any of the following acts:

(a) unlawful act of violence or detention or any act of depredation, or threat thereof, other than an act of piracy, committed for private ends and directed against a ship or against

---

[7] International Maritime Organization (IMO), *Code of Practice for the Investigation of the Crimes of Piracy and Armed Robbery against Ships*, IMO Doc. A 22/Res.922 (Jan. 22, 2009).

[8] Regional Cooperation Agreement on Combating Piracy and Armed Robbery against Ships in Asia, *available at* www.recaap.org/about/pdf/ReCAAP%20Agreement.pdf (last visited Feb. 10, 2010).

[9] Code of Conduct Concerning the Repression of Piracy and Armed Robbery against Ships in the Western Indian Ocean and the Gulf of Aden, Annex 1 to Resolution 1 adopted on January 29, 2009 at a high-level meeting of 17 States from the Western Indian Ocean, Gulf of Aden and Red Sea areas, convened by IMO in Djibouti to help address the problem of piracy and armed robbery against ships off the coast of Somalia and in the Gulf of Aden.

persons or property on board such a ship, within a State's internal waters, archipelagic waters and territorial sea;

(b) any act of inciting or of intentionally facilitating an act described in subparagraph (a).

Kenyan Merchant Shipping Act 2009[10]

Section 369(1) – Interpretation

In this Part –

"armed robbery against ships" means any unlawful act of violence or detention or any act of depredation, or threat thereof, other than an act of piracy, directed against persons or property on board such a ship, within territorial waters or waters under Kenya's jurisdiction;

Section 371 – Offences of piracy and armed robbery

Any person who –

(a) commits any act of piracy;

(b) in territorial waters, commits any act of armed robbery against ships

shall be liable, upon conviction, to imprisonment for life.

---

[10] Kenyan Merchant Shipping Act (entry into force on Sept. 1, 2009), Part XVI – Maritime Security, *available at* www.kenyalaw.org/kenyalaw/klr_home/ (last visited Feb. 10, 2010).

S.C. Res. 1816[11]

Adopted by the Security Council at its 5902nd meeting, on 2 June 2008

The Security Council,

Recalling its previous resolutions and the statements of its President concerning the situation in Somalia,

Gravely concerned by the threat that acts of piracy and armed robbery against vessels pose to the prompt, safe and effective delivery of humanitarian aid to Somalia, the safety of commercial maritime routes and to international navigation,

Expressing its concerns at the quarterly reports from the International Maritime Organization (IMO) since 2005, which provide evidence of continuing piracy and armed robbery in particular in the waters off the coast of Somalia,

Affirming that international law, as reflected in the United Nations Convention on the Law of the Sea of 10 December 1982 ("the Convention"), sets out the legal framework applicable to combating piracy and armed robbery, as well as other ocean activities,

Reaffirming the relevant provisions of international law with respect to the repression of piracy, including the Convention, and *recalling* that they provide guiding principles for cooperation to the fullest possible extent in the repression of piracy on the high seas or in any other place outside the jurisdiction of any state, including but not limited to boarding, searching, and seizing vessels engaged in or suspected of engaging in acts of piracy, and to apprehending persons engaged in such acts with a view to such persons being prosecuted,

Reaffirming its respect for the sovereignty, territorial integrity, political independence and unity of Somalia,

Taking into account the crisis situation in Somalia, and the lack of capacity of the Transitional Federal Government (TFG) to interdict pirates or patrol and secure either the international sea lanes off the coast of Somalia or Somalia's territorial waters,

Deploring the recent incidents of attacks upon and hijacking of vessels in the territorial waters and on the high seas off the coast of Somalia including attacks upon and hijackings of vessels operated by the World Food Program and numerous commercial vessels and the serious adverse impact of these attacks on the prompt, safe and effective delivery of food aid and other humanitarian assistance to the people of Somalia, and the grave dangers they pose to vessels, crews, passengers, and cargo,

Noting the letters to the Secretary-General from the Secretary-General of the IMO dated 5 July 2007 and 18 September 2007 regarding the piracy problems off the coast of Somalia and the IMO Assembly resolution A.1002 (25), which strongly urged Governments to increase their efforts to prevent and repress, within the provisions of international law, acts of piracy and armed robbery against vessels irrespective of where such acts occur, and *recalling* the joint communiqué of the IMO and the World Food Programme of 10 July 2007,

---

[11] S.C. Res. 1816, U.N. Doc. S/RES/1816 (June 2, 2008).

Taking note of the Secretary-General's letter of 9 November 2007 to the President of the Security Council reporting that the Transitional Federal Government of Somalia (TFG) needs and would welcome international assistance to address the problem,

Taking further note of the letter from the Permanent Representative of the Somali Republic to the United Nations to the President of the Security Council dated 27 February 2008, conveying the consent of the TFG to the Security Council for urgent assistance in securing the territorial and international waters off the coast of Somalia for the safe conduct of shipping and navigation,

Determining that the incidents of piracy and armed robbery against vessels in the territorial waters of Somalia and the high seas off the coast of Somalia exacerbate the situation in Somalia which continues to constitute a threat to international peace and security in the region,

Acting under Chapter VII of the Charter of the United Nations,

1. *Condemns and deplores* all acts of piracy and armed robbery against vessels in territorial waters and the high seas off the coast of Somalia;

2. *Urges* States whose naval vessels and military aircraft operate on the high seas and airspace off the coast of Somalia to be vigilant to acts of piracy and armed robbery and, in this context, *encourages*, in particular, States interested in the use of commercial maritime routes off the coast of Somalia, to increase and coordinate their efforts to deter acts of piracy and armed robbery at sea in cooperation with the TFG;

3. *Urges* all States to cooperate with each other, with the IMO and, as appropriate, with the relevant regional organizations in connection with, and share information about, acts of piracy and armed robbery in the territorial waters and on the high seas off the coast of Somalia, and to render assistance to vessels threatened by or under attack by pirates or armed robbers, in accordance with relevant international law;

4. *Further urges* States to work in cooperation with interested organizations, including the IMO, to ensure that vessels entitled to fly their flag receive appropriate guidance and training on avoidance, evasion, and defensive techniques and to avoid the area whenever possible;

5. *Calls upon* States and interested organizations, including the IMO, to provide technical assistance to Somalia and nearby coastal States upon their request to enhance the capacity of these States to ensure coastal and maritime security, including combating piracy and armed robbery off the Somali and nearby coastlines;

6. *Affirms* that the measures imposed by paragraph 5 of resolution 733 (1992) and further elaborated upon by paragraphs 1 and 2 of resolution 1425 (2002) do not apply to supplies of technical assistance to Somalia solely for the purposes set out in paragraph 5 above which have been exempted from those measures in accordance with the procedure set out in paragraphs 11 (b) and 12 of resolution 1772 (2007);

7. *Decides* that for a period of six months from the date of this resolution, States cooperating with the TFG in the fight against piracy and armed robbery at sea off the coast of Somalia, for which advance notification has been provided by the TFG to the Secretary-General, may:

(a) Enter the territorial waters of Somalia for the purpose of repressing acts of piracy and armed robbery at sea, in a manner consistent with such action permitted on the high seas with respect to piracy under relevant international law; and

(b) Use, within the territorial waters of Somalia, in a manner consistent with action permitted on the high seas with respect to piracy under relevant international law, all necessary means to repress acts of piracy and armed robbery;

8. *Requests* that cooperating states take appropriate steps to ensure that the activities they undertake pursuant to the authorization in paragraph 7 do not have the practical effect of denying or impairing the right of innocent passage to the ships of any third State;

9. *Affirms* that the authorization provided in this resolution applies only with respect to the situation in Somalia and shall not affect the rights or obligations or responsibilities of member states under international law, including any rights or obligations under the Convention, with respect to any other situation, and underscores in particular that it shall not be considered as establishing customary international law, and affirms further that this authorization has been provided only following receipt of the letter from the Permanent Representative of the Somalia Republic to the United Nations to the President of the Security Council dated 27 February 2008 conveying the consent of the TFG;

10. *Calls upon* States to coordinate their actions with other participating States taken pursuant to paragraphs 5 and 7 above;

11. *Calls upon* all States, and in particular flag, port and coastal States, States of the nationality of victims and perpetrators or piracy and armed robbery, and other States with relevant jurisdiction under international law and national legislation, to cooperate in determining jurisdiction, and in the investigation and prosecution of persons responsible for acts of piracy and armed robbery off the coast of Somalia, consistent with applicable international law including international human rights law, and to render assistance by, among other actions, providing disposition and logistics assistance with respect to persons under their jurisdiction and control, such victims and witnesses and persons detained as a result of operations conducted under this resolution;

12. *Requests* States cooperating with the TFG to inform the Security Council within 3 months of the progress of actions undertaken in the exercise of the authority provided in paragraph 7 above;

13. *Requests* the Secretary-General to report to the Security Council within 5 months of adoption of this resolution on the implementation of this resolution and on the situation with respect to piracy and armed robbery in territorial waters and the high seas off the coast of Somalia;

14. *Requests* the Secretary-General of the IMO to brief the Council on the basis of cases brought to his attention by the agreement of all affected coastal states, and duly taking into account the existing bilateral and regional cooperative arrangements, on the situation with respect to piracy and armed robbery;

15. *Expresses* its intention to review the situation and consider, as appropriate, renewing the authority provided in paragraph 7 above for additional periods upon the request of the TFG;

16. *Decides* to remain seized of the matter.

S.C. Res. 1846[12]

Adopted by the Security Council at its 6026th meeting, on 2 December 2008

The Security Council,

Recalling its previous resolutions concerning the situation in Somalia, especially resolutions 1814 (2008), 1816 (2008) and 1838 (2008),

Continuing to be gravely concerned by the threat that piracy and armed robbery at sea against vessels pose to the prompt, safe and effective delivery of humanitarian aid to Somalia, to international navigation and the safety of commercial maritime routes, and to other vulnerable ships, including fishing activities in conformity with international law,

Reaffirming its respect for the sovereignty, territorial integrity, political independence and unity of Somalia,

Further reaffirming that international law, as reflected in the United Nations Convention on the Law of the Sea of 10 December 1982 ("the Convention"), sets out the legal framework applicable to combating piracy and armed robbery at sea, as well as other ocean activities,

Taking into account the crisis situation in Somalia, and the lack of capacity of the Transitional Federal Government ("TFG") to interdict pirates or patrol and secure either the international sea lanes off the coast of Somalia or Somalia's territorial waters,

Taking note of the requests from the TFG for international assistance to counter piracy off its coasts, including the 1 September 2008 letter from the President of Somalia to the Secretary-General of the United Nations expressing the appreciation of the TFG to the Security Council for its assistance and expressing the TFG's willingness to consider working with other States and regional organizations to combat piracy and armed robbery at sea off the coast of Somalia, the 20 November 2008 letter conveying the request of the TFG that the provisions of resolution 1816 (2008) be renewed, and the 20 November request of the Permanent Representative of Somalia before the Security Council that the renewal be for an additional 12 months,

Further taking note of the letters from the TFG to the Secretary-General providing advance notification with respect to States cooperating with the TFG in the fight against piracy and armed robbery at sea off the coast of Somalia and from other Member States to the Security Council to inform the Council of their actions, as requested in paragraphs 7 and 12 of resolution 1816 (2008), and encouraging those cooperating States, for which advance notification has been provided by the TFG to the Secretary-General, to continue their respective efforts,

Expressing again its determination to ensure the long-term security of World Food Programme (WFP) maritime deliveries to Somalia,

Recalling that in its resolution 1838 (2008) it commended the contribution made by some States since November 2007 to protect (WFP) maritime convoys, and the establishment by the European Union (EU) of a coordination unit with the task of supporting the surveil-

---

[12] S.C. Res. 1846, U.N. Doc. S/RES/1846 (Dec. 2, 2008).

lance and protection activities carried out by some member States of the European Union off the coast of Somalia, as well as other international and national initiatives taken with a view to implementing resolutions 1814 (2008) and 1816 (2008),

Emphasizing that peace and stability within Somalia, the strengthening of State institutions, economic and social development and respect for human rights and the rule of law are necessary to create the conditions for a full eradication of piracy and armed robbery at sea off the coast of Somalia,

Welcoming the signing of a peace and reconciliation Agreement ("the Djibouti Agreement") between the TFG and the Alliance for the Re-Liberation of Somalia on 19 August 2008, as well as their signing of a joint ceasefire agreement on 26 October 2008, *noting* that the Djibouti Agreement calls for the United Nations to authorize and deploy an international stabilization force, and *further noting* the Secretary-General's report on Somalia of 17 November 2008, including his recommendations in this regard,

Commending the key role played by the African Union Mission to Somalia (AMISOM) in facilitating delivery of humanitarian assistance to Somalia through the port of Mogadishu and the contribution that AMISOM has made towards the goal of establishing lasting peace and stability in Somalia, and *recognizing* specifically the important contributions of the Governments of Uganda and Burundi to Somalia,

Welcoming the organization of a ministerial meeting of the Security Council in December 2008 to examine ways to improve international coordination in the fight against piracy and armed robbery off the coast of Somalia and to ensure that the international community has the proper authorities and tools at its disposal to assist it in these efforts,

Determining that the incidents of piracy and armed robbery against vessels in the territorial waters of Somalia and the high seas off the coast of Somalia exacerbate the situation in Somalia which continues to constitute a threat to international peace and security in the region,

Acting under Chapter VII of the Charter of the United Nations,

1. *Reiterates* that it condemns and deplores all acts of piracy and armed robbery against vessels in territorial waters and the high seas off the coast of Somalia;

2. *Expresses* its concern over the finding contained in the 20 November 2008 report of the Monitoring Group on Somalia that escalating ransom payments are fuelling the growth of piracy off the coast of Somalia;

3. *Welcomes* the efforts of the International Maritime Organization ("IMO") to update its guidance and recommendations to the shipping industry and to Governments for preventing and suppressing piracy and armed robbery at sea and to provide this guidance as soon as practicable to all Member States and to the international shipping community operating off the coast of Somalia;

4. *Calls upon* States, in cooperation with the shipping industry, the insurance industry and the IMO, to issue to ships entitled to fly their flag appropriate advice and guidance on avoidance, evasion, and defensive techniques and measures to take if under the threat of attack or attack when sailing in the waters off the coast of Somalia;

5. *Further calls upon* States and interested organizations, including the IMO, to provide technical assistance to Somalia and nearby coastal States upon their request to enhance the capacity of these States to ensure coastal and maritime security, including combating piracy and armed robbery at sea off the Somali and nearby coastlines;

6. *Welcomes* initiatives by Canada, Denmark, France, India, the Netherlands, the Russian Federation, Spain, the United Kingdom, the United States of America, and by regional and international organizations to counter piracy off the coast of Somalia pursuant to

resolutions 1814 (2008), 1816 (2008) and 1838 (2008), the decision by the North Atlantic Treaty Organization (NATO) to counter piracy off the Somalia coast, including by escorting vessels of the WFP, and in particular the decision by the EU on 10 November 2008 to launch, for a period of 12 months from December 2008, a naval operation to protect WFP maritime convoys bringing humanitarian assistance to Somalia and other vulnerable ships, and to repress acts of piracy and armed robbery at sea off the coast of Somalia;

7. *Calls upon* States and regional organizations to coordinate, including by sharing information through bilateral channels or the United Nations, their efforts to deter acts of piracy and armed robbery at sea off the coast of Somalia in cooperation with each other, the IMO, the international shipping community, flag States, and the TFG;

8. *Requests* the Secretary-General to present to it a report, no later than three months after the adoption of this resolution, on ways to ensure the long-term security of international navigation off the coast of Somalia, including the long-term security of WFP maritime deliveries to Somalia and a possible coordination and leadership role for the United Nations in this regard to rally Member States and regional organizations to counter piracy and armed robbery at sea off the coast of Somalia;

9. *Calls upon* States and regional organizations that have the capacity to do so, to take part actively in the fight against piracy and armed robbery at sea off the coast of Somalia, in particular, consistent with this resolution and relevant international law, by deploying naval vessels and military aircraft, and through seizure and disposition of boats, vessels, arms and other related equipment used in the commission of piracy and armed robbery off the coast of Somalia, or for which there is reasonable ground for suspecting such use;

10. *Decides* that for a period of 12 months from the date of this resolution States and regional organizations cooperating with the TFG in the fight against piracy and armed robbery at sea off the coast of Somalia, for which advance notification has been provided by the TFG to the Secretary-General, may:

(a) Enter into the territorial waters of Somalia for the purpose of repressing acts of piracy and armed robbery at sea, in a manner consistent with such action permitted on the high seas with respect to piracy under relevant international law; and

(b) Use, within the territorial waters of Somalia, in a manner consistent with such action permitted on the high seas with respect to piracy under relevant international law, all necessary means to repress acts of piracy and armed robbery at sea;

11. *Affirms* that the authorizations provided in this resolution apply only with respect to the situation in Somalia and shall not affect the rights or obligations or responsibilities of Member States under international law, including any rights or obligations under the Convention, with respect to any other situation, and underscores in particular that this resolution shall not be considered as establishing customary international law; and *affirms further* that such authorizations have been provided only following the receipt of the 20 November letter conveying the consent of the TFG;

12. *Affirms* that the measures imposed by paragraph 5 of resolution 733 (1992) and further elaborated upon by paragraphs 1 and 2 of resolution 1425 (2002) do not apply to supplies of technical assistance to Somalia solely for the purposes set out in paragraph 5 above which have been exempted from those measures in accordance with the procedure set out in paragraphs 11 (b) and 12 of resolution 1772 (2007);

13. *Requests* that cooperating States take appropriate steps to ensure that the activities they undertake pursuant to the authorization in paragraph 10 do not have the practical effect of denying or impairing the right of innocent passage to the ships of any third State;

14. *Calls upon* all States, and in particular flag, port and coastal States, States of the nationality of victims and perpetrators of piracy and armed robbery, and other States with

relevant jurisdiction under international law and national legislation, to cooperate in determining jurisdiction, and in the investigation and prosecution of persons responsible for acts of piracy and armed robbery off the coast of Somalia, consistent with applicable international law including international human rights law, and to render assistance by, among other actions, providing disposition and logistics assistance with respect to persons under their jurisdiction and control, such victims and witnesses and persons detained as a result of operations conducted under this resolution;

15. *Notes* that the 1988 Convention for the Suppression of Unlawful Acts Against the Safety of Maritime Navigation ("SUA Convention") provides for parties to create criminal offences, establish jurisdiction, and accept delivery of persons responsible for or suspected of seizing or exercising control over a ship by force or threat thereof or any other form of intimidation; *urges* States parties to the SUA Convention to fully implement their obligations under said Convention and cooperate with the Secretary-General and the IMO to build judicial capacity for the successful prosecution of persons suspected of piracy and armed robbery at sea off the coast of Somalia;

16. *Requests* States and regional organizations cooperating with the TFG to inform the Security Council and the Secretary-General within nine months of the progress of actions undertaken in the exercise of the authority provided in paragraph 10 above;

17. *Requests* the Secretary-General to report to the Security Council within 11 months of adoption of this resolution on the implementation of this resolution and on the situation with respect to piracy and armed robbery in territorial waters and the high seas off the coast of Somalia;

18. *Requests* the Secretary-General of the IMO to brief the Council on the basis of cases brought to his attention by the agreement of all affected coastal States, and duly taking into account the existing bilateral and regional cooperative arrangements, on the situation with respect to piracy and armed robbery;

19. *Expresses* its intention to review the situation and consider, as appropriate, renewing the authority provided in paragraph 10 above for additional periods upon the request of the TFG;

20. *Decides* to remain seized of the matter.

S.C. Res. 1851[13]

Adopted by the Security Council at its 6046th meeting, on 16 December 2008

The Security Council,

Recalling its previous resolutions concerning the situation in Somalia, especially resolutions 1814 (2008), 1816 (2008), 1838 (2008), 1844 (2008), and 1846 (2008),

Continuing to be gravely concerned by the dramatic increase in the incidents of piracy and armed robbery at sea off the coast of Somalia in the last six months, and by the threat that piracy and armed robbery at sea against vessels pose to the prompt, safe and effective delivery of humanitarian aid to Somalia, and *noting* that pirate attacks off the coast of Somalia have become more sophisticated and daring and have expanded in their geographic scope, notably evidenced by the hijacking of the M/V Sirius Star 500 nautical miles off the coast of Kenya and subsequent unsuccessful attempts well east of Tanzania,

Reaffirming its respect for the sovereignty, territorial integrity, political independence and unity of Somalia, including Somalia's rights with respect to offshore natural resources, including fisheries, in accordance with international law,

Further reaffirming that international law, as reflected in the United Nations Convention on the Law of the Sea of 10 December 1982 (UNCLOS), sets out the legal framework applicable to combating piracy and armed robbery at sea, as well as other ocean activities,

Again taking into account the crisis situation in Somalia, and the lack of capacity of the Transitional Federal Government (TFG) to interdict, or upon interdiction to prosecute pirates or to patrol and secure the waters off the coast of Somalia, including the international sea lanes and Somalia's territorial waters,

Noting the several requests from the TFG for international assistance to counter piracy off its coast, including the letter of 9 December 2008 from the President of Somalia requesting the international community to assist the TFG in taking all necessary measures to interdict those who use Somali territory and airspace to plan, facilitate or undertake acts of piracy and armed robbery at sea, and the 1 September 2008 letter from the President of Somalia to the Secretary-General of the UN expressing the appreciation of the TFG to the Security Council for its assistance and expressing the TFG's willingness to consider working with other States and regional organizations to combat piracy and armed robbery off the coast of Somalia,

Welcoming the launching of the EU operation Atalanta to combat piracy off the coast of Somalia and to protect vulnerable ships bound for Somalia, as well as the efforts by the North Atlantic Treaty Organization, and other States acting in a national capacity in cooperation with the TFG to suppress piracy off the coast of Somalia,

Also welcoming the recent initiatives of the Governments of Egypt, Kenya, and the Secretary-General's Special Representative for Somalia, and the United Nations Office on Drugs and Crime (UNODC) to achieve effective measures to remedy the causes, capabilities, and incidents of piracy and armed robbery off the coast of Somalia, and *emphasizing*

---

[13] S.C. Res. 1851, U.N. Doc. S/RES/1851 (Dec. 16, 2008).

the need for current and future counter-piracy operations to effectively coordinate their activities,

Noting with concern that the lack of capacity, domestic legislation, and clarity about how to dispose of pirates after their capture, has hindered more robust international action against the pirates off the coast of Somalia and in some cases led to pirates being released without facing justice, and *reiterating* that the 1988 Convention for the Suppression of Unlawful Acts Against the Safety of Maritime Navigation ("SUA Convention") provides for parties to create criminal offences, establish jurisdiction, and accept delivery of persons responsible for or suspected of seizing or exercising control over a ship by force or threat thereof or any other form of intimidation,

Welcoming the report of the Monitoring Group on Somalia of 20 November 2008 (S/2008/769), and *noting* the role piracy may play in financing embargo violations by armed groups,

Determining that the incidents of piracy and armed robbery at sea in the waters off the coast of Somalia exacerbate the situation in Somalia which continues to constitute a threat to international peace and security in the region,

Acting under Chapter VII of the Charter of the United Nations,

1.   *Reiterates* that it condemns and deplores all acts of piracy and armed robbery against vessels in waters off the coast of Somalia;

2.   *Calls* upon States, regional and international organizations that have the capacity to do so, to take part actively in the fight against piracy and armed robbery at sea off the coast of Somalia, in particular, consistent with this resolution, resolution 1846 (2008), and international law, by deploying naval vessels and military aircraft and through seizure and disposition of boats, vessels, arms and other related equipment used in the commission of piracy and armed robbery at sea off the coast of Somalia, or for which there are reasonable grounds for suspecting such use;

3.   *Invites* all States and regional organizations fighting piracy off the coast of Somalia to conclude special agreements or arrangements with countries willing to take custody of pirates in order to embark law enforcement officials ("shipriders") from the latter countries, in particular countries in the region, to facilitate the investigation and prosecution of persons detained as a result of operations conducted under this resolution for acts of piracy and armed robbery at sea off the coast of Somalia, provided that the advance consent of the TFG is obtained for the exercise of third state jurisdiction by shipriders in Somali territorial waters and that such agreements or arrangements do not prejudice the effective implementation of the SUA Convention;

4.   *Encourages* all States and regional organizations fighting piracy and armed robbery at sea off the coast of Somalia to establish an international cooperation mechanism to act as a common point of contact between and among states, regional and international organizations on all aspects of combating piracy and armed robbery at sea off Somalia's coast; and *recalls* that future recommendations on ways to ensure the long-term security of international navigation off the coast of Somalia, including the long-term security of WFP maritime deliveries to Somalia and a possible coordination and leadership role for the United Nations in this regard to rally Member States and regional organizations to counter piracy and armed robbery at sea off the coast of Somalia are to be detailed in a report by the Secretary-General no later than three months after the adoption of resolution 1846;

5.   *Further encourages* all states and regional organizations fighting piracy and armed robbery at sea off the coast of Somalia to consider creating a centre in the region to coordinate information relevant to piracy and armed robbery at sea off the coast of Somalia, to increase regional capacity with assistance of UNODC to arrange effective shiprider

agreements or arrangements consistent with UNCLOS and to implement the SUA Convention, the United Nations Convention against Transnational Organized Crime and other relevant instruments to which States in the region are party, in order to effectively investigate and prosecute piracy and armed robbery at sea offences;

6. In response to the letter from the TFG of 9 December 2008, *encourages* Member States to continue to cooperate with the TFG in the fight against piracy and armed robbery at sea, *notes* the primary role of the TFG in rooting out piracy and armed robbery at sea, and *decides* that for a period of twelve months from the date of adoption of resolution 1846, States and regional organizations cooperating in the fight against piracy and armed robbery at sea off the coast of Somalia for which advance notification has been provided by the TFG to the Secretary-General may undertake all necessary measures that are appropriate in Somalia, for the purpose of suppressing acts of piracy and armed robbery at sea, pursuant to the request of the TFG, provided, however, that any measures undertaken pursuant to the authority of this paragraph shall be undertaken consistent with applicable international humanitarian and human rights law;

7. *Calls on* Member States to assist the TFG, at its request and with notification to the Secretary-General, to strengthen its operational capacity to bring to justice those who are using Somali territory to plan, facilitate or undertake criminal acts of piracy and armed robbery at sea, and *stresses* that any measures undertaken pursuant to this paragraph shall be consistent with applicable international human rights law;

8. *Welcomes* the communiqué issued by the International Conference on Piracy around Somalia held in Nairobi, Kenya, on 11 December 2008 and *encourages* Member States to work to enhance the capacity of relevant states in the region to combat piracy, including judicial capacity;

9. *Notes* with concern the findings contained in the 20 November 2008 report of the Monitoring Group on Somalia that escalating ransom payments are fuelling the growth of piracy in waters off the coast of Somalia, and that the lack of enforcement of the arms embargo established by resolution 733 (1992) has permitted ready access to the arms and ammunition used by the pirates and driven in part the phenomenal growth in piracy;

10. *Affirms* that the authorization provided in this resolution apply only with respect to the situation in Somalia and shall not affect the rights or obligations or responsibilities of Member States under international law, including any rights or obligations under UNCLOS, with respect to any other situation, and underscores in particular that this resolution shall not be considered as establishing customary international law, and *affirms further* that such authorizations have been provided only following the receipt of the 9 December 2008 letter conveying the consent of the TFG;

11. *Affirms* that the measures imposed by paragraph 5 of resolution 733 (1992) and further elaborated upon by paragraphs 1 and 2 or resolution 1425 (2002) shall not apply to weapons and military equipment destined for the sole use of Member States and regional organizations undertaking measures in accordance with paragraph 6 above;

12. *Urges* States in collaboration with the shipping and insurance industries, and the IMO to continue to develop avoidance, evasion, and defensive best practices and advisories to take when under attack or when sailing in waters off the coast of Somalia, and *further urges* States to make their citizens and vessels available for forensic investigation as appropriate at the first port of call immediately following an act or attempted act of piracy or armed robbery at sea or release from captivity;

13. *Decides* to remain seized of the matter.

S.C. Res. 1897[14]

Adopted by the Security Council at its 6226th meeting, on 30 November 2009

The Security Council,

Recalling its previous resolutions concerning the situation in Somalia, especially resolutions 1814 (2008), 1816 (2008), 1838 (2008), 1844 (2008), 1846 (2008), and 1851 (2008),

Continuing to be gravely concerned by the ongoing threat that piracy and armed robbery at sea against vessels pose to the prompt, safe, and effective delivery of humanitarian aid to Somalia and the region, to international navigation and the safety of commercial maritime routes, and to other vulnerable ships, including fishing activities in conformity with international law and the extended range of the piracy threat into the western Indian Ocean,

Reaffirming its respect for the sovereignty, territorial integrity, political independence and unity of Somalia, including Somalia's rights with respect to offshore natural resources, including fisheries, in accordance with international law,

Further reaffirming that international law, as reflected in the United Nations Convention on the Law of the Sea of 10 December 1982 ("The Convention"), sets out the legal framework applicable to combating piracy and armed robbery at sea, as well as other ocean activities,

Again taking into account the crisis situation in Somalia, and the limited capacity of the Transitional Federal Government (TFG) to interdict, or upon interdiction to prosecute pirates or to patrol or secure the waters off the coast of Somalia, including the international sea lanes and Somalia's territorial waters,

Noting the several requests from the TFG for international assistance to counter piracy off its coast, including the letters of 2 and 6 November 2009 from the Permanent Representative of Somalia to the United Nations expressing the appreciation of the TFG to the Security Council for its assistance, expressing the TFG's willingness to consider working with other States and regional organizations to combat piracy and armed robbery at sea off the coast of Somalia, and requesting that the provisions of resolutions 1846 (2008) and 1851 (2008) be renewed for an additional twelve months,

Commending the efforts of the EU operation Atalanta, which the European Union is committed to extending until December 2010, North Atlantic Treaty Organization operations Allied Protector and Ocean Shield, Combined Maritime Forces' Combined Task Force 151, and other States acting in a national capacity in cooperation with the TFG and each other, to suppress piracy and to protect vulnerable ships transiting through the waters off the coast of Somalia,

Noting with concern that the continuing limited capacity and domestic legislation to facilitate the custody and prosecution of suspected pirates after their capture has hindered more robust international action against the pirates off the coast of Somalia, and in some cases has led to pirates being released without facing justice, regardless of whether there is sufficient evidence to support prosecution, *reiterating* that, consistent with the provisions of the

---

[14] S.C. Res. 1897, U.N. Doc. S/RES/1897 (Nov. 30, 2009).

Convention concerning the repression of piracy, the 1988 Convention for the Suppression of Unlawful Acts Against the Safety of Maritime Navigation ("SUA Convention") provides for parties to create criminal offences, establish jurisdiction, and accept delivery of persons responsible for or suspected of seizing or exercising control over a ship by force or threat thereof or any other form of intimidation, and *stressing* the need for States to criminalize piracy under their domestic law and to favourably consider the prosecution, in appropriate cases, of suspected pirates, consistent with applicable international law,

Commending the Republic of Kenya's efforts to prosecute suspected pirates in its national courts, and *noting* with appreciation the assistance being provided by the United Nations Office of Drugs and Crime (UNODC) and other international organizations and donors, in coordination with the Contact Group on Piracy off the Coast of Somalia ("CGPCS"), to support Kenya, Somalia and other States in the region, including Seychelles and Yemen, to take steps to prosecute or incarcerate in a third state after prosecution elsewhere captured pirates consistent with applicable international human rights law,

Noting the ongoing efforts within the CGPCS to explore possible additional mechanisms to effectively prosecute persons suspected of piracy and armed robbery at sea off the coast of Somalia,

Further noting with appreciation the ongoing efforts by UNODC and UNDP to support efforts to enhance the capacity of the corrections system in Somalia, including regional authorities, to incarcerate convicted pirates consistent with applicable international human rights law,

Welcoming the adoption of the Djibouti Code of Conduct concerning the Repression of Piracy and Armed Robbery against Ships in the Western Indian Ocean and the Gulf of Aden, and the establishment of the International Maritime Organization (IMO) Djibouti Code Trust Fund (Multi-donor trust fund – Japan initiated), as well as the International Trust Fund Supporting Initiatives of the CGPCS, and *recognizing* the efforts of signatory States to develop the appropriate regulatory and legislative frameworks to combat piracy, enhance their capacity to patrol the waters of the region, interdict suspect vessels, and prosecute suspected pirates,

Emphasizing that peace and stability within Somalia, the strengthening of State institutions, economic and social development and respect for human rights and the rule of law are necessary to create the conditions for a durable eradication of piracy and armed robbery at sea off the coast of Somalia, and further emphasizing that Somalia's long-term security rests with the effective development by the TFG of the National Security Force and Somali Police Force, in the framework of the Djibouti Agreement and in line with a national security strategy,

Determining that the incidents of piracy and armed robbery at sea off the coast of Somalia exacerbate the situation in Somalia, which continues to constitute a threat to international peace and security in the region,

Acting under Chapter VII of the Charter of the United Nations,

1. *Reiterates* that it condemns and deplores all acts of piracy and armed robbery against vessels in the waters off the coast of Somalia;

2. *Notes* again its concern regarding the findings contained in the 20 November 2008 report of the Monitoring Group on Somalia (S/2008/769, page 55) that escalating ransom payments and the lack of enforcement of the arms embargo established by resolution 733 (1992) are fuelling the growth of piracy off the coast of Somalia, and calls upon all States to fully cooperate with the Monitoring Group on Somalia;

3. *Renews* its call upon States and regional organizations that have the capacity to do so, to take part in the fight against piracy and armed robbery at sea off the coast of Somalia, in

particular, consistent with this resolution and international law, by deploying naval vessels, arms and military aircraft and through seizures and disposition of boats, vessels, arms and other related equipment used in the commission of piracy and armed robbery at sea off the coast of Somalia, or for which there are reasonable grounds for suspecting such use;

4. *Commends the work* of the CGPCS to facilitate coordination in order to deter acts of piracy and armed robbery at sea off the coast of Somalia, in cooperation with the IMO, flag States, and the TFG and *urges* States and international organizations to continue to support these efforts;

5. *Acknowledges* Somalia's rights with respect to offshore natural resources, including fisheries, in accordance with international law, and *calls upon* States and interested organizations, including the IMO, to provide technical assistance to Somalia, including regional authorities, and nearby coastal States upon their request to enhance their capacity to ensure coastal and maritime security, including combating piracy and armed robbery at sea off the Somali and nearby coastlines, and stresses the importance of coordination in this regard through the CGPCS;

6. *Invites* all States and regional organizations fighting piracy off the coast of Somalia to conclude special agreements or arrangements with countries willing to take custody of pirates in order to embark law enforcement officials ("shipriders") from the latter countries, in particular countries in the region, to facilitate the investigation and prosecution of persons detained as a result of operations conducted under this resolution for acts of piracy and armed robbery at sea off the coast of Somalia, provided that the advance consent of the TFG is obtained for the exercise of third state jurisdiction by shipriders in Somali territorial waters and that such agreements or arrangements do not prejudice the effective implementation of the SUA Convention;

7. *Encourages* Member States to continue to cooperate with the TFG in the fight against piracy and armed robbery at sea, notes the primary role of the TFG in the fight against piracy and armed robbery at sea, and *decides* that for a period of twelve months from the date of this resolution to renew the authorizations as set out in paragraph 10 of Resolution 1846 (2008) and paragraph 6 of Resolution 1851 (2008) granted to States and regional organizations cooperating with the TFG in the fight against piracy and armed robbery at sea off the coast of Somalia, for which advance notification has been provided by the TFG to the Secretary-General;

8. *Affirms* that the authorizations renewed in this resolution apply only with respect to the situation in Somalia and shall not affect the rights or obligations or responsibilities of Member States under international law, including any rights or obligations under the Convention, with respect to any other situation, and underscores in particular that this resolution shall not be considered as establishing customary international law; and *affirms further* that such authorizations have been renewed only following the receipt of the 2 and 6 November 2009 letters conveying the consent of the TFG;

9. *Affirms* that the measures imposed by paragraph 5 of resolution 733 (1992) and further elaborated upon by paragraphs 1 and 2 of resolution 1425 (2002) do not apply to weapons and military equipment destined for the sole use of Member States and regional organizations undertaking measures in accordance with paragraph 7 above or to supplies of technical assistance to Somalia solely for the purposes set out in paragraphs 5 above which have *been exempted* from those measures in accordance with the procedure set out in paragraphs 11 (b) and 12 of resolution 1772 (2007);

10. *Requests* that cooperating States take appropriate steps to ensure that the activities they undertake pursuant to the authorizations in paragraph 7 do not have the practical effect of denying or impairing the right of innocent passage to the ships of any third State;

11. *Calls on* Member States to assist Somalia, at the request of the TFG and with notification to the Secretary-General, to strengthen capacity in Somalia, including regional authorities, to bring to justice those who are using Somali territory to plan, facilitate, or undertake criminal acts of piracy and armed robbery at sea, and *stresses* that any measures undertaken pursuant to this paragraph shall be consistent with applicable international human rights law;

12. *Calls upon* all States, and in particular flag, port, and coastal States, States of the nationality of victims and perpetrators of piracy and armed robbery, and other States with relevant jurisdiction under international law and national legislation, to cooperate in determining jurisdiction, and in the investigation and prosecution of persons responsible for acts of piracy and armed robbery off the coast of Somalia, consistent with applicable international law including international human rights law, to ensure that all pirates handed over to judicial authorities are subject to a judicial process, and to render assistance by, among other actions, providing disposition and logistics assistance with respect to persons under their jurisdiction and control, such as victims and witnesses and persons detained as a result of operations conducted under this resolution;

13. *Commends* in this context the decision by the CGPCS to establish an International Trust Fund to support its initiatives and *encourages* donors to contribute to it;

14. *Urges* States parties to the Convention and the SUA Convention to fully implement their relevant obligations under these Conventions and customary international law and cooperate with the UNODC, IMO, and other States and other international organizations to build judicial capacity for the successful prosecution of persons suspected of piracy and armed robbery at sea off the coast of Somalia;

15. *Welcomes* the revisions by the IMO to its recommendations and guidance on preventing and suppressing piracy and armed robbery against ships, and *urges* States, in collaboration with the shipping and insurance industries, and the IMO, to continue to develop and implement avoidance, evasion, and defensive best practices and advisories to take when under attack or when sailing in the waters off the coast of Somalia, and further urges States to make their citizens and vessels available for forensic investigation as appropriate at the first port of call immediately following an act or attempted act of piracy or armed robbery at sea or release from captivity;

16. *Requests* States and regional organizations cooperating with the TFG to inform the Security Council and the Secretary-General within nine months of the progress of actions undertaken in the exercise of the authorizations provided in paragraph 7 above and further requests all States contributing through the CGPCS to the fight against piracy off the coast of Somalia, including Somalia and other States in the region, to report by the same deadline on their efforts to establish jurisdiction and cooperation in the investigation and prosecution of piracy;

17. *Requests* the Secretary-General to report to the Security Council within 11 months of the adoption of this resolution on the implementation of this resolution and on the situation with respect to piracy and armed robbery at sea off the coast of Somalia;

18. *Requests* the Secretary General of the IMO to brief the Security Council on the basis of cases brought to his attention by the agreement of all affected coastal States, and duly taking into account the existing bilateral and regional cooperative arrangements, on the situation with respect to piracy and armed robbery;

19. *Expresses* its intention to review the situation and consider, as appropriate, renewing the authorizations provided in paragraph 7 above for additional periods upon the request of the TFG;

20. *Decides* to remain seized of the matter.

S.C. Res. 1918[15]

Adopted by the Security Council at its 6301st meeting, on 27 April 2010

The Security Council,

Recalling its previous resolutions concerning the situation in Somalia, especially resolutions 1814 (2008), 1816 (2008), 1838 (2008), 1844 (2008), 1846 (2008), 1851 (2008) and 1897 (2009),

Continuing to be gravely concerned by the threat that piracy and armed robbery at sea against vessels pose to the situation in Somalia and other States in the region, as well as to international navigation and the safety of commercial maritime routes,

Reaffirming that international law, as reflected in the United Nations Convention on the Law of the Sea of 10 December 1982 ("the Convention"), in particular its articles 100, 101 and 105, sets out the legal framework applicable to combating piracy and armed robbery at sea, as well as other ocean activities,

Reaffirming also that the authorizations renewed in resolution 1897 (2009) apply only with respect to the situation in Somalia and shall not affect the rights, obligations or responsibilities of Member States under international law, including any rights or obligations under the Convention, with respect to any other situation, and *underscoring in particular* that resolution 1897 shall not be considered as establishing customary international law,

Stressing the need to address the problems caused by the limited capacity of the judicial system of Somalia and other States in the region to effectively prosecute suspected pirates,

Noting with appreciation the assistance being provided by the United Nations Office on Drugs and Crime (UNODC) and other international organizations and donors, in coordination with the Contact Group on Piracy off the Coast of Somalia ("CGPCS"), to enhance the capacity of the judicial and the corrections systems in Somalia, Kenya, Seychelles and other States in the region to prosecute suspected, and imprison convicted, pirates consistent with applicable international human rights law,

Commending the role of the EU operation Atalanta, North Atlantic Treaty Organization operations Allied Protector and Ocean Shield, Combined Maritime Forces' Combined Task Force 151, and other States acting in a national capacity in cooperation with the Transitional Federal Government (the TFG) and each other, in suppressing piracy and armed robbery at sea off the coast of Somalia, including by bringing persons suspected of piracy to justice,

Commending the efforts of the Republic of Kenya to date to prosecute suspected pirates in its national courts and imprison convicted persons, and *encouraging* Kenya to continue these efforts, while acknowledging the difficulties Kenya encounters in this regard,

Also commending the efforts to date of other States to prosecute suspected pirates in their national courts,

---

[15] S.C. Res. 1918, U.N. Doc. S/Res/1918 (April 27, 2010).

Acknowledging the decision of the Seychelles to engage in the prosecution of suspected pirates, and *welcoming in particular* their decision on 6 February 2010 to consider hosting a regional prosecution centre,

Commending the decision by the CGPCS to create the International Trust Fund supporting initiatives of the Contact Group on Piracy off the Coast of Somalia administered by the UNODC to defray the expenses associated with prosecution of suspected pirates and to support other counter-piracy initiatives, *welcoming* the contributions of participating States and *encouraging* other potential donors to contribute to the fund,

Welcoming the adoption of the CGPCS regional capability needs assessment report and *urging* States and international organizations to provide fullest possible support to enable early implementation of its recommendations,

Commending those States that have amended their domestic law in order to criminalize piracy and facilitate the prosecution of suspected pirates in their national courts, consistent with applicable international law, including human rights law, and *stressing* the need for States to continue their efforts in this regard,

Noting with concern at the same time that the domestic law of a number of States lacks provisions criminalizing piracy and/or procedural provisions for effective criminal prosecution of suspected pirates,

Acknowledging the ongoing efforts within the CGPCS to explore possible mechanisms to more effectively prosecute persons suspected of piracy and armed robbery at sea off the coast of Somalia,

Emphasizing that peace and stability within Somalia, the strengthening of State institutions, economic and social development and respect for human rights and the rule of law are necessary to create the conditions for a durable eradication of piracy and armed robbery at sea off the coast of Somalia, and further emphasizing that Somalia's long-term security rests with the effective development by the TFG of the National Security Force and Somali Police Force, in the framework of the Djibouti Agreement and in line with a national security strategy,

Being concerned over cases when persons suspected of piracy are released without facing justice and *determined* to create conditions to ensure that pirates are held accountable,

1. *Affirms* that the failure to prosecute persons responsible for acts of piracy and armed robbery at sea off the coast of Somalia undermines anti-piracy efforts of the international community;

2. *Calls on* all States, including States in the region, to criminalize piracy under their domestic law and favourably consider the prosecution of suspected, and imprisonment of convicted, pirates apprehended off the coast of Somalia, consistent with applicable international human rights law;

3. *Welcomes* in this context the progress being made to implement the IMO Djibouti Code of Conduct, and *calls upon* its participants to implement it fully as soon as possible;

4. *Requests* the Secretary-General to present to the Security Council within 3 months a report on possible options to further the aim of prosecuting and imprisoning persons responsible for acts of piracy and armed robbery at sea off the coast of Somalia, including, in particular, options for creating special domestic chambers possibly with international components, a regional tribunal or an international tribunal and corresponding imprisonment arrangements, taking into account the work of the CGPCS, the existing practice in establishing international and mixed tribunals, and the time and the resources necessary to achieve and sustain substantive results;

5. *Decides* to remain seized of the matter.

Council Joint Action Operation Atalanta[16]
(with Corrigenda)

THE COUNCIL OF THE EUROPEAN UNION,

Having regard to the Treaty on European Union, and in particular Article 14, the third sub-paragraph of Article 25 and Article 28(3) thereof,

Whereas:

(1) In its Resolution 1814 (2008) on the situation in Somalia, adopted on 15 May 2008, the United Nations Security Council (UNSC) has called on States and regional organisations, in close coordination with one another, to take action to protect shipping involved in the transport and delivery of humanitarian aid to Somalia and in activities authorised by the United Nations.

(2) In its Resolution 1816 (2008) on the situation in Somalia, adopted on 2 June 2008, the UNSC expressed its concern at the threat that acts of piracy and armed robbery against vessels pose to the delivery of humanitarian aid to Somalia, the safety of commercial maritime routes and international navigation. The UNSC encouraged, in particular, States interested in the use of commercial maritime routes off the coast of Somalia to increase and coordinate their efforts, in cooperation with the Transitional Federal Government of Somalia (TFG), to deter acts of piracy and armed robbery at sea. It authorised, for a period of six months from the date of the resolution, States cooperating with the TFG, of which advance notification had been given by the TFG to the UN Secretary-General, to enter the territorial waters of Somalia and to use, in a manner consistent with relevant international law, all necessary means to repress acts of piracy and armed robbery at sea.

(3) In its Resolution 1838 (2008) on the situation in Somalia, adopted on 7 October 2008, the UNSC commended the ongoing planning process towards a possible European Union (EU) naval operation, as well as other international or national initiatives taken with a view to implementing Resolutions 1814 (2008) and 1816 (2008), and urged States that have the capacity to do so, to cooperate with the TFG in the fight against piracy and armed robbery at sea in conformity with the provisions of Resolution 1816 (2008). The UNSC also urged States and regional organisations, in conformity with the provisions of Resolution 1814 (2008), to continue to take action to protect the World Food Programme (WFP) maritime convoys, which is vital to bring humanitarian assistance to the affected populations in Somalia.

(4) In its conclusions of 26 May 2008, the Council expressed its concern at the upsurge of piracy attacks off the Somali coast, which affect humanitarian efforts and international maritime traffic in the region and contribute to continued violations of the UN arms embargo. The Council also commended the sequenced initiatives of some Member States to provide protection to WFP vessels. It stressed the need for wider participation by the international community in these escorts in order to secure the delivery of humanitarian aid to the Somali population.

---

[16] Council Joint Action 2008/851/CFSP of 10 November 2008 on a European Union Military Operation to Contribute to the Deterrence, Prevention and Repression of Acts of Piracy and Armed Robbery off the Coast of Somalia, 2008 O.J. (L 301) 31–37 (EU).

(5) On 5 August 2008, the Council approved a crisis management concept for action by the EU to help implement UNSC Resolution 1816 (2008) and for peace and international security in the region.

(6) On 15 September 2008, the Council reaffirmed its serious concern at the acts of piracy and armed robbery off the Somali coast, deploring, in particular, their recent resurgence. As regards the EU's contribution to the implementation of UNSC Resolution 1816 (2008) on combating piracy off the Somali coast and to the protection, under Resolutions 1814 (2008) and 1816 (2008), of vessels chartered by the WFP and bound for Somalia, the Council decided to establish a coordination cell in Brussels with the task of supporting the surveillance and protection activities carried out by some Member States off the Somali coast. On the same day, it approved, on the one hand, a plan for the implementation of this military coordination action (EU NAVCO) and, on the other, a strategic military option for a possible EU naval operation for which those Member States wishing to cooperate with the TFG under Resolution 1816 (2008) would make available military resources for the deterrence and repression of acts of piracy and armed robbery off the Somali coast.

(7) On 19 September 2008, the Council adopted Joint Action 2008/749/CFSP on the European Union military coordination action in support of UN Security Council Resolution 1816 (2008) (EU NAVCO).

(8) On the launch of the Atalanta military operation, the tasks of the military coordination cell will be exercised under this Joint Action. The coordination cell should then be closed.

(9) The Political and Security Committee (PSC) should exercise political control over the EU military operation in order to help deter acts of piracy off the Somali coast, provide it with strategic direction and take the relevant decisions in accordance with third subparagraph of Article 25 of the Treaty.

(10) Under Article 28(3) of the Treaty, the operational expenditure, arising from this Joint Action, which has military or defence implications, should be borne by the Member States in accordance with Council Decision 2007/384/CFSP of 14 May 2007 establishing a mechanism to administer the financing of the common costs of European Union operations having military or defence implications (Athena) (hereinafter referred to as 'Athena').

(11) Article 14(1) of the Treaty calls for Joint Actions to lay down the means to be made available to the European Union. The financial reference amount, for a twelve-month period, for the common costs of the EU military operation constitutes the best current estimate and is without prejudice to the final figures to be included in a budget to be approved in accordance with the rules laid down in the decision regarding Athena.

(12) By letter dated 30 October 2008, the EU made an offer to the TFG, pursuant to point 7 of Resolution 1816 (2008), which contains proposals for States other than Somalia to exercise jurisdiction over persons captured in Somali territorial waters who have committed, or are suspected of having committed, acts of piracy or armed robbery.

(13) In accordance with Article 6 of the Protocol on the position of Denmark annexed to the Treaty on European Union and to the Treaty establishing the European Community, Denmark does not participate in the elaboration and implementation of decisions and actions of the European Union which have defence implications. Denmark does not participate in the implementation of this Joint Action and therefore does not participate in the financing of the operation,

HAS ADOPTED THIS JOINT ACTION:

Article 1 – Mission

1. The European Union (EU) shall conduct a military operation in support of Resolutions 1814 (2008), 1816 (2008) and 1838 (2008) of the United Nations Security Council (UNSC), in a manner consistent with action permitted with respect to piracy under Article 100 *et seq.* of the United Nations Convention on the Law of the Sea signed in Montego Bay on 10 December 1982 (hereinafter referred to as 'the United Nations Convention on the Law of the Sea') and by means, in particular, of commitments made with third States, hereinafter called 'Atalanta' in order to contribute to:

– the protection of vessels of the WFP delivering food aid to displaced persons in Somalia, in accordance with the mandate laid down in UNSC Resolution 1814 (2008),

– the protection of vulnerable vessels cruising off the Somali coast, and the deterrence, prevention and repression of acts of piracy and armed robbery off the Somali coast, in accordance with the mandate laid down in UNSC Resolution 1816 (2008),

2. The forces deployed to that end shall operate, up to 500 nautical miles off the Somali coast and neighbouring countries, in accordance with the political objective of an EU maritime operation, as defined in the crisis management concept approved by the Council on 5 August 2008.

Article 2 – Mandate

Under the conditions set by the relevant international law and by UNSC Resolutions 1814 (2008), 1816 (2008) and 1838 (2008), Atalanta shall, as far as available capabilities allow:

(a) provide protection to vessels chartered by the WFP, including by means of the presence on board those vessels of armed units of Atalanta, in particular when cruising in Somali territorial waters;

(b) provide protection, based on a case-by-case evaluation of needs, to merchant vessels cruising in the areas where it is deployed;

(c) keep watch over areas off the Somali coast, including Somalia's territorial waters, in which there are dangers to maritime activities, in particular to maritime traffic;

(d) take the necessary measures, including the use of force, to deter, prevent and intervene in order to bring to an end acts of piracy and armed robbery which may be committed in the areas where it is present;

(e) in view of prosecutions potentially being brought by the relevant States under the conditions in Article 12, arrest, detain and transfer persons who have committed, or are suspected of having committed, acts of piracy or armed robbery in the areas where it is present and seize the vessels of the pirates or armed robbers or the vessels caught following an act of piracy or an armed robbery and which are in the hands of the pirates, as well as the goods on board;

(f) liaise with organisations and entities, as well as States, working in the region to combat acts of piracy and armed robbery off the Somali coast, in particular the 'Combined Task Force 150' maritime force which operates within the framework of 'Operation Enduring Freedom'.

Article 3 – Appointment of the EU Operation Commander

Rear admiral Phillip Jones is hereby appointed EU Operation Commander.

Article 4 – Designation of the EU Operational Headquarters

The EU Operational Headquarters shall be located at Northwood, United Kingdom.

Article 5 – Planning and launch of the operation

The Decision to launch the EU military operation shall be adopted by the Council following approval of the Operation Plan and the Rules of Engagement and in the light of the notification by the TFG to the Secretary-General of the United Nations of the offer of co-operation made by the EU pursuant to point 7 of UNSC Resolution 1816 (2008).

Article 6 – Political control and strategic direction

1.   Under the responsibility of the Council, the Political and Security Committee (hereinafter referred to as the 'PSC') shall exercise the political control and strategic direction of the EU military operation. The Council hereby authorises the PSC to take the relevant decisions in accordance with Article 25 of the EU Treaty. This authorisation shall include the powers to amend the planning documents, including the Operation Plan, the Chain of Command and the Rules of Engagement. It shall also include the powers to take decisions on the appointment of the EU Operation Commander and/or EU Force Commander. The powers of decision with respect to the objectives and termination of the EU military operation shall remain vested in the Council, assisted by the Secretary-General/High Representative (hereinafter referred to as the 'SG/HR').

2.   The PSC shall report to the Council at regular intervals.

3.   The PSC shall receive reports from the chairman of the EU Military Committee (EUMC) regarding the conduct of the EU military operation, at regular intervals. The PSC may invite the EU Operation Commander and/or EU Force Commander to its meetings, as appropriate.

Article 7 – Military direction

1.   The EUMC shall monitor the proper execution of the EU military operation conducted under the responsibility of the EU Operation Commander.

2.   The EUMC shall receive reports from the EU Operation Commander at regular intervals. It may invite the EU Operation Commander and/or EU Force Commander to its meetings as appropriate.

3.   The chairman of the EUMC shall act as the primary point of contact with the EU Operation Commander.

Article 8 – Coherence of EU response

The Presidency, the SG/HR, the EU Operation Commander and the EU Force Commander shall closely coordinate their respective activities regarding the implementation of this Joint Action.

Article 9 – Relations with the United Nations, neighbouring countries and other actors

1.   The SG/HR, in close coordination with the Presidency, shall act as the primary point of contact with the United Nations, the Somali authorities, the authorities of neighbouring

countries, and other relevant actors. Within the context of his contact with the African Union, the SG/HR shall be assisted by the EU Special Representative (EUSR) to the African Union, in close coordination with the presidency.

2. At operational level, the EU Operation Commander shall act as the contact point with, in particular, ship-owners' organisations, as well as with the relevant departments of the UN General Secretariat and the WFP.

Article 10 – Participation by third States

1. Without prejudice to the decision-making autonomy of the EU or to the single institutional framework, and in accordance with the relevant guidelines of the European Council, third States may be invited to participate in the operation.

2. The Council hereby authorises the PSC to invite third States to offer contributions and to take the relevant decisions on acceptance of the proposed contributions, upon the recommendation of the EU Operation Commander and the EUMC.

3. Detailed modalities for the participation by third States shall be the subject of agreements concluded in accordance with the procedure laid down in Article 24 of the Treaty. The SG/HR, who shall assist the Presidency, may negotiate such agreements on behalf of the Presidency. Where the EU and a third State have concluded an agreement establishing a framework for the latter's participation in EU crisis management operations, the provisions of such an agreement shall apply in the context of this operation.

4. Third States making significant military contributions to the EU military operation shall have the same rights and obligations in terms of day-to-day management of the operation as Member States taking part in the operation.

5. The Council hereby authorises the PSC to take relevant decisions on the setting-up of a Committee of Contributors, should third States provide significant military contributions.

6. The conditions for the transfer to a State participating in the operation of persons arrested and detained, with a view to the exercise of jurisdiction of that State, shall be established when the participation agreements referred to in paragraph 3 are concluded or implemented.

Article 11 – Status of EU-led forces

The status of the EU-led forces and their personnel, including the privileges, immunities and further guarantees necessary for the fulfilment and smooth functioning of their mission, who:

– are stationed on the land territory of third States,
– operate in the territorial or internal waters of third States,

shall be agreed in accordance with the procedure laid down in Article 24 of the Treaty. The SG/HR, who shall assist the Presidency, may negotiate such arrangements on behalf of the Presidency.

Article 12 – Transfer of persons arrested and detained
with a view to their prosecution

1. On the basis of Somalia's acceptance of the exercise of jurisdiction by Member States or by third States, on the one hand, and Article 105 of the United Nations Convention on the Law of the Sea, on the other hand, persons having committed, or suspected of having

committed, acts of piracy or armed robbery in Somali territorial waters or on the high seas, who are arrested and detained, with a view to their prosecution, and property used to carry out such acts, shall be transferred:

- to the competent authorities of the flag Member State or of the third State participating in the operation, of the vessel which took them captive, or
- if this State cannot, or does not wish to, exercise its jurisdiction, to a Member States or any third State which wishes to exercise its jurisdiction over the aforementioned persons and property.

2. No persons referred to in paragraphs 1 and 2 may be transferred to a third State unless the conditions for the transfer have been agreed with that third State in a manner consistent with relevant international law, notably international law on human rights, in order to guarantee in particular that no one shall be subjected to the death penalty, to torture or to any cruel, inhuman or degrading treatment.

Article 13 – Relations with the flag States of protected vessels

The conditions governing the presence on board merchant ships, particularly those chartered by the WFP, of units belonging to Atalanta, including privileges, immunities and other guarantees relating to the proper conduct of the operation, shall be agreed with the flag States of those vessels.

Article 14 – Financial arrangements

1. The common costs of the EU military operation shall be administered by Athena.

2. The financial reference amount for the common costs of the EU military operation shall be EUR 8 300 000. The percentage of the reference amount referred to in Article 33(3) of Athena shall be 30%.

Article 15 – Release of information to the United Nations and other third parties

1. The SG/HR is hereby authorised to release to the United Nations and to other third parties associated with this Joint Action, classified EU information and documents generated for the purposes of the EU military operation up to the level of classification appropriate for each of them and in accordance with the Council's security regulations.

2. The SG/HR is hereby authorised to release to the United Nations and to other third parties associated with this Joint Action, unclassified EU documents relating to Council deliberations on the operation which are covered by the obligation of professional secrecy pursuant to Article 6(1) of the Council's Rules of Procedure.

Article 16 – Entry into force and termination

1. This Joint Action shall enter into force on the date of its adoption.

2. Joint Action 2008/749/CFSP shall be repealed as from the date of closure of the coordination cell put in place by that Joint Action. It shall be closed on the launch date of the operation referred to in Article 6 of this Joint Action.

3. The EU military operation shall terminate 12 months after the initial operating capability is declared, subject to the prolongation of UNSC Resolutions 1814 (2008) and 1816 (2008).

4. This Joint Action shall be repealed following the withdrawal of the EU force, in accordance with the plans approved for the termination of the EU military operation, and without prejudice to the relevant provisions of Athena.

Article 17 – Publication

1. This Joint Action shall be published in the *Official Journal of the European Union*.

2. The PSC's decisions on the appointment of an EU Operation Commander and/or EU Force Commander, as well as the PSC's decisions on the acceptance of contributions from third States and the setting-up of a Committee of Contributors shall likewise be published in the *Official Journal of the European Union*.

Done at Brussels, 10 November 2008.

For the Council
The President
B. KOUCHNER

Corrigenda to Council Joint Action Operation Atalanta[17]

On page 35, Article 2, introductory wording:

for: 'Under the conditions set by the relevant international law and by UNSC Resolutions 1814 (2008), 1816 (2008) and 1838 (2008), Atalanta shall, as far as available capabilities allow:',

read: 'Under the conditions set by applicable international law, in particular the United Nations Convention on the Law of the Sea, and by UNSC Resolutions 1814 (2008), 1816 (2008) and 1838 (2008), Atalanta shall, as far as available capabilities allow:';

on page 35, Article 12, paragraph 1, first indent:

for: '– to the competent authorities of the flag Member State or of the third State participating in the operation, of the vessel which took them captive, or',

read: '– to the competent authorities of the Member State or of the third State participating in the operation, of which the vessel which took them captive flies the flag, or'.

---

[17] Corrigendum to Council Joint Action 2008/851/CFSP of 10 November 2008 on a European Union military operation to contribute to the deterrence, prevention and repression of acts of piracy and armed robbery off the Somali coast, 2009 O.J. (L 253) 18 (EU).

Gemeinsame Aktion des Rates Operation Atalanta[18] (excerpts)

Artikel 12

Überstellung der aufgegriffenen und festgenommenen Personen zwecks Wahrnehmung der gerichtlichen Zuständigkeiten

(1) Personen, die seeräuberische Handlungen oder bewaffnete Raubüberfälle begangen haben oder im Verdacht stehen, diese Taten begangen zu haben, und die in den Hoheitsgewässern Somalias oder auf Hoher See aufgegriffen und im Hinblick auf die Strafverfolgung durch die zuständigen Staaten festgenommen wurden, sowie die Güter, die zur Ausführung dieser Taten dienten, werden auf Grundlage der Zustimmung von Somalia zur Ausübung von gerichtlicher Zuständigkeit durch Mitgliedstaaten oder durch Drittstaaten einerseits und andererseits auf Artikel 105 des VN-Seerechtsübereinkommens, an die

- zuständigen Behörden des Mitgliedstaats oder des an der Operation teilnehmenden Drittstaats übergeben, unter dessen Flagge das Schiff fährt, durch das die Gefangennahme erfolgte, oder

- sofern dieser Staat seine gerichtliche Zuständigkeit nicht wahrnehmen kann oder will, an einen Mitgliedstaat oder an jeden Drittstaat, der seine gerichtliche Zuständigkeit in Bezug auf diese Personen und Güter wahrnehmen möchte, übergeben.

(2) Die in Absatz 1 genannten Personen können nur dann an einen Drittstaat übergeben werden, wenn mit dem betreffenden Drittstaat die Bedingungen für diese Übergabe im Einklang mit dem einschlägigen Völkerrecht, insbesondere den internationalen Menschenrechtsnormen, festgelegt wurden, um insbesondere sicherzustellen, dass für niemandem das Risiko der Todesstrafe, Folter oder jeglicher anderen grausamen, unmenschlichen oder erniedrigenden Strafe oder Behandlung besteht.

Korrigendum[19]

Artikel 12, Titel und Absatz 1:

Statt: „Überstellung der aufgegriffenen und festgenommenen Personen zwecks Wahrnehmung der gerichtlichen Zuständigkeiten

(1) Personen, die seeräuberische Handlungen oder bewaffnete Raubüberfälle begangen haben oder im Verdacht stehen, diese Taten begangen zu haben, und die in den Hoheits-

---

[18] Gemeinsame Aktion 2008/851/GASP des Rates vom 10. November 2008 über die Militäroperation der Europäischen Union als Beitrag zur Abschreckung, Verhütung und Bekämpfung von seeräuberischen Handlungen und bewaffneten Raubüberfällen vor der Küste Somalias, 2008 Abl. (L 301) 33–37 (EU).

[19] Berichtigung der Gemeinsamen Aktion 2008/851/GASP des Rates vom 10. November 2008 über die Militäroperation der Europäischen Union als Beitrag zur Abschreckung, Verhütung und Bekämpfung von seeräuberischen Handlungen und bewaffneten Raubüberfällen vor der Küste Somalias, 2009 Abl. (L 10) 35 (EU).

gewässern Somalias oder auf Hoher See aufgegriffen und im Hinblick auf die Strafverfolgung durch die zuständigen Staaten festgenommen wurden, […]"

muss es heißen: „Überstellung der aufgegriffenen und festgehaltenen Personen zwecks Wahrnehmung der gerichtlichen Zuständigkeiten

(1) Personen, die seeräuberische Handlungen oder bewaffnete Raubüberfälle begangen haben oder im Verdacht stehen, diese Taten begangen zu haben, und die in den Hoheitsgewässern Somalias oder auf Hoher See aufgegriffen worden sind und im Hinblick auf die Strafverfolgung durch die zuständigen Staaten festgehalten werden, […]".

EU-Kenya Transfer Agreement[20] (excerpts)

Annex

Provisions on the Conditions of Transfer of Suspected Pirates and Seized Property from the EU-led Naval Force to the Republic of Kenya

1. Definitions

For the purposes of this Exchange of Letters:

(a) 'European Union-led naval force (EUNAVFOR)' means EU military headquarters and national contingents contributing to the EU operation 'Atalanta', their ships, aircrafts and assets;

(b) 'operation' means the preparation, establishment, execution and support of the military mission established by EU Council Joint Action 2008/851/CFSP and/or its successors;

(c) 'EU Operation Commander' means the commander of the operation;

(d) 'EU Force Commander' means the EU commander in the area of operations as defined within Article 1(2) of EU Council Joint Action 2008/851/CFSP;

(e) 'national contingents' means units and ships belonging to the Member States of the European Union and to other States participating in the operation;

(f) 'sending State' means a State providing a national contingent for EUNAVFOR.

(g) 'piracy' means piracy as defined in Article 101 of UNCLOS;

(h) 'transferred person' means any person suspected of intending to commit, committing, or having committed, acts of piracy transferred by EUNAVFOR to Kenya under this Exchange of Letters.

2. General principles

(a) Kenya will accept, upon the request of EUNAVFOR, the transfer of persons detained by EUNAVFOR in connection with piracy and associated seized property by EUNAVFOR and will submit such persons and property to its competent authorities for the purpose of investigation and prosecution.

(b) EUNAVFOR will, when acting under this Exchange of Letters, transfer persons or property only to competent Kenyan law enforcement authorities.

(c) The signatories confirm that they will treat persons transferred under this Exchange of Letters, both prior to and following transfer, humanely and in accordance with international human rights obligations, including the prohibition against torture and cruel, inhumane and degrading treatment or punishment, the prohibition of arbitrary detention and in accordance with the requirement to have a fair trial.

---

[20] Exchange of Letters between the European Union and the Government of Kenya on the conditions and modalities for the transfer of persons suspected of having committed acts of piracy and detained by the European Union-led naval force (EUNAVFOR), and seized property in the possession of EUNAVFOR, from EUNAVFOR to Kenya and for their treatment after such transfer, 2009 O.J. (L 79) 51–59 (EU). This Exchange of Letters was approved by the Council of the European Union, Council Decision 2009/293/CFSP, 2009 O.J. (L 79) 47–48 (EU).

3. Treatment, prosecution and trial of transferred persons

(a) Any transferred person will be treated humanely and will not be subjected to torture or cruel, inhuman or degrading treatment or punishment, will receive adequate accommodation and nourishment, access to medical treatment and will be able to carry out religious observance.

(b) Any transferred person will be brought promptly before a judge or other officer authorised by law to exercise judicial power, who will decide without delay on the lawfulness of his detention and will order his release if the detention is not lawful.

(c) Any transferred person will be entitled to trial within a reasonable time or to release.

(d) In the determination of any criminal charge against him, any transferred person will be entitled to a fair and public hearing by a competent, independent and impartial tribunal established by law.

(e) Any transferred person charged with a criminal offence will be presumed innocent until proved guilty according to law.

(f) In the determination of any criminal charge against him, every transferred person will be entitled to the following minimum guarantees, in full equality:

  (1) to be informed promptly and in detail in a language which he understands of the nature and cause of the charge against him;

  (2) to have adequate time and facilities for the preparation of his defence and to communicate with counsel of his own choice;

  (3) to be tried without undue delay;

  (4) to be tried in his presence, and to defend himself in person or through legal assistance of his own choice; to be informed, if he does not have legal assistance, of this right; and to have legal assistance assigned to him, in any case where the interests of justice so require, and without payment by him in any such case if he does not have sufficient means to pay for it;

  (5) to examine, or have examined, all evidence against him, including affidavits of witnesses who conducted the arrest, and to obtain the attendance and examination of witnesses on his behalf under the same conditions as witnesses against him;

  (6) to have the free assistance of an interpreter if he cannot understand or speak the language used in court;

  (7) not to be compelled to testify against himself or to confess guilt.

(g) Any transferred person convicted of a crime will be permitted to have the right to his conviction and sentence reviewed by or appealed to a higher tribunal in accordance with the law of Kenya.

(h) Kenya will not transfer any transferred person to any other State for the purposes of investigation or prosecution without prior written consent from EUNAVFOR.

4. Death penalty

No transferred person will be liable to suffer the death sentence. Kenya will, in accordance with the applicable laws, take steps to ensure that any death sentence is commuted to a sentence of imprisonment.

5. Records and notifications

(a) Any transfer will be the subject of an appropriate document signed by a representative of EUNAVFOR and a representative of the competent Kenyan law enforcement authorities.

(b) EUNAVFOR will provide detention records to Kenya with regard to any transferred person. These records will include, so far as possible, the physical condition of the transferred person while in detention, the time of transfer to Kenyan authorities, the reason for his detention, the time and place of the commencement of his detention, and any decisions taken with regard to his detention.

(c) Kenya will be responsible for keeping an accurate account of all transferred persons, including, but not limited to, keeping records of any seized property, the person's physical condition, the location of their places of detention, any charges against him and any significant decisions taken in the course of his prosecution and trial.

(d) These records will be available to representatives of the EU and EUNAVFOR upon request in writing to the Kenyan Ministry of Foreign Affairs.

(e) In addition, Kenya will notify EUNAVFOR of the place of detention of any person transferred under this Exchange of Letters, any deterioration of his physical condition and of any allegations of alleged improper treatment. Representatives of the EU and EUNAVFOR will have access to any persons transferred under this Exchange of Letters as long as such persons are in custody and will be entitled to question them.

(f) National and international humanitarian agencies will, at their request, be allowed to visit persons transferred under this Exchange of Letters.

(g) For the purposes of ensuring that EUNAVFOR is able to provide timely assistance to Kenya with attendance of witnesses from EUNAVFOR and the provision of relevant evidence, Kenya will notify EUNAVFOR of its intention to initiate criminal trial proceedings against any transferred person and the timetable for provision of evidence, and the hearing of evidence.

6. EUNAVFOR Assistance

(a) EUNAVFOR, within its means and capabilities, will provide all assistance to Kenya with a view to the investigation and prosecution of transferred persons.

(b) In particular, EUNAVFOR will:

    (1) hand over detention records drawn up pursuant to paragraph 5(b) of this Exchange of Letters;

    (2) process any evidence in accordance with the requirements of the Kenyan competent authorities as agreed in the implementing arrangements described in paragraph 9;

    (3) endeavour to produce statements of witness or affidavits by EUNAVFOR personnel involved in any incident in relation to which persons have been transferred under this Exchange of Letters;

    (4) hand over all relevant seized property in the possession of EUNAVFOR.

7. Relationship to other rights of transferred persons.

Nothing in this Exchange of Letters is intended to derogate, or may be construed as derogating, from any rights that a transferred person may have under applicable domestic or international law.

8. Liaison and disputes

(a) All issues arising in connection with the application of these provisions will be examined jointly by Kenyan and EU competent authorities.

(b) Failing any prior settlement, disputes concerning the interpretation or application of these provisions will be settled exclusively by diplomatic means between Kenyan and EU representatives.

9. Implementing arrangements

(a) For the purposes of the application of these provisions, operational, administrative and technical matters may be the subject of implementing arrangements to be approved between competent Kenyan authorities on the one hand and the competent EU authorities, as well as the competent authorities of the sending States, on the other hand.

(b) Implementing arrangements may cover, inter alia:

(1) the identification of competent law enforcement authorities of Kenya to whom EUNAVFOR may transfer persons;

(2) the detention facilities where transferred persons will be held;

(3) the handling of documents, including those related to the gathering of evidence, which will be handed over to the competent law enforcement authorities of Kenya upon transfer of a person;

(4) points of contact for notifications;

(5) forms to be used for transfers;

(6) provision of technical support, expertise, training and other assistance upon request of Kenya in order to achieve the objectives of this Exchange of Letters.

EU-Seychelles Transfer Agreement[21] (excerpts)

Exchange of Letters between the European Union and the Republic of Seychelles on the Conditions and Modalities for the Transfer of Suspected Pirates and Armed Robbers from EUNAVFOR to the Republic of Seychelles and for Their Treatment after such Transfer

A. *Letter from the Republic of Seychelles*

Your Excellency,

Reference is made to the working session held in Seychelles on the 18th and 19th August 2009 to discuss the EU Agreements on Piracy and Armed Robbery which involved the participation of representatives of the EU, the members of the Seychelles High Level Committee and other related institutions and to our subsequent letter of August 21, 2009.

In the course of the working session, the concerns of the different related institutions on the transfer of suspected pirates and armed robbers were tabled. The *'Guidance for the Transfer of Suspected pirates, armed robbers and seized property to Seychelles'* prepared by the Attorney General of the Republic of Seychelles, which is intended to ensure that any transfer of persons suspected of acts of piracy and armed robbery is done in accordance with the laws of Seychelles was approved in principle. It was also agreed that the Implementing Arrangements (which clarifies Article 10 of the proposed Transfer Agreement) could be agreed upon after the proposed Transfer Agreement has been finalised and that a common Guidance on the handover of suspected pirates, armed robbers and seized property is prepared. Furthermore, that the Republic of Seychelles will be provided with the necessary assistance for the detention, maintenance, investigation, prosecution trial and repatriation of the suspected pirates and armed robbers.

Following the working session and our letter, further discussions have taken place within the High Level Committee on the transfer of suspected pirates and armed robbers to the territory of the Republic of Seychelles.

The Government of the Republic of Seychelles would like to take this opportunity to renew its reassurance to the EU of its commitment to cooperate to its fullest possible extent, having regard to its available resources and infrastructure capacities, in the repression of piracy to accept the transfer of captured suspected pirates and armed robbers.

At the same time, the Government of the Republic of Seychelles would like to express its desire that the EU SOFA be signed as discussions continue on the proposed EU Transfer Agreement.

In view of ongoing negotiations and pending conclusion of a mutually acceptable arrangement between the EU and the Government of the Republic of Seychelles on the

---

[21] Exchange of Letters between the European Union and the Republic of Seychelles on the Conditions and Modalities for the Transfer of Suspected Pirates and Armed Robbers from EUNAVFOR to the Republic of Seychelles and for Their Treatment after such Transfer, 2009 O.J. (L 315) 37–43 (EU); this Exchange of Letters was approved by the Council of the European Union, Council Decision 2009/877/CFSP, 2009 O.J. (L 315) 35–36 (EU).

transfer of pirates and armed robbers to its territory, the Government of the Republic of Seychelles may authorize the EUNAVFOR to transfer suspected pirates and armed robbers captured in the course of its operations in the exclusive economic zone, territorial sea, archipelagic waters and internal waters of the Republic of Seychelles. This authorization is extended to the protection of Seychelles flagged vessels and Seychellois Citizens on a non-Seychelles flagged vessel beyond the limit aforementioned and in other circumstances on the high seas at the discretion of the Republic of the Seychelles.

Provided always that:

– The EU, aware of the limited capacities of the Republic of Seychelles to accept, try, detain and incarcerate suspected pirates and armed robbers and in consideration of the acceptance by the Republic of Seychelles of the transfer of any suspected pirates and armed robbers to its territory, shall provide the Republic of Seychelles with such full financial, human resource, material, logistical and infrastructural assistance for the detention, incarceration maintenance, investigation, prosecution, trial and repatriation of the suspected or convicted pirates and armed robbers;

– The Attorney General shall have at least 10 days from the date of transfer of the suspected pirates or armed robbers to decide on the sufficiency of the available evidence in view of prosecution,

– In the event that the Attorney General decides that there is insufficient evidence to prosecute, the EUNAVFOR shall take the full responsibility, including the financial costs, of transferring the suspected pirates and armed robbers back to their country of origin within 10 days of EUNAVFOR having been notified of such a decision;

– Any transfer of suspected pirates and armed robbers shall as far as possible be in accordance with the *'Guidance for the Transfer of Suspected pirates, armed robbers and seized property to Seychelles'*,

– The Government of the Republic of the Seychelles also confirms that:

– Any transferred person will be treated humanely and will not be subjected to torture or cruel, inhuman or degrading treatment or punishment, will receive adequate accommodation and nourishment, access to medical treatment and will be able to carry out religious observance.

– Any transferred person will be brought promptly before a judge or other officer authorised by law to exercise judicial power, who will decide without delay on the lawfulness of his detention and will order his release if the detention is not lawful,

– Any transferred person will be entitled to trial within a reasonable time or to release,

– In the determination of any criminal charge against him, any transferred person will be entitled to a fair and public hearing by a competent, independent and impartial tribunal established by law,

– Any transferred person charged with a criminal offence will be presumed innocent until proved guilty according to law,

– In the determination of any criminal charge against him, every transferred person will be entitled to the following minimum guarantees, in full equality:

(1) to be informed promptly and in detail in a language which he understands of the nature of the charge against him;

(2) to have adequate time and facilities for the preparation of his defence and to communicate with counsel of his own choice;

(3) to defend himself in person or through legal assistance of his own choice; to be informed, if he does not have legal assistance, of this right; and to have legal assistance assigned to him, in any case where the interests of justice so require,

and without payment by him in any such case if he does not have sufficient means to pay for it;

(4) to examine, or have examined, all evidence against him, including affidavits of witnesses who conducted the arrest, and to obtain the attendance and examination of witnesses on his behalf under the same conditions as witnesses against him;

(5) to have the free assistance of an interpreter if he cannot understand or speak the language used in court;

(6) not to be compelled to testify against himself or to confess guilt.

– Any transferred person convicted of a crime will be permitted to have the right to have its conviction and sentence reviewed by or appealed to a higher tribunal in accordance with the law of the Seychelles,

– The Seychelles will not transfer any transferred person to any other State without prior written consent from EUNAVFOR.

This arrangement has been discussed and agreed by the Seychelles authorities. The arrangements proposed herewith may come into force when the European Union indicates its agreement in writing.

Yours Sincerely,

Mr J. Morgan

THE MINISTER

Chairman of the High Level Committee of Piracy

B. *Letter from the European Union*

Your Excellency,

I have the honour to acknowledge receipt of your letter dated 29 September 2009 regarding the conditions and modalities for the transfer of suspected pirates and armed robbers from EUNAVFOR to the Republic of Seychelles and for their treatment after such transfer, which reads as follows:

[here the letter from the Republic of Seychelles as reprinted above is reproduced]

I have the honour to confirm, on behalf of the European Union, that the content of your letter is acceptable to the European Union. This Instrument will be applied provisionally by the European Union from the date of signature of this letter and will enter into force definitively once the European Union has completed its internal procedures for conclusion.

With regard to the reference in your letter to the consideration by the Seychelles Attorney General of the sufficiency of the available evidence in view of prosecution, the European Union understands that you have agreed that, since EUNAVFOR will communicate in each case all the evidence available to it at the time, such as logbooks, pictures and videos, this will allow the Seychelles Attorney General to take a decision on the sufficiency of such evidence before accepting the transfer of suspected pirates and armed robbers.

I also recall that, as mentioned in your letter, this Instrument will apply on a transitional basis, pending the conclusion of a mutually acceptable transfer agreement between the EU and the Republic of Seychelles on the transfer of pirates and armed robbers to the territory of the Republic of Seychelles.

Please, accept Sir, the assurance of my highest consideration.

For the European Union

J. SOLANA MADARIA

Declaration by the European Union on the occasion of the signature of the exchange of letters between the European Union and the Republic of Seychelles on the conditions and modalities for the transfer of suspected pirates and armed robbers from EUNAVFOR to the Republic of Seychelles and for their treatment after such transfer

1. The European Union (EU) notes that nothing in the Exchange of letters between the European Union and the Republic of Seychelles on the conditions and modalities for the transfer of suspected pirates and armed robbers is intended to derogate, or may be construed as derogating, from any rights that a transferred person may have under applicable domestic or international law.

2. The EU notes that representatives of the EU and of EUNAVFOR will be granted access to any persons transferred to the Republic of Seychelles (Seychelles) pursuant to the Exchange of Letters as long as such persons are held in custody there, and that representatives of the EU and of EUNAVFOR will be entitled to question them.

For this purpose, the EU notes that an accurate account will be made available to representatives of the EU and of EUNAVFOR of all transferred persons, including records of any seized property, the persons' physical condition, their place of detention, any charges against them and any significant decisions taken in the course of their prosecution and trial.

EUNAVFOR is willing to provide timely assistance to Seychelles through the attendance of witnesses from EUNAVFOR and the provision of relevant evidence. For this purpose, Seychelles should notify EUNAVFOR of its intention to initiate criminal proceedings against any transferred person and the timetable for the provision and hearing of evidence.

The EU notes that national and international humanitarian agencies will also be allowed, at their request, to visit persons transferred under the Exchange of Letters.

Djibouti Code of Conduct[22]

The Governments of Comoros, Djibouti, Egypt, Eritrea, Ethiopia, France, Jordan, Kenya, Madagascar, Maldives, Mauritius, Mozambique, Oman, Saudi Arabia, Seychelles, Somalia, South Africa, Sudan, the United Arab Emirates, the United Republic of Tanzania and Yemen (hereinafter referred to as "the Participants"),

DEEPLY CONCERNED about the crimes of piracy and armed robbery against ships in the Western Indian Ocean and the Gulf of Aden and the grave dangers to the safety and security of persons and ships at sea and to the protection of the marine environment arising from such acts;

REAFFIRMING that international law, as reflected in UNCLOS, sets out the legal framework applicable to combating piracy and armed robbery at sea;

NOTING that the Assembly of the International Maritime Organization (hereinafter referred to as "IMO"), at its twenty-fifth regular session, adopted, on 27 November 2007, resolution A.1002(25) on Piracy and armed robbery against ships in waters off the coast of Somalia which, among other things, called upon Governments in the region to conclude, in cooperation with IMO, and implement, as soon as possible, a regional agreement to prevent, deter and suppress piracy and armed robbery against ships;

NOTING ALSO that the General Assembly of the United Nations, at its sixth-third session, adopted, on 5 December 2008, resolution 63/111 on Ocean and the law of the sea which amongst others:

- recognizes the crucial role of international cooperation at the global, regional, subregional and bilateral levels in combating, in accordance with international law, threats to maritime security, including piracy, armed robbery at sea, terrorist acts against shipping, offshore installations and other maritime interests, through bilateral and multilateral instruments and mechanisms aimed at monitoring, preventing and responding to such threats, the enhanced sharing of information among States relevant to the detection, prevention and suppression of such threats, the prosecution of offenders with due regard to national legislation and the need for sustained capacity-building to support such objectives;
- emphasizes the importance of prompt reporting of incidents to enable accurate information on the scope of the problem of piracy and armed robbery against ships and, in the case of armed robbery against ships, by affected vessels to the coastal State, underlines the importance of effective information-sharing with States potentially affected by incidents of piracy and armed robbery against ships, and takes note of the important role of the IMO;

---

[22] Code of Conduct Concerning the Repression of Piracy and Armed Robbery against Ships in the Western Indian Ocean and the Gulf of Aden, Annex 1 to Resolution 1 adopted on January 29, 2009 at a high-level meeting of 17 States from the Western Indian Ocean, Gulf of Aden and Red Sea areas, convened by IMO in Djibouti to help address the problem of piracy and armed robbery against ships off the coast of Somalia and in the Gulf of Aden.

- calls upon States to take appropriate steps under their national law to facilitate the apprehension and prosecution of those who are alleged to have committed acts of piracy;
- urges all States, in cooperation with the IMO, to actively combat piracy and armed robbery at sea by adopting measures, including those relating to assistance with capacity-building through training of seafarers, port staff and enforcement personnel in the prevention, reporting and investigation of incidents, bringing the alleged perpetrators to justice, in accordance with international law, and by adopting national legislation, as well as providing enforcement vessels and equipment and guarding against fraudulent ship registration;
- welcomes the significant decrease in the number of attacks by pirates and armed robbers in the Asian region through increased national, bilateral and trilateral initiatives as well as regional cooperative mechanisms, and calls upon other States to give immediate attention to adopting, concluding and implementing cooperation agreements on combating piracy and armed robbery against ships at the regional level;
- expresses serious concern regarding the problem of increased instances of piracy and armed robbery at sea off the coast of Somalia, expresses alarm in particular at the recent hijacking of vessels, supports the recent efforts to address this problem at the global and regional levels, notes the adoption by the Security Council of the United Nations of resolutions 1816 (2008) of 2 June 2008 and 1838 (2008) of 7 October 2008, and also notes that the authorization in resolution 1816 (2008) and the provisions in resolution 1838 (2008) apply only to the situation in Somalia and do not affect the rights, obligations or responsibilities of Member States of the United Nations under international law, including any rights or obligations under the United Nations Convention on the Law of the Sea (hereinafter referred to as "UNCLOS"), with respect to any other situation, and underscores in particular that they are not to be considered as establishing customary international law;
- notes the initiatives of the Secretary-General of the IMO, following up on resolution A.1002(25) to engage the international community in efforts to combat acts of piracy and armed robbery against ships sailing the waters off the coast of Somalia; and
- urges States to ensure the full implementation of resolution A.1002(25) on acts of piracy and armed robbery against ships in waters off the coast of Somalia;

NOTING FURTHER that the Security Council of the United Nations has adopted resolutions 1816 (2008), 1838 (2008), 1846 (2008) and 1851 (2008) in relation to piracy and armed robbery in waters off the coast of Somalia,

RECALLING the Assembly of IMO, at its twenty-second regular session, adopted, on 29 November 2001, resolution A.922(22) on the Code of Practice for the Investigation of the Crimes of Piracy and Armed Robbery against Ships which amongst others invited Governments to develop, as appropriate, agreements and procedures to facilitate co-operation in applying efficient and effective measures to prevent acts of piracy and armed robbery against ships;

TAKING INTO ACCOUNT the Special measures to enhance maritime security adopted on 12 December 2002 by the Conference of Contracting Governments to the International Convention for the Safety of Life at Sea, 1974 as amended, including the International Ship and Port Facility Security Code;

INSPIRED by the Regional Cooperation Agreement on Combating Piracy and Armed Robbery against Ships in Asia adopted in Tokyo, Japan on 11 November 2004;

RECOGNIZING the urgent need to devise and adopt effective and practical measures for the suppression of piracy and armed robbery against ships;

RECALLING that the Convention for the Suppression of Unlawful Acts Against the Safety of Maritime Navigation (hereinafter referred to as "SUA Convention") provides for parties to create criminal offences, establish jurisdiction, and accept delivery or persons responsible for or suspected of seizing or exercising control over a ship by force or threat thereof or any other form of intimidation;

DESIRING to promote greater regional co-operation between the Participants, and thereby enhance their effectiveness, in the prevention, interdiction, prosecution, and punishment of those persons engaging in piracy and armed robbery against ships on the basis of mutual respect for the sovereignty, sovereign rights, sovereign equality, jurisdiction, and territorial integrity of States;

WELCOMING the initiatives of IMO, the United Nations Office on Drugs and Crime, the United Nations Development Programme, European Commission, League of Arab States, and other relevant international entities to provide training, technical assistance and other forms of capacity building to assist Governments, upon request, to adopt and implement practical measures to apprehend and prosecute those persons engaging in piracy and armed robbery against ships;

WELCOMING the creation in New York on 14 January 2009 of the Contact Group on Piracy off the coast of Somalia which will help mobilize and co-ordinate contributions to international efforts in the fight against piracy and armed robbery against ships in the waters off the coast of Somalia, pursuant to United Nations Security Council resolution 1851(2008);

NOTING FURTHER the need for a comprehensive approach to address the poverty and instability that create conditions conducive to piracy, which includes strategies for effective environmental conservation and fisheries management, and the need to address the possible environmental consequences of piracy;

Have agreed as follows:

Article 1 – Definitions

For the purposes of this Code of conduct, unless the context otherwise requires:

1. "*Piracy*" consists of any of the following acts:
(a) any illegal acts of violence or detention, or any act of depredation, committed for private ends by the crew or the passengers of a private ship or a private aircraft, and directed:
   (i) on the high seas, against another ship or aircraft, or against persons or property on board such ship or aircraft;
   (ii) against a ship, aircraft, persons or property in a place outside the jurisdiction of any State;
(b) any act of voluntary participation in the operation of a ship or of an aircraft with knowledge of facts making it a pirate ship or aircraft;
(c) any act of inciting or of intentionally facilitating an act described in subparagraph (a) or (b).

2. "*Armed robbery against ships*" consists of any of the following acts:
(a) unlawful act of violence or detention or any act of depredation, or threat thereof, other than an act of piracy, committed for private ends and directed against a ship or against persons or property on board such a ship, within a State's internal waters, archipelagic waters and territorial sea;
(b) any act of inciting or of intentionally facilitating an act described in subparagraph (a).

3.   "*Secretary-General*" means the Secretary-General of the International Maritime Organization.

Article 2 – Purpose and Scope

1.   Consistent with their available resources and related priorities, their respective national laws and regulations, and applicable rules of international law, the Participants intend to co-operate to the fullest possible extent in the repression of piracy and armed robbery against ships with a view towards:

(a) sharing and reporting relevant information;

(b) interdicting ships and/or aircraft suspected of engaging in piracy or armed robbery against ships;

(c) ensuring that persons committing or attempting to commit piracy or armed robbery against ships are apprehended and prosecuted; and

(d) facilitating proper care, treatment, and repatriation for seafarers, fishermen, other shipboard personnel and passengers subject to piracy or armed robbery against ships, particularly those who have been subjected to violence.

2.   The Participants intend this Code of conduct to be applicable in relation to piracy and armed robbery in the Western Indian Ocean and the Gulf of Aden.

Article 3 – Protection Measures for Ships

The Participants intend to encourage States, ship owners, and ship operators, where appropriate, to take protective measures against piracy and armed robbery against ships, taking into account the relevant international standards and practices, and, in particular, recommendations [MSC/Circ.622/Rev.1 on Recommendations to Governments for preventing and suppressing piracy and armed robbery against ships as it may be revised; MSC/Circ.623/Rev.3 on Guidance to shipowners and ship operators, shipmasters and crews on preventing and suppressing acts of piracy and armed robbery against ships as it may be revised] adopted by IMO.

Article 4 – Measures to Repress Piracy

1.   The provisions of this Article are intended to apply only to piracy.

2.   For purposes of this Article and of Article 10, "pirate ship" means a ship intended by the persons in dominant control to be used for the purpose of committing piracy, or if the ship has been used to commit any such act, so long as it remains under the control of those persons.

3.   Consistent with Article 2, each Participant to the fullest possible extent intends to co-operate in:

(a) arresting, investigating, and prosecuting persons who have committed piracy or are reasonably suspected of committing piracy;

(b) seizing pirate ships and/or aircraft and the property on board such ships and/or aircraft; and

(c) rescuing ships, persons, and property subject to piracy.

4.   Any Participant may seize a pirate ship beyond the outer limit of any State's territorial sea, and arrest the persons and seize the property on board.

5.   Any pursuit of a ship, where there are reasonable grounds to suspect that the ship is engaged in piracy, extending in and over the territorial sea of a Participant is subject to the

authority of that Participant. No Participant should pursue such a ship in or over the territory or territorial sea of any coastal State without the permission of that State.

6. Consistent with international law, the courts of the Participant which carries out a seizure pursuant to paragraph 4 may decide upon the penalties to be imposed, and may also determine the action to be taken with regard to the ship or property, subject to the rights of third parties acting in good faith.

7. The Participant which carried out the seizure pursuant to paragraph 4 may, subject to its national laws, and in consultation with other interested entities, waive its primary right to exercise jurisdiction and authorize any other Participant to enforce its laws against the ship and/or persons on board.

8. Unless otherwise arranged by the affected Participants, any seizure made in the territorial sea of a Participant pursuant to paragraph 5 should be subject to the jurisdiction of that Participant.

Article 5 – Measures to Repress Armed Robbery against Ships

1. The provisions of this Article are intended to apply only to armed robbery against ships.

2. The Participants intend for operations to suppress armed robbery against ships in the territorial sea and airspace of a Participant to be subject to the authority of that Participant, including in the case of hot pursuit from that Participant's territorial sea or archipelagic waters in accordance with Article 111 of UNCLOS.

3. The Participants intend for their respective focal points and Centres (as designated pursuant to Article 8) to communicate expeditiously alerts, reports, and information related to armed robbery against ships to other Participants and interested parties.

Article 6 – Measures in All Cases

1. The Participants intend that any measures taken pursuant to this Code of conduct should be carried out by law enforcement or other authorized officials from warships or military aircraft, or from other ships or aircraft clearly marked and identifiable as being in government service and authorized to that effect.

2. The Participants recognize that multiple States, including the flag State, State of suspected origin of the perpetrators, the State of nationality of persons on board the ship, and the State of ownership of cargo may have legitimate interests in cases arising pursuant to Articles 4 and 5. Therefore, the Participants intend to liaise and co-operate with such States and other stakeholders, and to coordinate such activities with each other to facilitate the rescue, interdiction, investigation, and prosecution.

3. The Participants intend, to the fullest possible extent, to conduct and support the conduct of investigations in cases of piracy and armed robbery against ships taking into account the relevant international standards and practices, and, in particular, recommendations [Resolution A.922(22) on the Code of Practice for the Investigation of the Crimes of Piracy and Armed Robbery against Ships as it may be revised] adopted by IMO.

4. The Participants intend to co-operate to the fullest possible extent in medical and decedent affairs arising from operations in furtherance of the repression of piracy and armed robbery against ships.

Article 7 – Embarked Officers

1. In furtherance of operations contemplated by this Code of conduct, a Participant may nominate law enforcement or other authorized officials (hereafter referred to as "the embarked officers") to embark in the patrol ships or aircraft of another Participant (hereafter referred to as "the host Participant") as may be authorized by the host Participant.

2. The embarked officers may be armed in accordance with their national law and policy and the approval of the host Participant.

3. When embarked, the host Participant should facilitate communications between the embarked officers and their headquarters, and should provide messing and quarters for the embarked officers aboard the patrol ships or aircraft in a manner consistent with host Participant personnel of the same rank.

4. Embarked officers may assist the host Participant and conduct operations from the host Participant ship or aircraft if expressly requested to do so by the host Participant, and only in the manner requested. Such request may only be made, agreed to, and acted upon in a manner that is not prohibited by the laws and policies of both Participants.

Article 8 – Coordination and Information Sharing

1. Each Participant should designate a national focal point to facilitate coordinated, timely, and effective information flow among the Participants consistent with the purpose and scope of this Code of conduct. In order to ensure coordinated, smooth, and effective communications between their designated focal points, the Participants intend to use the piracy information exchange centres Kenya, United Republic of Tanzania and Yemen (hereinafter referred to as "the Centres"). The Centres in Kenya and the United Republic of Tanzania will be situated in the maritime rescue co-ordination centre in Mombasa and the sub-regional co-ordination centre in Dar es Salaam, respectively. The Centre in Yemen will be situated in the regional maritime information centre to be established in Yemen based on the outcomes of the sub-regional meetings held by IMO in Sana'a in 2005 and Muscat in 2006 and Dar es Salaam. Each Centre and designated focal point should be capable of receiving and responding to alerts and requests for information or assistance at all times.

2. Each Participant intends to:

(a) declare and communicate to the other Participants its designated focal point at the time of signing this Code of conduct or as soon as possible after signing, and thereafter update the information as and when changes occur;

(b) provide and communicate to the other Participants the telephone numbers, telefax numbers, and e-mail addresses of its focal point, and, as appropriate, of its Centre and thereafter update the information as and when changes occur; and

(c) communicate to the Secretary-General the information referred to in subparagraphs (a) and (b) and thereafter update the information as and when changes occur.

3. Each Centre and focal point should be responsible for its communication with the other focal points and the Centres. Any focal point which has received or obtained information about an imminent threat of, or an incident of, piracy or armed robbery against ships should promptly disseminate an alert with all relevant information to the Centres. The Centres should disseminate appropriate alerts within their respective areas of responsibility regarding imminent threats or incidents to ships.

4. Each Participant should ensure the smooth and effective communication between its designated focal point, and other competent national authorities including search and rescue coordination centres, as well as relevant non-governmental organizations.

5. Each Participant should make every effort to require ships entitled to fly its flag and the owners and operators of such ships to promptly notify relevant national authorities, including the designated focal points and Centres, the appropriate search and rescue coordination centres and other relevant the contact points [For example the Maritime Liaison Office Bahrain (MARLO), the United Kingdom Maritime Trade Office Dubai (UKMTO)], of incidents of piracy or armed robbery against ships.

6. Each Participant intends, upon the request of any other Participant, to respect the confidentiality of information transmitted from a Participant.

7. To facilitate implementation of this Code of conduct, the Participants intend to keep each other fully informed concerning their respective applicable laws and guidance, particularly those pertaining to the interdiction, apprehension, investigation, prosecution, and disposition of persons involved in piracy and armed robbery against ships. The Participants may also undertake and seek assistance to undertake publication of handbooks and convening of seminars and conferences in furtherance of this Code of conduct.

Article 9 – Incident Reporting

1. The Participants intend to undertake development of uniform reporting criteria in order to ensure that an accurate assessment of the threat of piracy and armed robbery in the Western Indian Ocean and the Gulf of Aden is developed taking into account the recommendations [MSC/Circ.622/Rev.1 on Recommendations to Governments for preventing and suppressing piracy and armed robbery against ships as it may be revised; MSC/Circ.623/Rev.3 on Guidance to shipowners and ship operators, shipmasters and crews on preventing and suppressing acts of piracy and armed robbery against ships as it may be revised] adopted by IMO. The Participants intend for the Centres to manage the collection and dissemination of this information in their respective geographic areas of responsibility.

2. Consistent with its laws and policies, a Participant conducting a boarding, investigation, prosecution, or judicial proceeding pursuant to this Code of conduct should promptly notify any affected flag and coastal States and the Secretary-General of the results.

3. The Participants intend for the Centres to:

(a) collect, collate and analyze the information transmitted by the Participants concerning piracy and armed robbery against ships, including other relevant information relating to individuals and transnational organized criminal groups committing piracy and armed robbery against ships in their respective geographical areas of responsibility; and

(b) prepare statistics and reports on the basis of the information gathered and analyzed under subparagraph (a), and to disseminate them to the Participants, the shipping community, and the Secretary-General.

Article 10 – Assistance among Participants

1. A Participant may request any other Participant, through the Centres or directly, to cooperate in detecting any of the following persons, ships, or aircraft:

(a) persons who have committed, or are reasonably suspected of committing, piracy;

(b) persons who have committed, or are reasonably suspected of committing, armed robbery against ships;

(c) pirate ships or ships, where there are reasonable grounds to suspect that those ships are engaged in piracy; and

(d) ships or persons who have been subjected to piracy or armed robbery against ships.

2. A Participant may also request any other Participant, through the Centres or directly, to take effective measures in response to reported piracy or armed robbery against ships.

3. Co-operative arrangements such as joint exercises or other forms of co-operation, as appropriate, may be undertaken as determined by the Participants concerned.

4. Capacity building co-operation may include technical assistance such as educational and training programmes to share experiences and best practice.

Article 11 – Review of National Legislation

In order to allow for the prosecution, conviction and punishment of those involved in piracy or armed robbery against ships, and to facilitate extradition or handing over when prosecution is not possible, each Participant intends to review its national legislation with a view towards ensuring that there are national laws in place to criminalize piracy and armed robbery against ships, and adequate guidelines for the exercise of jurisdiction, conduct of investigations, and prosecutions of alleged offenders.

Article 12 – Dispute Settlement

The Participants intend to settle by consultation and peaceful means amongst each other any disputes that arise from the implementation of this Code of conduct.

Article 13 – Consultations

Within two years of the effective date of this Code of conduct, and having designated the national focal points referred to in Article 8, the Participants intend to consult, with the assistance of IMO, with the aim of arriving at a binding agreement.

Article 14 – Claims

Any claim for damages, injury or loss resulting from an operation carried out under this Code of conduct should be examined by the Participant whose authorities conducted the operation. If responsibility is established, the claim should be resolved in accordance with the national law of that Participant, and in a manner consistent with international law, including Article 106 and paragraph 3 of Article 110 of UNCLOS.

Article 15 – Miscellaneous Provisions

Nothing in this Code of conduct is intended to:

(a) create or establish a binding agreement, except as noted in Article 13;

(b) affect in any way the rules of international law pertaining to the competence of States to exercise investigative or enforcement jurisdiction on board ships not flying their flag;

(c) affect the immunities of warships and other government ships operated for non-commercial purposes;

(d) apply to or limit boarding of ships conducted by any Participant in accordance with international law, beyond the outer limit of any State's territorial sea, including boardings based upon the right of visit, the rendering of assistance to persons, ships and property in distress or peril, or an authorization from the flag State to take law enforcement or other action;

(e) preclude the Participants from otherwise agreeing on operations or other forms of co-operation to repress piracy and armed robbery against ships;

(f) prevent the Participants from taking additional measures to repress piracy and armed robbery at sea through appropriate actions in their land territory;

(g) supersede any bilateral or multilateral agreement or other co-operative mechanism concluded by the Participants to repress piracy and armed robbery against ships;

(h) alter the rights and privileges due to any individual in any legal proceeding;

(i) create or establish any waiver of any rights that any Participant may have under international law to raise a claim with any other Participant through diplomatic channels;

(j) entitle a Participant to undertake in the territory of another Participant the exercise of jurisdiction and performance of functions which are exclusively reserved for the authorities of that other Participant by its national law;

(k) prejudice in any manner the positions and navigational rights and freedoms of any Participant regarding the international law of the sea;

(l) be deemed a waiver, express or implied, of any of the privileges and immunities of the Participants to this Code of conduct as provided under international or national law; or

(m) preclude or limit any Participant from requesting or granting assistance in accordance with the provisions of any applicable Mutual Legal Assistance Agreement or similar instrument.

Article 16 – Signature and Effective Date

1. The Code of conduct is open for signature by Participants on 29 January 2009 and at the Headquarters of IMO from 1 February 2009.

2. The Code of conduct will become effective upon the date of signature by two or more Participants and effective for subsequent Participants upon their respective date of deposit of a signature instrument with the Secretary-General.

Article 17 – Languages

This Code of conduct is established in the Arabic, English and French languages, each text being equally authentic.

DONE in Djibouti this twenty-ninth day of January two thousand and nine.

IN WITNESS WHEREOF the undersigned, being duly authorized by their respective Governments for that purpose, have signed this Code of conduct.

Signed (signatures omitted) in Djibouti on 29 January 2009 by Djibouti, Ethiopia, Kenya, Madagascar, Maldives, Seychelles, Somalia, United Republic of Tanzania and Yemen.

Kenyan Merchant Shipping Act 2009[23] (excerpts)

Part XVI – Maritime Security

Section 369 – Interpretation

(1) In this Part –

"armed robbery against ships" means any unlawful act of violence or detention or any act of depredation, or threat thereof, other than an act of piracy, directed against persons or property on board such a ship, within territorial waters or waters under Kenya's jurisdiction;

"piracy" means –

(a) any act of violence or detention, or any act of depredation, committed for private ends by the crew or the passengers of a private ship or a private aircraft, and directed –

   (i) against another ship or aircraft, or against persons or property on board such ship or aircraft; or

   (ii) against a ship, aircraft, persons or property in a place outside the jurisdiction of any State;

(b) any voluntary act of participation in the operation of a ship or of an aircraft with knowledge of facts making it a pirate ship or aircraft; or

(c) any act of inciting or of intentionally facilitating an act described in paragraph (a) or (b);

"pirate ship or aircraft" means a ship or aircraft under the dominant control of persons who –

(a) intend to use such ship or aircraft for piracy; or

(b) have used such ship or aircraft for piracy, so long as it remains under the control of those persons;

"private ship" and "private aircraft" means a ship or aircraft that is not owned by the Government or held by a person on behalf of, or for the benefit of, the Government; and

"UNCLOS" means the United Nations Convention on the Law of the Sea, 1982.

(2) Piracy committed by a warship, government ship or government aircraft whose crew has mutinied and taken control of the ship or aircraft is assimilated to piracy committed by a private ship or aircraft.

(3) This Part applies to aircraft only when they are on the high seas, that is to say, in those parts of the sea to which Part VII of UNCLOS is applicable, in accordance with Article 86 of UNCLOS.

---

[23] Kenyan Merchant Shipping Act (entry into force on Sept. 1, 2009), Part XVI – Maritime Security, *available at* www.kenyalaw.org/kenyalaw/klr_home/ (last visited Feb. 10, 2010).

Offences Against Safety of Ships

Section 370 – Hijacking and destroying of ships

(1) Subject to subsection (5), a person who unlawfully, by the use of force or by threats of any kind, seizes a ship or exercises control of it commits the offence of hijacking a ship.

(2) Subject to subsection (5), a person commits an offence if he unlawfully and intentionally –

(a) destroys a ship;

(b) damages a ship or its cargo so as to endanger, or to be likely to endanger, the safe navigation of the ship;

(c) commits, on board a ship, an act of violence which is likely to endanger the safe navigation of the ship; or

(d) places or causes to be placed on a ship any device or substance which is likely to destroy the ship or is likely so to damage it or its cargo as to endanger its safe navigation.

(3) Nothing in subsection (2) (d) is to be construed as limiting the circumstances in which the commission of any act may constitute –

(a) an offence under subsection (2) (a), (b) or (c); or

(b) attempting or conspiring to commit, or aiding, abetting, counselling, procuring or inciting, or being of and part in, the commission of such an offence.

(4) Subject to subsection (5), subsections (1) and (2) shall apply –

(a) whether the ship referred to in those subsections is in Kenya or elsewhere;

(b) whether any such act as is mentioned in those subsections is committed in Kenya or elsewhere; and

(c) whatever the nationality of the person committing the act.

(5) Subsections (1) and (2) shall not apply in relation to any warship or any other ship used as a naval auxiliary or in customs or police service, or any act committed in relation to such a warship or such other ship unless the –

(a) person seizing or exercising control of the ship under subsection (1), or committing the act under subsection (2), as the case may be, is a Kenyan citizen;

(b) act is committed in Kenya; or

(c) ship is used in the customs service of Kenya or in the service of the police force in Kenya.

(6) A person who commits an offence under this section shall be liable, upon conviction, to imprisonment for life.

(7) In this section –

"act of violence" means any act done –

(a) in Kenya which constitutes the offence of murder, attempted murder, manslaughter, or assault; or

(b) outside Kenya which, if done in Kenya would constitute such an offence as is mentioned in paragraph (a); and

"unlawfully" –

(a) in relation to the commission of an act in Kenya, means so as (apart from this Part) to constitute an offence under the law of Kenya; and

(b) in relation to the commission of an act outside Kenya, means that the commission of the act would (apart from this Part) have been an offence under the law of Kenya if it had been committed in Kenya.

Section 371 – Offences of piracy and armed robbery

Any person who –

(a) commits any act of piracy;

(b) in territorial waters, commits any act of armed robbery against ships

shall be liable, upon conviction, to imprisonment for life.

Section 372 – Endangering safe navigation, threats, etc.

(1) Subject to subsection (8), it is an offence for any person unlawfully or intentionally to –

(a) destroy or damage any property to which this subsection applies; or

(b) interfere with the operation of any such property,

where the destruction, damage or interference is likely to endanger the safe navigation of any ship.

(2) Subsection (1) applies to any property used for the provision of maritime navigation facilities, including any land, building or ship so used, and including any apparatus or equipment so used, whether it is on board a ship or elsewhere.

(3) Subject to subsection (8), it is an offence for any person intentionally to communicate that which he knows to be false in a material particular, where the communication of the information endangers the safe navigation of any ship.

(4) It is a defence for a person charged with an offence under subsection (3) to prove that, when he communicated the information, he was lawfully employed to perform duties which consisted of or included the communication of information, and that he communicated the information in good faith in performance of those duties.

(5) A person commits an offence if –

(a) in order to compel any other person to do or abstain from doing any act, he threatens that he or some other person will do in relation to any ship an act which is an offence by virtue of section 372(2)(a), (b) or (c); and

(b) the making of that threat is likely to endanger the safe navigation of the ship.

(6) Subject to subsection (8), a person commits an offence if –

(a) in order to compel any other person to do or abstain from doing any act, he threatens that he or some other person will do an act which is an offence by virtue of subsection (1); and

(b) the making of that threat is likely to endanger the safe navigation of any ship.

(7) Except as provided by subsection (8), subsections (1), (3), (5) and (6) applies whether any such act as is mentioned in those subsections is committed in Kenya or elsewhere and whatever the nationality of the person committing the act.

(8) For the purposes of subsections (1), (3) and (6)(b), any danger, or likelihood of danger, to the safe navigation of a warship or any other ship used as a naval auxiliary or in customs or police service is to be disregarded unless the –

(a) person committing the act is a Kenyan citizen;

(b) act is committed in Kenya.

Bibliography

African Press Organization, Seychelles and the USA Sign Piracy Agreement, July 14, 2010, *available at* http://appablog.wordpress.com/2010/07/14/seychelles-and-the-usa-sign-piracy-agreement/ (last visited Aug. 30, 2010).

Agence France Press, Dutch Seek Extradition of Somali Pirates, Jan. 15, 2009, *available at* www.google.com/hostednews/afp/article/ALeqM5hMfTxjAVudEutFTdRutwzyRn5nKA (last visited Aug. 30, 2010).

Agence France Press/Expatica, Netherlands Proposes International Anti-Piracy Tribunal, May 30, 2009, *available at* www.expatica.com/nl/news/dutch-news/Netherlands-pro poses-international-anti_piracy-tribunal_53106.html (last visited Aug. 30, 2010).

Ambos, Kai, Internationales Strafrecht, 2nd ed. München 2008.

American Society of International Law (publ.), Supplement: Research in International Law, Competence of Courts in Regard to Foreign States, Part IV – Piracy, American Journal of International Law 26 (1932), 739–885 (cit. ASIL-Commented Harvard Draft Convention on Piracy).

American Society of International Law (publ.), Supplement: Research in International Law, Competence of Courts in Regard to Foreign States, Part V – A Collection of Piracy Laws of Various Countries, American Journal of International Law 26 (1932), 887–1013 (cit. ASIL, A Collection of Piracy Laws in Various Countries).

American Society of International Law (publ.), Supplement: Research in International Law, General Introduction, American Journal of International Law 26 (1932), 1–14 (cit. ASIL, Harvard Research, General Introduction).

American Society of International Law (publ.), Supplement: Research in International Law, Jurisdiction with Respect to Crime, American Journal of International Law 29 (1935), 439–651 (cit. ASIL-Commented Harvard Draft Convention on Jurisdiction with Respect to Crime).

Amnesty International, Abolitionist and Retentionist Countries, *available at* www.amnes ty.org/en/death-penalty/abolitionist-and-retentionist-countries (last visited Aug. 30, 2010).

Amnesty International, Dangerous Deals – Europe's Reliance on "Diplomatic Assurances" Against Torture, 2010, *available at* www.amnesty.org/en/library/asset/EUR01/012/2010/ en/608f128b-9eac-4e2f-b73b-6d747a8cbaed/eur010122010en.pdf (last visited Aug. 30, 2010).

Amnesty International, Somalia Pirates Hold 130 Hostages after Hijacking Nine Ships, Sept. 10, 2008, *available at* www.amnesty.org.uk/news_details.asp?NewsID=17875 (last visited Aug. 30, 2010).

Aust, Anthony, Lockerbie: The Other Case, International and Comparative Law Quarterly 49 (2000), 278–296.

Barston, Ronald, United Nations Conference on Straddling and Highly Migratory Fish Stocks, Marine Policy 19 (1995), 159–166.

BBC News, Five Somali Men Jailed for Piracy by Dutch Court, June 17, 2010, *available at* http://news.bbc.co.uk/2/hi/europe/10342547.stm (last visited Aug. 30, 2010).

BBC News, Kenya Ends Somali Pirate Trials, April 1, 2010, *available at* http://news.bbc.co.uk/2/hi/africa/8599347.stm (last visited Aug. 30, 2010).

BBC News, Q&A: What Do You Do With a Captured Pirate? June 24, 2010, *available at* http://news.bbc.co.uk/2/hi/africa/8664623.stm (last visited Aug. 30, 2010).

BBC News, Somali "Pirates" Face Dutch Court, Feb. 11, 2009, *available at* http://news.bbc.co.uk/2/hi/europe/10342547.stm (last visited Aug. 30, 2010).

BBC News, Yemen Sentences Somali Pirates to Death, May 18, 2010, *available at* http://news.bbc.co.uk/2/hi/middle_east/8689129.stm (last visited Aug. 30, 2010).

Bell, Caitlin, Reassessing Multiple Attribution: The International Law Commission and The Behrami and Saramati Decision, New York University Journal of International Law and Politics, 42 (2010), 501–548.

Bodeau-Livinec, Pierre/Buzzini, Gionata/Villalpando, Santiago, Agim Behrami & Bekir Behrami v. France; Ruzhdi Saramati v. France, Germany & Norway. Joined App. Nos. 71412/01 & 78166/01, AJIL 102 (2008), 323–331.

Boyle, Robert/Pulsifer, Roy, The Tokyo Convention on Offenses and Certain Other Acts Committed on Board Aircraft, Journal of Air Law and Commerce 30 (1964), 305–354.

Broda, Christian/Weinstein, David, Globalization and the Gains from Variety, Quarterly Journal of Economics 121 (2006), 541–585.

Brownlie, Ian, Principles of Public International Law, 7th ed. Cambridge 2008.

Byers, Michael, Policing the High Seas: The Proliferation Security Initiative, American Journal of International Law 98 (2004), 526–545.

Byers, Michael, Proliferation Security Initiative (PSI). In: Rüdiger Wolfrum (ed.), The Max Planck Encyclopedia of Public International Law, online edition, *available at* www.mpepil.com (last visited Aug. 30, 2010).

Cala, Andrés, The New York Times, Spain Arraigns Somalis Suspected of Piracy, Oct. 13, 2009, *available at* www.nytimes.com/2009/10/14/world/europe/14iht-spain.html (last visited Aug. 30, 2010).

Council of Europe, EU Accession to the European Convention on Human Rights, *available at* www.coe.int/t/dc/files/themes/eu_and_coe/default_EN.asp (last visited Aug. 30, 2010).

Council of Europe, European Commission for Democracy through Law, Opinion on Human Rights in Kosovo: Possible Establishment of Review Mechanisms, adopted by the Venice Commission at its 60th plenary session, Strasbourg, Oct. 11, 2004, Opinion No. 280/2004, CDL-AD 2004(033), *available at* www.venice.coe.int/docs/2004/CDL-AD%282004%29033-e.pdf (last visited Aug. 30, 2010).

Council of Europe, European Committee on Crime Problems, Extraterritorial Criminal Jurisdiction, Report reprinted in Criminal Law Forum 3 (1992), 441–480.

Council of Europe, Extradition – European Standards, Strasbourg 2006 (cit. Council of Europe, Extradition).

Crocket, Clyde, Toward a Revision of the International Law of Piracy, DePaul Law Review 26 (1976), 78–99.

Dahm, Georg, Das materielle Völkerstrafrecht. Göttingen 1956.

Dalton, Jane/Roach, Ashley/Daley, John, Introductory Note to United Nations Security Council: Piracy and Armed Robbery at Sea – Resolutions 1816, 1846 & 1851, ILM 48 (2009), 129–142.

Der Spiegel, Somalische Piraten in Deutschland eingetroffen, June 10, 2010, *available at* www.spiegel.de/politik/deutschland/0,1518,700035,00.html (last visited Aug. 30, 2010).

Deutscher Bundestag, 16. Wahlperiode, Antwort der Bundesregierung auf die Kleine Anfrage der Abgeordneten Birgit Homburger, Dr. Rainer Stinner, Elke Hoff, weiterer Abgeordneter und der Fraktion der FDP, Beteiligung deutscher Soldaten am geplanten EU-Einsatz "Atalanta," Drucksache 16/11088, 12.12.2008.

Dickinson, Edward, Is the Crime of Piracy Obsolete? Harvard Law Review 38 (1925), 334–360.

Diekhans, Antje, ARD, Die Anti-Piraten-Mission "Atalanta" – Erfolgreich oder über-fordert? Dec. 9, 2010, *available at* www.tagesschau.de/ausland/atalanta110.html (last visited Aug. 30, 2010).

Droege, Cordula, Transfers of Detainees: Legal Framework, Non-Refoulement, and Contemporary Challenges, IRRC 90 (2008), 669–701.

Dupuy, René/Vignes, Daniel, A Handbook on the New Law of the Sea. Dordrecht a.o. 1991.

Duttwiler, Michael/Petrig, Anna, Neue Aspekte der extraterritorialen Anwendbarkeit der EMRK, Aktuelle Juristische Praxis 10 (2009), 1247–1260.

Encyclopædia Britannica Online, Gulf of Aden, *available at* www.search.eb.com/eb/article-9003716 (last visited Feb. 10, 2010).

Erie, Steven, Globalizing L.A.: Trade, Infrastructure, and Regional Development. Stanford 2004 (cit. *Erie*, Globalizing L.A.).

European Space Agency, Earth from Space: The Gulf of Aden – The Gateway to Persian Oil, April 13, 2006, *available at* www.esa.int/esaEO/SEMWOXNFGLE_index_2.html (last visited Aug. 30, 2010).

European Union, Council of the European Union, EU Naval Operation against Piracy, Factsheet, Feb. 1, 2010, *available at* http://consilium.europa.eu/showPage.aspx?id=1521 &lang=en (last visited Aug. 30, 2010).

European Union, Council of the European Union, News in Brief, Pirates Head East to Counter EUNAVFOR Success, April 20, 2010, *available at* http://consilium.europa. eu/showPage.aspx?id=1567&lang=en (last visited Aug. 30, 2010).

European Union, Council of the European Union, Operation EUNAVFOR, Current Total Strength of EU-NAVFOR Atalanta, *available at* http://consilium.europa.eu/uedocs/cmsUpload/naviresOCTOBRE.pdf (last visited Aug. 30, 2010).

European Union, Council of the European Union, Press Release, Foreign Affairs, 3005th Council Meeting, 7828/1/10 REV 1 (Presse 73), March 22, 2010, *available at* www.consilium.europa.eu/uedocs/cms_data/docs/pressdata/EN/foraff/113482.pdf (last visited Aug. 30, 2010).

Financial Times, Piraten kommen nicht nach Deutschland, March 7, 2009, *available at* www.ftd.de/politik/international/:Festnahmen-am-Horn-von-Afrika-Deutscher-Haftbefehl-gegen-Piraten/483948.html (last visited Aug. 30, 2010).

Fischer-Lescano, Andreas, Bundesmarine als Polizei der Weltmeere? Zeitschrift für öffentliches Recht in Norddeutschland 12 (2009), 49–56.

Flintoff, Corey, NPR, Prosecuting Pirates May Not Be Easy, April 23, 2010, *available at* www.npr.org/templates/story/story.php?storyId=126218804 (last visited Aug. 30, 2010).

Freestone, David, International Cooperation against Terrorism and the Development of International Law Principles of Jurisdiction. In: Rosalyn Higgins/Maurice Flory (eds.), Terrorism and International Law. London a.o. 1997, 43–68 (cit. *Freestone*, in: Higgins/ Flory (eds.), Principles of Jurisdiction).

Frowein, Jochen, Der Terrorismus als Herausforderung für das Völkerrecht, Heidelberg Journal of International Law 62 (2002), 879–905.

Frowein, Jochen/Krisch, Nico, Article 42 UN-Charter. In: Bruno Simma (ed.), The Charter of the United Nations, A Commentary, Volume I, 2nd ed. Oxford 2002 (cit. *Frowein/ Krisch*, in: Simma (ed.), UN-Charter).

Frowein, Jochen/Peukert, Wolfgang, Europäische Menschenrechtskonvention – EMRK Kommentar, 3rd ed. Kehl 2009 (cit. *Frowein/Peukert*, EMRK-Kommentar).

Garner, Bryan, Black's Law Dictionary, 9th ed. St. Paul 2009.

Geiß, Robin, Failed States – Die normative Erfassung gescheiterter Staaten. Berlin 2005 (cit. *Geiß*, Failed States).

Geiß, Robin, Qualifying Armed Violence in Fragile States – Low Intensity Conflicts, Spill Over Conflicts and Sporadic Law Enforcement Operations by External Actors, IRRC 91 (2009), 127–142.

Gilmore, Wiliam, Agreement Concerning Co-Operation in Suppressing Illicit Maritime and Air Trafficking in Narcotic Drugs and Psychotropic Substances in the Carribbean Area, 2003. Norwich 2005 (cit. *Gilmore*, Caribbean Regional Agreement).

Globalsecurity.org, Limburg Oiltanker Attacked, *available at* www.globalsecurity.org/ security/profiles/limburg_oil_tanker_attacked.htm (last visited Aug. 30, 2010).

Globalsecurity.org, USS Cole Bombing, *available at* www.globalsecurity.org/security/ profiles/uss_cole_bombing.htm (last visited Aug. 30, 2010).

Goodwin, Joshua, Universal Jurisdiction and the Pirate: Time for an Old Couple to Part, Vanderbilt Journal of Transnational Law 39 (2006), 973–1011.

Gros-Verheyde, Nicolas, Comment les pirates arrêtés sont jugés? Le point ..., Jan. 10, 2010, *available at* http://bruxelles2.over-blog.com/article-comment-sont-juges-les-pira tes-arretes-le-point--42673756.html (last visited Aug. 30, 2010).

Guilfoyle, Douglas, Counter-Piracy Law Enforcement and Human Rights, International and Comparative Law Quarterly 59 (2010), 141–169.

Guilfoyle, Douglas, Shipping Interdiction and the Law of the Sea. Cambridge 2009 (cit. *Guilfoyle*, Shipping Interdiction).

Guilfoyle, Douglas, Treaty Jurisdiction over Pirates: A Compilation of Legal Texts with Introductory Notes, Prepared for the 3rd Meeting of Working Group 2 on Legal Issues, Copenhagen, 26–27 August 2009.

Guilfoyle, Douglas, UN Security Council Resolution 1816 and IMO Regional Counter-Piracy Efforts, International and Comparative Law Quarterly 57 (2008), 690–699.

Halberstam, Malvina, International Maritime Navigation and Installations on the High Seas. In: Bassiouni, Cherif (ed.), International Criminal Law, Volume I – Crimes. 2nd ed. New York 1992, 819–835 (cit. *Halberstam*, in: Bassiouni (ed.), International Maritime Navigation).

Halberstam, Malvina, Terrorism on High Seas: The Achille Lauro, Piracy and the IMO Convention on Maritime Safety, American Journal of International Law 82 (1988), 269–310.

Hayashi, Moritaka, Introductory Note – Regional Cooperation Agreement on Combating Piracy and Armed Robbery against Ships in Asia, International Legal Materials 4 (2005), 826–828.

Heintschel von Heinegg, Wolff, The Proliferation Security Initiative – Security vs. Freedom of Navigation? Israel Yearbook on Human Rights 35 (2005), 181–203.

Human Rights Watch, Not the Way Forward – The UK's Dangerous Reliance on Diplomatic Assurances, Oct. 22, 2008, *available at* www.hrw.org/en/node/75603/section/1 (last visited Aug. 30, 2010).

International Chamber of Commerce – International Maritime Bureau, Piracy and Armed Robbery against Ships, Annual Report 1 January – 31 December 2009 (cit. ICC-IMB, Piracy Report 2009).

International Chamber of Commerce – International Maritime Bureau, Piracy and Armed Robbery against Ships, Report 1 January – 30 September 2009 (cit. ICC-IMB, Piracy Report January-September 2009).

International Chamber of Commerce – International Maritime Bureau, Piracy Prone Areas and Warnings, *available at* www.icc-ccs.org (follow "IMB Piracy Reporting Center" hyperlink, then follow "Piracy Prone Areas and Warnings" hyperlink) (last visited Aug. 30, 2010) (cit. ICC-IMB, Piracy Prone Areas and Warnings).

International Chamber of Commerce – International Maritime Bureau, Worldwide Piracy Figures Surpass 400, Jan. 14, 2010, *available at* www.icc-ccs.org (follow "News" hyperlink) (last visited Aug. 30, 2010) (cit. ICC-IMB, Worldwide Piracy Figures Surpass 400).

International Commission of Jurists, Assessing Damage, Urging Action – Report of the Eminent Jurists Panel on Terrorism, Counter-Terrorism and Human Rights, May 4, 2009, *available at* www.icj.org (follow "Publications" hyperlink, then follow "Panel Series" hyperlink) (last visited Aug. 30, 2010).

International Maritime Organization, Code of Practice for the Investigation of the Crimes of Piracy and Armed Robbery against Ships, IMO Doc. A22/Res.922 (Jan. 22, 2009).

International Maritime Organization, High-Level Meeting in Djibouti Adopts a Code of Conduct to Repress Acts of Piracy and Armed Robbery against Ships, Jan. 30, 2009, *available at* www.imo.org/newsroom/mainframe.asp?topic_id=1773&doc_id=10933 (last visited Aug. 30, 2010).

International Maritime Organization, Piracy and Armed Robbery against Ships, Guidance to Shipowners and Ship Operators, Shipmasters and Crews on Preventing and Suppressing Acts of Piracy and Armed Robbery against Ships, IMO Doc. MSC/Circ.623/Rev.3 (May 29, 2002).

International Maritime Organization, Piracy and Armed Robbery against Ships, Recommendations to Governments for Preventing and Suppressing Piracy and Armed Robbery against Ships, IMO Doc. MSC/Circ.622/Rev.1 (June 16, 1999).

International Maritime Organization, Piracy and Armed Robbery against Ships in Waters off the Coast of Somalia, Information on Internationally Recommended Transit Corridor (IRTC) for ships Transiting the Gulf of Aden, IMO Doc. SN.1/Circ.281 (Aug. 3, 2009).

International Maritime Organization, Piracy and Armed Robbery against Ships in Waters off the Coast of Somalia, IMO Doc. MSC.1/Circ.1335 (Sept. 29, 2009).

International Maritime Organization, Report of the Legal Committee on the Work of its Nineteenth Session, IMO Doc. LEG 90/15 (May 9, 2005).

International Maritime Organization, Reports on Acts of Piracy and Armed Robbery Against Ships, Annual Report – 2006, IMO Doc. MSC.4/Circ.98 (April 13, 2007) (cit. IMO, Piracy Report 2006).

International Maritime Organization, Reports on Acts of Piracy and Armed Robbery Against Ships, Annual Report – 2009, IMO Doc. MSC.4/Circ.152 (March 29, 2010) (cit. IMO, Piracy Report 2009).

International Maritime Organization, Resolution A.1026(26), adopted on 2 December 2009, Piracy and Armed Robbery against Ships in Waters off the Coast of Somalia, IMO Doc. A.26/Res.1026 (Dec. 3, 2009).

International Maritime Organization, Saudi Arabia Signs Djibouti Anti-Piracy Code, Press Release, March 10, 2010, *available at* www.imo.org/inforesource/mainframe.asp?topic_id=1859&doc_id=12603 (last visited Aug. 30, 2010).

International Maritime Organization, Status of Multilateral Conventions and Instruments in Respect of which the International Maritime Organization (IMO) or its Secretary-General Performs Depositary or Other Functions as at 31 December 2009, *available at* www.imo.org (follow "legal" hyperlink, then follow "IMO Conventions" hyperlink, the follow "Depositary Information on IMO Conventions" hyperlink).

International Maritime Organization, United States of America Delegation, White Paper on Article 8*bis* of the SUA Convention (Dec. 22, 2003).

Jay, Carmella, Jurist, Seychelles Announces Creation of UN-backed Piracy Court, May 6, 2010, *available at* http://jurist.org/paperchase/2010/05/seychelles-announces-creation-of-un-backed-piracy-court.php (last visited Aug. 30, 2010).

Jessup, Philip, The Law of Territorial Waters and Maritime Jurisdiction, New York 1927.

Kamminga, Menno, Extraterritoriality. In: Rüdiger Wolfrum (ed.), The Max Planck Encyclopedia of Public International Law, online edition, *available at* www.mpepil.com (last visited Aug. 30, 2010) (cit. *Kamminga*, in: Wolfrum (ed.), EPIL-Extraterritoriality).

König, Doris, Flag of Convenience. In: Rüdiger Wolfrum (ed.), The Max Planck Encyclopedia of Public International Law, online edition, *available at* www.mpepil.com (last visited Aug. 30, 2010) (cit. *König*, in: Wolfrum (ed.), EPIL-Flag of Convenience).

Kontorovich, Eugene, International Legal Responses to Piracy off the Coast of Somalia, ASIL Insights 16 (2009), *available at* www.asil.org/insights090206.cfm (last visited Aug. 30, 2010).

Kontorovich, Eugene, The Piracy Analogy: Modern Universal Jurisdiction's Hollow Foundation, Harvard International Law Journal 45 (2004), 183–237.

Kramek, Joseph, Bilateral Maritime Counter-Drug and Immigrant Interdiction Agreements: Is This the World of the Future? Miami Inter-American Law Review 31 (2001), Appendix B.

Kreß, Claus, International Criminal Law. In: Rüdiger Wolfrum (ed.), The Max Planck Encyclopedia of Public International Law, online edition, *available at* www.mpepil.com (last visited Aug. 30, 2010) (cit. *Kreß*, in: Wolfrum (ed.), EPIL-International Criminal Law).

Kreß, Claus, Universal Jurisdiction over International Crimes and the Institut de Droit international, Journal of International Criminal Justice 4 (2006), 561–585.

Krieger, Heike, A Credibility Gap: The Behrami and Saramati Decision of the European Court of Human Rights, Journal of International Peacekeeping 13 (2009), 159–180.

Krieger, Heike, Die Verantwortlichkeit Deutschlands nach der EMRK für seine Streitkräfte im Auslandseinsatz, Heidelberg Journal of International Law 62 (2002), 669–702.

Krugman, Paul/Cooper, Richard/Srinivasan, T.N., Growing World Trade: Causes and Consequences, Brookings Papers on Economic Activity 1 (1995), 327–377.

L'Express.fr, Les six pirates du *Ponant* sont arrivés en France, April 16, 2008, *available at* www.lexpress.fr/actualite/monde/les-six-pirates-du-i-ponant-i-sont-arrives-en-france_472071.html (last visited Aug. 30, 2010).

Lagoni, Rainer, Piraterie und widerrechtliche Handlungen gegen die Sicherheit der Seeschiffahrt. In: Jörn Ipsen/Edzard Schmidt-Jortzig (eds.), Recht – Staat – Gemeinwohl, Festschrift für Dietrich Rauschning, Köln a.o. 2001, 501–534 (cit. *Lagoni*, in: Ipsen/Schmidt-Jortzig (eds.), Piracy).

Larsen, Kjetil, Attribution of Conduct of Peace Operations: The "Ultimate Authority and Control" Test, European Journal of International Law 19 (2008), 509–531.

LeMonde.fr, «Carré-d'As»: les six pirates somaliens placés en garde à vue en France, Sept. 23, 2008, *available at* www.lemonde.fr/afrique/article/2008/09/23/carre-d-as-les-six-pirates-somaliens-places-en-garde-a-vue-en-france_1098819_3212.html (last visited Aug. 30, 2010).

LeMonde.fr, Les trois pirates somaliens du «Tanit» placés en garde à vue en France, April 14, 2009, *available at* www.lemonde.fr/afrique/article/2009/04/14/les-trois-pirates-somaliens-du-tanit-places-en-garde-a-vue-en-france_1180728_3212.html (last visited Aug. 30, 2010).

Levinson, Marc, Container Shipping and the Economy – Stimulating Trade and Transformations Worldwide, Transportation Research Board of the National Academies, Washington, D.C., TR News 246 (2006), *available at* www.worldshipping.org/pdf/container_shipping_and_the_us_economy.pdf (last visited Feb. 10, 2010).

Maierhöfer, Christian, "Aut dedere – aut iudicare," Herkunft, Rechtsgrundlagen und Inhalt des völkerrechtlichen Gebotes zur Strafverfolgung oder Auslieferung. Berlin 2006 (cit. *Maierhöfer, aut dedere – aut iudicare*).

Maritime Liaison Office, History of MARLO, *available at* www.cusnc.navy.mil/marlo/History/marlo-history.htm (last visited Aug. 30, 2010).

Maritime Liaison Office, Marlo Mission, *available at* www.cusnc.navy.mil/marlo/Mission/marlo-mission.htm (last visited Aug. 30, 2010).

Matz-Lueck, Neele, Planting the Flag in Arctic Waters: Russia's Claim to the North Pole, Göttingen Journal of International Law 1 (2009), 235–256.

Meijers Committee, Standing Committee of Experts on International Immigration, Refugee and Criminal Law, Comment on the Agreement Between the EU and Kenya on the Transfer of Persons Suspected of Piracy to Kenya, *available at* www.commissie-mei jers.nl/commissiemeijers/pagina.asp?pagkey=92379 (follow "Comments on the Agreement Between the EU and Kenya on Piracy" hyperlink) (last visited Aug. 30, 2010).

Mejia, Maximo, Regional Cooperation in Combating Piracy and Armed Robbery against Ships: Learning Lessons from ReCAAP. In: Petrig (ed.), Sea Piracy Law – Droit de la piraterie maritime (cit. *Mejia*, in: Petrig (ed.), Sea Piracy Law – Droit de la piraterie maritime).

Menefee, Samuel, Foreign Naval Intervention in Cases of Piracy: Problems and Strategies, International Journal Marine and Coastal Law 14 (1999), 353–370.

Middleton, Roger, Piracy in Somalia, Threatening Global Trade, Feeding Local War, Chatham House, Africa Programme, Briefing Paper, London, Oct. 2008, *available at* www.chathamhouse.org.uk/files/12203_1008piracysomalia.pdf (last visited Aug. 30, 2010).

Middleton, Roger, Pirates and How to Deal With Them, Chatham House, Africa Programme and International Law Discussion Group, London, April 22, 2009, *available at* www.chathamhouse.org.uk/files/13845_220409pirates_law.pdf (last visited Aug. 30, 2010).

Milanovic, Marko, From Compromise to Principle: Clarifying the Concept of State Jurisdiction in Human Rights Treaties, Human Rights Law Review 8 (2008), 411–448.

Milanovic, Marko/Papic, Tatjana, As Bad As It Gets: The European Court of Human Rights Behrami and Saramati Decision and General International Law, International and Comparative Law Quarterly 58 (2009), 267–296.

Miley, Sarah, Jurist, Yemen Court Sentences 6 Somali Pirates to Death, May 18, 2010, *available at* http://jurist.org/paperchase/2010/05/yemen-court-sentences–12-pirates-6-to-death.php (last visited Aug. 30, 2010).

Morgan, David, Reuters, Kenya Agrees to Prosecute U.S.-Held Pirates: Pentagon, Jan. 29, 2009, *available at* www.reuters.com/article/worldNews/idUSTRE50S4ZZ20090129 (last visited Aug. 30, 2010).

Münchau, Mathias, Terrorismus auf See aus völkerrechtlicher Sicht. Frankfurt am Main a.o. 1994.

Nandan, Satya, Articles 86 to 132 and Documentary Annexes. In: Nordquist, Myron (ed.), United Nations Convention on the Law of the Sea 1982: A Commentary, Volume III, The Hague a.o. 1985 (cit. *Nandan*, in: Nordquist (ed.), UNCLOS-Commentary, Article).

NATO, Allied Maritime Component Command Naples, *available at* www.afsouth.nato.int/ organization/CC_MAR_Naples/operations/allied_provider/index.htm (last visited Feb. 10, 2010).

NATO, Counter-Piracy Operations, *available at* www.nato.int/cps/en/natolive/topics_ 48815.htm#Protector (last visited Feb. 10, 2010).

NATO, NATO Resumes Counter-Piracy Mission, News, March 24, 2009, *available at* www.nato.int/cps/en/natolive/news_52016.htm?selectedLocale=en (last visited Feb. 10, 2010).

NATO, NATO's Standing Maritime Group 2 takes over counter piracy mission, News, June 29, 2009, *available at* www.nato.int/cps/en/natolive/news_56035.htm?selected Locale=en (last visited Feb. 10, 2010).

NATO, Operation Allied Provider, *available at* www.manw.nato.int/page_operation_ allied_provider.aspx (last visited Feb. 10, 2010).

NATO, Operation Ocean Shield – Current News, *available at* www.manw.nato.int/page_ operation_ocean_shield.aspx (last visited Feb. 10, 2010).

Nolte, Georg, The different functions of the Security Council with respect to Humanitarian Law. In: Lowe, Vaughan (ed.), The United Nations Security Council and War, Oxford a.o. 2008, 519–534 (cit. *Nolte*, in: Lowe (ed.), Security Council and War).

Norway, Mission to the United Nations, Communiqué: The Contact Group on Piracy off the Coast of Somalia, Jan. 29, 2010, *available at* www.norway-un.org/NorwayandUN/ Selected_Topics/Regional-Issues/Somalia/COMMUNIQUE-Contact-Group-on-Piracy-off-the-Coast-of-Somalia/ (last visited Aug. 30, 2010).

Nowak, Manfred, U.N. Covenant on Civil and Political Rights: CCPR Commentary. 2nd ed. Kehl a.o. 2005 (cit. Nowak, ICCPR Commentary).

Nowak, Manfred/McArthur, Elizabeth, The United Nations Convention Against Torture, A Commentary, Oxford 2008 (cit. Nowak/McArthur, Convention Against Torture Commentary).

O'Connell, Daniel/Shearer, Ivan, The International Law of the Sea, Volume 2, Oxford a.o. 1984.

Petretto, Kerstin, Piraterie als Problem der internationalen Politik. In: Stefan Mair (ed.) Piraterie und maritime Sicherheit, SWP-Studie, July 2010, Berlin, *available at* www.swp-berlin.org/common/get_document.php?asset_id=7286 (last visited Aug. 30, 2010).

Petrig, Anna, Counter-Piracy Operations in the Gulf of Aden, Expert Meeting on Multinational Law Enforcement & Sea Piracy held at the Max Planck Institute for Foreign and International Criminal Law, Press Release, Max Planck Society for the Advancement of Science, Jan. 15, 2010, *available at* www.mpg.de/english/illustrationsDocumentation/ documentation/pressReleases/2010/pressRelease20100115/index.html (last visited Aug. 30, 2010).

Plant, Glen, Legal Aspects of Terrorism at Sea. In: Rosalyn Higgins/Maurice Flory (eds.), Terrorism and International Law. London a.o. 1997, 68–97 (cit. *Plant*, in: Higgins/Flory (eds.), Terrorism at Sea).

Princeton University, Princeton Project on Universal Jurisdiction, The Princeton Principles on Universal Jurisdiction, 2001, *available at* http://lapa.princeton.edu/hosteddocs/unive_ jur.pdf (last visited Feb. 10, 2010).

Radio Netherlands Worldwide, Medvedev Calls for Piracy Tribunal, Nov. 20, 2009, *available at* www.rnw.nl/international-justice/article/medvedev-calls-piracy-tribunal (last visited Aug. 30, 2010).

Regional Cooperation Agreement on Combating Piracy and Armed Robbery against Ships in Asia (ReCAAP), The ReCAAP ISC Makes Further Progress and Will Co-Operate with the IMO in the Effort against Piracy in the Western Indian Ocean and the Gulf of

Aden, Press Release, Feb. 27, 2009, *available at* www.recaap.org/news/pdf/press/2009/Press%20Release-3GC%20Mtg.pdf (last visited Aug. 30, 2010).

Regional Cooperation Agreement on Combating Piracy and Armed Robbery against Ships in Asia (ReCAAP), Report for August 2009, *available at* www.recaap.org/incident/pdf/reports/2009/ReportAug09_O_180909.pdf (last visited Aug. 30, 2010).

Richter, N./Höll, S., Piratenjagd überfordert Bundesregierung, April 9, 2009, *available at* www.sueddeutsche.de/politik/987/464586/text/ (last visited Aug. 30, 2010).

Rivera, Ray, The New York Times, Somali Man Pleads Guilty in 2009 Hijacking of Ship, May 19, 2010, *available at* http://query.nytimes.com/gst/fullpage.html?res=990CE6DB153EF93AA25756C0A9669D8B63&ref=abduwali_abdukhadir_muse (last visited Aug. 30, 2010).

Rosenne, Shabtai/Gebhard, Julia, Conferences on the Law of the Sea. In: Rüdiger Wolfrum (ed.), The Max Planck Encyclopedia of Public International Law, online edition, *available at* www.mpepil.com (last visited Aug. 30, 2010) (cit. *Rosenne/Gebhard*, in: Wolfrum (ed.), EPIL-Conferences on the Law of the Sea).

Rosenstock, Robert, International Convention against the Taking of Hostages, Another International Community Step to Counter Terrorism, Denver Journal of International Law and Policy 9 (1980), 169–196.

Rubin, Alfred, Piracy. In: Rudolf Bernhardt (ed.), Encyclopedia of Public International Law, Law of the Sea – Air and Space, Vol. 11. Amsterdam a.o. 1989, 259–262 (cit. *Rubin*, in: Bernhardt (ed.), EPIL-Piracy).

Rubin, Alfred, The Law of Piracy. 2nd ed. New York 1998 (cit. Rubin, Law of Piracy).

Sari, Aurel, Jurisdiction and International Responsibility in Peace Support Operations: The *Behrami* and *Saramati* Cases, Human Rights Law Review 8 (2008), 151–170.

Sarooshi, Daneesh, The United Nations and the Development of Collective Security: The Delegation by the UN Security Council of its Chapter VII Powers. Oxford 2000 (cit. *Sarooshi*, The Delegation by the UN Security Council of its Chapter VII Powers).

Satterthwaite, Margaret, The Legal Regime Governing Transfer of Persons in the Fight Against Terrorism, May 2010, *available at* http://ssrn.com/abstract=1157583 (last visited Aug. 30, 2010).

Schaller, Christian, Die Unterbindung des Seetransports von Massenvernichtungswaffen – Völkerrechtliche Aspekte der "Proliferation Security Initiative", SWP-Studie 2004/17, *available at* www.swp-berlin.org/common/get_document.php?asset_id=1292 (last visited Aug. 30, 2010).

Schwartz, John, The New York Times, Somalis No Longer Face Federal Piracy Charges, Aug. 17, 2010, *available at* www.nytimes.com/2010/08/18/us/18pirates.html?_r=1&ref=piracy_at_sea (last visited Aug. 30, 2010).

Shearer, Ivan, Piracy. In: Rüdiger Wolfrum (ed.), The Max Planck Encyclopedia of Public International Law, online edition, *available at* www.mpepil.com (last visited Aug. 30, 2010) (cit. *Shearer*, in: Wolfrum (ed.), EPIL-Piracy).

Süddeutsche Zeitung, Piraten greifen erstmals deutsches Kriegsschiff an, March 30, 2009, *available at* www.sueddeutsche.de/panorama/817/463425/text/ (last visited Aug. 30, 2010).

Tams, Christian, League of Nations. In: Rüdiger Wolfrum (ed.), The Max Planck Encyclopedia of Public International Law, online edition, *available at* www.mpepil.com (last visited Aug. 30, 2010) (cit. *Tams*, in: Wolfrum (ed.), EPIL-League of Nations).

The Committee on International Human Rights of the Association of the Bar of the City of New York and The Center for Human Rights and Global Justice, New York University School of Law, Torture by Proxy: International and Domestic Law Applicable to "Extraordinary Renditions," 2004, *available at* www.chrgj.org/docs/TortureByProxy.pdf (last visited Aug. 30, 2010).

The New York Times, French Troops Seize Somali Pirates after Hostages are Freed, April 11, 2008, *available at* www.iht.com/articles/2008/04/11/africa/yacht.php (last visited Aug. 30, 2010).

Thienel, Tobias, The Georgian Conflict, Racial Discrimination and the ICJ: The Order on Provisional Measures of 15 October 2008, Human Rights Law Review 9 (2009), 465–472.

Treves, Tullio, Piracy, Law of the Sea, and Use of Force: Developments off the Coast of Somalia, European Journal of International Law 20 (2009), 399–414.

United Kingdom, Foreign & Commonwealth Office, Answer to a Freedom of Information Request filed by Anna Petrig, 21 April 2009

United Kingdom, Foreign & Commonwealth Office, Prisoner Transfer Agreements, *available at* www.fco.gov.uk/en/global-issues/conflict-prevention/piracy/prisoners (last visited Aug. 30, 2010).

United Kingdom, Foreign & Commonwealth Office, The International Response to Piracy, CGPCS (Contact Group on Piracy off the Coast of Somalia), *available at* www.fco.gov.uk/en/global-issues/conflict-prevention/piracy/international-response (last visited Feb. 10, 2010).

United Kingdom, Royal Navy, Combined Maritime Forces, Combined Task Force 151, *available at* www.royalnavy.mod.uk/operations-and-support/operations/united-king dom-component-command-ukmcc/coalition-maritime-forces-cfmcc/ctf–151/combined-task-force–151 (last visited Aug. 30, 2010).

United Nations, Committee against Torture, Conclusions and Recommendations on the United Kingdom, UN Doc. CAT/C/CR/33/3 (Dec. 10, 2004).

United Nations, Committee against Torture, Consideration of Reports Submitted by States Parties Under Article 19 of the Convention, Concluding Observations of the Committee against Torture, Kenya, U.N. Doc. CAT/C/KEN/CO/1 (Jan. 19, 2009).

United Nations, Committee against Torture, Considerations of Reports Submitted by States Parties under Article 19 of the Convention, Conclusion and Recommendations of the Committee against Torture, Bosnia and Herzegovina, UN Doc. CAT/C/BIH/CO/1 (Dec. 15, 2005).

United Nations, Committee against Torture, Considerations of Reports Submitted by States Parties under Article 19 of the Convention, Conclusion and Recommendations of the Committee against Torture, Estonia, UN Doc. CAT/C/EST/CO/4 (Feb. 19, 2008).

United Nations, Committee against Torture, Considerations of Reports Submitted by States Parties under Article 19 of the Convention, Conclusion and Recommendations of the Committee against Torture, France, UN Doc. CAT/C/FRA/CO/3 (April 3, 2006).

United Nations, Committee against Torture, Considerations of Reports Submitted by States Parties under Article 19 of the Convention, Conclusion and Recommendations of the Committee against Torture, United States of America, U.N. Doc. CAT/C/USA/CO/2 (May 18, 2006).

United Nations, Committee against Torture, Considerations of Reports Submitted by States Parties under Article 19 of the Convention, Conclusion and Recommendations of the Committee against Torture, United States of America, UN Doc. CAT/C/USA/CO/2 (July 25, 2006).

United Nations, Committee against Torture, General Comment No. 01, U.N. Doc. A/53/44, Annex IX (1998) (cit. United Nations, Committee against Torture, General Comment No. 01).

United Nations, Committee against Torture, Summary Record of the 703rd meeting, U.N. Doc. CAT/C/SR.703 (May 12, 2006).

United Nations, Conference on the Law of the Sea, Feb. 24 – April 27, 1958, Official Records: Volume II: Plenary Meetings, U.N. Doc. A/CONF.13/38 (Feb. 24 – April 27, 1958).

United Nations, Conference on the Law of the Sea, Feb. 24 – April 27, 1958, Official Records: Volume IV: Second Committee (High Seas: General Régime), U.N. Doc. A/CONF.13/40 (Feb. 24 to April 27, 1958).

United Nations, Conference on the Law of the Sea, Summary Record of the 29th Meeting, U.N. Doc. A/CONF.13/C.2/L.78 (Feb. 24 to April 27, 1958).

United Nations, Department of Public Information, Piracy off Somali Coast Not Only Criminal, But Very Successful, Security Council Hears, Cautioned There Could Be No Peace at Sea Without Stability on Land, Press Release, Nov. 18, 2009, statement by Ronald Jumeau (Seychelles), *available at* www.un.org/News/Press/docs/2009/sc9793.doc.htm (last visited Aug. 30, 2010).

United Nations, Department of Public Information, Security Council Authorizes States to Use Land-Based Operations in Somalia, Press Release, Dec. 16, 2008, *available at* www.un.org/News/Press/docs/2008/sc9541.doc.htm (last visited Aug. 30, 2010).

United Nations, Department of Public Information, Security Council Condemns Acts of Piracy, Armed Robbery off Somalia's Coast, Authorizes for Six Months "All Necessary Means" to Repress Such Acts, Press Release, June 2, 2008, *available at* www.un.org/News/Press/docs/2008/sc9344.doc.htm (last visited Aug. 30, 2010).

United Nations, Economic and Social Council, Second Periodic Report of Israel to the Committee on Economic, Social and Cultural Rights, UN Doc. E/1990/6/Add.32, (Oct. 16, 2001).

United Nations, Human Rights Committee, Concluding Observations: Belgium, UN Doc. CCPR/C/79/Add.99 (Nov. 19, 1998).

United Nations, Human Rights Committee, Concluding Observations: Belgium, UN Doc. CCPR/CO/81/BEL (Aug. 12, 2004).

United Nations, Human Rights Committee, Concluding Observations: Netherlands, UN Doc. CCPR/CO/72/NET (Aug. 27, 2001).

United Nations, Human Rights Committee, Considerations of Reports Submitted by States Parties under Article 19 of the Convention, Conclusion and Recommendations of the Committee against Torture, France, UN Doc. CCPR/CO/84/THA (July 8, 2005).

United Nations, Human Rights Committee, General Comment No. 20, U.N. Doc. CCPR/C/21/Rev.1/Add.13 (May 26, 2004) (cit. United Nations, Human Rights Committee, General Comment No. 20).

United Nations, Human Rights Committee, General Comment No. 31, U.N. Doc. CCPR/C/21/Rev.1/Add.13 (May 26, 2004) (cit. United Nations, Human Rights Committee, General Comment No. 31).

United Nations, Human Rights Committee, Replies of the Government of the Netherlands to the Concerns Expressed by the Human Rights Committee, UN Doc. CCPR/CO/72/NET/Add.1 (Apr. 29, 2003).

United Nations, Human Rights Committee, Second Periodic Report of Israel to the Human Rights Committee, UN Doc. CCPR/C/ISR/2001/2 (Dec. 4, 2001).

United Nations, Human Rights Committee, Second and Third Periodic Reports of the United States of America, Consideration of Reports Submitted by States Parties under Article 40 of the Covenant, Annex I: Territorial Scope of the Application of the Covenant, UN Doc. CCPR/C/USA/3 (Nov. 28, 2005).

United Nations, Human Rights Council, Report of the Special Rapporteur on Torture and Other Cruel, Inhuman and Degrading Treatment or Punishment, UN Doc A/HRC/13/39 (Feb. 9, 2010).

United Nations, International Law Commission, Commentary on the Articles Concerning the Law of the Sea, Yearbook, 1956, Volume 2, 265–301 (cit. United Nations, International Law Commission, Commentary on the Law of the Sea Draft Convention).

United Nations, International Law Commission, Report of the International Law Commission on the Work of its 56th Session (3 May to 4 June and 5 July to 6 August 2004): United Nations, General Assembly, Official Records, 64th Session, Supplement No. 10, U.N. Doc. A/59/10 (2004) (cit. United Nations, International Law Commission, Report of the International Law Commission on the Work of its 56th Session, 2004).

United Nations, International Law Commission, Report of the International Law Commission on the Work of its 60th Session (5 May to 6 June and 7 July to 8 August 2008): United Nations, General Assembly, Official Records, 63rd Session, Supplement No. 10, U.N. Doc. A/63/10 (2008) (cit. United Nations, International Law Commission, Report of the International Law Commission on the Work of its 60th Session, 2008).

United Nations, International Law Commission, Report of the International Law Commission on the Work of its 61st Session (4 May to 5 June and 6 July to 7 August 2009): United Nations, General Assembly, Official Records, 64th Session, Supplement No. 10, U.N. Doc. A/64/10 (2009) (cit. United Nations, International Law Commission, Report of the International Law Commission on the Work of its 61st Session, 2009).

United Nations, International Law Commission, Responsibility of International Organizations: Comments and Observations Received from International Organizations, U.N. Doc. A/CN.4/545 (June 25, 2004).

United Nations, International Law Commission, Second Report on Responsibility of International Organizations by Mr. Giorgio Gaja, Special Rapporteur, U.N. Doc. A/CN.4/541 (April 2, 2004).

United Nations, International Law Commission, Yearbook of the International Law Commission, 1955, Volume 1.

United Nations, Monitoring Group on Somalia, Report of the Monitoring Group on Somalia pursuant to Security Council resolution 1811 (2008), U.N. Doc. S/2008/769 (Dec. 10, 2008) (cit. United Nations, Monitoring Group on Somalia, Report, Dec. 10, 2008).

United Nations, Monitoring Group on Somalia, Report of the Monitoring Group on Somalia pursuant to Security Council resolution 1853 (2008), U.N. Doc. S/2010/91 (March 10, 2010) (cit. United Nations, Monitoring Group on Somalia, Report, March 10, 2010).

United Nations, News Centre, UN Opens New Courtroom to Try Pirate Suspects in Kenyan Port, June 25, 2010, *available at* www.un.org/apps/news/story.asp?NewsID=35156 &Cr=UNODC&Cr1= (last visited Aug. 30, 2010).

United Nations, Security Council, Official Records, 64th Session, 6197th Meeting, U.N. Doc. S/PV.6197 (Oct. 8, 2009).

United Nations, Secretary-General, Report of the Secretary-General on Oceans and the Law of the Sea, *delivered to the General Assembly,* UN Doc. A 63/63 (March 10, 2008).

United Nations, Secretary-General, Report of the Secretary-General on possible options to further the aim of prosecuting and imprisoning persons responsible for acts of piracy and armed robbery at sea off the coast of Somalia, including, in particular, options for creating special domestic chambers possibly with international components, a regional tribunal or an international tribunal and corresponding imprisonment arrangements, taking into account the work of the Contact Group on Piracy off the Coast of Somalia, the existing practice in establishing international and mixed tribunals, and the time and resources necessary to achieve and sustain substantive results, U.N. Doc. S/2010/394 (July 26, 2010) (cit. United Nations, Secretary-General Report pursuant to S.C. Res. 1918, July 26, 2010).

United Nations, Secretary-General, Report of the Secretary-General on Somalia, U.N. Doc. S/2010/234 (May 11, 2010) (cit. United Nations Secretary-General Report on Somalia, May 11, 2010).

United Nations, Secretary-General, Report of the Secretary-General on the situation in Somalia, delivered to the Security Council, U.N. Doc. S/2009/684 (Jan. 8, 2010) (cit. United Nations, Secretary-General Report on Somalia, Jan. 8, 2010).

United Nations, Secretary-General, Report of the Secretary-General pursuant to Security Council resolution 1846 (2008), delivered to the Security Council, U.N. Doc. S/2009/146 (March 16, 2009) (cit. United Nations, Secretary-General Report on S.C. Res. 1846, March 16, 2009).

United Nations, Secretary-General, Report of the Secretary-General pursuant to Security Council resolution 1846 (2008), delivered to the Security Council, U.N. Doc. S/2009/590 (Nov. 13, 2009) (cit. United Nations, Secretary-General Report on S.C. Res. 1846, Nov. 13, 2009).

United Nations, Security Council, Statement by the President of the Security Council, U.N. Doc. S/PRST/2009/31 (Dec. 3, 2009).

United Nations, Security Council, Statement by the President of the Security Council, U.N. Doc. S/PRST/2009/32 (Dec. 8, 2009).

United Nations, Third United Nations Conference on the Law of the Sea (1973–1982), *available at* http://untreaty.un.org/cod/diplomaticconferences/lawofthesea-1982/lawofthe sea-1982.html (last visited Aug. 30, 2010).

United Nations, United Nations Conference on Trade and Development (UNCTAD), Review of Maritime Transport, 2009, Report by the UNCTAD Secretariat, *available at* www.unctad.org/en/docs/rmt2009_en.pdf (last visited Aug. 30, 2010).

United Nations, United Nations Office on Drugs and Crime, Annual Report 2009, *available at* www.unodc.org/documents/about-unodc/AR09_LORES.pdf (last visited Feb. 10, 2010).

United Nations, United Nations Office on Drugs and Crime, Counter Piracy Programme, November 2009, *available at* www.unodc.org/documents/easternafrica//piracy/UNO DC_Counter_Piracy_Programme.pdf (last visited Aug. 30, 2010).

United Nations, United Nations Office on Drugs and Crime, Piracy-Background, *available at* www.unodc.org/easternafrica/en/piracy/background.html (last visited Feb. 10, 2010).

United Nations, United Nations Office on Drugs and Crime, "Ship Riders": Tackling Somali Pirates at Sea, Press Release, Jan. 20, 2009, *available at* www.unodc.org/unodc/ en/frontpage/ship-riders-tackling-somali-pirates-at-sea.html (last visited Feb. 10, 2010).

United Nations, United Nations Office on Drugs and Crime, UNODC and Piracy, *available at* www.unodc.org/unodc/en/piracy/index.html (last visited Feb. 10, 2010).

United Nations, United Nations Office on Drugs and Crime, UNODC, Promoting Health, Security and Justice, Cutting the Threads of Drugs, Crime and Terrorism, 2010 Report, *available at* www.unodc.org/documents/frontpage/UNODC_Annual_Report_2010_ LowRes.pdf (last visited Aug. 30, 2010).

United Nations, United Nations Office on Drugs and Crime, UNODC Proposes Measures to Stop Piracy in the Horn of Africa, Press Release, Dec. 16, 2008, *available at* www.unodc.org/unodc/en/press/releases/2008–12.16.html (last visited Feb. 10, 2010).

United States of America, Africa Command, Policy Statement: Contact Group on Piracy off the Coast of Somalia, Jan. 14, 2009, *available at* www.africom.mil/getArticle. asp?art=2466 (last visited Feb. 10, 2010).

United States of America, Central Command, Pirate Attacks on Rise off Somalia Coast, Sept. 29, 2009, *available at* www.centcom.mil/en/press-releases/pirate-attacks-on-rise-off-somalia-coast.html (last visited Feb. 10, 2010).

United States of America, Central Intelligence Agency, The World Fact Book, Somalia, *available at* https://www.cia.gov/library/publications/the-world-factbook/geos/so.html (last visited Aug. 30, 2010).

United States of America, Department of Justice, United States Attorney's Office, Eastern District of Virgina, Alleged Somali Pirates Indicted for Attacks on Navy Ships, Press Release, April 23, 2010, *available at* http://norfolk.fbi.gov/dojpressrel/pressrel10/nf042310.htm (last visited Aug. 30, 2010).

United States of America, Department of Justice, United States Attorney's Office, Southern District of New York, Somalian Pirate Brought to U.S. to Face Charges for Hijacking the Maersk Alabama and Holding the Ship's Captain Hostage, Press Release, April 21, 2010, *available at* http://newyork.fbi.gov/dojpressrel/pressrel09/nyfo042109.htm (last visited Aug. 30, 2010)

United States of America, Department of State, Bureau of Democracy, Human Rights, and Labor, 2008 Human Rights Report: Kenya, Feb. 25, 2009, *available at* www.state.gov/ g/drl/rls/hrrpt/2008/af/119007.htm (last visited Aug. 30, 2010).

United States of America, Department of State, Bureau of Political and Military Affairs, First Plenary Meeting of the Contact Group on Piracy Off the Coast of Somalia, New York, Jan. 14, 2009, *available at* www.state.gov/t/pm/rls/fs/130610.htm (last visited Aug. 30, 2010).

United States of America, Department of State, Office of the Spokesman, Fourth Plenary Meeting of the Contact Group on Piracy off the Coast of Somalia, Sept. 11, 2009, *available at* www.state.gov/r/pa/prs/ps/2009/sept/129143.htm. (last visited Aug. 30, 2010).

United States of America, Department of State, Office of the Spokesman, Sixth Plenary Meeting of the Contact Group on Piracy off the Coast of Somalia, June 11, 2010, *available at* www.state.gov/r/pa/prs/ps/2010/06/143010.htm (last visited Aug. 30, 2010).

United States of America, The Commander's Handbook on the Law of Naval Operations, July 2007, Pursuit of Pirates Into Foreign Territorial Seas, Archipelagic Waters, or Airspace, Section 3.5.3.2, *available at* www.usnwc.edu/getattachment/a9b8e92d-2c8d-4779-9925-0defea93325c/1–14M_(Jul_2007)_(NWP) (last visited Aug. 30, 2010).

Van der Toorn, Damien, Attribution of Conduct by State Armed Forces Participating in UN-Authorised Operations: The Impact of *Behrami* and *Al-Jedda*, Australian International Law Journal 15 (2008), 9–27.

Van Dijk et al., Theory and Practice of the European Convention on Human Rights, 4th ed. Antwerpen 2006.

Wambua, Paul, The Legislative Framework for Adjudication of Piracy Cases in Kenya – Review of the Jurisdictional and Procedural Challenges and the Institutional Capacity. In: Petrig (ed.), Sea Piracy Law – Droit de la piraterie maritime (cit. *Wambua*, in: Petrig (ed.), Sea Piracy Law – Droit de la piraterie maritime).

Weinzierl, Ruth/Lisson, Urszula, Border Management and Human Rights. A study of EU Law and the Law of the Sea, German Institute for Human Rights, 2008, *available at* http://files.institut-fuer-menschenrechte.de/488/d75_v1_file_47c81c6053b74_Study_Border_Management_and_Human_Rights.pdf (last visited Aug. 30, 2010).

Werle, Gerhard, Völkerstrafrecht, 2nd ed. Tübingen 2007.

Wille, Jörn, Die Verfolgung strafbarer Handlungen an Bord von Schiffen und Luftfahrzeugen. Berlin/New York 1974.

Wood, Michael, The Convention on the Prevention and Punishment of Crimes against Internationally Protected Persons, Including Diplomats, International and Comparative Law Quarterly 23 (1974), 791–817.

Woolf, Marie, The Sunday Times, Pirates Can Claim UK Asylum, April 13, 2008, *available at* www.timesonline.co.uk/tol/news/uk/article3736239.ece (last visited Aug. 30, 2010).

Zimmermann, Andreas, Extraterritoriale Staatenpflichten und internationale Friedensmissionen, Anhörung des Bundestagsausschusses für Menschenrechte und Humanitäre Hilfe, Dec. 17, 2008, *available at* http://www.bundestag.de/bundestag/ausschuesse/a17/anhoerungen/Allg__Erkl__rung_MR__Extraterritoriale_Staatenpflichten/Prof__Dr__Andreas_Zimmermann__09_12_08.pdf (last visited Feb. 10, 2010).

Index